Drugs, Ethics, and Quality of Life

*Cases and Materials
on Ethical, Legal,
and Public Policy Dilemmas
in Medicine and Pharmacy Practice*

Drugs, Ethics, and Quality of Life

Cases and Materials
on Ethical, Legal,
and Public Policy Dilemmas
in Medicine and Pharmacy Practice

Bruce D. White

informa
healthcare

New York   London

Informa Healthcare USA, Inc.
52 Vanderbilt Avenue
New York, NY 10017

© 2008 by Informa Healthcare USA, Inc. (original copyright 2007 by The Haworth Press, Inc.)
Informa Healthcare is an Informa business

International Standard Book Number-10: 0-7890-2856-5 (Hardcover)
International Standard Book Number-13: 978-0-7890-2865-3 (Hardcover)

Library of Congress Cataloging-in-Publication Data

Drugs, ethics, and quality of life : cases and materials on ethical, legal, and public policy
    dilemmas in medicine and pharmacy practice / Bruce D. White.
    p. ; m. Includes index.
    ISBN-13: 978-0-7890-2856-3; ISBN-10: 0-7890-2856-5 (hard : alk. paper)
    ISBN-13: 978-0-7890-2857-0; ISBN-10: 0-7890-2857-3 (soft : alk. paper)
    1. Pharmaceutical ethics--United States. 2. Pharmacy--Law and legislation--United States.
    [DNLM: 1. legislation, Pharmacy--ethics--United States. 2. Decision Making--ethics--
United States. 3. Ethics, Pharmacy--United States. QV 733 AA1 W582d 2007]

    RS100.5.W45 2007
    174.2'951--dc22
                                                                                2007018318

Visit the Informa Web site at
www.informa.com

and the Informa Healthcare Web site at
www.informahealthcare.com

R. Clayton McWhorter
Joseph O. Dean Jr.
Mickey C. Smith

Pharmacists all, who as visionary leaders
set the highest ethical standard,
and thereby improved the quality of life
of countless others

CONTENTS

ABOUT THE AUTHOR

Bruce D. White, DO, JD, is a pharmacist, a board-certified pediatrician, and an attorney with fellowship training in clinical medical ethics. He came to St. Joseph's Hospital and Medical Center in Phoenix, Arizona, from Nashville, Tennessee, in March 2004 to serve as a member of the general pediatrics residency faculty; he currently is academic chair of the pediatrics department. He also directs the clinical ethics fellowship program for the hospital. He holds faculty appointments as Clinical Professor of Pediatrics in the University of Arizona College of Medicine; Clinical Professor of Pharmacy Practice and Science in the College of Pharmacy, Tucson, Arizona; and Clinical Professor of Pediatrics in the Creighton University School of Medicine, Omaha, Nebraska. He also serves as Professor and Director of the campus-wide, interdisciplinary Healthcare Ethics and Law (HEaL) Institute at Samford University in Birmingham, Alabama. He directs an interactive Web site—www.ethicsconsultant.com—which offers online clinical ethics coaching, mentoring, and educational services to a pilot group of hospitals and ethics committee members nationwide.

CONTRIBUTORS

Gretchen A. Fair, JD, MA, holds law and bioethics degrees from the University of Virginia. She was an associate with the Venable law firm in Washington, DC, for three years before serving as the 2005-2006 fellow in clinical ethics at St. Joseph's Hospital and Medical Center, Phoenix, Arizona.

Joseph L. Fink III, BS Pharm, JD, is Professor of Pharmacy at the University of Kentucky College of Pharmacy in Lexington, where he focuses on pharmaceutical public policy and pharmacy law, and is Professor of Public Health in the College of Public Health. He chaired the committee for the latest revision of the American Pharmacists Association Code of Ethics for Pharmacists. For more than twenty years he has been an editor of *Pharmacy Law Digest,* the most widely used pharmacy law text and reference in the United States.

Kenneth V. Iserson, MD, MBA, is Professor of Emergency Medicine in the College of Medicine and Director of the Arizona Bioethics Center at the University of Arizona, Tucson, where he also chairs the ethics committee of the University Medical Center. He is the author of over 300 scientific articles and nine books, including *Getting into a Residency: A Guide for Medical Students* (6th ed., 2003), *Grave Words: Notifying Survivors of Sudden, Unexpected Death* (1999), and *Ethics in Emergency Medicine* (2nd ed., 1995).

Jan M. Kovarik is a freelance copyeditor and proofreader (a.k.a. Jan K., The Proofer), and has been serving the publications industry at large since 1996. Her principal focus is academic-level research journals (in the accounting and computer technology fields). Jan also provides primary freelance editing services for postgraduates who are in their dissertation stage. Prior to becoming a freelancer, Jan worked for more than twenty years in the corporate accounting arena.

John Lachs, PhD, is Centennial Professor of Philosophy at Vanderbilt University, Nashville, Tennessee. His philosophical interests center on human nature, which takes him into metaphysics, philosophy of mind, political philosophy, and ethics. He is general editor of the *Encyclopedia of American Philosophy* and the author of seven books.

Edmund D. Pellegrino, MD, is the John Carroll Professor Emeritus of Medicine and Medical Ethics at Georgetown University, and Chairman of the President's Council on Bioethics, Washington DC. He is a Master of the American College of Physicians, Fellow of the American Association for the Advancement of Science, and Member of the Institute of Medicine of the National Academy of Sciences. Dr. Pellegrino formerly directed the Kennedy Institute of Ethics, Center for the Advanced Study of Ethics, and Center for Clinical Bioethics at Georgetown. He is the author of over 500 published items in medical science, philosophy, and ethics, and is a member of numerous editorial boards.

Somlynn Rorie is a freelance journalist residing in Phoenix, Arizona. She obtained her bachelor's degree in English from Arizona State University. She has written extensively on the topics of Internet technology, current events, fashion and beauty, natural health and healing, herbal supplements, pharmaceuticals, food ingredients, and organic food. Her articles have been featured in many publications, and she has served as editor for several magazines such as *Organic and Natural News, Natural Products Insider,* and *Health Supplement Retailer.* Currently, she provides marketing and public relations for a global digital media company that provides access controls and management for digital entertainment products.

Foreword

This is not your boring old professor's law or ethics tome. Dr. White's exciting new casebook offers students and practitioners a fascinating way to broach both the legal and moral realms surrounding health care and pharmaceutical manufacture, sales, and dispensing.

The book highlights topical issues involving drugs, their effect on patients and impact on health care professionals, and the influence of government and industry on their distribution. In so doing, Dr. White delves into the dusty shadows of decision making to illuminate the dilemmas and ethical and moral deviance that occur "in plain sight." While examining little-known details about the issues that frequently make headlines, the intricate legal and ethical details that are essential for true understanding emerge.

Dr. White is, of course, highly qualified to write this book, with his extensive experience in health care and pharmacy law, clinical ethics, and clinical medicine. In addition to formal training in each of these fields, he has also completed a senior fellowship at the University of Chicago's MacLean Center for Clinical Medical Ethics. An academic with appointments both at the University of Arizona and Samford University in Alabama, he brings both a scholarly and practical perspective to his writing.

Who should read this book? The answer is somewhat surprising. Students in the health care professions will derive immense benefit from this book—and enjoy it, even if it is "assigned reading." Health care professionals will enjoy learning the "nitty-gritty" details behind the issues that they struggle with daily, whether they come from the dispensing side (pharmacy) or the prescribing side (physicians, nurse practitioners, physician assistants, dentists, podiatrists, and others).

Lay readers will also find this book a fascinating and easy read, packed with real-world examples to which they can easily relate.

We have been waiting for this book for some time. We're glad that it has arrived.

Kenneth V. Iserson, MD, MBA

Preface

It is difficult to pick up a daily paper anywhere today and not see a headline that mentions drug use or abuse of some sort. Recent examples illustrate this point: "A Drug Scourge Creates Its Own Form of Orphan; Methamphetamine Is Sending Children to Strained Agencies"[1]; "'Targeted' Cancer Treatment Effective in Older Patients"[2]; "President Tells Insurers to Aid New Drug Plan; Confusion Over Benefits; Cost Caps for the Poor and 30 Days of Medicine Are Ordered"[3]; and "U.S. Regulators Approve Insulin in Inhaled Form; Alternative to Injection; Some Doctors Concerned About Lung Impact—Pfizer to Sell Soon."[4] These and other news stories show, perhaps better than any other way, how *drugs* directly and indirectly affect the *quality of life* of innumerable people. More distressing is the fact that decisions to use a drug often fail to include a thorough analysis of the ethics involved—a complete understanding of the *benefits* and *burdens* entailed.

In April 2004, University of Mississippi Professor Emeritus Mickey Smith suggested that I consider writing a text to help pharmacy and medical students, interested practitioners, and others better understand the ethics of drug use and impact of drugs on quality of life. The idea arose during a conversation we shared when he was in Birmingham receiving an academic medal from the Healthcare Ethics and Law Institute at Samford University "for contributions to healthcare ethics in the selfless spirit of Edmund D. Pellegrino."

At that time, we identified four pharmacy ethics books that were currently available as teaching texts. If there were more, we were not aware of them. The first ethics textbook was his own, *Pharmacy Ethics* (The Haworth Press, 1991), which was co-edited with three other pharmacy administration educators: Steven Strauss, John Baldwin, and the late Kelly Alberts. This anthology of essays explores ethical issues that are important to pharmacists and those studying pharmacy and medicine. The second textbook was *Ethical Responsibility in Pharmacy Practice* (American Institute of the History of Pharmacy, 1994; 2nd ed., 2004) by Bob Buerki and Lou Vottero. This book can be described as the Beauchamp and Childress of pharmacy ethics, recalling the seminal contribution that Tom Beauchamp and Jim Childress have had on the medical ethics field (with their book *Principles of Biomedical Ethics,* Oxford University Press, 5th ed., 2001). Buerki and Vottero's textbook provides decision-making tools needed for pharmacy practitioners and discusses ethical principles by using common problems and hypothetical vignettes. The third book, *Ethical Dimensions of Pharmaceutical Care* (The Haworth Press, 1996), was edited by Amy Haddad and Bob Buerki and takes a more theoretical and futuristic approach by featuring philosophers who discuss professionalism issues and pharmacists who explore the idea of expanding present-day pharmacy practice into the more clinical concept of pharmaceutical care. The fourth book by pharmacist-philosopher-ethicist Robert Veatch and Amy Haddad, called *Case Studies in Pharmacy Ethics* (Oxford University Press, 1999), approaches pharmacy ethics much like Beauchamp and Childress's biomedical ethics text, has extensive discussions of philosophical principles, and is illustrated with numerous cases.

This book's title describes its limited, but still relatively specific, focus: *Drugs, Ethics, and Quality of Life*. It differs in style and content from the other pharmacy ethics textbooks currently available. Since physicians, patients, and others—including drug company executives and representatives, federal and state regulators, and nurses—are involved in the drug product distribution system, the book has value to anyone who is generally interested in health care ethics and drugs. I have attempted to show that ethics is a very practical discipline and is about individuals making decisions when faced with a particular set of choices. As a general theme, I illustrate the benefits-burdens decisions process used: when pharmaceutical companies research, manufacture, and sell drug products; when the government approves medicines for market; and when physicians prescribe or administer, pharmacists dispense, and patients take *drugs*. Needless to say, all of these actions can directly impact an individual's *quality of life.* Decisions affecting drug use are made repeatedly, every single day, usually with little thought about the ethics involved. These drug use decisions demonstrate how important ethics is to a professional practice and how a simple act within a decision-making framework can affect a patient's life, either positively or negatively.

Actual cases and scenarios are used in this book to highlight certain ethical challenges. The real-life circumstances of each case are, for the most part, reviewed chronologically as a legal action unfolds. One should note that law cases are not used to show that judges and the courts ultimately make ethical decisions. There is a stark difference between ethics and law. Ethics can be represented as the ceiling of a room—lofty, aspirational conduct; the law can be represented as the floor—the basic level that must be achieved to satisfy legal conduct requirements in a civilized society. When judges and juries settle legal disputes or conflicts, they make decisions in a fashion similar to those who confront ethical dilemmas. In America, contentious issues may ultimately be resolved in the courts, which traditionally are the final arbiters of justice claims (moreover, some of society's more unusual end-of-life ethics dilemmas are also law cases, specifically *Quinlan, Cruzan,* and *Schiavo*).

Legal cases can be instructive in teaching ethics for at least two reasons. First, opposing points of view need rigorous analysis. Both sides of a legal issue make their arguments, often forcefully, in hopes of pressing what they each think is a better claim. Individuals facing a moral choice should weigh countervailing views with the same adversarial vigor. Second, at the end of a hearing or trial, the judge or jury has to make a decision, sometimes one that has unpleasant consequences. Similarly, after an ethical dilemma has been analyzed, an individual must select an option. In both legal and ethical decision making, those who must make the choice must be at peace with that resolution. They may try to avoid making a decision, they may not like the result, but they must learn to live with the decision. It is unfortunate that, in the legal system, one party is often thought of as "the loser"; however, the entire community usually gains, over time, through a balanced public policy that has evolved one decision at a time. Without question, ethics and law are interrelated. This dynamic demonstrates an obvious tension at the nexus of ethics, law, and public policy. The difficult choices discussed in these chapters (as represented by statutes, regulations, and previous judicial opinions) usually occur at a point where individual liberty, professional rights, and public policy collide.

The cases in this book may also be used to inform readers about how the law works procedurally (e.g., through civil and criminal prosecutions with their discovery processes and judgments; appellate review with judges writing majority and dissenting opinions; legislatures enacting statutes; and administrative agencies promulgating regulations and adjudicating interests). With resolution of substantive and procedural matters, legal rules evolve from the Anglo-American common law system and give voice to a uniform public policy as dramatic issues are settled between individual litigants.

Lastly, this book provides useful content and topics that can be implemented in a format that easily fits the way pharmacy and medical ethics and law courses are currently taught. Many pharmacy students learn ethics in law courses, and many medical students learn law in ethics courses. Books like this one can provide an invaluable adjunct to classroom presentations on ethics issues in a pharmacy law course or legal issues in a medical ethics class. More often than not, however, both pharmacists and physicians learn by debating these cases and hypothetical situations within the small group of peers they encounter every day in practice.

Arguably, there should be more formal law teaching in the current medical curriculum and more formal ethics instruction in pharmacy schools. Many who think that physicians have an undue fear of legal liability (perhaps from all the risks associated with medical malpractice) consider a structured medicolegal education as an option in calming professional anxiety. Pharmacy law classes heavily emphasize the regulatory aspects of practice (with federal food and drug law, federal controlled substances statutes and regulations, and state pharmacy practice acts and regulations), making it possible for pharmacy students to mistakenly think the law is purely black letter on a printed page and have little time to reflect on more ethical topics such as conflicts of interest, irrational prescribing, and health care delivery injustices.

In this book, I offer ethics materials as narrative (as used when teachers tell stories) and opportunities for casuistic (case-by-case, contextual) analysis. These materials emphasize that decisions must be made in a timely and rather pragmatic way. Discussion and systematic reviews can provide better learning opportunities for pharmacy and medical students than dry, didactic presentations. In this vein, students and teachers are greatly indebted to model clinical ethics textbooks like those by Greg Pence (*Classic Cases in Medical Ethics: Accounts of Cases That Have Shaped Medical Ethics, with Philosophical, Legal, and Historical Backgrounds,* McGraw-Hill, 4th ed., 2004)* and Al Jonsen, Mark Siegler, and Bill Winslade (*Clinical Ethics: A Practical Approach to Ethical Decisions in Clinical Medicine,* 5th ed., McGraw-Hill, 2002).**

The book begins with two introductions by eminent scholars; one written primarily for physicians, and the second principally for pharmacists. The first is compiled from previously published works of physician-ethicist Edmund D. Pellegrino, by myself and Gretchen A. Fair—with Dr. Pellegrino's collaboration and approval—and discusses physician virtues and introduces the current American Medical Association (AMA) *Principles of Medical Ethics* (2001). Dr. Pellegrino is considered by some as the modern "father of American bioethics" and in 2005 was named chair of the President's Council on Bioethics. The second introduction is by pharmacist-attorney Joseph L. Fink III, who likewise considers pharmacist virtues and practice values and introduces the current American Pharmacists Association (APhA) *Code of Ethics* (1994). Professor Fink edits the most widely used American pharmacy law text and reference and chaired the APhA committee that last revised the Code of Ethics for Pharmacists. After careful comparison, one will be struck by the similarities between the two. From a traditional point of view, it may be essential to begin a learned study of professional ethics for health care providers with conversations about practitioner virtues and codes of ethics. However, as both Pellegrino and Fink prove, this is simply the beginning for those interested in thoroughly understanding how ethical decision making is important in a real-world context.

---

*Pence GE. *Classic Cases in Medical Ethics: Accounts of the Cases That Have Shaped Medical Ethics, with Philosophical, Legal, and Historical Backgrounds.* New York, NY: McGraw-Hill, 2004. Copyright 2004. Excerpted material is reprinted with permission.

**Jonsen AR, Siegler M, Winslade WJ. *Clinical Ethics: A Practical Approach to Ethical Decisions in Clinical Medicine.* 5th ed. New York, NY: McGraw-Hill, 2002. Copyright 2002. Excerpted material is reprinted with permission.

This rest of the book is divided into three parts and two appendixes. The first four chapters deal with cases that permit students to understand foundational concepts: *drugs, ethics, quality of life, beneficence, nonmaleficence, autonomy,* and *justice*. The use of recent cases that involve tobacco, COX-2 inhibitors, medicinal marijuana, and emergency contraceptives provide excellent backdrops for these explanations. The following chapters look at issues related to drug use when quality of life is diminished, or when patients are dying or undeniably dwindling. The final chapter deals with drug experimentation; and the appendixes raise certain issues for further discussion topically with information concerning (1) law and decisions, and (2) resources about drug use decisions and situations when patients have acute or chronic illnesses, are trying to prevent contagious illnesses, wish to prevent and terminate pregnancies, or seek pleasure or enhanced performance.

In providing these various cases and scenarios, I hope that those reading this book will begin to see the important role that ethics plays in today's society—how it has shaped the laws and guidelines that dictate and define our daily activities. I have chosen controversial and thought-provoking subjects that I hope will generate discussion and analysis that will go beyond the classroom doors and into our day-to-day decision-making processes.

NOTE CONCERNING OMISSIONS IN QUOTED MATERIAL

Footnotes in some of the materials used in this book have been omitted without indication. Citations in some of the materials have been generally omitted without indication; some exceptions have been made when quoted material is involved. Other textual omissions have been indicated either by ellipses, asterisks, or bracketed insertions.

Acknowledgments

My professional debts are many. Bob Crumby and I were partners for more than fifteen years. We began working together at the Center for Clinical and Research Ethics at Vanderbilt University Medical Center in 1988. We are grateful to Dick Zaner for providing us with the opportunity to work with him as the center's outreach team. From 1995 to 2004, Bob and I were the clinical ethics teaching unit for Hospital Corporation of America (HCA) hospitals at the Center for Clinical Ethics in Summit Medical Center. Many of Bob's ideas are reflected in this book; I have learned much from him.

I would like to thank John Lachs, Ken Iserson, Jay Jacobson, Bob Walker, and Randy LaFevor for their many contributions to my professional growth. John is a great philosophy teacher and has been a strong ally and supporter; for a number of years he was the Vanderbilt connection for the Clinical Ethics Center at Saint Thomas Hospital. Ken, Jay, and Bob have been core faculty in the development and continuation of our clinical ethics education modules. Randy has been a best friend from law school days and our lunchtime discussions about the law, lawyering, and judging provide wonderful memories. In that same vein, those at the Nashville law firm where I served of counsel— both Bill Moodys, John Whitfield, and Mike Castellarin—permitted me the opportunity to see the law as a very practical tool to help people resolve problems.

I am thankful to Louis Bernard for allowing me to participate in the fellowship program at the University of Chicago Center for Clinical Medical Ethics (now the MacLean Center) while I was a pediatrics faculty member at Meharry Medical College. The experience was the most enriching and rewarding of all my educational years.

One cannot praise Mark Siegler enough for creating the center that has trained more clinical ethics program directors than any other in the country. It was a pleasure learning from the center's core faculty: John

Lantos, Ann Dudley Goldblatt, Stephen Toulmin, Mary Mahowald, and Carol Stocking. Others in my class have remained colleagues and strong influences: Ken Iserson, Gene Bereza, September Williams, and the late Marion Secundy.

Sister Almeda Golson and John Sergent honored me with the privilege of leading the new Clinical Ethics Center at Saint Thomas Hospital in Nashville. The "Clinical Ethics for Practitioners" series, which began as a pilot at Saint Thomas in 1991 with sixteen volunteer physicians, has evolved into an ongoing program with the participation to date of more than 1,500 physicians, nurses, chaplains, social workers, lawyers, and ethics committee members from more than half the states. It was a pleasure working too with John Johnson from 1996 to 1998; John succeeded John Sergent as Chair of Medicine and chair of the hospital's ethics committee. Besides having quick and brilliant minds and being distinguished rheumatologists, both Sergent and Johnson were supportive role models. Saint Thomas was very fortunate to have them leading their internal medicine residency programs and ethics efforts.

It was an honor working with the Daughters of Charity National Health System's East Central Region (now a part of the Ascension Health group) and their member hospitals; the late Sister Priscilla Grimes (Saint Thomas Hospital, Nashville) and Sisters Sharon Richardt (St. Vincent Hospital and Health Services, Indianapolis), Cathy Kelly (St. Mary's Medical Center, Evansville), Virginia Delaney (St. Vincent's Hospital, Birmingham), and Elise Boudreaux (Providence Hospital, Mobile) are remarkable mission servant-leaders and strong clinical ethics champions. It was a joy to serve with them in sharing the clinical ethics message with their staffs and friends.

Most recently, John Boyd and Sister Margaret McBride offered me the opportunity to work at Saint Joseph's Hospital and Medical Center in Phoenix as a pediatric faculty member and clinical ethics fellowship director. Through them, I have continued helping hospitals meet ethics committee leadership goals locally and regionally.

I first learned medical ethics literally at the feet of Ed Pellegrino and the late Dave Thomasma. Dr. Pellegrino was Chancellor of the University of Tennessee Medical Units in Memphis and Dr. Thomasma presided over Wednesday noon sessions at the Interfaith Center during my last year of pharmacy school. I later served on the Institutional

Review Board of the University of Tennessee Health Sciences Center (as it had been renamed because of Dr. Pellegrino's influence) with Dr. Thomasma, again literally by his side at the conference table. Their influence in my life has been profound.

The late Bill Swafford, Martin Hamner, Alan Rosenbluth, Mike Ryan, D. C. Huffman, Mickey Smith, and Joe Fink were pharmacy law and pharmacy administration colleagues and friends during my faculty tenure at the University of Tennessee. They helped me as a budding faculty member and I fondly recall our days together. Ed Elko and Mike Budd were key in my relocation to the Texas College of Osteopathic Medicine (TCOM) of North Texas State University, and I remain grateful to them; I am indeed thankful for their trust and encouragement. The late Clyde Gallehugh was my medical humanities chair at TCOM; he proved an advisor, teacher, and friend over and over.

Nationally, clinical ethics education has had no greater champion than Clayton McWhorter. Clayton provided the initial grant to create the HealthTrust-Saint Thomas Hospital Clinical Ethics Initiative when he was Chairman of that national network of eighty hospitals. He opened the doors at HCA to create the Summit Center for Clinical Ethics. From 1998 to 2003, I served as clinical ethics director for his assisted-living company LifeTrust. He also gave Samford University the challenge grant to establish the Healthcare Ethics and Law (HEaL) Institute that offered clinical ethics education opportunities to Alabama's institutional ethics committees. Clayton is a quiet and unassuming visionary who has promoted clinical ethics education in health care at every opportunity. He sincerely believes that clinical ethics education enhances corporate, institutional, and bedside care and should be supported because "it's the right thing to do." I wish the world had more stalwarts like him. In cooperation with Clayton, Joe Dean at Samford led the effort to give the HEaL Institute a firm foundation and extend the distance learning possibilities through www.ethicsconsultant.com.

At Saint Joseph's Hospital and Medical Center in Phoenix, administrative assistants Kerstin Boyer and Jodi Tichi helped prepare the manuscript and checked references; their gracious spirits and attention to detail were invaluable. Charlie Daschbach reviewed chapters and made very helpful suggestions. Gretchen Fair read parts of the manuscript, compiled Dr. Pellegrino's introduction, and briefed *Gonzales v. Oregon* for the assisted suicide chapter. I appreciate their contributions and their friendship very much. Carol Bayley, who serves as vice president for ethics and justice education at Catholic Healthcare West, reviewed Parts I and II of the book; I sincerely appreciate her insights and suggestions. Farr Curlin, an internist and medical ethicist at the University of Chicago, and Rob Vischer, professor of law at the University of St. Thomas in Minneapolis, reviewed Chapter 4; Farr offered extensive suggestions which I readily adopted. Their ideas were offered graciously and I sincerely acknowledge their assistance. Both Randy Heidenreich, Department of Pediatrics (Medical Genetics) at the University of Arizona, Tucson, and Art Caplan, Director of the University of Pennsylvania Center for Bioethics, Philadelphia, reviewed Chapter 8 and offered helpful insights. I gratefully thank my friend-neighbor-philosopher Paul Kelley for his final review of the entire manuscript.

It has been a pleasure to work with Somlynn Rorie whose editorial and wordsmithing talents have improved the first four chapters tremendously. Jan K. Kovarik reviewed every chapter and appendix and suggested changes for clarity, grammatical errors, inconsistencies, and logical presentation of the subject matter. Somlynn and Jan did a marvelous job in helping make the ethical, legal, and medical and pharmacy concepts more intelligible for students and laypersons. Their ideas and independent research extending my efforts have added rich value.

Lastly, to my wife Sarah, who uses clinical ethics skills daily in geriatrics practice, both in direct patient care and administration, and who continues to provide pride and purpose to life; I owe her everything.

Introduction

Pellegrino on Professionalism: A Human Values Basis for the Healing Arts

In today's increasingly complicated health care delivery environment, medical, legal, and biological progress challenge traditional ethics. Yet these developments must be confronted without the ethical compass points of a consensus on values or common religious beliefs. We are now a morally heterogeneous society, divided on the most fundamental ethical issues, particularly about the meaning of life and death. Without a common conception of human nature we cannot agree on what constitutes a good life and the virtues that ought to characterize it. As a result, the ethics of the professions, especially of the medical profession, have turned to the analysis of ethics puzzles and of the process of ethical decision making. For many, ethics consists primarily in a balancing of rights, duties, and prima facie principles and the resolution of conflicts among them. Procedural ethics has replaced normative ethics. This avoids the impasses generated when patients, clients, and professionals hold fundamentally opposing moral viewpoints.[1]

This introduction was compiled from edited excerpts selected from Dr. Edmund Pellegrino's previously published works by Bruce D. White, DO, JD, with the assistance of Gretchen A. Fair, JD, MA. Occasional—but otherwise unindicated—minor modifications, insertions, or deletions of a few words, phrases, or sentences to the original texts were made to maintain continuity and flow and to weave the quotations into a cohesive whole. The final text of the introduction was reviewed and approved by Dr. Pellegrino prior to publication.

Practitioners also rely on codes of professional ethics that are becoming less committed morally and more legalistic in spirit.* They seem designed more to protect against litigation than as voluntary statements of recognized obligations. To be sure, new codes have appeared to protect patients against the dangers of human experimentation, but little has been added to refine the far more subtle but common moral dangers in everyday clinical decisions.[2]

However reliance on process and codes cannot substitute for character and virtue even though it provides conceptual clarity. Moral acts are the acts of human agents. Their quality is determined by the characters of the persons doing the analysis. The physician's character shapes the way he defines a moral problem, selects what we think is an ethical issue, and decides which principles, values, and technical details are determinative.[3]

A theory of the good in medicine provides an ordering principle whereby conflicts between social and individual good, between autonomy and beneficence, can be resolved. Such a theory is requisite also for ordering the health care professional's obligations, which are necessary both to the individual and to society.[4] Health care delivered by professional caregivers is an inherently moral and ethical enterprise. Patients and practitioners make daily decisions that require evaluation and prioritization of competing values.

Professional knowledge does not exist for its own sake. The professional is a member of a moral community, that is, a collective human association whose members share the privileges of special knowledge and together pledge their dedication to use it to advance health. The professional is, therefore, not a moral island. He belongs to a group which has been given a monopoly on special knowledge and holds it in trust for all who need it.[5]

In common usage, professions have often been defined in the following terms: possession of a body of special knowledge, practice within some ethical framework, fulfillment of some broad societal

*The *Principles of Medical Ethics* (really "nine standards of conduct which define the essentials of honorable behavior for the physician") promulgated by the American Medical Association (AMA)—which is an integral part of the association's code of ethics—is reprinted at the end of this chapter. *See* AMA Council on Ethical and Judicial Affairs. *Code of Medical Ethics: Current Opinions with Annotations, 2004-2005 Edition.* Chicago, Ill: American Medical Association, 2004.

need, and a social mandate which permits a significant discretionary latitude in setting standards for education and performance of its members.[6] Physicians and pharmacists meet the criteria for sociologically defined professions but they also occupy a special niche among the vast number of occupations that now lay claim to professionhood. That special claim lies less in their expertise than in their dedication to something other than self-interest while providing their services. That something else is a certain degree of altruism of suppression of self-interest when the welfare of those they serve requires it. Every time a physician or a pharmacist sees a patient and asks "what can I do for you, what is wrong, what is the problem?" he or she is professing (committing oneself) to two things: one is competence (i.e., having the knowledge and skill to help) and the other is to use that competence in the best interest of the patient. This "profession" or commitment, by its very declaration, invites trust.[7]

The first written use of the word "profession" in relation to medicine was in 47 AD in a book of prescriptions written by Scribonius, physician or pharmacist in the court of the Roman Emperor Claudius. In a few short pages having to do with the reluctance of his contemporaries to use medications, Scribonius referred to the "profession" of medicine. This he defined as a commitment to compassion or clemency in the relief of suffering. He did this in the context of one of the first references to the Hippocratic Oath in ancient literature, arguing that the proper use of drugs was consistent with the Hippocratic injunction to help and heal the patient.[8]

Public profession of a commitment to heal establishes a promise to work for the good of the patient with respect to matters of health.[9] Medicine, as a human activity, is of necessity a form of beneficence. It is a response to the need and plea of a sick person for help, without which the patient might die or suffer unnecessary pain or disability. When one is a professed healer, one possesses knowledge and skill that society has permitted one to acquire precisely because they can benefit others. One also promises to help and to act on behalf of the good of the patient.[10]

Principles and duties are the letter of medical ethics. It remains to virtue to live according to the spirit of medical ethics, which has been and should remain focused on the good of the sick person. Principles and duties enable health care professionals to do good, virtues enable them to be good, to make the difference that can make a competent professional a noble one.[11]

Among the professional virtues are: fidelity to trust, compassion, *phronesis,* intellectual honesty, justice, fortitude, temperance, self-effacement, and integrity. In an ethic of trust, the health care professional is impelled to develop a relationship with the patient from the very outset that includes becoming familiar with who and what the patient is and how she wants to meet the serious challenges of illness, disability, and death.[12] Similarly, a good physician does not just apply cognitive data from the medical literature to the particular patient by reason of a catalogue or "cook-book" of indications. Rather, the good physician cosuffers with the patient, thus exhibiting compassion. To be compassionate is to be disposed to see and feel what a trial, tribulation, or illness has wrought in the life of this person's here-and-now suffering.[13]

Aristotle described the third virtue, *phronesis,* the virtue of practical wisdom, as the capacity for deliberation, judgment, and discernment in difficult moral situations.[14] Similarly, the virtue of intellectual honesty requires that the professional accept that he does not know the answer and have the humility to admit it and obtain assistance. The virtue of justice, one of the most complex of all the virtues, is the strict habit of rendering what is due to others.[15] Justice has its deepest roots in love; it is an extension of the charity we should show to others.[16]

The sixth virtue, fortitude, is a sustained courage. As in all the virtues, the emphasis is on sustainability—not individual and isolated acts, but on the disposition to act continuously in a certain way.[17] So too, medical temperance is defined as the constant disposition of physicians toward responsible use of power for the good of their patients, avoiding on the one hand underuse of technology and other interventions with its consequent abandonment of patients, and, on the other, overuse of interventions and technology.[18]

The eighth virtue, self-effacement, requires among other things that practitioners take responsibility for professional ethics, act as an advocate for patients, and maintain a role for character development in the process of technical education.[19] Lastly, there is the virtue of integrity, which by its very connotation defines for us the nature of the individual who integrates all the virtues. To say that someone possesses integrity is to claim that that person is almost predictable without responses to specific situations, that he or she can integrate all the virtues into a whole and can prudentially judge the relative importance in each situation of principles, rules, guidelines, precepts, and the other virtues in reaching a decision to act.[20]

Society demands, and the responsibility of their role requires, that health care practitioners provide care in a fashion that addresses patient preferences while exhibiting the nine virtues: fidelity to trust, compassion, *phronesis*, intellectual honesty, justice, fortitude, temperance, self-effacement, and integrity.[21] In summary, society expects health care professionals to practice ethically.

APPENDIX:
PRINCIPLES OF MEDICAL ETHICS OF THE AMERICAN MEDICAL ASSOCIATION (2001)

Preamble

The medical profession has long subscribed to a body of ethical statements developed primarily for the benefit of the patient. As a member of this profession, a physician must recognize responsibility to patients first and foremost, as well as to society, to other health professionals, and to self. The following principles adopted by the American Medical Association are not laws, but standards of conduct which define the essentials of honorable behavior for the physician.

Principles of Medical Ethics

I. A physician shall be dedicated to providing competent medical care, with compassion and respect for human dignity and rights.

II. A physician shall uphold the standards of professionalism, be honest in all professional interactions, and strive to report physicians deficient in character or competence, or engaging in fraud or deception, to appropriate entities.

III. A physician shall respect the law and also recognize a responsibility to seek changes in those requirements which are contrary to the best interests of the patient.

IV. A physician shall respect the rights of patients, colleagues, and other health professionals, and shall safeguard patient confidences and privacy within the constraints of the law.

V. A physician shall continue to study, apply, and advance scientific knowledge, maintain a commitment to medical education, make relevant information available to patients, colleagues, and the public, obtain consultation, and use the talents of other health professionals when indicated.

VI. A physician shall, in the provision of appropriate patient care, except in emergencies, be free to choose whom to serve, with whom to associate, and the environment in which to provide medical care.

VII. A physician shall recognize a responsibility to participate in activities contributing to the improvement of the community and the betterment of public health.

VIII. A physician shall, while caring for a patient, regard responsibility to the patient as paramount.

IX. A physician shall support access to medical care for all people.

Adopted by the American Medical Association's House of Delegates on June 17, 2001.

Source: Code of Medical Ethics of the American Medical Association, copyright 2001. Reprinted with permission.

Special Additional Introduction

Ethics and a Code of Ethics in Pharmacy Practice

Joseph L. Fink III

How should a pharmacist respond when a patient presents a pre-scription requesting dispensing of a medication the use of which clashes with the pharmacist's personal beliefs? What should be the appropriate role of a pharmacist in a state where the legislature has authorized physicians to prescribe medications to hasten the death of a terminally ill patient? Should a pharmacist participate in prepar-ing lawfully distributed medications to be used to carry out a court-ordered execution of a criminal?

Upon its founding in 1852, the American Pharmaceutical (now Pharmacists) Association adopted a Code of Ethics to guide members of the profession when confronted with challenging situations. A code of ethics has been defined as "a formal statement by a group that establishes and prescribes moral and nonmoral standards and behaviors for members of that group."[1] That original Code has now been revised six times: in 1922, 1952, 1968, 1975, 1981, and most recently during 1994.[2] It is noteworthy that four of the six updates have occurred during the past half century, reflecting the rapid advances in pharmacy practice, the changing roles of the pharmacist, and changing practice attitudes and philosophies. This most recent revision was based on a list of the purposes of a professional code compiled by the members of the Revision Committee:[3]

A code of ethics for the profession of pharmacy should:

- Explain the training, duties, and responsibilities of pharmacists to the public;
- Provide guidance to practitioners on ethical and moral dilemmas;
- Lead to professional accountability;
- Educate practitioners and students; and
- Authorize a structure for enforcing and interpreting the code.

Using this list as a basis, the Revision Committee compiled what it viewed as key values for the code to contain:

- Respect for patient autonomy;
- Trust;
- Caring, as well as curing (continuity of care);
- Honesty and integrity;
- Social responsibility;
- Confidentiality;
- Concern for the patient's welfare;
- Distributive justice when resources are limited;
- Fairness;
- Faithfulness;
- Protection of the patient;
- Competence;
- Stewardship—managing resources in a responsible manner;
- Professional autonomy of the pharmacist;
- Nondiscrimination;
- Cooperation with other professions;
- Dignity;
- Self-determination or empowerment; and
- Compassion.

The members of the Revision Committee were selected to be broadly representative of the profession, both by geography and specialty:

- Joseph Fink—Kentucky—pharmacist/lawyer/educator;
- Elizabeth Keyes—West Virginia—pharmacy student;
- Calvin Knowlton—New Jersey—pharmacist/ethicist;
- Michael Manolakis—Tennessee—pharmacist/ethicist;
- Beverly Mendoza—New Jersey—pharmacy student;
- David Miller—Maryland—pharmacy association executive;
- Phyllis Moret—Mississippi—pharmacy association executive;

- Jesse Vivian—Michigan—pharmacist/lawyer/educator;
- Louis Vottero—Ohio—pharmacist/ethicist/educator; and
- William Zellmer—Maryland—pharmacist/journalist.

In addition to having the group working on the revision be broadly representative of the profession, the Committee solicited comments and suggestions from members of the American Pharmacists Association, from other national pharmacy and health-related organizations, from state boards of pharmacy, and from colleges and schools of pharmacy. Comments from national thought leaders in the specialties of bioethics and professional ethics were also solicited. Finally, the draft of the current Code was the subject of an open hearing at the 1993 APhA Annual Meeting.

A major challenge in using a code of ethics is that the broad general statements or guidelines in the code usually need to be applied to very specific factual situations arising in the context of professional practice. Moreover, the individual health professional confronted with the situation must leaven his or her approach to the conundrum with personal attitudes, beliefs, and morals.

Buerki and Vottero* have reminded us that

> [c]odes [of ethics] are not comprehensive. By their very nature, most professional codes of ethics are self-limited and restricted in scope. Brief codes of ethics are too abstract or idealized to be useful and may avoid dealing with sensitive areas. Such codes are designed primarily for their public relations value and are usually described as being "suitable for framing and display in your place of practice."[4]

They provide an insightful list of typical shortcomings of codes of ethics:

1. Codes are not all-encompassing.
2. Codes may be ambiguous.
3. Codes are difficult to enforce.
4. Codes usually lack patient input.[5]

---

*Buerki, RA and Vottero, LD (2002). *Ethical Responsibility in Pharmacy Practice.* 2nd ed. Madison, WI: American Institute of the History of Pharmacy. Reprinted with permission.

In the view of those commentators "[t]he ideal code of ethics usually consists of a concise, generalized code supplemented by a manual of interpretations or case histories. Medicine, nursing, and law now use this latter approach, which is also intended to be developed for the 1994 Code of Ethics for Pharmacists as this Code continues to be fully implemented." Note that the text of the Code of Ethics for Pharmacists appearing at the end of this chapter has a bold-font, "black letter," broad-brush ethical statement which is amplified in a paragraph to facilitate application of the broad principle by the user.

The role of a code of ethics in providing guidance and perhaps reassurance that the pharmacist is on-track with his or her approach to a challenging situation cannot be overemphasized. However, codes have their limits: "Some pharmacists prefer to appeal to some external authority, such as a code of ethics, to help them resolve their ethical dilemmas. Unfortunately, as we have noted, some codes of ethics are so general and vague that they are not very useful in resolving specific problems."[6] Moreover, ethical issues arising in professional practice can be as many and varied as the patients we serve. These issues are rarely neat and clean with distinct, clear-cut choices or alternatives. In the end, the health profession must be guided by personal and professional beliefs, attitudes and standards of behavior that enable him or her to be comfortable with the decision reached.

APPENDIX:
CODE OF ETHICS FOR PHARMACISTS
OF THE AMERICAN PHARMACISTS
ASSOCIATION (1994)

Preamble

Pharmacists are health professionals who assist individuals in making the best use of medications. This Code, prepared and supported by pharmacists, is intended to state publicly the principles that form the fundamental basis of the roles and responsibilities of pharmacists. These principles, based on moral obligations and virtues, are established to guide pharmacists in relationships with patients, health professionals, and society.

Code of Ethics for Pharmacists

I. **A pharmacist respects the covenantal relationship between the patient and pharmacist.** Considering the patient-pharmacist relationship as a covenant means that a pharmacist has moral obligations in response to the gift of trust received from society. In return for this gift, a pharmacist promises to help individuals achieve optimum benefit from their medications, to be committed to their welfare, and to maintain their trust.

II. **A pharmacist promotes the good of every patient in a caring, compassionate, and confidential manner.** A pharmacist places concern for the well-being of the patient at the center of professional practice. In doing so, a pharmacist considers needs stated by the patient as well as those defined by health science. A pharmacist is dedicated to protecting the dignity of the patient. With a caring attitude and a compassionate spirit, a pharmacist focuses on serving the patient in a private and confidential manner.

III. **A pharmacist respects the autonomy and dignity of each patient.** A pharmacist promotes the right of self-determination and recognizes individual self-worth by encouraging patients to participate in decisions about their health. A pharmacist communicates with patients in terms that are understandable. In all cases, a pharmacist respects personal and cultural differences among patients.

IV. **A pharmacist acts with honesty and integrity in professional relationships.** A pharmacist has a duty to tell the truth and to act with conviction of conscience. A pharmacist avoids discriminatory practices, behavior, or work conditions that impair professional judgment, and actions that compromise dedication to the best interests of patients.

V. **A pharmacist maintains professional competence.** A pharmacist has a duty to maintain knowledge and abilities as new medications, devices, and technologies become available and as health information advances.

VI. **A pharmacist respects the values and abilities of colleagues and other health professionals.** When appropriate, a pharmacist asks for the consultation of colleagues or other health professionals or refers the patient. A pharmacist acknowledges that colleagues and other health professionals may differ in the beliefs and values they apply to the care of the patient.

VII. **A pharmacist serves individual, community, and societal needs.** The primary obligation of a pharmacist is to individual patients. However, the obligations of a pharmacist may at times extend beyond the individual to the community and society. In these situations, the pharmacist recognizes the responsibilities that accompany these obligations and acts accordingly.

VIII. **A pharmacist seeks justice in the distribution of health resources.** When health resources are allocated, a pharmacist is fair and equitable, balancing the needs of patients and society.[7]

Adopted by the American Pharmacists Association membership, October 27, 1994. © APhA, 1994. Reprinted with permission.

PART I:
FOUNDATIONAL BASICS

Chapter 1

Tobacco and Choices: How Values and Definitions Impact Decision Making

Why begin a medical and pharmacy ethics book with a discussion about tobacco? One might think that it would be best to begin with reflections about Schiavo, Cruzan, *or* Quinlan, *or at least with an analysis of an intensive care unit case. What's so special about the FDA and cigarette advertising, and what does it have to do with drugs, ethics, and quality of life? In a word, everything.*

In 1996, the federal Food and Drug Administration (FDA) declared that tobacco, more specifically its active chemical agent nicotine, was a drug.[1] Several years later in 2000, the U.S. Supreme Court ruled in a decision with five of the nine justices in the majority that the FDA was wrong.[2] How could such a ruling occur when the FDA is *the* federal consumer protection agency that regulates the availability of prescription drug products and assures their quality, safety, and effectiveness? How is it that the nation's responsible administrative authority on drugs could be wrong about such a critically fundamental—if not pivotal—definitional issue? The answer lies in the fact that a *drug* (an agent or chemical with pharmacologic activity) may not be considered a drug, according to certain federal regulatory definitions.

FDA'S 1996 TOBACCO REGULATIONS AND FDA v. BROWN & WILLIAMSON

On August 11, 1995, the FDA issued final rules in the Federal Register titled Regulations Restricting the Sale and Distribution of

Cigarettes and Smokeless Tobacco to Protect Children and Adolescents. The final regulations were published after the agency issued
a proposed rule under the same title,[3] and after analyzing more than
700,000 comments concerning the proposed regulation (more than
"at any other time in its history on any other subject"[4]).

In its final rule, the FDA noted that nicotine is a "drug," and cigarettes and smokeless tobacco products are "drug delivery devices."[5]
The federal Food, Drug, and Cosmetic Act (FDCA), the enabling legislation enacted in 1938 that created the modern FDA and initially
granted its primary powers, defined a *drug* as an "[article] (other than
food) intended to affect the structure or any function of the body."[6]
Moreover, the FDA claimed in its final rule that, because nicotine is a
drug, the agency had the right to regulate nicotine and nicotine delivery devices under the authority of the FDCA. The novelty of this 1996
FDA assertion was that—for the first time in its or its predecessor
agency's* ninety-year history—it claimed regulatory jurisdiction over
a tobacco product.

In promulgating the final rule, it was undisputed that the FDA was
motivated by sincerely held and even noble public policy considerations as indicated by the following statements:

- "[O]ne of the most troubling public health problems facing our
  Nation today [results in] thousands of premature deaths that occur each year because of tobacco use."[7]
- "Tobacco consumption is 'the single leading cause of prevent-
  able death in the United States.'"[8]
- "[M]ore than 400,000 people die each year from tobacco-related
  illnesses, such as cancer, respiratory illnesses, and heart disease."[9]
- "[T]he only way to reduce the amount of tobacco-related illness
  and mortality [is] to reduce the level of addiction, a goal that
  [can] be accomplished only by preventing children and adolescents from starting to use tobacco."[10]

---

*The FDA's predecessor was the Division (1862-1901) and later the Bureau of
Chemistry in the Department of Agriculture (1901-1927), which became the Food,
Drug. and Insecticide Administration in 1927, and whose name was shortened to Food
and Drug Administration in 1930. In 1940, the agency was transferred to the new Federal Security Agency, and then in 1953 to the new Department of Health, Education, and
Welfare. See "FDA History" on the federal government's FDA Web site. Available at
http://www.fda.gov/oc/history/default.htm (accessed May 27, 2006).

- It is known "that 82% of adult smokers had their first cigarette before the age of 18, and more than half had already become regular smokers by that age."[11]
- "As many as 75% of adult smokers believe that smoking 'reduces nervous irritation.'"[12]
- About "73% of young people (10- to 22-year-olds) who begin smoking say they do so for 'relaxation.'"[13]
- Authorities understand that "children [are] beginning to smoke at a younger age, that the prevalence of youth smoking [has] recently increased, and that similar problems existed with respect to smokeless tobacco."[14]
- "[L]ess than 3% of the 70% of smokers who want to quit each year succeed."[15]
- It is the opinion of experts "that if 'the number of children and adolescents who begin tobacco use can be substantially diminished, tobacco-related illness can be correspondingly reduced because data suggest that anyone who does not begin smoking in childhood or adolescence is unlikely ever to begin.'"[16]

With the agency's self-declared statutory jurisdiction over nicotine as a drug and the uncontested findings about its use and potential health hazards, the FDA promulgated a final rule designed to limit tobacco product promotion and accessibility to children and young adults and required very specific label warnings on all tobacco product packages. Before the regulations went into effect, a group of tobacco manufacturers, retailers, and advertisers filed a lawsuit in the U.S. District Court for the Middle District of North Carolina challenging the regulation's validity.[17] The plaintiffs asked that the regulations be struck down for the following reasons: (1) the FDA lacked jurisdiction to regulate tobacco products as customarily marketed; (2) the regulations exceeded the agency's statutory authority as delineated in the FDCA; and (3) the promotional and advertising regulations violated the commercial free speech liberties guaranteed by the First Amendment.[18] The district court granted plaintiffs' motion for summary judgment in part and denied it in part. The court upheld the FDA's jurisdiction and the regulations surrounding the accessibility and labeling of nicotine, but found that the promotional and advertising regulations exceeded the agency's authority. The court prevented the FDA from implementing the regulations it found valid; and then certified its order for immediate interlocutory appeal to the U.S. Court of Appeals for the Fourth Circuit to expedite quick resolution of the issues before a higher court.

The Court of Appeals reversed the district court ruling based on the fact that Congress had not granted the FDA jurisdictional authority to regulate tobacco products.[19] Having resolved the jurisdictional question against the FDA, the appellate court did not consider whether the agency had exceeded its authority under the FDCA or violated the First Amendment. The U.S. Supreme Court granted the FDA's petition for certiorari* as a way to determine the authority of the agency under the FDCA to regulate tobacco products as customarily marketed.[20]

The Supreme Court heard arguments in December 1999 and issued its opinion in March 2000 via a published thirty-five-page document. Justice Sandra Day O'Connor authored the twenty-page majority opinion (on behalf of herself, Chief Justice William H. Rehnquist, and Justices Antonin Scalia, Anthony M. Kennedy, and Clarence Thomas). Justice Stephen G. Breyer wrote the fifteen-page dissenting opinion (for himself and Justices John Paul Stevens, David H. Souter, and Ruth Bader Ginsburg). In summary, the Court supported the Court of Appeals' decision, proclaiming that the FDA did not have proper jurisdiction to regulate tobacco products. The majority offered several reasons for this decision:

- The Congress had not expressly granted authority to the FDA— or any other federal agency—to regulate tobacco products.[21] Moreover, the Congress had implicitly refused that authority to the FDA to regulate tobacco products by failing to enact specific

---

*This particular petition is often referred to simply as a *"cert."* If a party wants its case reviewed on appeal, one petitions the Supreme Court to order the lower court to supply the records with a writ of certiorari. The Latin certiorari means "to be ascertained"; it is the present passive infinitive for *certioro*, which is a contraction of *certiorem facio*, "to make more certain." Soukhanov AH, ex ed. *The American Heritage Dictionary of the English Language*. 3rd ed. Boston: Houghton Mifflin Company, 1992, p. 314. Most cases come to the U.S. Supreme Court on petitions for writ of certiorari, but very few cases are actually heard. See "The Justices' Caseload," on the Web site for the Supreme Court of the United States for more information. Available at http://www.supremecourtus.gov/about/justicescaseload.pdf (accessed Feb 2, 2006).

legislation—on multiple occasions—that would have granted that necessary regulatory authority to the agency.[22] Since tobacco products are of such a vital economic interest to the Nation, the Congress would not have left tobacco regulation to the FDA by implication (i.e., without a specific legislative grant of authority directing the FDA to regulate tobacco products).*

- The FDA had heretofore expressly stated—through its principal officers over the decades—that it did not have the authority to regulate tobacco products as customarily marketed (i.e., without the tobacco products manufacturers intentionally making some health or therapeutic claim in marketing or advertising).[23]
- The Congress, over the years (but primarily since 1965), with the apparent historical understanding that the FDA did not have authority to regulate tobacco products, had created its own legislative plan to regulate tobacco products.[24]
- Given the evidence, the Court held that if the FDA did have authority to regulate tobacco products, it would have to ban these products outright because they were not "safe" within the meaning of the federal FDCA.[25]
- Regarding the FDA's own interpretation of its regulatory authority, the Court found that "Congress [had] directly spoken to the issue [specifically] and precluded the FDA's jurisdiction to regulate tobacco products."[26] Without demeaning or questioning "the seriousness of the problem that the FDA sought to address,"[27] the FDA cannot supersede the intent of the Congress by attempting to regulate in an area that the Congress has reserved for itself.

---

*Speaking to this issue, Justice O'Connor stated in the majority opinion:

Congress, however, has foreclosed the removal of tobacco products from the market. A provision of the United States Code currently in force states that "the marketing of tobacco constitutes one of the greatest basic industries of the United States with ramifying activities which directly affect interstate and foreign commerce at every point, and stable conditions therein are necessary to the general welfare. 7 U.S.C. § 1311(a).

FDA v. Brown & Williamson, 120 S.Ct 1291 (2000) at 1303.

The opinion of the four justices in the minority, which was presented in the dissent by Justice Breyer, felt that the FDA did have authority to regulate tobacco products based on the following reasons:

- Tobacco products—as drugs—fall within the regulatory scope of the FDCA (if one interprets the statute literally, giving plain word meaning to the language) and the FDA's jurisdiction.[28]
- The FDCA's basic purpose—the protection of the public health—supports the notion that nicotine-containing products should be subject to regulation by the FDA.[29]

Justice Breyer added that two of the majority's following "propositions" were not persuasive enough. The first proposition was that the FDA would be compelled to prohibit tobacco distribution outright if it did have jurisdiction because nicotine is so unsafe. The second proposition was the implication that Congress had precluded the FDA from regulating tobacco because there was no specific statutory authority grant (which was coupled with the fact that Congress had developed a separate regulatory machinery for tobacco products). Justice Breyer concluded his dissent with the following paragraph:

> The upshot is that the Court today holds that a regulatory statute aimed at unsafe drugs and devices does not authorize regulation of a drug (nicotine) and a device (a cigarette) that the Court itself finds is unsafe. Far more than most, this particular drug and device risks the life-threatening harms that administrative regulation seeks to rectify. The majority's conclusion is counter-intuitive. And, for the reasons set forth, I believe the law does not require it.[30]

DEFINITIONS

In America, patients, health care providers, and regulators often reach a point where issues involving drugs, ethics, and quality of life merge. For example, once a drug is available, the patient or consumer considers the benefits and burdens of its use. Then the patient and society must contend with the consequences of how that person's life may have changed, for better or worse, as a result of the drug's use.

As demonstrated in *FDA v. Brown & Williamson,* there is no better example to illustrate this ethical and political conundrum than tobacco. Is tobacco a drug? Are there moral implications to the use of tobacco as a drug? Does tobacco as a drug improve the consumer's personal satisfaction with life? Reflecting on these questions provides the opportunity to consider in greater detail the central themes and underlying definitions of words and phrases such as *drugs, ethics,* and *quality of life.*

What is a drug?

> **drug** (drŭg) *n.* **1.a.** A substance used in the diagnosis, treatment, or prevention of a disease or as a component of a medication. **b.** Such a substance as recognized or defined by the U.S. Food, Drug, and Cosmetic Act. **2.** A chemical substance such as a narcotic or hallucinogen, that affects the central nervous system, causing changes in behavior and often addiction. **3.** *Obsolete.* A chemical or dye. —**drug** *tr.v.* **drugged, drug•ging, drugs. 1.** To administer a drug to. **2.** To poison or mix (food or drink) with a drug. **3.** To stupefy or dull with or as if with a drug: *drugged with sleep.* [Middle English *drogge,* from Old French *drogue,* drug, perhaps from Middle Dutch *droge (vate),* dry (cases), pl. of *drog,* dry.][31]

Howard Ansel, Loyd Allen, and Nicholas Popovich begin the seventh edition of their standard pharmacy school text, *Pharmaceutical Dosage Forms and Drug Delivery Systems,* with another definition of the word: "[a] drug is defined as an agent intended for use in the diagnosis, mitigation, treatment, cure, or prevention of disease in humans or in other animals."[32] Their definition is deceptively straightforward and simple, noting that some agents and chemicals that would be labeled as drugs or "recreational" drugs—such as alcohol, caffeine, tobacco, Ecstasy, performance-enhancing steroids, or compounds used for terminal sedation at end-of-life—would not be considered *drugs* within this definitional scope since their use is not necessarily tied to "disease."

Might a drug be better defined by what it does? This is the approach suggested by Wesley Clark, Craig Brater, and Alice Johnson in the thirteenth edition of *Goth's Medical Pharmacology.* They wrote:

> Chemical agents not only provide the structural basis and energy supply of living organisms but also regulate their functional activities. Interactions between potent chemicals and living systems contribute to our knowledge of biologic processes and provide effective methods for treatment, prevention, and diagnosis of many diseases. Compounds used for these purposes are called drugs, and their actions on living systems lead to drug effects.[33]

The ambiguous and hard-to-pin-down definition of *drug* is further illustrated in the following passage from Andrew Weil and Winifred Rosen's *From Chocolate to Morphine:*

> A common definition of the word *drug* is any substance that in small amounts produces significant changes in the body, mind, or both. This definition does not clearly distinguish drugs from some foods. The difference between a drug and a poison is also unclear. All drugs become poisons in high enough doses. Is alcohol a food, drug, or poison? The body can burn it as a fuel, just like sugar or starch, but it causes intoxication and can kill in overdoses. Many people who drink alcohol crusade against drug abuse, never acknowledging that they themselves are involved with a powerful drug. In the same way, many cigarette addicts have no idea that tobacco is a strong drug, and many people depend [*sic*] on coffee do not realize that they are addicted to a stimulant.[34]

It can be said historically that individuals knew what drugs *did* before they actually knew what drugs *were*. In the prescientific period, there are numerous examples of natural drug products used as extracts or derivatives for their known effects—poisons, drinks during religious or other rituals, and cosmetics.[35] Substances such as opium, belladonna, cinchona bark, ergot, curare, nutmeg, Calabar bean, foxglove, and squill were used for various reasons before their pharmacologic effects were studied and documented.*

Paracelsus (1493 to 1541), a Swiss physician, made the first recorded challenge against the empiric use of herbs as medicine and urged alchemists of the day to use their knowledge to develop chemical medicines, particularly from minerals. Herbal medicine reached its zenith in Europe during the seventeenth century, with physicians turning to experimentation to test and validate their purported remedies. By the late eighteenth century, chemical experimentation had led to the identification and the discovery of new drugs.

Tobacco was introduced into European culture in the early fifteenth century.[36] Columbus and other early explorers watched as Indians "drank the smoke" from rolled, dried tobacco leaves. Magellan's crew smoked tobacco and left seeds on their circumnavigation voyage. As tobacco smoking spread throughout England, the demand often exceeded the supply. By 1614, there were more than 7,000 tobacco shops in London alone. It was during this time that the addictive nature of tobacco was reported by Sir Francis Bacon. He noted, "the use of tobacco is growing greatly and conquers men with a certain secret pleasure, so that those who have once become accustomed thereto can later hardly be restrained therefrom."[37]

Nicotine, the active ingredient in tobacco, produces stimulation and has a powerfully addictive quality.[38] There were numerous anecdotal stories throughout the ages about the addictive nature of tobacco and nicotine—Sigmund Freud's cigar-smoking habit is legendary. The first studies proving addiction appeared in the 1940s, and the English medical journal *Lancet* carried an article on the subject in 1942.

Pharmacologically, tobacco or nicotine is considered a drug because it produces physiologic effects. But for U.S. legal and regulatory purposes, it is not a "drug" as other substances are labeled because

---

*Of course, there were many ancient uses for the natural drug products listed. But as a point of interest and reference: opioids were often used for pain; belladonna or deadly nightshade leaf, an anticholinergic, was used for cosmetic purposes; cinchona bark was used for fever; ergot, a vasodilator, was given for headache and seizures; curare, a muscle paralyzer, was used as a poison; nutmeg, a spice, was used to ward off plague; Calabar bean, a poison, was given to those on trial for witchcraft; foxglove (digitalis) was administered for dropsy (generalized swelling, as caused by heart failure); and squill was used for cough.

Congress has said it is not. How is it that tobacco or nicotine was identified as such while in 1984 the FDA allowed Nicorette® gum, a nicotine replacement therapy, to be dispensed by prescription only for nicotine addiction?[39] Clearly the definition of "drug," like the regulation of tobacco and nicotine, is arbitrary and contextual.

What is ethics?

> **eth•ic** (eth´ik) n. **1.a.** A set of principles of right conduct. **b.** A theory or a system of moral values: *"An ethic of service is at war with a craving for gain"* (Gregg Easterbrook). **2. ethics.** *(used with a sing. verb).* The study of the general nature of morals and of the specific moral choices to be made by a person; moral philosophy. **3. ethics.** *(used with a sing. or pl. verb).* The rules or standards governing the conduct of a person or the members of a profession: *medical ethics.* [Middle English *ethik,* from Old French *ethique* (from Late Latin *ethica,* from Greek *ethika,* ethics) and from Latin *ethice* (from Greek *ethike*), both from Greek *ethikos,* ethical, from *ethos,* character.][40]

In *Understanding Ethics,** David Bruce Ingram and Jennifer Parks expanded on the notion that ethics are tools for proper conduct. They wrote:

> *Ethics* is a subfield of philosophy that aims at clarifying the nature of right and wrong, good and bad. Besides clarifying the meaning and justification of ethical ideas, ethics tells us how we ought to behave.[41]

By definition, is ethics similar to morality? A passage from Tom Morris's book, *Philosophy,* builds upon this point:

> Many people use the terms ethics and morality differently. Roughly speaking, they use the term ethics when they're talking about professional obligations and rules of conduct—as in the

---

*Excerpts from THE COMPLETE IDIOT'S GUIDE TO UNDERSTANDING ETHICS by David Bruce Ingram and Jennifer A. Parks, copyright © 2002 by David Bruce Ingram & Jennifer A. Parks. Used by permission of Alpha Books, an imprint of Penguin Group (USA) Inc.

phrases legal ethics and medical ethics—and restrict the term morality to refer to matters of private behavior. Some people even say, "Hey, I wear one hat at work, and another at home," implying that a person's professional ethics can diverge from her private commitments of morality. But I've always reminded people that they wear those hats on the same head. So I think of personal life and professional conduct as deeply continuous, rather than compartmentalized. Because of this, I use the terms ethics and morality interchangeably.[42]

Ethics can be viewed as an individualized guidance map designed to help individuals or communities make better decisions about life and living. These models can guide an individual or communities toward choices that are intended to "do the right thing" and also build the type of character that allows them to flourish within the world. As a preliminary step in decision making, one must first list and then prioritize important values. Ingram and Parks defined a *value* as "something that has worth, at least for some people" or "a standard typically shared by others in a given community for judging the goodness or badness of something or some action."[43] The authors also wrote that individuals may find something valuable in the value itself (an "intrinsic" value), or it will serve as a way to reach some other value or good (an "instrumental" value). A few professional and personal values that one might enumerate include: strength, justice, courage, integrity, equality, freedom, happiness, health, and respect for nature.[44] Not surprisingly, this list includes a number of character traits or virtues identified by Aristotle (384 to 322 BC) in his book, *The Nicomachean Ethics*.[45] In modern pharmacy and medical practice, one might add the concepts of truth-telling (honesty), confidentiality, privacy, and fidelity to the mix.

When philosophers discuss Aristotle, it is often in the context of *virtue-based ethics*.[46] Aristotle regarded decision making in life as a tension or struggle to maintain a mean or moderate character between extreme traits (virtues and vices). For example, Aristotle felt that man should strive for courage as a balance between the two behavioral extremes of base cowardliness and rash foolhardiness, and temperance as a mean between being licentious or prodigal. Aristotle's great drive was to focus on moderation during life with ultimate happiness at life's end.[47]

A pharmacy ethics text called *Ethical Responsibility in Pharmacy Practice,* by Robert Buerki and Louis Vottero, begins not with a dictionary definition of *ethics* but with a chapter entitled "Professional Values in Pharmacy Practice."[48] According to the authors, if one were to catalog the professional values pharmacists would regard as important, the list might include: a recommitment to human dignity of the individual patient; the patient's expectation of effective drug therapy; technical competence in compounding, dispensing, counseling, and advising; observing legal boundaries; and evolving to meet societal expectations of good "pharmaceutical care" delivery. As noted earlier, the authors of *Goth's Medical Pharmacology* attempt to define drugs by their actions. Buerki and Vottero suggest a standard of pharmacy ethics based on actions to which "good" or exemplary pharmacy practitioners aspire. Philosophers may consider this approach as one that illustrates *normative ethics.*[49] Paraphrased, "good ethics" are descriptive of how "good" practitioners behave or solve dilemmas. They are known to set the norm or the conduct standard. Ingram and Parks noted, "Norms are regular ways of doing things that everybody agrees on. Unlike other conventions, ethical norms regulate all aspects of our lives in ways that are crucial for society. They also create a core part of who we are."[50]

What a norm is or what determines behavioral standards of conduct that one must meet in thought and action can be considered an aspect of ethics. Philosophers have studied these issues throughout the ages. The ancient Greeks like Socrates (469 to 399 BC), Plato (427 to 347 BC), and Aristotle dissected and wrote extensively about ethics, moral conflicts, and the meaning of a "good life" in the hope of helping others make better decisions. However, even they had critics who challenged their theories, such as the Roman Epictetus (50 to 130 AD). Early on, the overarching theme of this school of thought centered on the fact that there was an identifiable standard in a society (even with seemingly impossible conflicting behavior options), and one was better off if the standard was met. It was accepted that when one deviated from the accepted community standard or the norm, there was a potential for conflict or trouble. However, critics contended that it was difficult to decipher what the norm was in many cases, and it was ridiculous for individuals making critical decisions to wait until the normative conduct was recognizable.

During the thirteenth century, Saint Thomas Aquinas (1225 to 1274) added Christianity to the milieu of normative conduct, standards, and right-wrong decision making. His ideas were instrumental in developing the notion of *natural law theory*[51] with a theological check. According to Aquinas, there are universal standards that man could find through reason, and if man violated these norms, then he was immoral. Some later theologians, for example, Bishop Joseph Butler (1692 to 1752), urged that scripture established a universal standard for society.[52]

Virtue-based ethics and natural law theory assume that humans strive naturally to reach a state of happiness and contentment, unfettered by materialistic constraints. Thomas Hobbes (1588 to 1679), a seventeenth century British philosopher, questioned these notions by assuming the very opposite. He argued that in the real world, individuals never have enough security and are constantly striving for more wealth and power. He made the point that the world was not peaceful and harmonious (the true natural state). He wrote that if man were to achieve happiness, then it would begin with the individual serving in everyone's best interest—through universal recognition and trust in one another for mutually beneficial purposes (the *social contract theory*[53]). The societal norm is rooted in fairness and interdependency. If this theory is taken to heart, then individuals can make better rather than worse decisions because ultimately it is in their own best interests.

In the 1700s, philosophers began focusing their ethical decision-making dialogues on individual behavior and moral reflection rather than societal norms. Immanuel Kant (1724 to 1804), a German philosopher, promoted the idea of critical thinking and reasoning as the cornerstone of individual epistemology (the branch of philosophy that studies the nature of knowledge). Kant noted that individuals make moral choices by "doing their duty" (*duty-based* or *deontological theory*[54]), whether they wanted to or not.[55] He considered duties as obligations that must be met. As a result, Kant regarded the role of duties as the core of ethics. He also wrote that individuals would make moral choices after asking themselves, "What if everyone did that?" This question underlies Kant's categorical imperative, which suggests that there is a single moral obligation from which all other duties flow. It is similar to the Golden Rule: one should treat other people with the same regard as he or she would like to be treated. This way of thinking, according to Kant, demonstrated respect for other people. In this sense Kant felt that people should never be used as means to ends; individuals were an end, complete unto themselves.

One of the drawbacks of the duty-based theory is that it allows an assessment of right or wrong conduct based on intent and action, without regard to the outcome or consequences of the act. Jeremy Bentham (1748 to 1832), a British philosopher, embraced the idea that outcomes or consequences of actions are important ethical considerations *(outcomes-based* or *teleological theory; consequentialism)*. John Stuart Mill (1806 to 1873), another English philosopher, expanded on Bentham's ideas of utilitarianism[56] (a moral theory that treats pleasure or happiness as the only absolute moral good; in which quality may be more valuable than quantity). Mill's ideas may be very important to persons reflecting on the quality of life. One should also note that there are divisions of thought among those espousing utilitarianism as a guide to standards of conduct. For some, the critical difference is that the decision maker should act in order to maximize benefit *(act-utilitarianism);* others might assert that the decision maker should create and prioritize rules regarding actions to maximize benefit *(rule-utilitarianism)*.[57]

If one were to make better rather than worse decisions, then philosophers argue that it is important to be self-critical, perhaps even cynical. The German philosopher Karl Marx (1818 to 1883) cautioned decision makers not to view themes such as community, equality, freedom, and justice as empty slogans. Friedrich Nietzsche (1844 to 1900), another German philosopher—perhaps the most extreme defender of anti-ethics—opposed familiar ethical ideas, but was more vehement against ethical hypocrisy.[58]

Since many individuals in the community contribute to the development and availability of health care and drugs, these are considered collective societal goods. As a result, individualized decision making may not be enough to achieve ethical fairness among possible beneficiaries. In the twentieth century, American John Rawls (1921 to 2002) suggested *justice-based ethics*[59] as a means of combining social contract theory and individual decision making to improve the human condition. Rawls commented on the idea that a truly fair society would allow each person an equal opportunity by minimizing the impact of luck (the accidental privileges of birth and intellect), permitting a more just distribution of collective benefits based on merit and need. In a similar vein, *feminist ethics*[60] promotes a community-wide ethics of care based on relationships. This approach rejects the absolutist, objective, and impartial approaches to ethics and emphasizes the higher moral good of inclusiveness and caring for (and about) others.[61] Both justice-based ethics and feminist ethics may be criticized because they are contextual and depend on relativism (since they make no universal claims).

However, one might argue that in trying to solve a single problem, it is the context that makes the dilemma unique. A drug responds differently in every individual—absorption varies, distribution throughout the body differs, and the peak serum concentration is not the same after specific periods of time. It is this same framework that is required when looking at an ethics decision making context—different circumstances lead to different outcomes. There are several schools of thought regarding ethics analysis that may offer some insight to decision makers. *Narrative ethics,* a way of teaching others (particularly health care providers[62]) about ethics decision making, offers the opportunity to see that dilemmas are resolved just as storytellers share their stories. Like narrative ethics, *casuistry*[63]—an opportunity to evaluate ethical dilemmas case-by-case, in an almost freestanding manner without regard to the way similar cases have been analyzed in the past—has much appeal to some ethicists and ethics teachers. However, using casuistry to resolve ethical dilemmas leaves many bewildered because it opens decision makers to the charge of being *relativistic,* and ungrounded in immutable standards.[64] *Case-based ethics* simply allows decision makers to take the unique circumstances of the case into consideration.[65] Similarly, *principalism* and *pragmatism* contribute to decision making frameworks. By trying to identify and prioritize the *principles*[66] (such as beneficence, nonmaleficence, autonomy [respect for persons], and justice) that are associated with a clinical ethics context, one might attempt to make a better, rather than worse, decision. Or, once coming to the conclusion that a decision must be made, one may be quite *pragmatic,* just to get it over with, move on, and deal with any fallout.

In summary, ethics is about decision making. As one identifies values, the process of ranking these values (or beliefs, virtues, character traits, and principles) leads to an evaluation and, finally, a conflict resolution. Hopefully, any evaluation will lead to better rather than worse decision making if one takes into consideration those critical values that matter most. For pharmacists and physicians—who are continually making decisions that impact a patient's quality of life—peace of mind comes from doing the best they can in any given circumstance.

What does quality of life *mean?*

> **quality of life** *n.* The degree of emotional, intellectual, or cultural satisfaction in a person's every day life as distinct from the degree of material comfort: "programs that . . . make a big difference in the quality of life here in the city" (Henry Geldzahler).[67]

Albert Jonsen, Mark Siegler, and William Winslade wrote one of the most widely used textbooks in medical ethics, *Clinical Ethics: A Practical Approach to Ethical Decisions in Clinical Medicine.** In the introduction, the authors stated their purpose for writing the book, "[F]irst to offer an approach that facilitates thinking about the complexities of the [ethical dilemmas] that clinicians actually face and, second, to assemble concise representative opinions about typical ethical problems that occur in the practice of medicine."[68] Of the book's four chapters, Chapter 3 focuses on "Quality of Life."[69] The authors discuss the importance of quality of life considerations in resolving bedside medical ethics dilemmas:

> Any injury or illness threatens persons with actual or potentially reduced quality of life, manifested in the signs and symptoms of their disease. One goal of medical intervention is to restore, maintain, or improve quality of life. *Thus, in all medical interventions, the topic of quality of life must be considered.* Many questions surround this topic: What does the phrase "quality of life" mean in general? How should it be understood in particular cases? How do persons other than the patient perceive the patient's quality of life, and of what ethical relevance are their perceptions? Above all, what is the relevance of quality of life to ethical judgment? This topic, important as it is in clinical judgment, opens the door for bias and prejudice. Still, it must be confronted in the analysis of clinical ethical problems. [emphasis added][70]

---

*Jonson AR, Siegler M, and Winslade WJ (2002). *Clinical Ethics: A Practical Approach to Ethical Decisions in Clinical Medicine.* 5th ed. New York, NY: McGraw-Hill. Excerpts reprinted with permission of The McGraw-Hill Companies.

In Chapter 3, the authors offer a more comprehensive definition of the term in their subsection "Meaning of Quality of Life":

> Despite the importance of quality of life in clinical medicine, the phrase is not easy to define. The phrase expresses a value judgment: The experience of living, as a whole or in some aspect, is judged to be "good" or "bad," "better," or "worse." In recent years, efforts have been made to develop measures of quality of life that can be used to evaluate outcomes of clinical interventions. Such measures list a variety of physical functions, such as mobility, performance of activities of daily living, absence or presence of pain, social interaction, and mental acuity. Scales are devised to rate the range of performance and satisfaction with these aspects of living. These various measures attempt to provide an objective description of what is inevitably a highly subjective and personal evaluation. Also, many surveys inquiring about personal appraisal of quality of life and that of others have been made. Even when measures are based on empirical surveys of what persons consider valuable, individuals may depart, often in striking ways, from the general view. Empirical studies of this subject are difficult to design and are limited in application.
>
> Quality of life judgments, then, are not based on a single dimension, nor are they entirely subjective or objective. They must consider personal and social function and performance, symptoms, prognosis, and the subjective values that patients ascribe to quality of life. Several important questions must be addressed: (1) Who is making the evaluation—the person living the life or the observer? (2) What criteria are being used for evaluation? And finally, the crucial ethical question: (3) What types of clinical decisions, if any, are justified by reference to quality of life judgments?[71]

It may be reasonable, simple, and direct—from a medical decision-making perspective at least—to just assert that *Health-Related Quality of Life* (HRQOL) is "what the patient can do and what the patient thinks about what he or she can do."[72] What the patient can do is be tied inextricably to his or her functional capacities, activities of daily living, and physical and intellectual capabilities. The concept is entirely subjective to the individual and contextual, that is, it is completely dependent upon circumstances at the time. HRQOL research attempts to create objective measures or metrics for comparisons and standardization.[73]

Illustrating this point about objectivity and subjectivity is a recent study that measured quality of life for prostate cancer survivors and was presented to the American Urological Association in May 2004.[74] The University of Michigan Health System in Ann Arbor and Beth Israel Deaconess Medical Center in Boston tracked nearly 1,000 patients for approximately eight years. The study found that quality of life for some prostate cancer survivors gets significantly worse over time:

- Most prostate cancer survivors gave their overall emotional and physical health high scores about the same as those who had never had cancer.
- Prostate cancer survivors rated their sexual function 50 percent lower than those who had never had cancer.
- Two years after treatment with external radiation, fewer than one percent of cancer survivors reported urinary incontinence severe enough to require pads; after six years, about 3 percent.
- Among men who had radioactive implants, 5 percent had problems with urinary incontinence, compared with about 10 percent after six years.
- Surgical patients reported no large changes in their quality of life over time.

In this study, researchers found that the complications of surgery appear immediately, whereas problems with radiation (from burns) and radioactivity (from scarring) show up slowly over time. However, one researcher said, "We're just scratching the tip of the iceberg in terms of learning what happens in the long-term."

Building on this individual perception of functionality and quality of life, a recent issue of the *JAMA* published a Patient Page to facilitate physicians' and patients' communications about the subject.[75] The article begins:

> Quality of life refers to a person's perceived physical and mental well-being. Many factors can contribute to quality of life, including those that influence the "goodness" of life, a person's

happiness, and the ability to function independently and to enjoy life. Health-related quality of life (HRQOL) refers to those issues that can be affected by illnesses and their treatments. For example, pain associated with an illness and limitations in functioning that require being dependent on others to help with usual daily activities can decrease a person's quality of life.

Obviously, quality of life considerations are important in drug therapy. Drugs are often used to help cure disease and restore or maintain health. However, one of the limitations of the Jonsen-Siegler-Winslade argument for quality of life is that their decision-making model focuses on individual patients to the exclusion of a drug's impact within the community. It is equally important to evaluate drugs at a broader societal level based on these issues:

- The community as a whole (including scientists, researchers, manufacturers, wholesalers, retail pharmacies, institutional pharmacies, physicians, marketers, third-party payers, regulators, and all potential users) is a stakeholder in a drug's availability and distribution.
- As drug prices increase, individuals pay a tiny fraction of the cost for drug availability and distribution.
- Unless used properly, drugs are unsafe and ineffective.
- Like other commodities available in the health care system, drugs are considered "community goods," therefore, it is valuable to consider quality of life as it impacts a community and each individual separately.

CONTINUING DILEMMAS WITH TOBACCO

Just because the Supreme Court struck down the FDA rules in *FDA v. Brown & Williamson* does not mean that tobacco is unregulated in the United States. There are many rules. The Department of Agriculture essentially controls supply via grower subsidies, manufacturers must follow advertising regulations that govern marketing, and the states manage or increase tobacco taxes.[76] Tobacco product manufacturers continue to be assaulted in the United States from a number of directions:

- In 1998, several state attorney generals signed an omnibus settlement agreement with the nation's five largest tobacco manufacturers.[77] Over a twenty-five-year period, the states will receive approximately $206 billion in compensation for any claims (such as increased health care costs to state Medicaid programs) for tobacco-related injuries.
- In 2004, the Senate overwhelmingly approved new federal regulation of tobacco products and advertising as part of a deal to buy out the nation's tobacco growers and end price supports that date from the depression.[78]
- Smoking (because of the studies demonstrating the dangers of second-hand smoke) is being banned from increasingly more public places: government buildings, workplaces, restaurants, bars, and even prisons.[79]
- Worldwide, countries are demanding that cigarette and tobacco product package warnings and labeling be considerably more blunt (England uses "Smoking kills" as a warning) and graphic (Canadian cigarette packages come with stark images of decayed teeth).[80]
- In June 2005, the federal government concluded a nine-month racketeering trial against the nation's leading cigarette companies.[81]
- Voter initiatives in November 2005 in Washington, Indiana, and California (San Francisco) sought to extend the indoor smoking ban to 25 feet beyond building entrances, exits, and windows that open.[82]

There continue to be areas of concern and ethical dilemmas for tobacco suppliers and those intent on reducing smoking and tobacco-related health risks. Issues that have been highlighted include:

- Cigarette and tobacco manufacturers are clearly designing products and packaging with children in mind (brand names appear in chocolate, vanilla, and "Twista Lime" flavors; packaging is more cartoonish and colorful).[83]
- Cigarette and tobacco manufacturers are sponsoring parties at bars and nightclubs near college campuses, linking smoking to alcohol, music, and socializing.[84]

- The United States Postal Service is refusing to cooperate—citing privacy concerns and postal clerk unease with policing parcels—with states attempting to thwart the illegal trade of cigarettes via the Internet (even though New York has persuaded the major credit card companies not to accept online payments and passed a statute prohibiting private carriers, like FedEx, from shipping cigarettes).[85]

On the whole, some antitobacco efforts promoted by quality of life action groups and regulators have created effective change. Californians voted in 1988 to raise cigarette taxes by 25¢ a pack with 5¢ going toward tobacco education and research programs. California banned smoking from most workplaces in 1995 and extended the ban to include bars in 1998. State health officials marked the fifteenth anniversary of the anticigarette law by releasing statistics showing dramatic results:[86]

- California's lung and bronchi cancer rates, which were higher than the national average in 1988, have fallen three times faster than rates in the rest of the country.
- Since 1988, the number of adults who smoke has fallen from 23 percent to 16 percent, one of the lowest rates in the nation.
- High school smoking rates have fallen from 22 percent in 2000 to 13 percent in 2004; middle school smoking rates have dropped from 7 percent to 4 percent in the same period.
- More than 90 percent of children in California live in smoke-free homes.
- A spokesman for the Office on Smoking and Health at the Centers for Disease Control and Prevention reminded states that they have a strong incentive to curb smoking. On average, each pack of cigarettes sold increases a state's Medicaid costs by $1.30. He also said that tobacco causes about 440,000 deaths annually and adds nearly $160 billion to medical costs each year.

As the continuing battle with tobacco regulation goes on, the clarification of terms such as drugs, ethics, and quality of life continue to be fine-tuned and altered in accordance with our changing society. There may be no better illustration of how values and definitions evolve and merge through decision making, personal choice, and public policy than from the ethical dilemmas surrounding tobacco, a drug that impacts quality of life today for millions in America and around the world.

Chapter 2

COX-2 Inhibitors and Conflict: How Balancing Beneficence and Nonmaleficence Influences Decision Making

How do pharmacists, physicians, pharmaceutical manufacturers, and others make decisions about product availability and use given that a particular drug may have wondrous promise to provide good benefits, while at the same time an undeniable potential to do harm? Moreover, what response should be given when some believe that in the decision-making process self-interest or profit took priority over patients' best interests?

On September 30, 2004, Merck & Co., Inc. voluntarily removed VIOXX® (rofecoxib), its product commonly prescribed as an arthritis pain reliever, from the market.[1] Merck's Chairman and Chief Executive Officer (CEO) Raymond V. Gilmartin, in an open letter to patients and physicians published on that date, provided this reason for the worldwide withdrawal:

> This decision is based on new data from a three-year clinical study. In this study, there was an increased risk for cardiovascular (CV) events, such as heart attack and stroke, in patients taking VIOXX 25 mg compared to those taking placebo (sugar pill). While the incidence of CV events was low, there was an increased risk beginning after 18 months of treatment . . .

> We are taking this action because we believe it best serves the interests of patients. That is why we undertook this clinical trial to better understand the safety profile of VIOXX. And it's why we instituted this voluntary withdrawal upon learning about these data.
>
> Be assured that Merck will continue to do everything we can to maintain the safety of our medicines.[2]

At the time of the withdrawal, VIOXX represented 11 percent of Merck's revenue for the previous year, with total sales of about $2.5 billion. After news of the withdrawal, Merck's stock plunged by 27 percent.

Within months, the hundreds of individual and class-action lawsuits that were filed in federal courts were consolidated in the U.S. District Court for the Eastern District of Louisiana in New Orleans.[3] By early 2005, analysts estimated that Merck's total liabilities in state and federal cases could reach as high as $30 billion. The company set aside $675 million as a reserve for legal expenses, to cover the foreseeable costs of removing the product from the market and releasing the above statement. On May 6, 2005, the nation's leading newspapers reported that Gilmartin had resigned as Merck's chairman and CEO. His troubled, decade-long tenure collapsed in the wake of the VIOXX recall and the threatened loss of the company's reputation as one of the world's leading drug researchers and manufacturers.[4]

These lawsuits helped bring to the forefront the controversy surrounding VIOXX and other COX-2 inhibitors. Reports surfaced as early as 1999 that COX-2 inhibitors might be linked to an increased risk of heart attacks and strokes in patients.[5] In March 2000, Merck executives learned that VIOXX posed a significant risk for a cardiovascular incident. This information came as an incidental finding from their company-sponsored VIGOR study (VIOXX Gastrointestinal Outcomes Research—a clinical trial designed specifically to compare the gastrointestinal safety of VIOXX to naproxen, another commonly used nonsteroidal anti-inflammatory drug or NSAID).[6] Merck officials disclosed the data almost immediately, but explained that the fivefold increased risk difference was based on their belief that naproxen had a strong protective effect on the heart (in the same way that aspirin, also an NSAID, has an anti-platelet, anti-clotting benefit). Individuals, not believing the company's theory, began to investigate the cardiovascular side effects of the COX-2 class of drugs.

In May 2000, Merck's top research and marketing executives considered sponsoring a clinical trial that would directly evaluate the possibility of an increased heart risk with VIOXX use and for a number of reasons decided not to proceed with such an investigation. A slide presentation prepared by the group to discuss the possible VIOXX link with heart risk carried these statements: "At present, there is no compelling marketing need for such a study" and "the implied message is not favorable."[7] Around this time, Merck executives chose to focus on the measurable positive benefits of COX-2 inhibitor use as compared to frequently used NSAIDs in patients with intestinal polyps, colon cancer, and prostate cancer. One of the studies was called APPROVe (Adenomatous Polyp Prevention on VIOXX). The investigation was a prospective, randomized, placebo-controlled trial— considered by many the statistical gold standard for this type of investigation—of more than 24,000 patients diagnosed with or without known cardiovascular disease. As part of the APPROVe study, investigators monitored cardiovascular data closely, but still indirectly.

The VIGOR study results were published in the *New England Journal of Medicine* in late 2000.[8] In February 2001, the Arthritis Drugs Advisory Committee of the FDA met to discuss the VIGOR study findings,[9] and Merck representatives presented their explanation regarding the protective effects of naproxen. An FDA medical reviewer and others expressed concern about Merck's opinion. The committee voted unanimously that physicians should be advised of the cardiovascular concerns as noted in the VIGOR study. Curiously, the day after the advisory committee met, Merck sent a bulletin to its VIOXX sales force of more than 3,000 representatives that read: "DO NOT INITIATE DISCUSSIONS OF THE FDA ADVISORY COMMITTEE . . . OR THE RESULTS OF THE . . . VIGOR STUDY" [emphasis in original].[10] Furthermore, the bulletin suggested that if a physician should ask about the VIGOR study, the representative was to remind the doctor that the drug showed a gastrointestinal benefit and then say, "I cannot discuss the study with you."[11]

Soon, other articles appeared suggesting an increased risk of heart attack and stroke to patients taking COX-2 inhibitors.[12] Meanwhile, Merck continued to market VIOXX with remarkable success. There were 20.6 million VIOXX prescriptions in 2000, 25.4 million in 2001, 22.0 million in 2002, 20.0 million in 2003, and 14.0 million in the first nine months of 2004.[13]

Why did Merck executives make and support a decision not to further investigate the possible cardiovascular risks right away? And, why did they continue to assertively market the drug for years, downplaying the possible negative consequences to patients?

COX-2 INHIBITORS AND THEIR EFFECTS

Selective COX-2 inhibitors work by blocking an enzyme called cyclooxygenase-2 (COX-2) in the body.[14] When COX-2 is inhibited, fewer prostaglandin precursors are formed in individuals suffering from painful conditions like arthritis. These prostaglandin precursors can cause multiple chemical reactions that ultimately result in local swelling, heat, redness (inflammation), and pain in joints and other parts of the body. COX-2 inhibitors are listed as NSAIDs and are used to reduce inflammation, kill pain (as an analgesic), and lower fever (as an antipyretic). However, unlike most NSAIDs, such as ibuprofen (MOTRIN®, McNeil PPC, Inc.), COX-2 inhibitors do not inhibit the cyclooxygenase-1 (COX-1) isoenzyme in humans taking therapeutic doses. The COX-1 enzyme is vital in protecting the intestinal lining and is helpful to those taking pain medicines. Consequently, a primary sales point for COX-2 inhibitor drugs is that they are less likely to cause bleeding, stomach ulcers, and digestive tract complications during short- and long-term use.[15]

The first COX-2 inhibitor to be approved by the Food and Drug Administration (FDA) was CELEBREX® (celecoxib, G. D. Searle & Co. and Pfizer Inc.) in December 1998. CELEBREX was initially approved for the treatment of osteoarthritis and rheumatoid arthritis. The FDA approved VIOXX shortly afterward in May 1999 for osteoarthritis, acute pain, and menstrual cramps.

THE FDA'S DRUG APPROVAL PROCESS AND VIOXX

The FDA approves products after manufacturer submissions are reviewed for specific indications.[16] In cases such as VIOXX, studies are compiled to show that the drug product is safe and effective for the intended use and indications. The supporting investigatory data is submitted to the FDA with a new drug application asking for market approval. Once a product is approved and then made publicly available, prescribers may elect to use the approved product for an unapproved ("off label") indication.[17] For example, a physician might prescribe VIOXX for rheumatoid arthritis even though the FDA did not approve the product for that medical indication. The clinician might reason that all COX-2 inhibitors work the same way, and if one drug in this class has proven effectiveness in relieving the pain associated with rheumatoid arthritis, then another will as well. This reasoning can be particularly appealing if the clinician has prescribed CELEBREX to a patient with little benefit, and VIOXX is an available option.

The FDA does not regulate individual prescriber activity for a vast majority of drugs. Instead, its primary role is to approve and monitor the manufacture and delivery of drug products in the marketplace for specific indications after the evidence is reviewed and shows that the product is safe and effective when used as recommended. Moreover, it is the responsibility of product manufacturers to decide which studies to conduct in support of the new drug's indications. The manufacturer may limit the initial research to a small number of indications in order to speed up the process—knowing that additional uses can be added later with amended applications once the drug has reached the market.

Not long after the FDA approved VIOXX, in November 2001, the agency also approved BEXTRA® (valdecoxib, Pfizer Inc.) for osteoarthritis, rheumatoid arthritis, and menstrual pain. CELEBREX, VIOXX, and BEXTRA were the only three COX-2 inhibitors approved by the FDA for the U.S. market. At least two others, PREXIGE® (lumiracoxib, Novartis) and ARCOXIA® (etoricoxib, Merck & Co., Inc.) were sold in other countries.

Once VIOXX was released, Merck began an aggressive marketing campaign to compete with Pfizer's earlier approved CELEBREX.[18] Internal documents, released to the public due to public investigations and lawsuits, revealed that Merck officials planned to offer clinical trials, grants, lucrative consulting, and advisory panel positions to physicians in an attempt to increase support for VIOXX.[19] (The internal documents were made available to the public because federal investigators, state officials, congressional committees, and plaintiffs' lawyers obtained the information while pursuing investigations and lawsuits.) One questionable effort involved enticing a nationally recognized rheumatologist with a $25,000 grant to fund a drug trial—the internal memo included a handwritten, scribbled "show me the money" notation by the physician's name.[20] One may ask if this directed marketing effort blurred the line between legitimate promotion and financial inducements as a way to entice targeted doctors to recommend and prescribe VIOXX.

When early studies of CELEBREX and VIOXX and their potential adverse effects became available, physicians compared the newer drugs with the older ones and were disappointed that neither appeared better than the other NSAIDs already on the market. Some of these, in fact, are available over-the-counter (OTC) without a prescription and cost only a few cents compared to these COX-2 inhibitors, which cost around $3 per pill.

When a critical article from the cardiovascular section of the Cleveland Clinic appeared in the *JAMA* in 2001, Dr. Eric Topol (one of the authors) called for additional investigation.[21] Both Pfizer and Merck rejected the idea, questioning the *JAMA* article's study design.[22] In September 2001, the FDA issued a warning letter advising Gilmartin to send a letter to doctors to "correct false or misleading impressions and information" about VIOXX's safety and efficacy. The FDA letter admonished the company for "engag[ing] in a promotional campaign for VIOXX that minimize[d] the potentially serious cardiovascular findings that were observed in the VIOXX Gastrointestinal Outcomes Research (VIGOR) study."[23]

By April 2002, upon advice from the FDA and an advisory panel recommendation, Merck decided to revise the product's labeling to include potential heart effects as well as reduced ulcer risks.

In October 2002, a year after the alarm-raising *JAMA* report was published, Dr. Wayne A. Ray, a Vanderbilt University Medical Center epidemiologist, published a study in *Lancet,* which found that Tennessee Medicaid patients who took high doses of VIOXX long-term had significantly more heart attacks and strokes than patients who took lower doses.[24] Soon after, Ray commented on the study's findings in a *New York Times* interview. He said, "a heart attack in exchange for an ulcer is a poor treatment."[25]

As problematic reports regarding COX-2 appeared more frequently in the medical literature canon, some individuals in the FDA became concerned that VIOXX might conceivably damage the heart. An opportunity came in 2001 for an FDA official—Dr. David J. Graham, Associate Director for Science, Office of Drug Safety (ODS)—to speak with researchers at Kaiser Permanente California HMO about a project that would gather information on COX-2 inhibitors and cardiovascular effects from Kaiser's extremely large and extensive patient database.[26] The FDA provided funding to partially support this pilot scientific collaboration in August 2001 and again in August 2002. The protocol was designed to study the risk of myocardial infarction among users of selective (COX-2) and nonselective nonsteroidal anti-inflammatory agents (NSAIDs). Graham was the ODS project officer designated to work with Kaiser Permanente counterparts. Later, Ray from Vanderbilt was added, based on his particular expertise and qualifications as an epidemiologist. The results of this study were first revealed to the FDA's senior management team when Graham shared a poster session draft in August 2004. FDA researchers in the ODS and the Office of New Drugs (OND) within the agency's Center for Drug Evaluation and Research (CDER) questioned some of Graham's statements and conclusions. Graham later presented the revised results at a meeting in Bordeaux, France, on August 23-24, 2004, and participated in a press conference that discussed the unfavorable findings. Graham forwarded a publishable manuscript of his work to FDA supervisors on September 30, 2004.[27] On November 18, 2004, Dr. Graham testified before Congress. The following day the *New York Times* reported his testimony on its front page*:

Federal drug regulators are "virtually incapable of protecting America" from unsafe drugs, a federal drug safety reviewer told a Congressional panel on [November 18], and he named five drugs now on the market whose safety "needs to be seriously looked at."

---

*Copyright © 2004 by The New York Times Co. Reprinted with permission.

In testimony before the Senate Finance Committee, Dr. David Graham, the reviewer in the Food and Drug Administration's office of safety research, used fiery language to denounce his agency as feckless and far too likely to surrender to demands of drugs makers.

"We are faced with what may be the single greatest drug safety catastrophe in the history of this country or the history of the world," Dr. Graham concluded.

Dr. Steven Galson, the director of the FDA's center for drug evaluation and research and one of the agency's top civil servants, later said that Dr. Graham's new numbers constitute "junk science" and were "irresponsible." Dr. Graham, with more than 20 years service with the Food and Drug Administration, cited the anti-cholesterol drug Crestor, the pain pill Bextra, the obesity pill Meridia, the asthma drug Serevent and the acne drug Accutane. Makers of each drug defended the medicines as safe.[28]

A BALANCING ACT:
BENEFICENCE, NONMALEFICENCE,
AND PROFIT AND OTHER MOTIVES

The 2005 mission statement for Merck & Co., Inc. read as follows:

> The mission of Merck is to provide society with superior products and services by developing innovations and solutions that improve the quality of life and satisfy customer needs, and to provide employees with meaningful work and advancement opportunities, and investors with a superior rate of return.[29]

One might infer from this statement that Merck's overall goals were:

- To try to do good ("provide society with superior products and services," "[develop] innovations and solutions," "improve the quality of life," and "provide employees with meaningful work and advancement opportunities");
- To avoid harm ("superior products"; "improve quality of life"; and "meaningful work"); and

- To make a profit ("satisfy customer needs" and "provide . . . investors with a superior rate of return").

With such a broad statement, Merck could prioritize its principal goals day-to-day and balance its competing interests such as making and selling drugs and making a profit. Merck also explicitly stated that it sees its "innovations and solutions" (particularly vaccines and medicines) as improving quality of life within society. It is unstated but implied that Merck anticipated a *net* improvement in quality of life.

Health care delivery—of which medical and pharmaceutical care are essential elements—involves numerous treatment choices, all with the overall aim of benefiting the patient. *Beneficence* is defined as attempting to do good (being beneficent, "producing benefit, beneficial"[30]). In medicine and pharmacy, prescribing a drug in hope of a good physiological result almost always comes with some risk of harm. This risk of harm may be characterized as *maleficence* ("the doing of evil or harm or mischief"[31]); making an effort to avoid that risk is *nonmaleficence*. Health care entities such as drug manufacturers, physicians, pharmacists, and the FDA are responsible for dispensing safe and effective drugs to patients and must balance the good (beneficence) against efforts to reduce risk of harm (nonmaleficence) with each prescription. With every prescription, pharmacists and physicians balance the possibility of good effects against the risk of side effects and make a very deliberate choice in the patient's best interests.

Mickey Smith and David Knapp reflected on this balancing act in the fifth edition of their pharmacy school text, *Pharmacy, Drugs and Medical Care.* They wrote,

> Drugs have been described as a two-edged sword, combining the potential benefit of therapy with the risk of therapeutic misadventure. A figure of 10 percent is frequently cited as the incidence in which an unwanted reaction to a drug may occur . . .
>
> Although medicinal chemists invest considerable effort in modifying the structure of drugs to maximize benefits and minimize risk, they will likely never succeed in developing products that are completely risk-free. The ultimate responsibility for determining and evaluating the risk-to-benefit ratio for a particular patient belongs to the prescribing physician. Society accorded

this responsibility to physicians with the establishment of the legal category of prescription drugs in the early 1950s. In order for society to receive the largest net benefit from prescription drugs, physicians must take care to use them appropriately.

Drug products themselves are inanimate objects—powerful tools with great potential to do good or to cause harm. How they are used is of ultimate importance. Harmful adverse results cannot legitimately be blamed on drugs if they are prescribed inappropriately, any more than computers can legitimately be blamed for errors caused by inappropriate programming.[32]

Pharmaceutical company management teams must continuously balance—philosophically and pragmatically—beneficence and nonmaleficence (individual patients' best interests) against the possibility of a commercial success (profit). This balance can be seen in Merck's mission statement, which attempts to define two key identified goals: trying to do good and still make a profit. Less frequently discussed are the challenges physicians, medical groups, hospitals, and pharmacists (pharmacies) must face when balancing—albeit on a much smaller scale—the necessity of providing patients with care and goods and services (their business purpose) against a profit motive in the same way as drug manufacturers. Even the FDA must balance beneficence and nonmaleficence (making safe and effective drugs available to Americans) with the burden of excessive regulatory demands (resulting in a decreased drug supply and increased overall consumer costs). These competing interests and tensions can result in ethical dilemmas and resolutions that can potentially impact the quality of life for patients. In the VIOXX lawsuits already filed, it seems likely that plaintiffs' lawyers will argue—philosophically at least—that Merck weighed beneficence and nonmaleficence against profit and decided that company profit (or some other self-interest) was more important than the individual patient's quality of life.

COST-BENEFIT ANALYSIS, STAKEHOLDERS, AND ISSUES MANAGEMENT ANALYSIS

Business entities like Merck, when faced with ethical dilemmas, usually use one of three approaches when resolving their concerns:

- Cost-benefit analysis;
- Cost-effectiveness analysis (CEA); or
- Stakeholder and issues management analysis.

These methodologies are also used within physician practice groups, hospitals, and pharmacies when making nonclinical business and management decisions.

Cost-benefit analysis is explained by David Bruce Ingram and Jennifer Parks in the chapter titled "Business Ethics" in their book, *Understanding Ethics*. They wrote:

> **The Case of the Exploding Ford Pinto:** Do you remember this case from the 1970s? The Ford Pinto was a sub-compact that was marketed to average folks as an affordable new car. Lee Iacocca came up with the idea, demanding that the Pinto weigh no more than 2,000 pounds and cost no more than $2,000. During design and production, however, crash tests showed that the gas tank ruptured, even at lower speeds of 25 miles per hour. Fixing the Pinto would have required changes to the car's design.
>
> Iacocca did not want to invest money in changes, and by lobbying the government, managed to convince them to delay regulations on gas tanks for eight years. One argument Ford used was based on cost-benefit analysis: according to their estimates, the rupturing tanks would cause 180 burn deaths, 180 serious burn injuries, and 2,100 burned cars each year. Ford estimated it would have to pay [annually] $200,000 per death, $67,000 per injury, and $700 per car for a total of $49.5 million. But it would cost more than that to make the cars safe for people to drive: changes to the car would cost $11 each, which comes to $173 million per year. Ford's argument to the government was basically that it would be cheaper to let people burn!
>
> This is just one case that makes us think about ethics and business. What the heck is going on? It sounds like the business world needs a little ethics.[33]

From one point of view, cost-benefit analysis can be seen as an example of a straightforward mathematical equation rather than ethical reasoning. It seemingly unifies the business purpose (of making and selling drugs) with a profit motive that allows only accounting determinations to resolve dilemmas impacting the company's financial statements and bottom line. Complex ethical reasoning and honored ethical concepts and ideals such as virtue, social contract, fairness, and care are removed from the formula. This approach can be encapsulated in the Latin phrase *caveat emptor* or "let the buyer beware." This take-it-or-leave-it marketing attitude places a heavy burden on purchasers to be savvy enough not to buy goods unless they know exactly what they are getting in the exchange. In this situation, the consumers are required to act responsibly, researching the usefulness and quality of the purchase, and later dealing with the consequences if a problem occurs.

Cost-benefit analysis does not provide an optimal way of assessing ethical dilemmas regarding drug delivery and use. In addition, a patient can never fully understand the benefits and burdens of most pharmaceuticals. The legal doctrine of informed consent demands that physicians and patients converse with each other about the diagnosis, prognoses, treatment options (even the possibility of forgoing treatment), and together agree on a plan.[34] It is a general duty of pharmacists to also inform patients about the benefits and burdens of individual drug use.[35]

Of course, companies may voluntarily assume greater obligations to patients than what normally would be expected (as with various philanthropic projects) by calculating net impact and weighing a business purpose with some minimal profit in mind. For example, Merck, in its mission statement, said that it will "provide society with superior products and services by developing innovations and solutions that improve the quality of life." Such a statement implies more than just an interest in the economic bottom line.

Although cost-benefit analysis is somewhat related, it is quite different from CEA. CEA is known as "a technique for selecting among competing wants wherever resources are limited."[36] The concept was initially developed for the military and later suggested for health care application in the mid-1960s.[37] It is CEA and not cost-benefit analysis that permits researchers to calculate the overall net savings of a health care system. Items such as requiring a particular immunization,[38] raising taxes on a pack of cigarettes,[39] or assessing the effect of obesity on an individual's lifetime health care costs[40] are determined by CEA. The calculations are far more imposing than the less complex cost-benefit analyses, but come closer to including some notions of individuality and fairness in the equation. Like cost-benefit analysis, it is an attempt to place a dollar amount or quantify business strategies or risks and their possible impact on overall operations.

Many physicians, perhaps none more vehemently than Edmund Pellegrino, John Carroll Professor Emeritus of Medicine and Medical Ethics at the Center for Clinical Bioethics at Georgetown University Medical Center and the present (2005) Chair of the President's Council on Bioethics, attested to the fact that doctors should never pit their business purpose (i.e., doctoring, of which prescribing drugs is an integral part) against profit or other motives (earning a living; remaining in practice; prestige; and career advancement) in an attempt to resolve ethical dilemmas. Pellegrino noted, "[a]t its very core, the practice of medicine is an inherently moral enterprise rooted in the physician-patient covenant. In his mind, medicine and healthcare are not commodities that are bought and sold in the marketplace."[41] He identified three important points that distinguish medicine as a unique moral enterprise:

1. *The nature of illness itself.* Sick persons are particularly vulnerable. When they seek medical attention, they bare their frailties and infirmities; compromise their dignity; and reveal intimacies of mind, body, and soul. The predicament of illness requires that patients trust physicians, pharmacists, and drug manufacturers in a relationship that is more or less forced upon them. According to Pellegrino, healthcare providers have a special obligation to act in a patient's best interest and not their own self-interest.

2. *A physician's or a pharmacist's knowledge is not proprietary.* Physicians and pharmacists are privileged by society to learn medicine and pharmacy—many at state-supported universities and hospitals. Medical and pharmacy students do not even pay fair market value for their training since their education is in great part subsidized. According to Pellegrino, those who accept the privilege of medical and pharmacy education and practice make a covenant with mankind to use their knowledge for the benefit of society.

3. *Physicians and pharmacists take an oath.* This covenantal relationship is often acknowledged publicly when physicians and

pharmacists take the ceremonial oath of Hippocrates or Asclepius upon graduation. The oath is a public promise—an affirmation of professionalism—that the healthcare provider understands the seriousness of the calling, pledges to remain competent, and uses that competence in the interests of the sick.

These three points are what set health care providers apart from overtly commercial enterprises and define the healing arts as a moral community. Unfortunately for the public, the prevailing social mindset runs counter to this fundamental belief about medical practice, as championed by Pellegrino.[42] He wrote that the legitimization of the profit motive in health care delivery has transformed the physician-patient *covenant* into the physician-patient *contract*. He argued persuasively that if today's physicians must choose between doing good and pursuing profit, then they must act in the patient's best interests rather than their own. He added a patient's trust can be broken if the covenant between the two turns into a contract. "The end result is a physician who is an employee whose loyalties are divided between organization and patient, and whose interests are pitted against the patient to curb costs or make profits."

To be a health care professional, one makes and keeps a promise to help and serve individuals who are ill and to act in a vulnerable patient's best interest without regard to the ethos of the marketplace.

A third methodology used in business enterprise ethical decision making is one articulated by Joseph Weiss and explained in the third edition of the textbook, *Business Ethics: A Stakeholder and Issues Management Approach*.[43] Weiss recommended a stakeholder and issues management approach to create a win-win collaboration as opposed to a win-lose (offering no net gain or loss) or a lose-lose possibility. Given the complex and highly interdependent relationships of those who have a constituent interest or claim (the stakeholders) in the outcome of the ethical dilemma, this matrix has much appeal. Weiss offers a seven-step plan:

1. Map stakeholder relationships.
2. Map stakeholder coalitions.
3. Assess the nature of each stakeholder's interest.
4. Assess the nature of each stakeholder's power.
5. Identify stakeholder ethical and moral responsibilities.

6. Develop specific strategies and tactics.
7. Monitor shifting coalitions.

Using the VIOXX case under consideration as an example, one might work through a stakeholder and issues management analysis in the following way:

1. The primary stakeholders are: Merck; its management team and shareholders (those who manufactured and sold VIOXX); physicians (who prescribed the drug); pharmacists (who dispensed the product); patients (who took the medicine); and the FDA (which approved and regulated the availability of the pain reliever in the marketplace). The list of secondary stakeholders could include: Merck employees; communities where Merck facilities are located; pharmaceutical product trade and professional associations (the Pharmaceutical Research and Manufacturers Association of America and the American Medical Association); special interest groups (the Arthritis Foundation and the American Heart Association); third parties who might have been injured (including patient family members of deceased patients); those who represented parties in court and tried cases (primarily lawyers and judges); lawmakers (U.S. senators, representatives, state legislators); regulators (including state boards of medical examiners and pharmacy, and the U.S. Patent Office); other health care providers and business entities in the drug distribution chain (pharmacies, hospitals, nurses, drug wholesalers and suppliers, health care insurance providers, and commercial carriers); the media; taxpaying citizens; and the remainder of society.

2. Coalitions may be harder to assess in the VIOXX case, but it appears that the primary camps are: Merck and other pharmaceutical manufacturers; doctors and other health care providers; patients and their supporters; and the government (regulators *and* lawmakers).

3. The stakeholders' interest in this example are apparent; however, it might be helpful to use a cost-benefit analysis to reflect on each stakeholder's specific involvement and claim.

4. The stakeholders' power appears somewhat obvious. Merck was in a position to study VIOXX's safety and effectiveness and remove the drug from the market; physicians were in a position to advise patients and regulators; patients could file lawsuits to recover

damages; and the federal government could use criminal and civil sanctions to back up their recommendations. Another critical power (perhaps easily overlooked) lies with consumers and shareholders—if Merck failed to act responsibly in their eyes, the company's reputation could become so tarnished as to irrevocably damage future business prospects entirely.

5. In determining the ethics and moral responsibility of each stakeholder, one can refer to Merck's mission statement, the physicians' codes of ethics and standards of care, and the federal statutes that created and empowered the FDA.

6. Since Merck faced several choices at various points, it is not necessary to list them all in order to illustrate strategies and tactics. The more important decisions center around the importance of:

   a. sponsoring a specific study to consider the cardiovascular effects of VIOXX (confronted around May 2000), or

   b. voluntarily removing VIOXX from the market (decided in September 2004).

Both these decisions offer two immediate answers—yes or no—with supporting alternatives along the spectrum. Recall when Gilmartin said, "we are taking this action because we believe it best serves the interests of patients."

7. As fault-finding and liability questions unfold, the coalitions will shift in a way that might leave Merck alone on one side to deal with the consequences. The shifting coalitions that needed to be monitored in the VIOXX case also occurred within the FDA and federal government. When Graham offered evidence to his superiors that VIOXX might not be as safe as they thought, he was rebuffed by agency colleagues. As a result, he reported his beliefs in an indirect way and gained worldwide attention. He testified before Congress and questioned whether the entire drug approval system was "broken,"[44] and triggered a legislative and public storm that resulted in the removal of another COX-2 inhibitor from the market.[45] As a result *Forbes Magazine* honored Graham with the Face of the Year award for his "steadfast advocacy of drug safety and his willingness to blow the whistle on his bosses."[46] The magazine noted Graham's comments, "The FDA had ignored warnings that the pain pill VIOXX was killing people by causing heart attacks and strokes" and "the agency was incapable of defending the public against another drug disaster." "I could have given

a very mealy-mouthed statement," he said. "But, then I would have been part of the problem."[47] Other coalitions shifted as well. Patients clamored for effective pain medicines even when the risks were high.[48] Pharmaceutical manufacturers rallied support in defense of their claims and attempted to extend their market share,[49] and plaintiffs' lawyers selected a steering committee to manage the class action lawsuits.[50] However, none seemed as dramatic as the Graham-FDA episode.

Weiss noted that there are several "quick ethical tests" that one might consider once a plan of action is developed after analysis:

- *The Golden Rule:* "Do unto others as you would have them do unto you." This includes not knowingly doing harm to others.
- *The Intuition Ethic:* We know apart from reason [intuition] what is right. We have a moral sense about what is right and wrong. We should follow our "gut feeling" about what is right.
- *The Means-Ends Ethic:* We may choose unscrupulous but efficient means to reach an end if the ends are really worthwhile and significant. Be sure the ends are not the means.
- *The Test of Common Sense:* "Does the action I am getting ready to take really make sense?" Think before acting.
- *The Test of One's Best Self:* "Is this action or decision I'm getting ready to take compatible with my concept of myself at my best?"
- *The Test of Ventilation:* Do not isolate yourself with your dilemma. Get additional feedback before acting or deciding.
- *The Test of the Purified Idea:* "Am I thinking this action or decision is right just because someone with appropriate authority or knowledge says it is right?" An action may not be right because someone in a position of power or authority states it is right. You may still be held responsible for taking the action.[51]

Those trying to resolve an ethical dilemma using Weiss's strategy might criticize the usefulness of the stakeholder and issues management approach since it does not point to the most appropriate resolution. However, models are tools that do require valid judgments and subjectivity on the part of the decision maker, thus providing a range of ethical options, depending on the contextual features of the problem.

CONTINUING DILEMMAS WITH COX-2 INHIBITORS

Early in November 2004, the Senate Finance Committee concluded hearings that included David Graham's bombshell testimony. On the following Sunday, November 14, 2004, the *New York Times* published an extensive article on the VIOXX debacle; that same issue of the paper also carried a full-page "Open Letter from Merck" released by CEO Gilmartin.[52] In his letter, Gilmartin wanted "to take this opportunity to set the record straight" about certain "events," which included the company's "business practices surrounding VIOXX" and "Merck's scientific integrity and . . . commitment to ensuring patient safety." He vigorously defended the management team's decision making process by highlighting these key points:

- **We extensively studied** VIOXX before seeking regulatory approval to market it.
- **We promptly disclosed** the clinical data about VIOXX.
- When questions arose, we took additional steps, including conducting further prospective, controlled studies to gain more clinical information about the medicine.
- When information from these additional prospective, controlled trials became available **we acted promptly** and made the decision to voluntarily withdraw VIOXX.
- These actions are consistent with putting the interests of patients first, as well as with faithful adherence to the best principles of scientific discipline and transparency.
- Throughout our history, it is those fundamental priorities that have enabled us to bring new medicines to patients who need them [emphasis in original].[53]

When the withdrawal of VIOXX occurred, attention immediately shifted to CELEBREX and BEXTRA, the two remaining COX-2 inhibitors that were sold in the U.S. marketplace. In December 2004, Pfizer released information that CELEBREX more than tripled the risk of heart attacks, strokes, and sudden death among those taking high doses.[54] In response, Dr. Lester Crawford, the FDA's acting commissioner, said the agency had "great concerns" about the COX-2 drug class and that physicians should consider switching patients taking

CELEBREX to an alternative. Within weeks, Pfizer removed consumer-directed ads for CELEBREX.[55] A month later, a public interest group petitioned the FDA to ban both drugs outright.[56] With these developments, there was speculation that Pfizer would be awash in personal injury lawsuits much like Merck, even though their product remained on the market.[57]

In February 2005, members of the FDA arthritis and drug safety and risk management advisory panels met for three days in Gaithersburg, Maryland.[58] Several pertinent issues were discussed, including the inability of researchers to evaluate the COX-2 inhibitors against placebos. Some members questioned the ethics of giving study patients a sugar pill for pain control. In addition, the complexity of comparing the drugs with older NSAIDs was brought to the table since the cardiovascular risk of NSAIDs had not been evaluated. With the available data, the experts voted unanimously to not only advise the FDA that COX-2 inhibitors can cause heart problems, but also recommended against banning the drugs by narrow margins.[59] By April 2005, the FDA—acting contrary to their own expert panels' suggestions—asked Pfizer to remove BEXTRA from the market. In their announcement, the FDA claimed that risks associated with BEXTRA, including a rare but sometimes fatal skin disorder, outweighed its benefits. Pfizer complied immediately with the FDA's request.

Not everyone was happy with the FDA's actions. Some lawmakers and physicians wondered why the agency did not act sooner.[60] Patients suffering with pain symptoms and doctors who cared for these patients became concerned that the list of available drugs was now shorter.[61] By June 2005, FDA officials were openly admitting that the nation's drug safety system had "pretty much broken down" and there was room for "a lot of improvement" in the government's approach to identifying problems with drug products already on the market.[62] Proposals have circulated for years to give the FDA more authority and funding to improve postmarketing surveillance efforts, but Congress has been reluctant to do so.

After the VIOXX and BEXTRA withdrawals, a noticeable marketing shift and an opportunity appeared for other drug manufacturers to fill in the gaps. As confidence in COX-2 drugs waned, prices for other painkillers rose by an average of 10 percent.[63] Within six months of the VIOXX withdrawal, sales of the analgesic MOBIC® (meloxicam,

Boehringer Ingelheim) increased from a 4.4 percent market share to 9.9 percent with a 10.6 percent price increase. The price for Wyeth's pain drug LODINE® (etodolac) rose 13.3 percent from September 2004 to March 2005, even though the company did not raise the drug's price, which suggests that wholesalers or pharmacies were responsible for the increase. Moreover, Astra Zeneca International (the manufacturer of the "purple pill" NEXIUM®, esomeprazole) began a consumer-directed advertising campaign for patients who "may have switched to another pain reliever such as ibuprofen, naproxen, or aspirin" and are "concerned about the possibility of stomach ulcers."[64] Their product name was not mentioned, but NEXIUM is, according to company marketing information, "the number one prescribed drug of its kind by specialists."[65]

Only three of the more than 7,000 lawsuits filed have been tried as of December 10, 2005. One Texas jury awarded a plaintiff's decedent $253 million (under state law the award will be reduced to $26 million); and a New Jersey trial ended with a verdict for Merck.[66] In mid-December 2005, the first federal trial regarding VIOXX was heard, involving the heart attack and subsequent death of fifty-three-year-old Richard "Dicky" Irvin. According to defense witness, Dr. Thomas Wheeler (pathologist) of Baylor College of Medicine, the cause of Irvin's death was the result of a plaque rupture in his coronary artery. Wheeler added that the rupture led to the formation of a blood clot that eventually blocked the flow of blood in Irvin's coronary artery, which was the cause of Irvin's death, not the VIOXX painkiller.[67] In addition, Dr. David Silver, a Los Angeles rheumatologist who received research grants from Merck & Co., testified on behalf of the drug manufacturer. Silver noted that after reviewing FDA documents and several clinical studies, he did not believe VIOXX causes heart attacks. "The FDA says it does not increase the risk at all . . . and the overall benefits of VIOXX do outweigh the risks," Silver said. He added that VIOXX does not cause bleeding ulcers and other stomach problems the way earlier painkillers do.[68]

Merck stood by its claim that it did not know VIOXX had the potential for putting people at risk for heart attack until 2004, and voluntarily withdrew the drug from the market at that time. On the opposing side, two prominent scientists testified and made the claim that VIOXX does increase the risk of heart attacks. Dr. Wayne Ray (who conducted the study published in *Lancet* regarding Tennessee Medicaid patients) said that patients could be at risk from VIOXX within a day of taking the drug, regardless of the dosage prescribed or the length of time the drug is taken.[69] Cardiologist Eric Topol also took the stand and testified that Merck was aware of the scientific evidence that showed VIOXX's cardiac dangers as far back as 1999—almost five years before the drug was withdrawn from the market. Topol, known as one of the most outspoken critics of Merck's handling of VIOXX and one of the several Cleveland Clinic authors who first raised concerns, told the court that Merck had evidence of two scientific studies, including the VIGOR study, that showed VIOXX as unsafe for the heart. Topol also presented to the jury correspondences from Dr. Alise Reicin, a senior Merck scientist, who had attempted to "tone down" and rework the paper that Topol cowrote that claimed the VIGOR study most likely showed that VIOXX increased the risk of heart attacks. In addition, Topol asserted that Gilmartin approached Malachi Mixon, chairman of the board of trustees at the Cleveland Clinic, to complain about Topol.[70]

During deliberations of the federal trial, another blow for the drug company was delivered when the *New England Journal of Medicine* said Merck withheld information about the cardiac side effects of VIOXX.[71] The medical journal determined that Merck not only concealed heart attacks suffered by three patients during the study, but it had also deleted data on "cardiovascular outcomes" prior to submitting the VIGOR manuscript. According to those who reported the incident, "[t]he evidence has raised questions about the integrity of the data on adverse cardiovascular events in the [original] article and about some of the article's conclusions."[72]

A *USA Today* article entitled "Merck Loses VIOXX Verdict; Will Consumers Also Lose?" published on August 23, 2005,[73] outlined how these lawsuits and the VIOXX withdrawal has taken a toll on the drug manufacturer. According to the article, Merck's stock price dropped almost 9 percent within days of the $253 million verdict and 40 percent in almost one year once it withdrew VIOXX from the market. Merck announced on November 28, 2005 that it was taking initial steps toward global restructuring.[74] "The actions we are announcing today are an important first step in positioning Merck to meet the challenges the company faces now and in the future," said Richard T.

Clark, chief executive officer and president of Merck & Co. The company intends to close or sell five of its thirty-one manufacturing plants and will cut around 7,000 jobs (11 percent) of its global workforce by the end of 2008.

In the wake of the surrounding COX-2 investigations, pharmaceutical manufacturers have reconsidered changing business and lobbying practices and other approaches such as direct-consumer advertising campaigns,[75] voluntarily posting information about ongoing clinical trials,[76] research relationships within medical schools,[77] and phase IV postmarketing clinical trials.[78] The FDA has also started to evaluate its current system and is currently exploring ways to improve communications about side effects and risks associated with prescription drugs. In addition, Congress has put pressure on the FDA to improve its drug safety system and provided a $10 million increase for FDA's drug safety activities in the FY2006 appropriations bill.[79]

In a December 2005 press release, the FDA noted that there is an urgent need for devising a modern system for communicating drug safety information. "It is imperative that FDA lead a collaborative effort to develop a comprehensive and effective approach to risk communication by engaging experts from a variety of disciplines," said Dr. Steven Galson, director of Center for Drug Evaluation and Research (CDER).[80] "Ensuring the safe and effective use of drugs throughout their lifecycle requires us to work closely with medical and patient groups to make sure they have the most up-to-date information about risks and benefits in order to make educated decisions about the products they use."

Perhaps the most interesting turn of events comes on the heels of a new research study that was published on December 1, 2005 in the *British Medical Journal,* which found that COX-2 inhibitors are just as harmful to the stomach as NSAIDs.[81] The British researchers also reported that there was no evidence to support the claims that COX-2 inhibitors are less harmful to the stomach lining than many traditional NSAIDs, such as aspirin. When one recalls that the major design and marketing push for COX-2 drugs was that they provided pain relief without the serious gastrointestinal side effects associated with traditional NSAIDS, it may be easy to understand the confusion and frustration that this fosters. It is unknown how this new development will shape the future lawsuits for Merck and whether it will create a domino effect for this entire class of anti-inflammatory drugs.

On February 20, 2005, a federal jury awarded Merck another court victory, clearing it of any responsibility in the death of Richard Irvin. In a *USA Today* article, Andy Birchfield, a lawyer for Irvin's wife, Evelyn Plunkett, said that "the biggest problem was a ruling by Judge Eldon Fallon, shortly before the trial, that two of the plaintiff's experts—a cardiologist and a pathologist—could not testify that VIOXX was to blame for Mr. Irvin's heart attack. They were experts in their fields, but not about VIOXX, the judge ruled."[82]

In conclusion, the VIOXX case shows how everyone in the drug distribution supply chain—researchers, manufacturers, marketers, physicians, pharmacists, and patients—must continually reassess risks and benefits. Moreover, the case shows how ethical dilemmas arise continuously as stakeholders make decisions, how they must balance beneficence and nonmaleficence in the process, and how an individual's quality of life can change as a result of these decisions.

Chapter 3

Marijuana, Individual Liberty, and Police Power: How Autonomy Drives Decision Making

Why shouldn't patients have access to a drug that relieves burdensome symptoms and improves their quality of life? More particularly, when patients' use of this drug doesn't really harm anyone else, what difference does it make? What if the drug is marijuana?

California voters approved Proposition 215, also known as the Compassionate Use Act, in 1996 and legalized the statewide use of marijuana for medicinal purposes.[1] This law allowed seriously ill Californians to obtain and use marijuana for medical purposes in specified situations. Pursuant to the law, a physician can determine if a person's health status would benefit from the use of marijuana in the treatment of ailments and diseases such as cancer, anorexia, AIDS, chronic pain, glaucoma, arthritis, and migraines. Furthering implementation of the law, the California legislature enacted S.B. 420[2] in 2003, which clarified and operationalized provisions of the Compassionate Use Act and protected medical marijuana patients and their primary caregivers from criminal prosecution or sanction.[3]

Hundreds of Californians have taken advantage of this law and reported an improved quality of life.[4] One patient, an Oakland resident named Angel McClary Raich, was diagnosed with an inoperable brain tumor and scoliosis with accompanying nausea, fatigue, and pain.[5] Raich, a mother of two, credited marijuana with allowing her to leave her wheelchair and regain mobility. Another Californian, Oroville resident Diana Monson, claimed that aerosolized marijuana helped relieve suffering caused by severe chronic back spasms that were not alleviated with prescription drugs.[6] Both patients used the drug with their physicians' approval. According to the law, the physicians could not *provide* the drug but could *recommend* its use. Both Raich's and Monson's physicians found that marijuana provided these patients with therapeutic benefit. Raich's physician believed that forgoing cannabis treatment would cause her excruciating pain and might very well prove fatal.[7]

In August 2002, the rights of these two women and other California citizens to use an otherwise illegal drug for legal medical purposes was threatened when county deputy sheriffs and federal Drug Enforcement Administration (DEA) agents raided Monson's house; the DEA officers destroyed all six of her homegrown marijuana plants while the local officers stood by after protesting the action in a three-hour standoff.[8] The U.S. Supreme Court later ruled in June 2005 that the federal government's comprehensive drug abuse laws trumped local California law and held the DEA agents' actions permissible, even though it deprived patients of an effective drug therapy.[9]

Why did the Supreme Court not permit California and other states the latitude necessary to regulate the availability and use of marijuana by their residents? After all, in the 1600s and 1700s when the American colonies were still British colonies and drafting the laws for what eventually was to become the United States, it was their ideal to promote and sustain local laws that protected the health, safety, and welfare of their citizens, and the morals of their communities. This particular inherent governmental authority is referred to as *police power,* which is defined as the right of a government to make laws necessary for the general well-being of the populace.[10] Moreover, states have used police power to regulate pharmacists, physicians, and other healing arts practitioners since licensing laws were first enacted in most jurisdictions before the turn of the twentieth century. Until the 1930s, states rather matter-of-factly regulated drug use and availability—including marijuana—with little federal interference or involvement.

Why not allow medical marijuana, particularly when its accessibility and benefit, as contemplated under the California law, is purely local in character, and, in its most simple and direct application, does not directly impact anyone other than one patient and one doctor in one state? Why keep suffering patients from a drug that they believe improves their quality of life?

Could the prohibition of the use of medical marijuana be somehow related to a national concept of licit and illicit drug use and how central governmental authority (federalism) can sometimes conflict and affect notions of personal freedom and independent state power?

MARIJUANA

Marijuana is the popular name for a hemp plant called *Cannabis sativa*.[11] Its flowering tops and leaves contain the highest concentration of chemicals, mainly cannabinols, which produce physiological effects in humans. One of the cannabinols, delta-9-tetrahydrocannabinol (THC), is considered the major active ingredient. An aromatic, sticky resin that exudes from the plant contains large amounts of this active ingredient (when dried, the resin is known as hashish).

Marijuana has been used for its euphoric effects since ancient times.[12] It was first described in a Chinese medical compendium dated around 2737 BC. Later, its cultivation spread to India, then to North Africa, and eventually Europe as early as AD 500. Nineteenth century medical practitioners prescribed cannabis tincture for a variety of ailments including migraines, neuralgia, gout, rheumatism, convulsions, depression, and insanity. As one famous example, court physicians gave it to Queen Victoria for her menstrual cramps. In 1850, the *United States Pharmacopoeia* (U.S.P.) listed Extractum Cannabis or Extract of Hemp, and included the product as an entry in the official drug compendium until 1942 when it was removed to the *National Formulary*.

Over the centuries, the *sativa* species has been used to produce valuable fiber, edible seed, oil, and medicine.[13] Its fiber was crafted to make nautical ropes, canvas, and clothes. The seed was used as animal and bird feed. In colonial America, the plant was grown by farmers— including George Washington and Thomas Jefferson—as a major cash crop. It was extensively cultivated in the United States during World War II, when Asian hemp supplies were cut off.

As a drug, marijuana is in a class by itself.[14] It is neither a stimulant nor depressant, but it possesses features of both. It is psychoactive, but not a true hallucinogen. Its use as an intoxicant was commonplace from the 1850s to the 1930s. Smoking marijuana was first seen in the United States among the migrant Mexican workers in the western United States and then appeared in southern cities after World War I. Prominent jazz musicians of the 1920s were notorious users, as were those in the Beat Generation in the early 1960s. A campaign conducted in the 1930s by the U.S. Federal Bureau of Narcotics sought to portray marijuana as a powerful, addicting substance that would lead users into drug abuse and narcotics addiction. By the mid- to late 1960s, the use of marijuana by college students and "hippies" was regarded as a symbol of rebellion against authority.

The acute effects of cannabis consumption can vary according to dosage, the variety of the plant, the method of administration, the individual, and the environment.[15] In general, some of the effects are: mild euphoria; relaxation; increased appreciation for humor, music, and other art; enhanced physical pleasure; loss of inhibition; reduced motor skills; memory difficulties; pain relief; increased appetite; dry mouth; reduced nausea; faster heart rate; bloodshot eyes; or lower intraocular pressure. No fatal overdose due solely to use of marijuana has been documented. For those who smoke cannabis for prolonged periods, there are adverse effects on the respiratory system since marijuana has more tar and carcinogenic additives than tobacco. However, there is new data that suggest a positive correlation between occasional marijuana smoking and lung cancer prevention, with enhancement of the immune system theorized as a possible mechanism.

MARIJUANA CONTROL IN THE UNITED STATES

It may have been a change in the laws rather than a change in the drug or in human nature that resulted in the large-scale marketing of recreational marijuana in the United States during the early twentieth century.[16] With its large Hispanic migrant worker population who used the drug openly, California was one of the first states to prohibit inappropriate marijuana use in 1913.[17]

The enactment of the Eighteenth Amendment and the Volstead Act of 1920 (which defined and regulated intoxicating liquors) began the Prohibition Period, which lasted from 1919 to 1933. During this time, the manufacture, transportation, import, export, and sale of *alcoholic beverages* were restricted or illegal. As a result, the rising prices and inferior quality of illegal alcoholic beverages made available by "bootleggers" ushered in a blossoming commercial trade for marijuana. By 1926, more than 500 marijuana "tea pads" existed in New York City and a state narcotic officer in New Orleans reported that 60 percent of the crimes committed there were by marijuana users in 1928.

To counterattack its growing use, numerous newspaper articles were written about the supposed evils of marijuana abuse, and by the late 1920s and early 1930s, many states reacted to the "marijuana menace" by enacting laws that made its possession and sale illegal. California had already outlawed the drug and, in 1937, it added cannabis cultivation as a separate offense. In a brief pamphlet published in 1940 called "Marijuana: Our Newest Narcotic Menace," the California Division of Narcotic Enforcement portrayed the drug as such:

> Up to about ten years ago . . . this dangerous drug was virtually unknown in the United States. . . . Marihuana [*sic*] . . . is an excitant drug. It attacks the central nervous system and violently affects the mentality and the five physical senses . . . Marihuana has no therapeutic or medicinal value that can not [*sic*] better be replaced by other drugs. It serves no legitimate purposes whatsoever. . . . Fortunately marihuana is not habit forming to the extent that other drugs are . . . [W]hen deprived of his drug . . . the marihuana user will at most feel a mere hankering or craving much like the user of tobacco or alcohol. Considering the dangers involved, there can be no excuse for using or peddling marihuana: anyone guilty of either should be brought promptly to the most severe punishment provided by law.[18]

By the end of the 1930s, forty-six of the forty-eight states and the District of Columbia had laws against marijuana possession.[19] Most state laws allowed marijuana users to be punished similarly to those convicted of morphine, heroin, and cocaine abuse.

In 1937, acting on a bill drafted and recommended by the Treasury Department with a regulatory strategy paralleling the Harrison Narcotic Act of 1914, Congress enacted the Marijuana Tax Act (MTA).[20] The law levied a token tax on all buyers, sellers, importers, growers, physicians, veterinarians, and any other persons who dealt with marijuana commercially, prescribed it professionally, or possessed it. Enforcement responsibility was vested in the U.S. Bureau of Narcotics within the Treasury Department, which was already responsible for the enforcement of the Harrison Narcotic Act. (The Harrison Narcotic Act was initially set up as "an Act to provide for the registration of, with collectors of internal revenue, and to impose a special tax upon all persons who produce, import, manufacture, compound, deal in, dispense, sell, distribute, or give away opium or coca leaves, their salts, derivatives, or preparations, and for other purposes."[21]) The MTA did not ban marijuana outright but limited its availability for medicinal use to prescribers, dispensers, compounders, growers, importers, and manufacturers who paid a license fee. Only the nonmedicinal, untaxed possession, or sale of marijuana was outlawed under the MTA. However, through the concerted efforts of the Bureau's Assistant Prohibition Commissioner, Harry J. Anslinger, and other antimarijuana leaders, the medicinal use of marijuana markedly declined over the years. By the end of the 1970s, only thirty-eight American physicians paid the tax to prescribe the drug.[22]

Curiously, the constitutionality of the MTA was not questioned until 1969 in *Leary v. United States,* a case ultimately decided by the U.S. Supreme Court, thirty years after the statute was enacted.[23] The petitioner was none other than Dr. Timothy F. Leary, a prominent hallucinogenic drug researcher-psychologist and counterculture icon (who coined the phrase "Turn on, tune in, drop out," which came to symbolize the 1960s). Leary challenged the federal antimarijuana statute on U.S. Constitution Fifth Amendment self-incrimination grounds. He noted that the tax application, reporting, and registration requirements were potentially self-revealing, self-incriminatory, and could expose law-abiding citizens to possible prosecution in the federal and state courts. The Supreme Court agreed with Leary's reasoning and struck down certain provisions of the MTA and other narcotics laws, much to the dismay of law enforcement officials.

By the late 1960s and early 1970s, illicit drug use in America reached a fever pitch. Syndicated drug trafficking and connections with organized crime were a major law enforcement focus of the era. In an attempt to improve and streamline federal policing, President Johnson in 1968 reorganized the two responsible national drug control entities—the Food and Drug Administration's (FDA's) Bureau of Drug Abuse and Control in the Department of Health, Education, and Welfare (HEW) and the Department of the Treasury's Bureau of Narcotics—into the Bureau of Narcotics and Dangerous Drugs (BNDD) and placed it administratively within the Department of Justice, the nation's chief law enforcement department. In 1969, the newly inaugurated President Nixon declared a national "war on drugs." He asked Congress to consolidate the several drug laws into a "comprehensive statute [and to] provide meaningful regulation over legitimate sources to prevent diversion into illegal channels, and strengthen law enforcement tools against the traffic in illicit drugs." The Congress enacted the Comprehensive Drug Abuse Prevention and Control Act of 1970.[24] Title II of that Act is the Controlled Substances Act (CSA). This newly crafted legislation "devised a closed regulatory system making it unlawful to manufacture, distribute, dispense, or possess any controlled substance except in a manner authorized by the [law]."[25] Individuals who had contact with the drug or its precursors in the manufacture, sale, or "usual course of professional practice"—such as manufacturers, wholesalers, physicians, and pharmacists—were required to register with the government and receive a unique number to identify transactions. An audit trail was thus established for each dosage unit to track use and prevent diversion to illicit channels. Within the CSA, known dangerous drugs were grouped into five schedules (categorized as I, II, III, IV, and V) based on their accepted medical uses, potential for abuse, and psychological and physiological dependency characteristics. This act classified marijuana, along with heroin and lysergic acid diethylamide (LSD), as Schedule I drugs, which were drugs that had a high potential for abuse, no acceptable medical use, and could not be used safely without medical intervention because of their propensity for severe psychological or physiological dependency.

In addition to combining several of the drug laws, Nixon initiated another reorganization of federal drug control agencies in 1973 and created the Drug Enforcement Administration (DEA) as a unit within

the Department of Justice, to replace the BNDD. This new administration was responsible for suppressing drug trafficking and the sale
of recreational drugs by enforcing the Controlled Substances Act of
1970. According to a 2005 statement, the DEA's mission is:

> [T]o enforce the controlled substances laws and regulations
> of the United States and bring to the criminal and civil justice
> system of the United States, or any other competent jurisdiction,
> those organizations and principal members of organizations, in-
> volved in the growing, manufacture, or distribution of controlled
> substances appearing in or destined for illicit traffic in the United
> States; and to recommend and support non-enforcement pro-
> grams aimed at reducing the availability of illicit controlled sub-
> stances on the domestic and international markets.[26]

Many of the state legislatures—utilizing their inherent police
power—quickly revised their jurisdictional drug control statutes to
align with federal law and the CSA's terminology and regulatory
framework. However, the vast majority of corresponding state statutes contain minor variations from the federal law. For example, in
Tennessee, marijuana is listed as a Schedule VI controlled substance,
with different fines and prison sentences for those convicted under
federal law;[27] and at least nine states require Schedule II controlled
substances prescriptions to be written on specially supplied triplicate
forms for the prescription to be considered valid. As long as state laws
have standards that are more strict—that is, the state laws accept the
federal law as a threshold that is raised for particular local reasons—
there is no conflict between the two potentially controlling laws.
Thus, in Tennessee's Schedule VI marijuana classification and some
states' triplicate prescription forms, prescribers and dispensers can
follow the local laws and also be in compliance with the less stringent
federal statutes and regulations that apply. Moreover, if a person violates the state law, then the same act may be a concurrent violation of
federal law. As a consequence, an individual could be subjected to
criminal prosecution in both state and federal courts. It is, however,
prohibited by the Federal Constitution Fifth Amendment for an individual to be tried twice for the same offence (known as "double jeop-
ardy"). Quite naturally, the DEA and the principal officer of the
Department of Justice (i.e., the Attorney General of the United States)

treat state and local laws that conflict with the federal law and its national purposes with suspicion and as a potential threat to federal law enforcement dominance and priority.[28]

As the United States contends with its attempt at drug control, the issue of medicinal marijuana continues to sit in the middle of a state and federal crossfire. Unlike the prohibition of alcohol and opiates, the outlawing of marijuana was not brought to the forefront due to public outcry or widespread concern. Instead, it was lumped into the larger antinarcotic effort. In an article titled "The Origins of Cannabis Prohibition in California," author Dale Gieringer gathered some interesting statistics that represented the surge of marijuana use in California. He said, "Arrests for marijuana soared from 140 in 1935 to 5,155 per year in 1960. Over the next decade, the trend exploded into a mass phenomenon, propelled by the sixties counterculture. By 1974, arrests had skyrocketed to a record 103,097, almost all of them felonies. Overwhelmed by the law enforcement costs, the state legislature passed the Moscone Act of 1975, eliminating prison sentences for minor marijuana offenders. Arrests promptly plummeted to about half their previous level. Since then, they have continued at an average rate of about 18,000 felonies and 34,000 misdemeanors per year."[29]

PERSONAL FREEDOM, AUTONOMY, AND THE CALIFORNIA COMPASSIONATE USE ACT

From a clinical perspective, patients and doctors should be able to make their own decisions regarding treatment options, including the use of medical marijuana. Medical decision making and informed consent are cherished concepts in American law and society and evolve from notions of personal autonomy.[30] The word *autonomy* comes from the near transliteration and the combining of two Greek words: *auto* (meaning "self") and *nomos* (meaning "law").[31] As a general rule, individuals in a free society are autonomous or "a law unto themselves" and are capable of self-determination as long as they do not harm themselves or others.[32] One accepted statement of autonomy appears in the *Belmont Report* (drafted by a panel of experts in 1979 to offer guidance regarding ethically acceptable clinical research). It states:

> An autonomous person is an individual capable of deliberation about personal goals and of acting under the direction of such de-

liberation. To respect autonomy is to give weight to autonomous persons' considered opinions and choices while refraining from obstructing their actions unless they are clearly detrimental to others. To show lack of respect for an autonomous agent is to repudiate that person's considered judgments, to deny an individual the freedom to act on those considered judgments, or to withhold information necessary to make a considered judgment, when there are no compelling reasons to do so.[33]

For patients to make autonomous decisions, it is assumed that they are competent and have decision-making capacity. The law presumes that persons are competent when they "have sufficient ability ... possessing the requisite natural or legal qualifications" to engage in a particular activity or endeavor.[34] *Competency* is a term of art within the law: competent persons have the "mental ability and cognitive capabilities to complete a legally recognized act" (such as to make a contract, write a will, stand trial, and decide upon medical treatments).[35] Individuals are legally competent unless declared incompetent by a court. *Capacity* is a clinical determination made by practitioners at the bedside when obtaining informed consent from patients for treatment. Capacity is much like the term competency, but is still somewhat different. A patient may be competent but lack capacity (e.g., a stage two Alzheimer's disease patient who has waxing and waning capacity). Psychiatrist Raphael Leo suggested that in determining capacity, clinicians should assess the patient's ability to (1) explain or evidence a choice between treatment options and no treatment at all; (2) understand relevant information; (3) appreciate the situation and its likely consequences; and (4) manipulate information rationally.[36] Leo wrote, "Capacity assessment essentially determines the validity of a patient's decision to undergo or forgo a particular proposed treatment."[37] In addition, Leo added that a clinician should feel certain that the patient understands (1) the medical condition; (2) the natural course of the medical condition; (3) the proposed treatment intervention; (4) the risks and potential benefits; (5) the consequences of treatment or intervention refusal; and (6) any viable alternatives. Clinicians assess capacity because they respect autonomy. Unless patients have capacity, they cannot make autonomous choices.

In America, the government acts both to protect and limit individual autonomy. Federal, state, and local law creates the legal framework to permit citizens the freedom to act in their own best interests—allowing all the latitude to pursue the Declaration of Independence's thematic "Life, Liberty, and the pursuit of Happiness." Correspondingly, one of the roles of government is ". . . to establish justice, insure domestic tranquility . . . promote the general welfare, and secure the blessings of liberty to ourselves and our posterity."[38] Part of this constitutional liberty allows patients to have the right to accept or refuse proffered medical treatment.[39] On the other hand, it is the government's responsibility to protect vulnerable persons—those who are not competent, such as children, demented adults, the frail and elderly, prisoners, and research subjects—who may not be able to make autonomous decisions.

Individual liberty and autonomous decision making are circumscribed to guarantee freedom and safety for all citizens. The state creates and enforces laws that organize the functions of government to guard individual contract, property, tort rights, business, and trade relationships, as well as define and punish criminal activities. Crimes are acts that violate the peace and dignity of the community and are prosecuted in the name of the state and its citizens. The marijuana laws are an example of criminal prohibitions.* It is the phrase—"except as otherwise provided by law" which is written into some criminal statutes (like those in California)—that allowed exemption for the use of marijuana for medical purposes in that state. In the federal system, marijuana possession is illegal outside approved research projects.[40]

Since 1996, a majority of voters in Alaska, California, Colorado, the District of Columbia, Maine, Montana, Nevada, Oregon, and Washington have voted in favor of ballot initiatives that either eased or eliminated criminal penalties for those who grow or possess medical marijuana.[41] Several polls have found that public approval of these laws has increased since they went into effect and have consistently shown between 60 and 80 percent support for legal access to medical marijuana. A study of midlife and older Americans regarding the medical uses of marijuana was undertaken on behalf of *AARP*

---

*Two California criminal statutes are printed at the end of the chapter to illustrate the laws in force to control and punish marijuana sales, trafficking, and use. One can see that "except as provided by law" appears often.

The Magazine in 2004.[42] Of the 1,706 U.S. residents aged forty-five and older surveyed, the study found that:

- 72 percent agree that adults should be allowed to legally use marijuana for medical purposes if a physician recommends it;
- 59 percent believe that marijuana has medical benefits;
- 55 percent say they would obtain marijuana for a suffering loved one;
- 33 percent think that adults should be allowed to grow marijuana for medical purposes; and
- 23 percent think that marijuana should be legalized.

In California, a section of Proposition 215 provides further explanation (called "legislative intent") about the law's purpose and goals in protecting those who recommend (really, prescribe) and use medicinal marijuana:

(b) (1) The people of the State of California hereby find and declare that the purposes of the Compassionate Use Act of 1996 are as follows:

(A) To ensure that seriously ill Californians have the right to obtain and use marijuana for medical purposes where that medical use is deemed appropriate and has been recommended by a physician who has determined that the person's health would benefit from the use of marijuana in the treatment of cancer, anorexia, AIDS, chronic pain, spasticity, glaucoma, arthritis, migraine, or any other illness for which marijuana provides relief.

(B) To ensure that patients and their primary caregivers who obtain and use marijuana for medical purposes upon the recommendation of a physician are not subject to criminal prosecution or sanction.

(C) To encourage the federal and state governments to implement a plan for the safe and affordable distribution of marijuana to all patients in medical need of marijuana.

(2) Nothing in this act shall be construed to supersede legislation prohibiting persons from engaging in conduct that endangers others, nor to condone the diversion of marijuana for non-medical purposes.

(c) Notwithstanding any other provision of law, no physician in this state shall be punished, or denied any right or privilege, for having recommended marijuana to a patient for medical purposes.[43]

STATE POLICE POWER AND FEDERALISM: GONZALES v. RAICH

In the United States, a strong federal government is central to the functioning of the national legal framework. Some authorities have said that federalism is one of the three pillars of the U.S. Constitution. The other two are (1) the separation of powers among the three branches of government—the legislative, executive, and judicial—and (2) the protection of individual civil liberties. The authors of the *Federalist Papers* explained in essay numbers 45 and 46 how they expected state governments to exercise checks and balances on the national government to maintain limited government over time.[44] The U.S. Constitution does not define or explain federalism in any one section, but rather makes numerous references to the rights and responsibilities of state governments and state officials vis-à-vis the federal government. The federal government has certain express powers (called enumerated powers) that include the right to raise taxes, coin money, declare war, and regulate interstate and foreign commerce. In addition, it has implied power to enact any law "necessary and proper" for the execution of its express powers. Powers that the Constitution does not give to the federal government or forbid to the states—the reserved powers—are retained by the people or the states. The tension between federal and state authority and individual liberty is played out daily in the United States, but not as dramatically as in the 2005 case, *Gonzales v. Raich*.

With her personal source of marijuana destroyed after the August 2002 raid, Diana Monson, along with Angel Raich and those who supplied her with the drug, filed a lawsuit in a California federal district court against the Attorney General and the DEA administrator, seeking injunctive and declaratory relief.[45] "In their complaint and supporting affidavits, Raich and Monson described the severity of their afflictions, their repeatedly futile attempts to obtain relief with conventional medications, and the opinions of their doctors concerning their need for marijuana."[46] Raich and Monson claimed that federal enforcement of the CSA against them would violate the Commerce Clause, the Due Process Clause of the Fifth Amendment, and the Ninth and Tenth Amendments of the Constitution, as well as the doctrine of medical necessity.

The use of the Commerce Clause by Congress to justify its legislative power over citizens has been the subject of political controversy for some time. The clause empowers the U.S. Congress "to regulate Commerce with foreign Nations, and among the several States."[47] This clause has been also used, in part, to define the balance of power between the federal government and individual states. As such, it has made a direct impact on the lives of U.S. citizens.

It was the Commerce Clause that the Congress cited in 1970 as the authority for enacting the CSA in the first place.[48] Under Article I, Section 8 of the Constitution, Congress has the authority "[t]o make all Laws which shall be necessary and proper for carrying into Execution" its authority to "regulate Commerce with foreign Nations, and among the several States."[49] According to the Tenth Amendment, the federal government only has the power to regulate matters specifically delegated to it by the Constitution. Without a grant of power to do so, the federal government's authority to regulate marijuana and other drugs could be questioned. (Recall that the American national government is limited and can act only under power enumerated by the Constitution or one reasonably inferred from a specific grant. Other governmental powers are reserved to individual states, and the remaining liberties are reserved to individual citizens.) However, the Supreme Court has ruled on several occasions that drug availability and control within the United States is a proper exercise of Congressional power under the Commerce Clause.[50]

When the *Raich* case was brought to the district court, the judge found that "federal enforcement interests 'wane[d]' when compared to the harm that California residents would suffer if denied access to medically necessary marijuana, [but the court] concluded that [plaintiffs] could not demonstrate a likelihood of success on the merits" as is an essential finding if an injunction is to be issued.[51] The district court judge, therefore, declined to issue an injunction. Raich and Monson appealed.

On appeal, a split panel of judges (two to one) of the United States Court of Appeals for the Ninth Circuit reversed the district court judgment and ordered an injunction issued.[52] The appeals court found that Raich and Monson had "demonstrated a strong likelihood of success on their claim [and] that, as applied to them, the CSA is an unconstitutional exercise of the Congress' Commerce Clause authority."[53] The circuit court of appeals "distinguished . . . [other] cases upholding the CSA in the face of Commerce Clause challenges by focusing on what it deemed to be the 'separate and distinct class of activities' at issue in [the] case [at bar]." The difference, they opined, is that these facts involve "the intrastate, noncommercial cultivation and possession of cannabis for personal medical purposes as recommended by a patient's physician pursuant to valid California law."[54] The two judges in majority cited two recent U.S. Supreme Court decisions—*U.S. v. Lopez* and *U.S. v. Morrison*—in support of their argument that "this separate class of purely local activities was beyond the reach of federal power" to control.[55] The Attorney General appealed the decision to the U.S. Supreme Court.

The Ninth Circuit used both the *Lopez* case and the *Morrison* case as precedent for their decision in *Raich*. In the *Lopez* case, the Supreme Court held the federal Gun-Free School Zones Act of 1990—a law passed by Congress under the authority of the Commerce Clause—unconstitutional because it did not regulate an economic activity. Even though the Gun-Free School Zone Act had a noble governmental purpose, the Court could not find "any connection to past interstate activity or a predictable impact on future commercial activity," as stated in the Commerce Clause.[56]

In the *Morrison* case, the Court struck down a federal statute, one that attempted to create a law for the victims of violent gender-motivated crimes called the Violence Against Women Act of 1994. Once again, the reason for the Court's decision rested on the fact that when Congress enacted the law, it was not regulating economic activity outright and the conduct that substantially affects interstate commerce as emphasized in the Commerce Clause.[57]

The Supreme Court agreed to hear the *Raich* appeal on June 28, 2004.[58] The case was argued before the Court on November 29, 2004,[59] and the decision was rendered on June 6, 2005.[60] The Supreme Court reversed the decision of the Ninth Circuit by vacating their opinion and remanding the case for further consideration. The Court ruled that the U.S. government could prosecute California cannabis patients and growers even though they are using the drug as prescribed by the state's Compassionate Use Act.

Justice John Paul Stevens wrote the opinion for the six-justice majority. Several key passages explain the Court's reasoning:

- In assessing the scope of Congress' authority under the Commerce Clause, we stress that the task before us is a modest one. We need not determine whether [Raich and Monson's] activities, taken in the aggregate, substantially affect interstate commerce in fact, but only whether a "rational basis" exists for so concluding. [Citations omitted.] Given the enforcement difficulties that attend distinguishing between marijuana cultivated locally and marijuana grown elsewhere [statutory citation omitted], and concerns about diversion into illicit channels, we have no difficulty concluding that Congress had a rational basis for believing that failure to regulate the intrastate manufacture and possession of marijuana would leave a gaping hole in the CSA.[61]

- [T]he fact that marijuana is used "for personal medical purposes on the advice of a physician" cannot itself serve as a distinguishing factor. [Citation omitted.] The CSA designates marijuana as contraband for any purpose; in fact, by characterizing marijuana as a Schedule I drug, Congress expressly found that the drug has no acceptable medical uses. Moreover, the CSA is a comprehensive regulatory regime specifically designed to regulate which controlled substances can be utilized for medicinal purposes, and in what manner. Indeed, most of the substances classified in the CSA "have a useful and legitimate medical purpose." [Citation omitted].[62]

- The exemption for cultivation by patients and caregivers can only increase the supply of marijuana in the California market. The likelihood that all such production will promptly terminate when patients recover or will precisely match the patients' medical needs during their convalescence seems remote; whereas the danger that excesses will satisfy some of the admittedly enormous demand for recreational use seems obvious. Moreover, that the national and international narcotics trade had thrived in the face of vigorous criminal enforcement efforts suggests that no small number of unscrupulous people will make use of the California exemptions to serve their commercial ends whenever it is feasible to do so.[63]

Three members of the Court, Chief Justice William H. Rehnquist and Justices Sandra Day O'Connor and Clarence Thomas, dissented. The thrust of Justice O'Connor's dissenting opinion centered around the limits of the federal government's regulatory reach and encroachment into relatively local issues. At the onset of her dissent, she reminded other members of the Court that "[o]ne of federalism's chief virtues, of course, is that it promotes innovation by allowing for the possibility that 'a single courageous State may, if its citizens choose, serve as a laboratory; and try novel social and economic experiments without risk to the rest of the country. *New State Ice Co. v. Liebmann*, 285 U.S. 262, 311 (1932) (Brandeis, J., dissenting)."[64]

In the next paragraph, Justice O'Connor summarized her seventeen-page opinion:

> This case exemplifies the role of States as laboratories. The States' core police powers have always included authority to define criminal law and to protect the health, safety, and welfare of their citizens. [Citations omitted.] Exercising these powers, California (by ballot initiative and then by legislative codification) has come to its own conclusion about the difficult and sensitive question of whether marijuana should be available to relieve pain and suffering. [With this decision] the Court sanctions an application of the federal Controlled Substances Act that extinguishes that experiment, without any proof that the personal cultivation, possession, and use of marijuana for medicinal purposes, if economic activity in the first place, has a substantial effect on interstate commerce and is therefore an appropriate subject of federal regulation. In so doing, the Court announces a rule that gives Congress a perverse incentive to legislate broadly pursuant to the Commerce Clause—nestling questionable assertions of its authority into comprehensive regulatory schemes—rather than with precision. That rule and the result it produces in this case are irreconcilable with our decisions in [*U.S. v. Lopez* and *U.S. v. Morrison*—the two cases cited as authority by the Ninth Circuit panel].[65]

The U.S. Supreme Court was composed of the same justices who heard all three cases: *Lopez, Morrison,* and *Raich.* The *Lopez* and *Morrison* cases concluded with five-to-four decisions—Chief Justice Rehnquist and Justices O'Connor, Antonin Scalia, Anthony M. Kennedy, and Thomas in the majority. The *Raich* case was determined by a six-to-three decision with Justices Stevens, Scalia, Kennedy, David H. Souter, Ruth Bader Ginsburg, and Stephen G. Breyer in the majority. In a concurring opinion, Justice Scalia noted that it was appropriate for Congress to use their power under the Commerce Clause, with adjunctive authority under the Necessary and Proper Clause, to regulate illegal drug trafficking that impacts the entire nation. Justice Scalia noted that he felt somewhat differently than the others in the majority about the scope of congressional power. He added:

> [Their] category of "activities that substantially affect interstate commerce" [citation omitted] is incomplete because the authority to enact laws necessary and proper for the regulation of interstate commerce is not limited to laws governing intrastate activities that substantially affect interstate commerce. Where necessary to make a regulation of interstate commerce effective, Congress may regulate even those intrastate activities that do not themselves substantially affect interstate commerce.[66]

As noted in the lower court hearings, Raich and Monson provided additional arguments and claims other than the Commerce Clause argument. However, Justice Stevens' majority opinion dealt solely with the Commerce Clause issue since it was the only one brought before the Supreme Court. Raich and Monson, in their initial complaint, said that there were other legal reasons for concluding that the CSA should not be applied to them, but the Ninth Circuit did not address these questions in their deliberation. Raich and Monson asserted that enforcing the CSA against them would violate their rights under the Due Process Clause of the Fifth Amendment, the Ninth and Tenth Amendments of the Constitution, as well as the doctrine of medical necessity. However, because the circuit judges focused only on the Commerce Clause issue, the other arguments were addressed only in passing. Under a provision in the Fifth Amendment, "[no person shall be] deprived of life, liberty, or property, without due process of law."[67]

In the Ninth Amendment "[t]he enumeration in the Constitution, of certain rights, shall not be construed to deny or disparage others retained by the people."[68] And, in the Tenth Amendment, "[t]he powers not delegated to the United States by the Constitution, nor prohibited by it to the States, are reserved to the States respectively, or to the people."[69] The doctrine of medical necessity is occasionally presented as a defense in a criminal action as having evolved from the more general defense doctrine of necessity. "The defense 'traditionally cover[s] the situation where physical forces beyond the actor's control' [render] illegal conduct the lesser of two evils."[70] (Raich and Monson suggested that they are confronted by two "evil" choices: suffer needlessly or violate federal law substance.) These additional claims are to be addressed by the Ninth Circuit—if at all—on remand and resolved in a manner not inconsistent with the Supreme Court's *Raich* opinion.

Justice Stevens offered another possible remedy. He suggested that it remains within the discretion and purview of Congress to amend the CSA to accommodate the use of marijuana for medical purposes at the national level.[71] Thus, Congress could potentially resolve the legal conflict between federal and state policies. This possibility is embodied in a bill cosponsored by U.S. Rep. Barney Frank (D-Mass), who said that the proposed law "would give Congress' blessing for states to make their own medical marijuana laws."[72] Congressman Ron Paul (R-Texas) commented on the bill in a *USA Today* article, saying, "I think support [for the proposed law] is strong. However, people are still frightened a little bit about the politics of it. If you have a secret vote in Congress, I'll bet 80 percent would vote for it."[73]

The Bush administration did not support revising the CSA and "has made marijuana a priority in its war on drugs, casting it as an entry-level drug with no scientifically proven benefits that leads many users to try more dangerous ones such as cocaine and heroin."[74]

CONTINUING DILEMMAS
WITH MEDICAL MARIJUANA

The *Raich* decision came as a great disappointment to many. Sandra H. Johnson, a law professor and health care ethicist at St. Louis University said, "In the war on drugs, we have had a war on patients. This is a tremendous setback. Untreated pain is a public health issue."[75] Sandee Burbank, director of the non-profit Mothers Against Misuse and Abuse (MAMA) in Oregon where medical marijuana is permitted, commented, "It's going to make it harder for doctors and patients to have access [to the drug] because of the fear."[76] White House federal drug czar John Walters offered a different viewpoint. "The medical marijuana farce is done," Walters said. "I don't doubt that some people feel better when they use marijuana, but that's not modern science. That's snake oil."[77]

Immediately after the Supreme Court decision was announced, California Attorney General Bill Lockyer tried to reassure his constituents that nothing would change. "People shouldn't panic," Lockyer said. "There aren't going to be many changes . . . in terms of real-world impact." However, within days, newspapers carried reports of federal raids against California marijuana cooperatives.[78] The first sentence from one newspaper account read, "Federal agents executed search warrants at three medical marijuana dispensaries on [June 22, 2005] as part of a broad investigation into marijuana trafficking in San Francisco, setting off fears among medical marijuana advocates that a federal crackdown on the drug's use by sick people was beginning."

The result of another raid was reported in *USA Today* and claimed that 20 people were indicted and 9,300 plants, worth $5 million on the street, were seized. U.S. Attorney Kevin Ryan defended the raids, stating that the dispensaries or clubs "operated as fronts for marijuana and Ecstasy trafficking."[79] He also warned that federal drug laws would be strictly enforced even in cities tolerant of medical marijuana.[80] No one suggested, except for an editorial in the *New York Times,* that the DEA should not have the power to stop drug trafficking. The newspaper also argued that because patients benefit from marijuana, stronger federal regulation might help strike proper balance between medical marijuana availability and outright prohibition.[81]

Some state lawmakers were undeterred from pushing ahead with medical marijuana legislation even in the face of the *Raich* opinion.[82] Legislators in at least seven states—Alabama, Connecticut, Minnesota, New Jersey, New Mexico, Rhode Island, and Wisconsin—plan to continue efforts to pass laws in their states to permit marijuana for medical reasons. Rogene Waite, a spokesperson for the DEA, said that the *Raich* ruling will not impact the agency's enforcement pattern, "We don't go after the sick and dying. We go after the large-scale organizations, traffickers, and distributors." However, she added, "People should not be breaking the law. There's always the possibility they could come under the radar."

Law Professor Lawrence Gostin suggested a compromise: Reclassify medical marijuana as a Schedule II controlled substance and beef up federal regulation of those physicians who would like to prescribe it in the states that permit patients access.[83] However, for this to happen the federal government would need to make a policy shift. As Gostin also points out, current federal regulation is flawed because it is "not an appropriate model for regulating drugs with potential medical benefit." Moreover, changing the federal regulatory scheme for medical marijuana, as Gostin suggested, seems more consistent with an evidence-based approach to quality patient-centered care.

The *Raich* decision stands for the proposition that those who follow California's legal steps in accessing marijuana for relief can face federal prosecution. However, at least one inconsistency exists, even at the federal level.[84] A national research project supplies medical marijuana to a few patients across the country for "compassionate use." Under this FDA-sponsored research program, seven patients receive about 300 THC cigarettes each month from the University of Mississippi marijuana farm. The research project began in 1982, but was eliminated ten years later during the George H. W. Bush presidency. The thirteen patients enrolled were grandfathered into the program—some have since died, but as of 2005, seven patients are still involved in the program with the federal government's written permission. (One might ask are any of these patients living in states that prohibit marijuana use—even for medical purposes—and are they subject to state criminal prosecution?) White House National Drug Control Policy spokesperson Tom Riley defended the research project as part of a federal effort to investigate the medical use of marijuana. Riley noted that the government "would be receptive to a nonaddictive marijuana derivative with medical benefits, but . . . subject to FDA approval." He also said proponents of medical marijuana want to circumvent that process.

There are currently two marijuana products that are of interest and being investigated for possible legitimate distribution. Marijuana-flavored lollipops or candies flavored with marijuana oil are under consideration by Chronic Candy, a Corona, California- based company.[85] The "Pot Suckers" deliver THC in an oral dosage formulation. The problems with this alternative delivery system may lie in standardization, absorption, and distribution for patients since the drug is so lipophilic. However, in this form marijuana can be taken without smoking or having it aerosolized into a vaporizer. Another alternative was approved in Canada for medical use.[86] SAVITEX® (GW Pharmaceuticals) is available by prescription only for multiple sclerosis patients and is an under-the-tongue marijuana spray that contains the whole plant extract with THC and cannabidiol (CBD) as the active ingredients. According to Dr. Andrew Mittison, co-director of the Center for Medicinal Cannabis Research at the University of California, San Diego, "This is a burgeoning field. There's probably going to be great potential with the SATIVEX® compound."

The available medical data on the benefits of medicinal marijuana are difficult to assess.[87] The Institute of Medicine undertook a literature review in 1999 and concluded "[t]he evidence is just not there" to support medical marijuana for multiple sclerosis, glaucoma, epilepsy, AIDS, and nausea caused by chemotherapy. Even with products like SATIVEX®, there remain questions and concerns regarding dose uniformity. Because the product is a whole plant extract (and not an extract from just the flower, new leaf tips, or other presumed drug-concentrated parts), there may be more of a standardized opportunity to investigate its value more scientifically and less anecdotally.

The *Raich* decision will have a chilling effect on some patients. Many will choose not to use marijuana as a result, fearing that they will break the law and/or risk prosecution. However, both Angel McClary Raich and Diana Monson have said that they will continue to use medical marijuana because it is for them a matter of life with it, or severe disability or death without it.

APPENDIX:
EXAMPLES OF CALIFORNIA'S CRIMINAL STATUTES CONTROLLING MARIJUANA
CALIF. HEALTH & SAFETY CODE §§ 11357 AND 11358 (WEST 2004)

(a) Except as authorized by law, every person who possesses any concentrated cannabis shall be punished by imprisonment in the county jail for a period of not more than one year or by a fine of not more than five hundred dollars ($500), or by both such fine and imprisonment, or shall be punished by imprisonment in the state prison.

(b) Except as authorized by law, every person who possesses not more than 28.5 grams of marijuana, other than concentrated cannabis, is guilty of a misdemeanor and shall be punished by a fine of not more than one hundred dollars ($100). Notwithstanding other provisions of law, if such person has been previously convicted three or more times of an offense described in this subdivision during the two-year period immediately preceding the date of commission of the violation to be charged, the previous convictions shall also be charged in the accusatory pleading and, if found to be true by the jury upon a jury trial or by the court upon a court trial or if admitted by the person, the provisions of Sections 1000.1 and 1000.2 of the Penal Code shall be applicable to him, and the court shall divert and refer him for education, treatment, or rehabilitation, without a court hearing or determination or the concurrence of the district attorney, to an appropriate community program which will accept him. If the person is so diverted and referred he shall not be subject to the fine specified in this subdivision. If no community program will accept him, the person shall be subject to the fine specified in this subdivision. In any case in which a person is arrested for a violation of this subdivision and does not demand to be taken before a magistrate, such person shall be released by the arresting officer upon presentation of satisfactory evidence of identity and giving his written promise to appear in court, as provided in Section 853.6 of the Penal Code, and shall not be subjected to booking.

(c) Except as authorized by law, every person who possesses more than 28.5 grams of marijuana, other than concentrated cannabis, shall be punished by imprisonment in the county jail for a period of not more than six months or by a fine of not more than five hundred dollars ($500), or by both such fine and imprisonment.

(d) Except as authorized by law, every person 18 years of age or over who possesses not more than 28.5 grams of marijuana, other than concentrated cannabis, upon the grounds of, or within, any school providing instruction in kindergarten or any of grades 1 through 12 during hours the school is open for classes or school-related programs is guilty of a misdemeanor and shall be punished by a fine of not more than five hundred dollars ($500), or by imprisonment in the county jail for a period of not more than 10 days, or both.

(e) Except as authorized by law, every person under the age of 18 who possesses not more than 28.5 grams of marijuana, other than concentrated cannabis, upon the grounds of, or within, any school providing instruction in kindergarten or any of grades 1 through 12 during hours the school is open for classes or school-related programs is guilty of a misdemeanor and shall be subject to the following dispositions:

(1) A fine of not more than two hundred fifty dollars ($250), upon a finding that a first offense has been committed.

(2) A fine of not more than five hundred dollars ($500), or commitment to a juvenile hall, ranch, camp, forestry camp, or secure juvenile home for a period of not more than 10 days, or both, upon a finding that a second or subsequent offense has been committed. Calif. Health & Safety Code § 11357 (West 2004).

Every person who plants, cultivates, harvests, dries, or processes any marijuana or any part thereof, except as otherwise provided by law, shall be punished by imprisonment in the state prison. Calif. Health & Safety Code § 11358 (West 2004).

Chapter 4

The "Morning-After" Pill and Systematic Ethics and Public Policy Analysis: How Justice Tempers Decision Making

Pharmacists are taught that they have a "right" not to fill every prescription that is presented at the counter. They can assert that this "right" is grounded in law, standards, and honor. However, patients also feel that they have a "right" to have their lawful prescriptions filled. How should a clash of "rights" between a pharmacist and a patient be resolved when the pharmacist refuses to fill—as a matter of conscience—a prescription for emergency contraceptives when time is of the essence?

On June 8, 2005, pharmacist Luke D. Vander Bleek filed a lawsuit against Illinois Governor Rod R. Blagojevich, who had effected a new regulation that assured the unfettered availability of prescription contraceptives within the state.[1] In his formal complaint, Vander Bleek alleged that the governor violated state law—a remarkable charge given that the governor is the chief executive officer of the state and sworn to faithfully execute the law.[2] The governor (a lawyer himself) must have believed that the emergency regulation and his actions were in accord with the law; his personal and direct intervention into what one might consider a relatively inconsequential pharmacy practice issue obviously was based on what he felt was a serious complaint:

> [A few weeks earlier] two women called in prescriptions to their local pharmacy in the [downtown Chicago] South Loop to purchase contraceptives. . . . Each woman had a prescription from her doctor. Both women only sought to buy contraceptives. And yet both were denied. Why? Because the pharmacist refused to fill the prescription [*sic*]. Unfortunately, this story is not unique to Chicago or to Illinois. Cases like this have been popping up all over the country. It's happened in Wisconsin, Texas, New Hampshire, North Carolina, Ohio, California, and in other states around the country . . . [At a press conference] announcing the new law, the governor added that: "[t]hose involved in this effort may be getting away with this in other states, but here in Illinois, we are not going to let that happen."[3]

Broadly, the governor considered the pharmacists' refusals[4] as an overt threat by "[t]hose involved" to interfere with the ability of women to obtain oral contraceptives for daily or emergency use.[5] To counter this perceived peril, the governor's office drafted an emergency rule amending Board of Pharmacy regulations to "[require] *pharmacies* that sell contraceptives to fill prescriptions for birth control without delay" [emphasis added].[6] (Note that the regulatory burden was placed on pharmacies and not individual pharmacists.)

In Illinois, executive departments, such as the governor's office, can establish *emergency rules* if they are deemed absolutely (and immediately) necessary to protect the public welfare. These rules can be set in place without being promulgated under otherwise applicable administrative procedures that require opportunity for timely notice, public hearings, and comment or debate. Also, under the Illinois Administrative Procedures Act, emergency rules are only valid for 150 days or until superseded by regulations adopted in the regular administrative fashion.[7]

In defense of the new rule, Governor Blagojevich offered this explanation:

> Our regulation says that if a woman goes to a pharmacy with a prescription for birth control, the pharmacy is not allowed

to discriminate who they sell it to and who they won't. The pharmacy will be expected to accept that prescription and fill it the same way, and in the same period of time, they would fill any other prescription. No delays. No hassles. No lectures. Just fill the prescription.[8]

Vander Bleek, both a pharmacist and the owner of two northwestern Illinois pharmacies (one located in Morrison and one in Prophetsville), asked the court for a declaratory judgment holding the governor's actions null and void and for injunctive relief to prevent enforcement. More specifically, Vander Bleek claimed that the governor's actions were unjust and forced pharmacists who oppose "morning-after" and birth control pills to dispense the medicine, causing them to act against their own ethical and religious beliefs, that is, to act against their own consciences.[9] In his complaint, Vander Bleek noted that he "is a practicing Catholic, who after prayerful reflection and consideration, informed his beliefs and conscience upon which he relies and which holds that life begins at conception and therefore does not allow him to dispense the 'morning-after' pill and/ or 'Plan B'* because of their abortifacient mechanism of action [*sic*]."[10] In a letter to his employed pharmacists (and attached as an appendix supporting his petition), Vander Bleek wrote that it has been a "long-standing policy" at his pharmacies to "immediately return the prescription to the patient" if a prescription for an emergency contraceptive is ever presented.[11]

In summary, Governor Blagojevich took the stance that women have a right to have their contraceptive prescriptions filled at pharmacies and promulgated a regulation that would make this policy the law. Vander Bleek felt it is his personal and professional right as a pharmacist to refuse to fill prescriptions that might cause an abortion.[12]

How might this conflict be resolved? The issue at hand is about a regulation that requires pharmacies that stock contraceptives to fill such prescriptions "without delay." As proposed by the governor,

---

*PLAN B®, a product manufactured by DuraMed Pharmaceuticals, Inc., contains two tablets, each with levonorgesterol 0.75 mg, is a prescription-only drug, and is marketed as an emergency contraceptive. PLAN B brochure. DuraMed Pharmaceuticals, Inc., 2005. Available at http://www.go2planb.com/Plan_B.pdf (accessed Oct. 11, 2005).

the regulation allows a woman who wishes to avoid an unwanted pregnancy the right to have her emergency contraceptives prescription filled without a hassle or, by implication, even a stony stare or sense of moral indignation from the pharmacist. However, what about the rights of individual professionals, the pharmacists, standing on the other side of the counter? Should not pharmacists, and other health care professionals, have the option not to participate in actions that "violate their conscience"?

EMERGENCY CONTRACEPTIVES AND RIGHTS

Combination (estrogen-progestin) birth control pills (BCPs) or oral contraceptive pills (OCPs) have been available in the United States for about fifty years.[13] These products provide a safe and effective means of pregnancy prevention. Even so, studies show that 3.5 million unwanted pregnancies occur annually in the United States. Teenage mothers account for roughly one-third of the total. Nearly half of these unintended pregnancies end in abortion.[14] Some family-planning specialists contend that the widespread availability and use of emergency contraception pills (ECPs or "morning-after" pills) can potentially prevent one million abortions and two million unwanted pregnancies each year in the United States.[15]

ECPs have been available as a patient option since 1974. Dr. Albert Yuzpe and his Canadian obstetrics and gynecology colleagues first suggested that available OCPs—products intended for daily use, that were already on the market, and available by prescription—could be employed as an effective postcoital contraceptive. A study conducted by Dr. Yuzpe's group resulted in the "off-label" recommendation that ethinyl estradiol 100 mcg and norgestrel 0.1 mg (administered as two tablets with 50 mcg of the estrogen and 0.5 mg of the progestin) be taken within seventy-two hours of unprotected sexual intercourse, followed by a second dose twelve hours after the first.[16] In a 1997 document offering comments about the "Yuzpe method" (as this off-label emergency OCP regimen use had come to be known), the FDA reported that at least 225,000 American women had been treated safely and effectively—primarily in emergency rooms, reproductive health clinics, and university health centers—and had avoided unwanted pregnancies for the preceding twenty years.[17]

Currently, there is one commercially available prescription-only, dedicated ECP product in the U.S. market: PLAN B. The first ECP marketed in the United States, the PREVEN™ Emergency Contraceptive Kit* (Gynetics, Inc.) is no longer available. The superior efficacy and tolerability of PLAN B and the ease of using combined estrogen-progestin OCPs as ECPs is the reason PREVEN is not now considered commercially feasible.[18] PLAN B** (described earlier; the equivalent to two doses of 20 tablets of the available OVRETTE®, Wyeth, with 0.075 mg norgesterel each).[19] (Note that levonorgesterel—the *levo-* or *l*-isomer—is the active ingredient found in racemic norgesterel, which contains both *d-* and *l*-isomers; the therapeutic dose of levonorgesterel is one half the dose of racemic norgesterel.) PREVEN is a combination ECP; PLAN B contains a progestin only.

In contrast to OCPs and ECPs, RU-486 (a progesterone antagonist, mifepristone, which works by interrupting an established pregnancy) is used in some countries to cause an abortion early in the pregnancy.[20]

Whether administered as a combination or progestin-only product, oral daily contraceptives and ECPs have four possible mechanisms of action, that of inhibiting:

- ovulation (by suppressing the mid-cycle luteinizing hormone [LH] surge, which is necessary for follicular growth and ovulation);
- fertilization (by interfering with sperm and egg movement);
- transport of the fertilized egg through the fallopian tube to the uterus; and
- implantation of the blastocyst in the endometrium by rendering the lining of the uterus unreceptive.

Because ECPs, in theory, act before fertilization and implantation and cannot disrupt an established pregnancy, many experts do not refer to them as abortifacients.[21] Using the same logic, OCPs are not con-

---

*The PREVEN Emergency Contraceptive Kit contains four tablets, each containing ethinyl estradiol 50 mcg and levonorgesterel 0.25 mg, Gynetics, Inc.; the equivalent of four tablets of the available oral contraceptive OVRAL®, with ethinyl estradiol 50 mcg and norgesterel 0.5 mg, Wyeth.

**PLAN B contains the equivalent of two doses of 20 tablets of the available oral contraceptive OVRETTE®, Wyeth, with 0.075 mg norgesterel each.

sidered abortifacients since their primary mechanism of action is to prevent ovulation. OCPs are known for their ability to regulate menstrual flow and relieve cramps, in addition to their presumed primary mechanism of action. As a result, many reasonably infer that physicians who prescribe and women who use the product do so to inhibit ovulation and not to cause abortions.

Theoretically speaking, the drug does not allow an egg to be released from the ovaries, and consequently no egg would be available to any sperm that might be present. Should one believe that life begins with fertilization of the egg—with union of the ovum and sperm, and before implantation or further development—then OCPs might be a birth control option since no union or fertilization occurs. On the other hand, one might also argue that both ECPs and OCPs are *potential* abortifacients—their known secondary mechanisms of action confirm and strengthen this proposition. Since OCPs are only 99 percent effective, even with the most conscientious care, one can reasonably assume that in certain instances some women may ovulate, and the egg might be fertilized by available sperm.[22] The data on this occurrence or the possible number of spontaneous abortions in such circumstances is currently unavailable. However, the theorized number of failed conceptions or spontaneous abortions is predicted to be as high as 78 percent.[23] Of course, most occur before the woman even knows she is pregnant (e.g., when the fertilized egg fails to implant for whatever reason, the endometrium sloughs prematurely after implantation, and a miscarriage occurs).

Regarding the effectiveness of ECPs, a 2005 brochure for PLAN B makes this statement: "After a single act of unprotected sex, Plan B reduces the average risk of pregnancy among users from about eight percent to one percent. Thus, the correct use of PLAN B reduces the risk of pregnancy by 89 percent."[24]

BALANCING "RIGHTS":
ETHICS AND PUBLIC POLICY

Some patients are under the impression that once they receive an ECP or OCP prescription from their physician, they have a "right" to have that prescription filled at the pharmacy of their choice. In cases such as this, social and distributive justice arguments are often conveniently couched in "rights" language.[25] However, as Ingram and Parks wrote in *Understanding Ethics:*

> *Rights,* then, are demands we impose on others. Furthermore, because demands that cannot be enforced are empty demands, there is the expectation (or at least the hope) implicit in every rights-based demand that others should not only heed the demand but be ready and willing to enforce it [emphasis in original].[26]

If one person has a "right," then does another entity or person have a corresponding "duty" or obligation to sustain or perform such that the first individual's "right" is to be honored? Corroborating the belief that patients have an inherent "right" to have their legally valid prescriptions filled, the following quotation from Julee Lacey, a patient, appeared in a *USA Today* article that discussed the issues associated with pharmacists in Fort Worth, Texas, who refused to fill OCPs prescriptions: "I was shocked . . ." Lacey said. "[The pharmacists'] job is not to regulate what people take or do. It's just to fill the prescription that was ordered by my physician."[27] One dictionary defines *rights,* as used in the above context, as:

> *n.* . . . **6.** Something that is due to a person or governmental body by law, tradition, or nature: *"Certain rights can never be granted to the government, but must be kept in the hands of the people"* (Eleanor Roosevelt). **7.** A just or legal claim or title.[28]

When commenting upon Governor Blagojevich's new regulation, Carolyn A. Webber, MD, president of the American Medical Women's Association, suggested that women have a legal and ethical "right" to have their OCP prescriptions filled. "Contraceptive drugs lawfully prescribed by a physician should be available to anyone with a valid prescription without delay or other interference . . ." she said. Dr. Webber concluded her prepared statement:

> There shouldn't be anything even remotely controversial about going to the drug store to pick up your birth control prescription, but the anti-choice movement's willingness to intrude on our personal lives does not know any bounds. It is beyond nonsensical,

and it's time to stand up for women's *right* to control our personal decisions and take personal responsibility for reproductive health [emphasis added].[29]

Traditionally, pharmacists and pharmacy students are taught that they have neither an ethical obligation nor a legal duty to fill every prescription that is presented at the pharmacy counter.[30] They are taught, rather, that they have a "right"—and even an obligation—to refuse to fill prescriptions when they have sufficient reason to do so. It is the case that some patients have a contractual right or legal entitlement to have their prescriptions filled under a particular insurance plan at assigned pharmacies. However, pharmacists make a valid point when they say they have the right to refuse to fill some prescriptions. Dubious prescriptions for controlled substances, for example, should be refused. Pharmacy practitioners have a "corresponding responsibility," together with the prescribing practitioners, to assure that some drugs are properly ordered and dispensed.[31] If a pharmacist believes that a prescription might lead to harm, then the pharmacist has a duty of care (under common law, but in some jurisdictions by statutory or regulatory requirement) to intervene by not filling the prescription, at least until their concerns are addressed, in order to protect the patient.[32] Since these safety valve principles are embodied in the law, pharmacists do possess a "right" not to fill certain prescriptions; a right which then forswears the possibility of patients having a right to have all of their prescriptions filled.

Of course, pharmacists may not arbitrarily refuse to fill prescriptions; they must have just cause. For example, if their discrimination is based on sex, race, color, national origin, or age, their refusal would certainly violate the spirit—if not the letter—of some federal and state laws designed to provide equal protection and equal justice.[33] However, if refusals have a rational basis in the law (such as when the pharmacist does not participate contractually in a patient's pharmacy benefits or drug insurance program or the state's Medicaid program), then the refusal is probably valid if applied equally to all of those who are within those limited categories. Moreover, since pharmacies and pharmacists gain income (the "profit motive") for filling presented prescriptions, pharmacists have an economic incentive to fill any prescription that can be justified on reasonable and appropriate grounds. When they refuse to fill a prescription for reasons of conscience—as a matter of personal honor—they accept a financial loss (and perhaps adverse publicity with negative future market implications) in exchange.

Some states have statutes that permit health care professionals the right to refuse to fill prescriptions because of a "conscientious objection." The Illinois Health Care Right of Conscience Act, enacted in 1998, is typical of such statutes and includes the following provisions:

. . .

Sec. 2. Findings and policy. The General Assembly finds and declares that people and organizations hold different beliefs about whether certain health care services are morally acceptable. It is the public policy of the State of Illinois to respect and protect the right of conscience of all persons who refuse to obtain, receive or accept, or who are engaged in, the delivery of, arrangement for, or payment of health care services and medical care whether acting individually, corporately, or in association with other persons; and to prohibit all forms of discrimination, disqualification, coercion, disability or imposition of liability upon such persons or entities by reason of their refusing to act contrary to their conscience or conscientious convictions in refusing to obtain, receive, accept, deliver, pay for, or arrange for the payment of health care services and medical care.

Sec. 3. Definitions. As used in this Act, unless the context clearly requires otherwise:

(a) **"Health care"** means any phase of patient care, including but not limited to, testing, diagnosis, prognosis, ancillary research, instructions, family planning, counselling [*sic*], referrals, or any other advice in connection with the use or procurement of contraceptives and sterilization or abortion procedures; medication; or surgery or other care or treatment rendered by a physician or physicians, nurses, paraprofessionals or health care facility, intended for the physical, emotional, and mental well-being of persons;

. . .

    (c) **"Health care personnel"** means any nurse, nurse's aide, medical student, professional, paraprofessional or any other person who furnishes, or assists in the furnishing, of heath care services;*

. . .

    (e) **"Conscience"** means a sincerely held set of moral convictions arising from belief in and relation to God, or which, though not so derived, arises from a place in the life of its possessor parallel to that filled by God among adherents to religious faiths;

. . .

Sec. 6. Duty of physicians and other health care personnel. Nothing in this Act shall relieve a physician from any duty, which may exist under any laws concerning current standards, or normal medical practices and procedures, to inform his or her patient of the patient's condition, prognosis, risks, provided, however, that such physician shall be under no duty to perform, assist, counsel, suggest, recommend, refer or participate in any way in any form or medical practice or health care service that is contrary to his or her conscience. Nothing in this Act shall be construed so as to relieve a physician or other health care personnel from obligations under the law of providing emergency medical care.

. . .

Sec. 13. Liability for refusal to provide certain health care. Nothing in this Act shall be construed as excusing any person,

---

*One will readily note that "pharmacist," by name, is not included in the statutory listing of health care personnel; but for that matter neither is "physician." However, "medical student" is. It seems ridiculous to some that authorities would argue that physician is not intended when a medical student is clearly included. Similarly, one might reasonably assume that pharmacists are included in the broader term "professional" when it appears that the statute is meant to be broad enough to include a "nurses' aide" and "paraprofessionals" specifically in the listing.

public or private institution, or public official from liability for refusal to permit or provide a particular form of health care service if:

(a) the person, public or private institution, or public official has entered into a contract specifically to provide that particular form of health care service; or

(b) the person, public or private institution, or public official has accepted federal or state funds for the sole purpose of, and specifically conditioned upon, permitting or providing that particular form of health care service. [All emphases in original.][34]

. . .

The primary support for conscientious objection statutes and clauses came from supporters of health care professionals who were threatened with being dismissed or disciplined for refusing to participate in some acts or procedures because it would violate their deeply held personal beliefs. One of the pharmacists who was disciplined in 1996 was Karen L. Brauer, MS, RPh, who worked for a Kmart pharmacy in Delhi, Ohio, and was fired for refusing to fill a birth control prescription. (Currently, she serves as president of the national group Pharmacists for Life.[35])

A *conscience clause* may be defined as: "a clause in a law that relieves persons whose conscientious or religious scruples forbid compliance."[36] Recent conscience clause laws may be more of a new twist on an old issue since the Joint Commission on Accreditation of Healthcare Organizations has asked for many years that accredited hospital human resource policies contain provisions for personnel to opt out of procedures that would violate their conscience (e.g., a Jehovah Witness nurse who might refuse to administer a blood product; or a surgical technician who is unwilling to participate in a pregnancy termination).[37] However, with specific statutes for jurisdictions that enact the laws, many more patient care delivery settings and situations will be included than those within the quasi-regulatory reach of the Joint Commission.

JUSTICE AND CONSCIENTIOUS OBJECTION

When an individual makes an ethical claim based on a social or distributive justice argument, it may be preceded by a statement such as, "That doesn't seem fair!" In the situation regarding the woman who has been denied having her ECP prescription filled, it is easy to imagine her frustration after being turned away from the pharmacy counter and her comments, such as, "This is not right. I should be able to get this medicine that I need now. I have a legitimate prescription from my doctor." Likewise, one can visualize the pharmacist on the other side of the counter in that same hypothetical situation remarking, "It is not fair that I should have to fill that ECP prescription. In good conscience, I cannot do that."

One dictionary entry defines the word *justice* as:

> *n.* **1.** The quality of being just, fairness. **2.a.** The principle of moral rightness, equity. **b.** Conformity to moral rightness in action or attitude; righteousness. **3.a.** The upholding of what is just, especially fair treatment and due reward in accordance with honor, standards, or law. **b.** *Law.* The administration and procedure of law. **4.** Conformity to truth, fact, or sound reason: *The overcharged customer was angry, and with justice. . . .* [Middle English, from Old French, from Latin, *iustitia,* from *iustus,* just.][38]

In the health care context, justice discussions appear most often in conversations regarding: (1) treating similar and similarly situated people the same or avoiding discrimination; and (2) rationing, or distributing limited or scarce goods and services fairly.[39] With respect to a pharmacist's conscientious refusals to fill ECP prescriptions, justice considerations on both sides of the discussion are real and dramatic.

In the cited dictionary definition of *justice* lies the notion of "upholding . . . what is just, especially fair treatment and due reward in accordance with *honor, standards, or law*" [emphasis added].[40] From this, one might assert that a pharmacist can refuse to fill a presented prescription because of (1) law, (2) standards, or (3) honor. A pharmacist may refuse to fill questionable controlled substances prescriptions because to do so would be illegal (law). A pharmacist might reject a prescription if the prescribed dose is too high because of the perceived risks of harm to the patient and malpractice liability (standards). A pharmacist might refuse to fill an ECP prescription because of a conscientious objection, that is, as a matter of personal honor or integrity.

At first glance, this dictionary definition of *justice* can be read to support the position of women bearing valid prescriptions for ECPs. It does not seem quite *fair* or *equitable* that different pharmacies (which, in many respects, are very similar in professional and business practices) would treat women with ECP prescriptions differently— that is, one pharmacy filling, and another refusing the same type of prescription. Moreover, many individual pharmacies are units within regional and national pharmacy chains (such as CVS Corporation, Eckerd Corporation, Kmart Corporation, Longs Drug Stores, Rite Aid Corporation, Target Pharmacy, Walgreens Co., and Wal-Mart Stores, Inc.), which are situated in more than 35,000 locations across the country.[41] It does not seem right or just that women with the same prescription could be treated so dissimilarly at pharmacies that are part of the same chain—whether they live in an urban setting with access to many pharmacies or in a rural area with only one pharmacy outlet.

These considerations lead some to call for the government to take charge—as in Governor Blagojevich's emergency rule regarding contraceptives—to assure equitable access to ECPs. Moreover, it would seem a greater justice burden, one causing perhaps more discrimination, for individual pharmacies and pharmacists, to attempt differentiation based on the "innocence" or "worthiness" of the individual patient's needs (e.g., by filling prescriptions for patients who may have been the victims of sexual assault; but refusing them for women who have, arguably, less weighty reasons to use oral contraceptives, such as an acne treatment or menses regulation).

Given the gravity of the consequences, if pharmacists assert a conscientious objection to filling an ECP prescription, they should have genuine and substantive reasons for doing so, reasons that are not arbitrary or capricious but rather grounded in deeply rooted religious or other firm moral convictions. The pharmacist should—with reference to the dictionary definition—be acting on a point of personal integrity or "honor."

Support for protecting a deep-seated belief may be found in the philosophical writings of Immanuel Kant (1724 to 1804). As Ingram and Parks noted in *Understanding Ethics,* "Kant was one of the very few moral philosophers who thought in terms of absolutes: according to him, morality is about following absolute rules."[42] These authors summarized some of his ideas as follows:

> . . . Kant totally rejected outcomes as a way of judging acts: because things can turn out well even when we don't intend them to, and things can turn out terribly, even when we mean well! . . . Kant's duty-based theory holds the following things:
>
> - Duties are absolute obligations that you must follow through with, regardless of your personal feelings or inclinations.
> - Duties apply to all of us in the exact the same way (no exceptions!).
> - The only thing good in itself is good will; it's the only "good" that cannot be used for a bad purpose.
> - Your will determines the morality of an act—not the outcome.[43]

Yet, the Kantian or deontological approach is problematic for at least three reasons: (1) Outcomes are not always irrelevant and immaterial to the decision-making process. (2) Duties are not all universal, nor can they all be applied without exception. And (3) a duty-based ethic has little power to resolve dilemmas in which rights and rules appear to be in conflict—as is the case when pharmacists refuse to fill ECP prescriptions for reasons of conscience.[44]

CONFLICT AND SYSTEMATIC ETHICAL ANALYSIS

Ingram and Parks have written thus: "An ethical dilemma forces us to choose in a way that involves breaking some ethical norm or contradicting some ethical value."[45] One might characterize an ethical dilemma as a decision which involves conflict between two or more principles or values. In almost every treatment decision, physicians attempt to strike a balance between the often competing principles of beneficence ("do good") and nonmaleficence ("do no harm").[46] When pharmacists conscientiously refuse to fill ECP prescriptions, in the face of woman's rights claims against them, the dilemma involves competing interpretations of a single principle, namely *justice*.

In their pharmacy ethics textbook, *Ethical Responsibility in Pharmacy Practice,* Buerki and Vottero suggest a decision-making framework for anyone who is facing an ethical dilemma.[47] One might suggest a modification of the action sequence they recommend:

1. Identify the problem(s).
   a. Identify technical facts.
   b. Identify moral parameters.
   c. Identify legal constraints.
   e. Identify relevant human values.
2. Develop alternative courses of action.
   a. Identify relevant ethical principles for each alternative.
   b. Recognize ethical assumptions for each alternative.
   c. Assess additional emerging ethical problems.
3. Select the one best course of action that permits the decision maker to have the greatest peace of mind or that which most satisfies the demands of conscience.
   a. Justify the selection.
   b. Defend the choice upon ethical grounds.
4. Anticipate logical, rational objections to the selected course of action.
   a. Be prepared to defend the selection against objections arising from factual errors.
   b. Be prepared to defend the selection against objections arising from faulty reasoning.
   c. Be prepared to defend the selection against objections arising from conflicting values.

In the hypothetical situation given above, pharmacists and women with ECP prescriptions will both work through frameworks similar to this one in order to make their conscientious decisions. In the end, if their basic premises and values with respect to ECPs differ, some women will have to obtain contraceptives from other outlets. If the woman lives in a remote area or otherwise has limited access to pharmacies, she may not be able to obtain the prescribed ECPs within the

seventy-two-hour window that permits maximum therapeutic effectiveness. The pharmacist's refusal thus may reduce the likelihood that
the woman will successfully avoid an unwanted pregnancy. The decision-making model attempts to support the pharmacist-patient and
physician-patient relationship by giving primacy to the moral judgments of individuals.

Another decision-making model, proposed by Jonsen, Siegler, and
Winslade, encourages the decision maker to consider the "four boxes"
or "four topics" of (1) medical indications, (2) patient preferences,
(3) quality of life, and (4) contextual features.[48] This model is similar
in that physician and patient are independent decision makers who
work to reach a mutually acceptable accommodation when their principles, values, and judgments are in conflict. Both are free moral
agents: neither party can coerce the other. Either or both may decide
that the other's proposed course of action is morally objectionable and
personally inappropriate. In such cases, if no mutually acceptable accommodation can be reached, the physician is free to withdraw from
the case (apart from cases of medical emergency, or urgency, or abandonment) and the patient is free to seek medical care from another
provider (and terminating the extant physician-patient relationship
by creating a new one). The Buerki-Vottero framework and Jonsen-
Siegler-Winslade model thus complement one another and may be
used jointly to systematically resolve ethical dilemmas.

CONTINUING DILEMMAS
WITH EMERGENCY CONTRACEPTIVES

Physicians who prescribe drugs and pharmacists who fill prescriptions are morally accountable for their actions. This may be more
recognized today than in the past. One might recall Elvis Presley's
pharmacist Jack Kirsch who lamely stated, "I only fill them," to explain why he dispensed more than 5,684 pills during the seven-month
period just prior to the singer's death. In an office right across the
street from Kirsch's pharmacy, Dr. George C. Nichopolous, Presley's
physician, wrote 199 prescriptions for more than 10,000 doses of
sedatives, amphetamines, and narcotics—all in Presley's name—in
1977 alone. Both Kirsch and Nichopolous were subsequently disciplined by their respective licensing boards.[49] One might wonder if

Governor Blagojevich's regulation is an attempt to turn back time, presumably to an era when druggists filled prescriptions almost reflexively and hesitated to ask questions about the legitimacy of physicians' prescription orders.[50]

Some pharmacists might or perhaps *should* feel professionally threatened by the regulatory mandate to fill contraceptive prescriptions "without delay." In fact, within days of the Illinois emergency rule announcement, pharmacy organizations obtained a clarification from the governor's office regarding a possible conflict between the new regulatory standard and state pharmacy laws that required pharmacists to conduct a complete and proper drug utilization review of each patient's medication profile and to counsel patients about medicines when new prescriptions are presented. Organizations such as the American Pharmacists Association (APhA), the Illinois Pharmacists Association (IPhA), and the American Society of Health-System Pharmacists (ASHP) wrote an open letter, dated April 5, 2005, to the governor to warn him of several negative consequences, including those emanating from the pharmacist's mandatory patient drug utilization profile review and counseling requirements.[51]

The governor and the Illinois Department of Financial and Professional Regulation (the state agency responsible for pharmacy and pharmacist regulation through the board of pharmacy) quickly clarified that they did not intend to interfere in any way with legitimate pharmacist functions that involved professional judgment.[52] However, the governor's sincerity can be seen as questionable as regards the pharmacy's contribution to patient care, since only a few days earlier his office had implied that pharmacists were not "health care personnel," as covered by the broad sweep of the state's 1998 Health Care Right of Conscience Act.[53]

The governor either naively or disingenuously stated that the emergency rule affects only pharmacies directly and not the individual pharmacists simply because pharmacies are the entities subject to fines and other legal remedies. Vander Bleek rightly pointed out in his complaint that he is the owner of *and* pharmacist in charge of one of his pharmacies, and that he is therefore individually subject to sanction if his pharmacy is found in violation of the law. However, the governor and women's health advocates might understandably question whether individual complaints like those of Vander Bleek are representative of more structural and organized resistance. Vander Bleek's lawsuit is sponsored in part by the conservative bioethics advocacy group Americans United for Life[54] and is one of at least three such lawsuits filed by pro-life or religious groups on behalf of individual health care providers. One lawsuit was filed by the American Center for Law and Justice, representing nurse Andrea Nead at Eastern Illinois University, who claimed she had been denied a promotion because she refused to dispense the "morning-after" pill.[55] Another lawsuit was filed by the Center for Law and Religious Freedom representing a Chicago pharmacist.[56]

Of course, pharmacists are not new to the birth control and contraception debate. At one time, pharmacies could not stock condoms or birth control pills because some states made the sale and use of contraceptives a crime.[57] In 1965, the landmark U.S. Supreme Court decision—*Griswold v. Connecticut*[58]—overturned the state criminal conviction of a Planned Parenthood employee and a Yale physician for providing contraceptives to a married couple. It was the *Griswold* decision that first articulated the federal constitutional "right to privacy." Condoms are now widely available as OTC products, and pharmacists who sell them are moral participants in the birth control debate, quite apart from whether they dispense OCPs or ECPs.*

The distinction between "morning-after" pills and other contraceptives may be blurred, but the United States Conference of Catholic Bishops carefully discriminates between the two in its publication, *Ethical and Religious Directives for Catholic Health Care Services*.[59] The seventy-two directives are published as a pamphlet. Part Four of the booklet, "Issues in Care for the Beginning of Life"[60] includes Directive 52: "Catholic health institutions may not promote or condone contraceptive practices but should provide, for married couples and the medical staff who counsel them, instruction both about the Church's teaching on responsible parenthood and in methods of natu-

---

*Other products besides condoms have been seriously debated as items properly sold by pharmacists because of moral and public health concerns. After years of almost continual debate the American Pharmacists Association Policy Review Committee in 1996 reaffirmed their opposition to the sale of tobacco and non-medicinal alcohol in pharmacies. *Journal of the American Pharmacists Association*. 1996; NS36:396.

ral family planning."[61] However, Part Three, titled "The Professional-Patient Relationship," includes Directive 36 which states:

> Compassionate and understanding care should be given to a person who is the victim of sexual assault. Health care providers should cooperate with law enforcement officials, offer the person psychological and spiritual support and accurate medical information. A female who has been raped should be able to defend herself against a potential conception from sexual assault. If, after appropriate testing, there is no evidence that conception has occurred already, she may be treated with medications that would prevent ovulation, sperm capacitation, or fertilization. It is not permissible, however, to initiate or to recommend treatments that have as their purpose or direct effect the removal, destruction, or interference with the implantation of a fertilized ovum.[62]

After reviewing the *Directives,* one might have at least two questions for pharmacist-litigant Vander Bleek, who admits to being a practicing Catholic in his complaint[63] and whose pharmacies dispense BCPs but not ECPs. First, since the bishops say that Catholic "health care institutions may not promote or condone contraceptive practices," how can he in good conscience stock and dispense BCPs? Are those who receive BCPs from his pharmacies married, or should that really matter? Is it because Vander Bleek's pharmacy is not a Catholic "institution"? Second, if his pharmacies will not stock ECPs, then what "medications that would prevent ovulation, sperm capacitation, or fertilization" would they dispense, if any, for victims of sexual assault?

Catholic health care institutions are permitted to provide procedures that have the secondary effect of causing fetal death in circumstances where specific conditions are met. Directive 47 sanctions "[o]perations, treatments, and medications that have as their direct purpose the cure of a proportionately serious pathological condition of a pregnant woman . . . when they cannot be safely postponed until the unborn child is viable, even if they will result in the death of the unborn child."[64] This Directive expresses the *doctrine of double effect* and one of its conditions, *proportionality,* both of which emerged from Catholic moral theology but have been adopted widely among bioethicists.[65] Jonsen, Siegler, and Winslade in their book *Clinical Ethics* define the doctrine of double effect as follows:

> The principal of double effect recognizes that, occasionally, persons are faced with a decision that cannot be avoided and, in the circumstances, the decision will cause both desirable and undesirable effects. These effects are inextricably linked. One of these effects is intended by the agent and is ethically permissible [for example, curing the mother's medical problem], the other is not intended by the agent and is ethically undesirable [for example, the death of the fetus] . . . Roman Catholic medical ethics employs this argument to justify clinically appropriate pain medication for relief of pain, even if the unintended foreseen effect is the shortening of the patient's life.[66]

Directives 32 and 33 explicate the notion of proportionality as follows:

> 32. While every person is obliged to use ordinary means to preserve his or her health, no person should be obliged to submit to a health care procedure that the person has judged, with a free and informed conscience, not to provide a reasonable hope of benefit without excessive risks and burdens on the patient or excessive expense to family or community.*
> 33. The well-being of the whole person must be taken into account in deciding about any therapeutic intervention or use of technology. Therapeutic procedures that are likely to cause harm or undesirable side-effects can be justified only by a proportionate benefit to the patient.[67]

If a pregnant mother's life is threatened, then there may be proportionate cause to justify a procedure that ends a pregnancy, so long as other conditions are met. The *Directives* are clear, however, that even sexual assault is not a sufficient condition to warrant deliberately de-

---

*[Note 18 in original] Declaration on Euthanasia. Part IV [Referring to Part IV of the Declaration on Euthanasia published by the Congregation for the Doctrine of the Faith in 1980. Rome, Italy: The Sacred Congregation for the Doctrine of the Faith, 1980. Available at http:// www.vatican.va/roman-curia/congregations/cfaith/documents/rc_con_cfaith_doc_1980 0505_euthanasia_en.html (accessed July 5, 2007)]; cf. directives 56-57.

stroying a nascent human life at any point from fertilization forward. The *Directives* specifically caution that "there [be] no evidence that conception has occurred" before "medications" are offered the victim (Directive 36). This view seems consistent with the *Directives,* taken as a whole, and calls into question the justification for termination because a woman has been raped (a view incorporated into some abortion statutes[68]). If pharmacists do not want to dispense ECPs because they believe such medicines may terminate an "innocent unborn human life" (i.e., in a nutshell, the "sanctity of human life" argument), then they may not distinguish between the "innocent" life that is conceived as the result of a rape and that which is conceived as the result of consensual marital sex.

Allowing others to freely live out their religious commitments, worship, and practice, according to the dictates of conscience, is a foundational American tradition.[69] Another Illinois statute, the Illinois Religious Freedom Restoration Act, makes that tradition explicit by prohibiting the government from "substantially burdening" a person's exercise of religion "unless it demonstrates that the application of the burden is in furtherance of a compelling governmental interest and is the least restrictive means of furthering that interest."[70] However, the Act does not specify clearly whether it is intended to address matters of conscience in professional duties, or rather is limited to more general matters of religious worship and observance.

In California, the state Supreme Court recently ruled in *Catholic Charities of Sacramento, Inc., v. California,*[71] that a religious organization with a partly "secular" mission must act and operate similarly to other businesses by providing "its employees in the state with medical coverage for birth control [according to state law], despite the church's religious objections."[72]

It is an open question whether hospitals and pharmacists should provide patients with advance notice or warning of those medical therapies and procedures that they will not provide for reasons of conscience. Perhaps impacted pharmacies should prominently display a sign that states, "This pharmacy does not fill emergency contraceptive prescriptions."* Emergency departments could likewise post a sign at

---

*Or more positively, David A. Apgar, PharmD, of the University of Arizona College of Pharmacy faculty, has suggested that pharmacists might prefer to wear a button which reads: "I will dispense emergency contraception." Personal communication, July 29, 2006. Used with permission.

the triage desk that states, "Physicians in this hospital emergency department do not write prescriptions for emergency contraceptives except in cases of sexual assault where conception has not yet occurred." Some would find such policies ridiculous and unseemly, but how else will patients learn about "long-standing" policies like the one described in Vander Bleek's complaint appendix? How is the patient to know that the pharmacists in Morrison and Prophetsville, Illinois, "must immediately return the [ECP] prescription to the patient"?[73]

The APhA suggested that pharmacists may decline to fill prescriptions when doing so would violate conscience "as long as they make other arrangements for [patients]" by handing back the prescription, asking a colleague to fill the prescription, or transferring the prescription to another pharmacy.[74] This is certainly preferable to the actions of some pharmacists which were reported by Adam Sonfield of the Alan Guttmacher Institute in New York*:

> There are pharmacists who will only give birth control pills to a woman if she's married. There are pharmacists who mistakenly believe contraception is a form of abortion and refuse to [dispense] it to anyone. There are even cases of pharmacists holding prescriptions hostage, where they won't even transfer it to another pharmacist when time is of the essence.[75]

These actions certainly appear to go beyond the limits as established by the policies of organized pharmacy[76] and they raise the possibility of legal liability at the state board or personal injury (tort) level. It may be argued, for example, that such actions constitute outrageous conduct that intentionally inflicts emotional distress on patients. Regardless of organized pharmacy's established position, the dilemma persists, as noted in the following *USA Today* editorial**:

> When you hand a prescription to a pharmacist, you expect to receive medication in return, not a lecture on your lifestyle or a debate about religion. . . . No business should be obligated to

---

*© 2005 *The Washington Post*. Reprinted with permission.
**From *USA Today*, a division of Gannett Co., Inc. Reprinted with permission.

employ people who chase customers away and refuse to follow its policies. Last year, when three pharmacists at an Eckerd store in Denton, Texas, wouldn't give a "morning-after" pill to a rape victim, they were fired. The "conscience" law proposed in Austin would protect their jobs. That would be a mistake. Pharmacists who insist on imposing their views on others don't deserve state-enforced job protection. They may have to pay a price for their principles by finding another line of work.[77]

Another compromise has been suggested: permit the sale of ECPs over-the-counter (OTC), or without a prescription, as do about forty countries around the world.[78] If the products are OTC, then patients can readily and easily purchase them (as they do condoms and early pregnancy test kits) at pharmacies that elect to carry them without patients having to deal with moralizing physicians and pharmacists. The FDA, in a decision that met with widespread charges of political gerrymandering,[79] rejected that idea, much to the chagrin of proponents[80] and relief of opponents.[81] The FDA is considering permitting the OTC sale of emergency contraceptives to persons over age seventeen but has delayed action to date pending review of more data.[82] However, some advocacy groups have continued the debate and pressure in an attempt to forestall any crises; for example, the American Academy of Pediatrics recently issued a policy statement that "reiterate[s] the Academy's support for over-the-counter availability of emergency contraception for all adolescents and women of reproductive age."[83]

Currently, a number of states have adopted a modified version of the OTC compromise whereby pharmacists, acting under protocol or collaborative practice agreements authorized by a prescriber, are permitted to dispense ECPs.[84] Even in this instance, supporters have found opposition at the statehouse just as they have at the pharmacy counter and the FDA. In July 2005, Massachusetts Governor Mitt Romney vetoed a bill that would have allowed his state's pharmacists to dispense "morning-after" pills without a prescription.[85] Similarly, in August 2005, New York Governor George E. Pataki vetoed legislation for his state that would make the "morning-after" pill available without a prescription because it did not make special provision to prevent minors' access to the drug.[86]

In rejecting pharmacy conscience arguments, some women's rights advocates may make emotional appeals based on hypothetical circumstances. In debate about access, they will paint a very grim imaginary picture for effect. The patient—they will declare—is an older teenager with limited financial resources, raped while unconscious at a drunken party, who is afraid to share the situation with her parents, and crying when she presents the prescription at the only pharmacy within fifty miles on a Saturday night, now with only a few hours to take the medicine before the optimal seventy-two-hour window lapses. They will describe then, a confrontation before a stern pharmacist who asks inappropriate questions, and then preaches about abstinence and the sins of premarital sex. However, one should recall that pharmacists are perhaps the most accessible health care professionals; and that PLAN B is after all, a prescription drug. Such a theoretical state of affairs may happen, but it plainly seems insincere to say that one is more able to find a physician to write a prescription for an ECP than it is to find a compassionate pharmacist who is willing to fill it.

In addition to rights arguments and other moral and philosophical concerns, prior law bears on whether pharmacists can be required to dispense ECPs. In fact, Governor Blagojevich's emergency rule is likely to be overturned in the courts in the first instance because he did not follow specified administrative procedures in promulgating the regulation. In order to meet the legal standard of an *emergency rule,* Illinois requires the government to show there exists sufficient "threat to the public interest, safety, or welfare" to justify promulgating the regulation without opportunity for public notice and comment.[87] Moreover, as stated earlier, the emergency rule appears to be in conflict with the state's explicit law encoded in the Health Care Provider Right of Conscience Act.

Acting on the authority of the emergency rule in Illinois, Walgreens asked its Illinois pharmacists to sign a pledge that acknowledged that they would follow the law and dispense contraceptives. At least four pharmacists refused and were suspended indefinitely without pay.[88] Walgreens defended their action, citing the governor's emergency regulation. "We are required to follow the law. We don't have any choice in the matter," was the statement from Walgreens' spokesman Michael Polzin. The pharmacists have filed a lawsuit in state court, and with the federal Equal Employment Opportunity Commission, alleging a violation of their rights under Illinois and federal law.

The challenge to find compromise and balance is daunting when justice arguments appear to cancel one another out, or are at equipoise. At such times, it is helpful to recall that appeals to justice only make sense—or are intelligible—when made within a community context. An action is judged fair or unfair according to community standards, not in reference to a single individual's conscience—even if that conscience is informed by widely held religious beliefs. It is to this community standards notion that pharmacists are referring when they assert a right to not fill an ECP or OCP prescription.

However, it is the community, or society, that grants and recognizes professional status and sets expectations. It is the community that holds professionals accountable when expectations are not met. When standards and laws seem contradictory or at odds, legislatures, executives, and courts—community agents, not individuals—resolve the conflict or settle the dispute. It may not be a valid defense that a substantial minority, or even a majority, of reasonable practitioners might or might not act in a particular way when faced with given circumstances. Physicians and pharmacists may be sanctioned by their respective licensing boards for violating a standard or engaging in unprofessional conduct. They may be held liable in a malpractice suit if their actions are the proximate cause of a patient's injury. It remains then for peer practitioners to craft an acceptable response to the conflict of "rights" between providers and patients that will accommodate affected professionals' consciences, while meeting societal expectations and patients' individual medical needs.

PART II:
PAIN MEDICINES
AND END-OF-LIFE DRUGS

Chapter 5

Pain Medicines
and Palliative Care Drugs

Hospice and palliative care researchers Richard Chapman and Jonathan Gavrin wrote that "[d]ying is a natural and inevitable aspect of living."[1] They reported too that barriers exist to preventing patient suffering: deficient care provider knowledge and skills, misguided attitudes and beliefs among providers, and public attitudes and patient behaviors.[2] According to historian Philippe Ariès, persons at the moment of death—at least in Western cultures down through the ages—have a relatively simple goal: to die at home, surrounded by loved ones, peacefully and pain free.[3] Yet, in America today health care providers still struggle with comfort issues and the problems that arise from the appropriate use of pain medicines and other palliative care drugs for patients who are near their end-of-life.

Through the centuries, adequate pain control has remained a primary goal of medicine.[4] Hippocrates (460 BC to 380 BC)—recognized by many as the Father of Western Medicine—prescribed willow bark and leaves to women for pain relief during childbirth.[5] (Willow, of the genus *Salix*, contains a form of salicylic acid; aspirin, acetylsalicylic acid, is a derivative.) In the nineteenth century, physicians referred to opioids and morphine as "God's own medicine."[6] Due to the growing emphasis on hospice and palliative care for dying and failing chronically ill patients, physicians have been even more attentive to pain control and symptom management.[7] Albert Jonsen, Mark Siegler, and William Winslade, in their book *Clinical Ethics*, list "[r]elief of symptoms, pain, and suffering" second only to "[p]romotion of health and prevention of disease" in their "goals of medicine" inventory.[8] In America, physicians and other health care providers recognize adequate pain control as a moral—and ethical—obligation.[9]

Unfortunately, through the centuries physicians have continually struggled with both the technical and moral aspects of controlling their patients' pain. Two of the haunting, lingering messages from Leo Tolstoy's 1886 novella, *The Death of Ivan Ilyich*, are how truly ineffective was the patient's medical assistance, and how agonizing were the patient's last weeks and days due to the excruciating pain he suffered.[10] Given medicine's priority for relieving patients' pain and the ready availability of pain-relieving drugs, one might question why, in a 1993 study of 897 physicians caring for cancer patients, 86 percent of the physician respondents felt that most cancer patients were undertreated for their pain.[11] A 1995 paper revealed that non-cancer patients received even less adequate pain management than patients who had cancer-related pain; the same study also showed that minorities, the elderly, and women were more likely than other groups of patients to be inadequately treated for pain. Perhaps not surprisingly, at about that same time, an editorial by cancer and pain specialist Stratton Hill appeared in a volume of the *JAMA* titled, "When Will Adequate Pain Control Be the Norm?"[12] The editorial accompanied two other articles in that issue: "The WHO [World Health Organization] Analgesic Ladder for Cancer Pain Management: Stepping Up the Quality of Its Evaluation"[13] and "Quality Improvement Guidelines for the Treatment of Acute Pain and Cancer Pain."[14] All three of these *JAMA* pieces had a central theme: "Inadequate treatment of pain continues to be a problem despite more knowledge about its causes and control and despite widespread efforts of governments and multiple medical and voluntary organizations to disseminate this knowledge, particularly at the postgraduate level."[15] However, even so, one must still wonder about the circumstances that led a California jury in 2001 to award $1.5 million to the surviving children of a cancer patient whose physician inadequately controlled the patient's pain during his final days.[16] Though reported to be the first successful private prosecution of a physician for failing to treat a patient's pain, *Bergman v. Chin* was—at its legal core—an elder abuse or mistreatment case rather than an actual medical malpractice case.[17]

BERGMAN v. CHIN

At the time he sought medical assistance, William Bergman was an eighty-five-year-old retired railroad worker and lifelong smoker.[18] He was admitted to Eden Medical Center, Castro Valley, on February 16, 1998, with severe lower back pain. His daughter, Beverly, had taken him to the medical center's emergency department after she found him at home sitting in a chair experiencing such severe pain that he was unable to move. His attending physician during the hospitalization was Dr. Wing Chin, an internist. Bergman was initially admitted for weight loss and suspected compression fractures of the lower spine. In his admission orders, Chin prescribed DEMEROL® (meperidine, Sanofi-Aventis) 25-50 mg by mouth as needed for pain. Upon further evaluation, a chest X-ray revealed a spot on a lung. Subsequent biopsy results were suggestive of cancer, but not conclusive; concomitantly, it was also suspected that the spine lesions were metastatic. With this information, Bergman refused additional tests and the prospect of possible curative treatments, preferring to go home and avail himself of hospice care. During Bergman's hospital stay, when Beverly Bergman told Chin that VICODIN® (hydrocodone, Abbott Laboratories) had not controlled her father's back pain well in the past, the physician ordered a DEMEROL injection and a continuous-release fentanyl (DURAGESIC®, Janssen Pharmaceuticals) transdermal patch. On discharge, Chin prescribed VICODIN tablets, even though Bergman could not swallow very well and the tablets alone failed to fully control his pain while in the hospital.

During his five-day hospitalization, Bergman's nurses consistently rated his pain as seven to ten (on a ten-point scale, where ten is "the most severe pain ever experienced"). Notes by Chin and respiratory therapists recorded Bergman "felt okay" or that his back pain was tolerable. However, Beverly Bergman stated, "Every time I saw my father, he was in pain . . . I had to . . . get the nurse and ask her to give my dad a pain shot." For three days after his discharge from the hospital, Bergman suffered from severe back and abdominal pain. His daughter crushed the VICODIN tablets in an attempt to help Bergman to swallow the medicine, but Bergman had little success in getting them down. On the third day, a hospice nurse assessed Bergman's pain at ten and called Chin with a request for liquid morphine, which the doctor elected not to prescribe. Later that afternoon, Beverly contacted a physician who had treated Bergman in the past and that physician gave her a prescription for a single dose of liquid morphine and two more transcutaneous pain patches. The patient's daughter recalled, "[t]hen he was finally out of pain." Bergman died the following day on February 24, 1998.

Beverly Bergman—who worked as a mental health advocate in Oakland—was terribly upset and frustrated by her father's inadequate pain control and suffering during the last days of his life. She recalled that she spent two nights listening to him moan and had watched him writhe in agony. She remarked, "I think the extreme pain he was in just wore him out." She felt that his pain management was less than appropriate and could not understand why Dr. Chin would not prescribe liquid morphine, a standard treatment for patients who have metastatic bone cancer pain. Because of her concerns, she filed a complaint against Chin with the Medical Board of California. The medical board declined to take any action. They wrote, "[T]here is insufficient evidence at this time to warrant pursuing further action in this case." However, the letter also stated, "Our medical consultant did agree with you that pain management for your father was indeed inadequate." Candis Cohen, a spokesperson for the medical board, told a reporter that California law requires clear and convincing evidence of inappropriate conduct before the state medical board can pursue disciplinary action against a physician. "Clear and convincing evidence" is a higher standard of proof than "a preponderance of evidence," which is the proof standard required in most civil trials and administrative proceedings.

Saddened, and feeling helpless about the situation, Beverly Bergman—along with her brother and sister, Robert Bergman and Alice Edlinger—sought help from the Portland, Oregon, not-for-profit advocacy group Compassion in Dying Federation. With the group's assistance, the children (as the deceased patient's survivors) filed a personal injury lawsuit against Chin and Eden Medical Center, alleging the medical team failed to treat their father's pain appropriately. Under California medical malpractice law, only the patient can claim damages for pain and suffering, so Bergman's children filed a case for compensation pursuant to the state's Elder Abuse and Dependent Adult Civil Protection Act.[19] They, in effect, alleged that Dr. Chin "abused" their father. However, in order to be awarded damages for alleged elder abuse, the family would have to prove that Chin's conduct was not simply "below the standard of care" (as would be the requisite in a typical malpractice case), but was something worse—"reckless." According to the Federation's legal affairs director, Kathryn Tucker, this case represents "a new type of liability for physicians in an area where they have not up to now been held accountable, in the area of pain management."[20]

The hospital settled its portion of the lawsuit without acknowledging fault. As part of that settlement, however, the medical center agreed to provide pain management classes to its physicians and staff.

The jury trial against Dr. Chin began May 14, 2001, in an Alameda County superior court before Judge David E. Hunter.[21] Plaintiff's expert witnesses testified that "the modern course of treatment for a patient in intractable pain, such as Bergman, was to provide around-the-clock pain medication, with additional pain medication 'as needed' for breakthrough pain." It was the considered opinion of the plaintiffs' experts that the care rendered by Chin was "appalling" and "egregious." On the other hand, the defense experts felt that Chin's pain management efforts were well within the applicable standard of care. On the fourth day of deliberation, the jury found, nine-to-three, for the plaintiffs and awarded damages totaling $1.5 million for Bergman's pain and suffering. The jury found that Chin's conduct was reckless and constituted elder abuse. However, the jury was not able to reach a decision on the plaintiffs' additional claim for "intentional infliction of emotional distress."

Chin's attorney, Robert Slattery, discussed the case with the media following the trial. He reminded reporters that the medical team had not positively diagnosed cancer and that Chin had been treating Bergman for suspected "compression fractures in his low back."[22] Slattery suggested that Bergman had died from a narcotics overdose, not lung cancer. He felt that after taking the pain medicines prescribed, the patient "fell asleep and didn't wake up." During the trial, defense counsel noted that Bergman had been given morphine in the emergency department when he had first arrived at the hospital, but since it suppressed his respirations there, Dr. Chin had been disinclined to prescribe it again. Slattery also questioned the plaintiffs' use of the elder abuse statute as the basis for their action. Despite all this, Chin chose not to appeal the jury verdict.

Regrettably, the California medical board's letter to Beverly Berg-man caused consternation within the physician community. Sandra Bressler, director of professional standards and quality of care for the California Medical Association said, "The board found there wasn't sufficient evidence to proceed against Dr. Chin in any way, so it was gratuitous to term his care inadequate. He had no due-process rights or chance to respond."[23] Alameda-Contra Costa Medical Association president and vascular surgeon Sharon Drager responded similarly, suggesting Chin—known as a competent and compassionate physi-cian in the East Bay Area, and as having a "solid reputation"—was "victimized" by the media, an emotionally charged jury, and an out-of-state advocacy group "that saw the case as an opportunity to further their agenda for legalized euthanasia."

WHEN WILL ADEQUATE PAIN CONTROL
BE THE NORM?

One might ask: If Bergman had decided to forgo further medical evaluation of his condition, along with the possibility of curative treat-ment—regardless of the ultimate diagnosis, cancer or otherwise—and was now a hospice patient, why should Chin not have been willing to prescribe liquid morphine or any other medicine necessary to control the patient's pain and other symptoms? There are at least two ex-planations. A physician might use the argument that it may be in the *patient's* best interests to withhold pain and palliative care medicines; the second argument is that it may be in the *physician's* best interests to be more guarded about prescribing narcotics.

First, it may be that Chin might have felt uncomfortable about pre-scribing medicines because Bergman's final diagnosis was unclear. As a general rule in clinical medicine and clinical ethics, doctors should not treat symptoms when the underlying illness is undiagnosed or the medical indications for definitive treatment are uncertain—unless there is an otherwise compelling reason to do so.[24] Doctors should not prescribe medicines empirically (some might say, "in the dark") without good cause; they should not treat unless they know *what* they are treating. Empirical or symptomatic treatment may either mask important clues that would aid other physicians or health care professionals in making a more accurate diagnosis of or even prevent recovery from the underlying medical problem. However, if a competent adult patient fully understands the consequences of a medical team not making a definitive diagnosis and is willing to assume the associated risks—even a possibly shorter lifespan—of forgoing some medical treatments in order to receive palliative care, then that is an individual choice that should be respected because it is a "liberty interest" (or right) embedded in the United States Constitution.[25]

From about 1990 to the present, there has been an increasing educational emphasis in medical, pharmacy, and nursing schools and postgraduate training programs regarding hospice and palliative care. One educational effort that has been recognized nationally is the Education on Palliative and End-of-Life Care (EPEC) Project. The first "train-the-trainers" programs were offered by project principals Drs. Linda Emanuel, Charles von Guten, Frank Ferris, and Russell Portenoy, with initial funding from The Robert Wood Johnson Foundation, Princeton, New Jersey.[26] The project's continuing mission is to "educate all healthcare professionals on the essential clinical competencies in palliative care." The principals reported that by 2005, more than 300,000 physicians, nurses, and other caregivers had participated in at least one EPEC educational program.

Some believe that the modern hospice movement began in England with the founding of St. Christopher's Hospice in 1967 by Dame Cicely Saunders, OM, DBE, FRCP, FRCS.[27] From this beginning, the hospice movement has grown dramatically.[28] In the United States, Medicare reimbursement for hospice services has been relatively generous in comparison with its reimbursement for other physician and medical services.[29] The purpose of the Medicare hospice benefit is to provide for the palliation or management of a terminal illness and its related conditions. Under federal guidelines, the hospice benefit is available to individuals who have been certified by a physician to be terminally ill. These same federal guidelines say that an individual is terminally ill if the patient has a medical prognosis with a life expectancy of six months or less. Some states have incorporated this notion of six-month survival into their statutory and regulatory law as well. For example, in Texas, "terminal illness" is defined in their advance directives legislation as:

> an incurable condition caused by injury, disease, or illness that
> according to reasonable medical judgment will produce death

within six months, even with available life-sustaining treatment provided in accordance with the prevailing standard of medical care. A patient who is admitted to a program under which the person received hospice services provided by home and community support services licensed under [the law] is presumed to have a terminal illness for purposes of this [statute].[30]

By way of definition and common usage, *palliative care* is not as limited as *hospice care*. One working explanation of palliative care, as offered by the National Hospice and Palliative Care Organization (NHPCO) in their *Standards of Practice for Hospice Programs,* is:

> [Palliative care offers] treatment that enhances comfort and improves the quality of an individual's life during the last phase of life. The test of palliative care lies in the agreement between the individual, physicians, primary caregiver, and the hospice team that the expected outcome is relief from distressing symptoms, the easing of pain, and/or the enhancing the quality of life. The decision to intervene with active palliative care is based on an ability to meet stated goals rather than affect the underlying disease. An individual's options are explored and evaluated in the context of the individual's values and symptoms. The individual's choices and decisions regarding care are paramount and must be followed.[31]

A similar, but perhaps more task-specific, definition of palliative care is used by the United Nations World Health Organization:

> Palliative care is an approach that improves the quality of life of patients and their families facing the problem associated with life-threatening illness, through the prevention and relief of suffering by means of early identification and impeccable assessment and treatment of pain and other problems, physical, psychosocial and spiritual. Palliative care:
>
> • provides relief from pain and other distressing symptoms;
> • affirms life and regards dying as a normal process;
> • intends neither to hasten nor postpone death;
> • integrates the psychological and spiritual aspects of patient care;

- offers a support system to help patients live as actively as possible until death;
- offers a support system to help the family cope during the patient's illness and in their own bereavement;
- uses a team approach to address the needs of patients and their families, including bereavement counseling [*sic*], if indicated;
- will enhance quality of life, and may also positively influence the course of illness;
- is applicable early in the course of illness, in conjunction with other therapies that are intended to prolong life, such as chemotherapy or radiation therapy, and includes those investigations needed to better understand and manage distressing clinical complications.[32]

Featured prominently in both the NHPCO and WHO palliative care definitions are goals and treatment options as they positively impact a patient's quality of life.

Whether Bergman was willing to accept strong pain medicines with undesirable but anticipated side effects, such as respiratory depression and a clouded sensorium, was a matter for conversation, discussion, and agreement with Chin. In the final analysis, it remained a quality of life assessment for the patient. Such an individual patient assessment is supported widely by physicians, pharmacists, and medical ethicists. One statement reflective of this broad support is found in the United States Conference of Catholic Bishops' *Ethical and Religious Directives for Catholic Health Care Services,* at Directives 23, 26, 27, 32, and 33*:

23. The inherent dignity of the human person must be respected and protected regardless of the nature of the person's health problem or social status . . .

. . .

26. The free and informed consent of the person or the person's surrogate is required for medical treatments and procedures, except in an emergency situation when consent cannot be ob-

---

*Reprinted with permission of USCCB Publishing.

tained and there is no indication that the patient would refuse consent to the treatment.

27. Free and informed consent requires that the person or the person's surrogate receive all reasonable information about the essential nature of the proposed treatment and its benefits; its risks, side-effects, consequences, and costs; and any reasonable and morally legitimate alternatives, including no treatment at all.

. . .

32. While every person is obliged to use ordinary means to preserve his or her health, no person should be obliged to submit to a health care procedure that the person has judged, with a free and informed conscience, not to provide a reasonable hope of benefit without imposing excessive risks and burdens on the patient or excessive expense to the family or community.*

33. The well-being of the whole person must be taken into account in deciding about any therapeutic intervention or use of technology. Therapeutic procedures that are likely to cause harm or undesirable side-effects can be justified only by a proportionate benefit to the patient.[33]

Second, it may be that Chin was concerned that he might be investigated or prosecuted by federal, state, or local authorities for inappropriately prescribing narcotics and other controlled substances.[34] Some would say this particular concern is more than a mere passing one. The federal Drug Enforcement Administration (DEA) has been responsible for a number of high-profile physician prosecutions over the past several years, for what amounts to physician narcotic trafficking.[35] New York Beth Israel Medical Center pain and palliative care physician, Russell Portenoy, has remarked, "Fifteen years of progress in treating patients in chronic pain could really be wiped away if these prosecutions continue."

---

*[Note 18 in original] Declaration on Euthanasia. Part IV [Referring to Part IV of the Declaration on Euthanasia published by the Congregation for the Doctrine of the Faith in 1980. Rome, Italy: The Sacred Congregation for the Doctrine of the Faith. 1980. Available at http:// www.vatican.va/roman-curia/congregations/cfaith/documents/rc_con_cfaith_ doc_19800505_euthanasia_en.html (accessed July 5, 2007)]; cf. directives 56-57.

Notable among the physician prosecutions have been legal actions against: William E. Hurwitz, MD, JD, McLean, Virginia, beginning in 1996 (as featured in a CBS *60 Minutes* report); Frank Fisher, MD, Shasta County, California, beginning in 1999 (as reported in the *New York Times*); and Jeri B. Hassman, MD, Tucson, Arizona, beginning in 2001 (as reported in *The Washington Post*). Hurwitz's Virginia medical license was summarily suspended after it was reported that two of his patients died after he had prescribed excessive doses of opioid analgesics. As an immediate consequence of the Virginia board action, his District of Columbia medical license and DEA registration were also suspended. Later, a federal jury found him guilty of controlled substances violations, predicated upon the assertion that many of the prescriptions that he had written were "outside the bounds of medicine."[36] He received a prison sentence. Fisher was arrested for overprescribing high doses of narcotic pain relievers to his patients. It was alleged that five of his patients died as a consequence of narcotics overdoses.[37] As a result of his conviction for a drug trafficking offense, Fisher lost his medical license and his home. Dr. Fisher served five months of his prison sentence before it was determined that his patients had actually died as the result of accidents or illnesses and not the narcotics he had prescribed. Dr. Hassman, a pain and rehabilitation specialist, was indicted on "362 counts of prescribing controlled substances outside the scope of normal medical practice" after an undercover investigation.[38] Had she—a single mother of two—been convicted, Hassman would have faced the prospect of being sentenced to serve up to twenty-eight years in prison. She pleaded guilty in January 2004 to four counts of "accessory after the fact" for assisting patients and non-patients in unlawfully obtaining controlled substances by misrepresentation or deception.[39]

As it happens, all three physicians were allegedly prescribing very high numbers of prescriptions for OXYCONTIN® tablets (oxycodone controlled-release tablets, Purdue Pharma L.P.) to hundreds of patients. The chilling effect of these and other prosecutions on physician prescribing and pharmacist dispensing has been the subject of many debates among academics and practitioners.[40] Moreover, Purdue—OxyContin's manufacturer—has been named as defendant in a number of personal liability lawsuits.[41] The plaintiffs claim in this action was that "the company dishonestly marketed the pain pill by failing to tell doctors, pharmacists, and patients about the drug's addictive qualities." This theory seems outlandish at first blush because many think that the addictive potential of any opioid is relatively common knowledge, much like the addictive potential of tobacco.

The federal Controlled Substances Act (CSA) of 1970 created a closed system of distribution for narcotics and dangerous drugs.[42] Identified individuals and entities that manufacture, distribute, prescribe, administer, and dispense controlled substances register periodically with the DEA.[43] The comprehensive statute was designed primarily to prevent the diversion of controlled substances to illicit channels while maintaining the integrity of the drug delivery system for ultimate users—that is, patients—who might benefit from proper, supervised controlled substances' availability and use. Many states have local regulatory arrangements that mirror the federal system.[44] Severe penalties are provided for those convicted of trafficking controlled substances.[45] The Department of Justice, the DEA, state and local criminal authorities, and state medical arts professional licensing agencies exercise—for the most part—concurrent jurisdiction over the controlled substances closed distribution system. Many investigations are joint operations among the various authorities. For example, in 1994 state medical boards took 403 disciplinary actions against physicians for controlled substances violations, according to the Federation of State Medical Boards.[46] In 2002, 362 such actions were taken. However, according to one survey of thirty-eight state medical boards, when asked questions about the number of complaints, investigations, and disciplinary actions for overprescribing opioids between 1997 and 2001: 14 percent reported increased complaints during that time period; 15 percent reported increased investigations; and 14 percent reported increased disciplinary actions.

In an attempt to better clarify the line between appropriate and inappropriate prescriptions of pain-relieving medications, the Federation of State Medical Boards (FSMB) published (originally in 1998 and revised in 2004) proposed model guidelines for the use of controlled substances in the treatment of pain.[47] The FSMB's revised guidelines view both overprescribing for and undertreatment of pain as serious regulatory issues. The model policy suggests that suspect physician behavior be judged on the basis of individual circumstances and available documentation, and in consultation with subject area experts, rather than on more simple and arbitrary markers such as excessive quantities. The guidelines recommend that relevant patient documentation record the nature and intensity of the individual's pain, current and past therapies, and the effect of the pain and its relief on physical and psychological function, along with other objective criteria to evaluate treatment success or failure.

Similarly, the DEA has attempted to reassure physicians that there is no cause for worry if they practice good medicine, with respect to controlled substances and pain control and other symptom palliation. In this regard, the federal agency is primarily concerned about whether each prescription is (1) legally valid and (2) therapeutically appropriate. These two concepts are embodied in the definition of a valid controlled substances prescription: an order for a medicine that has been issued for a "legitimate medical purpose" by an authorized prescriber who is acting in the "usual course of professional practice."[48] DEA Diversion Control Office spokesperson Patricia Good was reported as saying that there are many misconceptions about the enforcement agency's role, leading to an unwarranted aura of fear that physicians will be targeted if they prescribe opioids. Good said that in the first quarter of 2003, only 557 physicians from across the country were investigated (with actions taken against 441), with less than fifty physicians actually being arrested for improperly prescribing narcotics. In an attempt to alleviate physician worries about harassment or unjustified prosecution stemming from prescribing controlled substances, the DEA cooperated with several of the nation's leading pain experts (including Beth Israel's Dr. Russell Portenoy, and the University of Wisconsin-Madison's medical social worker David E. Joranson) in developing a series of frequently asked questions (FAQs), and providing answers that are "designed to improve pain treatment while attacking the growing problem of prescription drug abuse."[49] The DEA suggests that there is a social policy balance that can be struck in the patient-physician-pharmacist triad: addiction and diversion prevention, while providing adequate pain relief. As pharmacist-attorney David Brushwood has written:

> The principle of balance mandates that [physicians and] pharmacists resolve ambiguities of an opioid analgesic prescription in an equitable way that doesn't consistently result in the refusal of a prescription. [Practitioners] must struggle with the uncertain-

ties and complexities of both substance abuse and pain management therapy. They must do their best to meet the potentially conflicting challenges posed by the therapeutic imperative to optimize patient outcomes and the regulatory imperative to prevent drug diversion. . . . Only through balance can the needs of legitimate patients be met, while also deterring controlled substance diversion.[50]

In continuously balancing these needs, physicians and pharmacists should be constantly on the alert for (1) patients and purported patients who might be seeking drugs for nonlegitimate medical purposes; and (2) patients who use pain medicines legitimately at first, but then develop an addiction.[51] If the prescribing physician or dispensing pharmacist—using reasonable professional judgment—comes to believe that a patient has developed an addiction, then a different action plan than just continuing to provide the drug is necessary. The physician is now treating the patient not only for pain, but also for another indication. Physicians may not prescribe controlled substances in the usual course of professional practice to individuals in order to maintain or detoxify addicts.[52] Physicians who care for patients with controlled substances addictions or drug dependencies must register separately with the DEA as a narcotic treatment program (NTP) or, more recently styled, an opioid treatment program (OTP).[53] OTPs are reaccredited and recertified every three years. Only methadone and levo-alpha-acetyl-methadol (LAAM) are approved for the treatment of narcotic addiction in these treatment programs. The DEA regulations have very specific definitions for "maintenance treatment" and "detoxification treatment":

> The term "maintenance treatment" means: the dispensing of an opioid agonist treatment medication at stable dosage levels for a period in excess of 21 days, in the treatment of an individual for opioid addiction.[54]

> The term "detoxification treatment" means: the dispensing of an opioid agonist treatment medication in decreasing doses to an individual to alleviate adverse physiological or psychological effects incident to withdrawal from the continuous or sustained use of an opioid drug and as a method of bringing the individual to a narcotic drug-free state within such period.[55]

Physicians and pharmacists will not be able to defend their ongoing prescription and dispensing of controlled substances to suspected addicts based on the ethical notions of "trying to help" (beneficence) while attempting to prevent further harm (nonmaleficence) because societal will, as expressed in the statutes and regulations, is very clear. Physicians and pharmacists must confront possible problems and help patients seek assistance through established legitimate channels. There is an exception—albeit strictly regulatory—regarding the treatment of addicts. The Congress enacted the Drug Addiction Treatment Act (DATA) in 2000 to ease some of the hardship for patients suffering from addiction problems (particularly those in rural areas without access to outpatient treatment programs) caused by the more stringent regulatory standards and a lack of physicians qualified in addiction medicine.[56] DATA allows for "qualifying physicians" to engage in office-based treatment of opioid-dependent patients by using Food and Drug Administration (FDA)-approved drugs. Two such drugs are SUBUTEX® (buprenorphine sublingual tablets, Reckitt Benckiser plc) and SUBOXONE© (buprenorphine-naloxone tablets, Reckitt Benckiser plc). Qualifying physicians must obtain a special DEA number and may not treat more than thirty patients at a time.

However, and as with the threat of medical malpractice claims, what gives physicians and pharmacists pause may not be the fear of losing a contest with the DEA or the state board of medical examiners, as much as just the thought of having to be involved with resolving and reporting allegations. Concerns about inconsequential complaints turning into "negative actions" that may be reported to the hospitals in which the physician practices, or to the state board of medical examiners (which might be then reviewed during initial licensure or renewal applications review), or even to the National Practitioner Data Bank (NPDB) loom large in some physicians' minds. The NPDB's statutory purpose—as explained on their Web site—is as follows:

> The legislation[57] that led to the creation of the NPDB was enacted because the U.S. Congress believed that the increasing occurrence of medical malpractice litigation and the need to improve the quality of medical care had become nationwide problems that warranted greater efforts than any individual State could undertake. The intent is to improve the quality of health care by encouraging State licensing boards, hospitals and other health

care entities, and professional societies to identify and discipline those who engage in unprofessional behavior; and to restrict the ability of incompetent physicians, dentists, and other health care practitioners to move from State to State without disclosure or discovery of previous medical malpractice payment and adverse action history. Adverse actions can involve licensure, clinical privileges, professional society membership, and exclusions from Medicare and Medicaid.

The NPDB is primarily an alert or flagging system intended to facilitate a comprehensive review of health care practitioners' professional credentials. The information contained in the NPDB is intended to direct discrete inquiry into, and scrutiny of, specific areas of a practitioner's licensure, professional society memberships, medical malpractice payment history, and record of clinical privileges. The information contained in the NPDB should be considered together with other relevant data in evaluating a practitioner's credentials; it is intended to augment, not replace, traditional forms of credentials review.[58]

More than the reporting to regulatory bodies and organizations—and the threat of the endless hassle associated with continuous explanations to peers for the remainder of a professional lifetime—is the more widespread possibility of negative general publicity and notoriety that may occur within an affected physician's practice community.[59] With state legislatures considering laws that would permit public disclosure of mere allegations or complaints of misconduct or substandard practice, professionals are even more concerned about the possible negative impact on their practices and careers.

Regardless, from an ethical point of view, it is difficult to defend a physician's decision to withhold pain medicines and palliative treatment from patients—especially those patients who may be dying or enrolled in a hospice program—because of the concern about possible allegations of inappropriate conduct (with regard to prescribing pain-relieving narcotics) and its attendant negative professional consequences.[60] One would think that if a physician feels ill at ease with a particular patient's medication needs, then open discussion and perhaps withdrawal from the physician-patient relationship (thus permitting the patient to find alternative medical assistance) would be an option for the physician.

CONTINUING DILEMMAS WITH PAIN MEDICINES AND PALLIATIVE CARE DRUGS

At the time of the *Bergman* case, *The Washington Post* reported that there had been at least two other lawsuits seeking damage awards for the undertreatment of pain (the source for the information was Compassion in Dying Foundation legal affairs director Kathryn Tucker).[61] In 1990, a North Carolina jury issued a $15 million verdict against a nursing home in which a nurse failed to administer prescribed pain-relief medicines to a terminally ill patient. In 1997, a South Carolina judge awarded $200,000 in damages for pain and suffering caused by inadequate treatment of a cancer patient's pain.

Moreover, after the *Bergman* case, the California medical board dealt much differently with a very similar family complaint regarding a dying patient's alleged inadequate pain control.[62] Ginger Tomlinson (who called Compassion in Dying after reading a newspaper article about the *Bergman* case) filed a complaint with the medical board revealing that her father suffered a total of twenty days of neglect and abuse while under the care of two physicians in two separate facilities. The advocacy team for Compassion in Dying assisted her with the complaints to the board, the federal Centers for Medicare and Medicaid Services (CMS), and a state court. The California medical board instituted action against one physician for unprofessional conduct and incompetence in failing to provide proper pain control. CMS decided to punish one facility as well. (One physician and a hospital settled claims with the family out of court.)

In this regard, the California medical board is following the lead of the Oregon medical board, which was the first in the nation to discipline a physician for failure to adequately treat a patient's pain.[63] In accepting an agreed order* stipulation disciplining Roseburg pulmonologist Dr. Paul Bildner, the chairman of the Oregon Board of Medical Examiners reportedly said, "[T]here is no longer room for doctors in Oregon that won't aggressively treat pain particularly in dying pa-

---

*An "agreed order" often results from a settlement of the disciplinary action without benefit of a convened hearing before the entire board or a panel of members. A close cousin of the criminal law is a "plea bargain agreement," which results in the disposition of a criminal complaint without a trial.

tients." Bildner acknowledged that his pain treatment of nine patients "showed unprofessional or dishonorable conduct and gross or repeated acts of negligence." As its sanction, the board required Bildner to participate in the state's Physicians Evaluation Education Renewal (PEER) program. (Oregon's PEER system is a one-year program in which another doctor works with the disciplined physician to assess practice patterns and suggest quality improvement strategies.) Bildner was also required to complete a course on physician-patient communication and to continue meeting with a psychiatrist, who was asked to make regular reports to the board for at least a year. (Sadly, the board's Web site reported that in 2003 Bildner was disciplined again, given ten years' probation, and ordered to continue psychiatric care with quarterly progress reports.[64])

Pharmacists also struggle with many of the same issues that physicians face. Moreover, they report feeling even more caught in the middle: between the doctor who has written a prescription for a controlled substance and the patient who thinks that she or he has a "right" to have the prescription filled.[65] In an attempt to sidestep the problem entirely, some pharmacies have elected not to stock certain products at all in order to avoid any controversy. And—at the other end of the spectrum—some pharmacists have been chided and disciplined for being too aggressive in monitoring prescription validity and therapeutic appropriateness.[66]

Professional monitoring by the state healing arts boards seems preferable to dealing with the associated issues more globally, than through legal actions taken by individual patients or their survivors for medical malpractice or elder abuse. In practice, individuals may be better compensated for damages under these liability theories (as well as for intentional infliction of emotional distress or outrageous conduct actions), but the results are certain to be more isolated, piecemeal, and less just. Moreover, having to demonstrate that a physician's conduct is "reckless" (or "grossly negligent") in order to establish baseline liability for inadequate pain control seems to miss the point. It may technically allow for a jury to award compensation for damages to the aggrieved party in a lawsuit, but does so indirectly and, thus, encourages plaintiffs and lawyers to be even more creative in stretching liability theories or bending legislative intent for an undesigned purpose. (It seems awkward and circuitous to compel plaintiffs to use a statute designed to prevent inappropriate and abusive care in a long-term care or residential facility to hold physicians responsible for providing inadequate pain control as in the *Bergman* case.) In addition, it sends a public message that legislators and regulators seem disinterested in dealing with proper pain management as an important societal concern—and is one best left for crafty lawyers to resolve.

Appropriate narcotic use is an extension of an issue that regulatory boards have been grappling with for a long time: physicians and pharmacists who are themselves abusing controlled substances.[67] This, too, is a major public issue and one that achieved an even higher level of scrutiny when it was revealed that Vice President Dick Cheney's personal physician participated in a treatment program for prescription drug addiction.[68]

There still is a great deal to be done in terms of educating physicians, nurses, and pharmacists on the delicate balance between adequate pain control and abuse of narcotics. Much remains, as well, to provide the personnel and mechanisms necessary for patient access to quality medical care that includes good pain control management. *American Medical News* reported that in 2004 there were only about 10,000 pain management physician specialists in the country and that they care for a very small percentage of patients—presumably these are the patients who suffer from the most debilitating types of pain, but this is really unproven.[69] Another recent study reported that only about one out of every five patients who suffer with chronic pain actually sees a physician pain management specialist.[70] It is also unfortunate that some patients—who are dying and who have had an otherwise very strong and positive relationship with their personal physicians—may fail to achieve a peaceful, pain-free, dignified end because doctors are ill-prepared to deal with and control pain adequately at the final stage of life.[71]

Chapter 6

Drugs Used for Assisted Suicide

At a time when practitioners knew more about poisons than almost any other drug category, one of Hippocrates' disciples included this sentence in a version of the Oath: "To please no one will I prescribe a deadly drug nor give advice which may cause his death."[1] Should today's physicians and pharmacists hold this same view as did Greek healers in the fourth century BC? And if so, then why? Should this hold true for the patient who is dying of an incurable or terminal illness, and who may be suffering in the process? If physicians choose not to honor this part of the Oath, then should society legally recognize (and accept as a standard of care) physician-assisted suicide? If so, then to what degree should health care provider involvement in a patient's intentional death be regulated?

In the nineteenth century, there were four commonly prescribed sedatives and hypnotics—bromide salts, chloral hydrate, paraldehyde, and alcohol—all potentially fatal following excessive use or overdose.[2] Bromide was effective in "calming the nerves" and as a sleep aid, but not favored because of the risk of chronic bromide poisoning. Chloral hydrate and paraldehyde have quite objectionable odors and tastes. Many patients preferred not to drink alcoholic beverages or take alcohol in any form because they were "teetotalers" and had "taken the pledge" to abstain from intoxicating liquors. In the late 1800s, physicians were searching for better medicines than those available to treat insomnia and to depress the central nervous system. However, physicians also recognized that any newer agents—like the others currently in use—might cause a patient's death if not dosed correctly.

In 1863, Adolph von Bayer, whose pharmaceutical firm also first synthesized aspirin and heroin, chemically produced barbituric acid by combining urea and malonic acid.[3] (The date of the discovery was the Feast Day of Saint Barbara, so von Bayer named his drug "Barbara's urates"—later contracted to "barbiturates"—in her honor.) Two other German scientists, Joseph von Mering and Emil Fischer, created a derivative they called barbital and introduced it into medical practice in 1903 under the tradename VERONAL® (Bayer & Co.). Tested on both animals and humans, barbital seemed to have just the right effect as a sleep aid. A second barbituric acid derivative, phenobarbital, was marketed under the trade name LUMINAL® (Bayer & Co. and Winthrop-Breon Laboratories) in 1912. Over the years, more than 2,500 other barbiturates were synthesized, with over fifty eventually reaching the market as sleeping pills or for other medical purposes.

It is believed that barbiturates act to enhance or mimic the inhibitory synaptic activity of gamma-aminobutyric acid (GABA) and thereby nonselectively depress the central nervous system (CNS).[4] The drugs can produce all levels of CNS alteration from mild excitation to sedation, hypnosis, anesthesia, coma, and even death. The effects are dose-dependent. However, as a class and when used appropriately for such medical problems as insomnia and seizures, the barbiturates improve the quality of life of many patients.

The barbiturate sedative-hypnotics may be categorized as long-acting, intermediate-acting, short-acting, and ultra-short-acting, depending on the timing of their onset of action. Phenobarbital is long-acting because it reaches its onset of activity about sixty minutes after oral ingestion, its duration of action is about ten to twelve hours, and its half-life range is about 52-118 hours. Pentobarbital (NEMBUTAL®, Abbott Laboratories) and secobarbital (SECONAL®, Eli Lilly & Co.) are short-acting drugs, each with an onset of action about ten-fifteen minutes after ingestion, with a duration of action of about three to four hours, and are completely metabolized in about fifteen to twenty hours. An example of an ultra-short-acting barbiturate is thiopental (PENTOTHAL®, Abbott Laboratories), which is so fast-acting and rapidly metabolized that it is used primarily to induce anesthesia. (One might note that in his initial case, Dr. Jack Kevorkian's "suicide machine" or Mercitron infused thiopental, thus allowing the patient to doze to a half-sleep or near unconsciousness before tripping the lever that administered a potassium chloride solution six seconds later.[5])

Those physicians who write lethal doses of barbiturates for patients to use in taking their own lives sometimes prescribe secobarbital to be taken orally.[6] On average, these patients lapse into unconsciousness within five minutes after ingesting the drug, and die about twenty-five minutes later. Derek Humphry, a journalist and author of *Jean's Way* (about his wife's terminal illness and suicide) and founder of the Hemlock Society (an advocacy group supporting guidelines for assisted death and providing information for the dying and their families) has published a formula to concoct a lethal barbiturate-based oral preparation.[7]

Benzodiazepines are a class of drugs marketed as antianxiety agents, sedatives-hypnotics, anticonvulsants, and muscle relaxants.[8] Like barbiturates, they depress the central nervous system globally in higher doses by acting on the $GABA_A$ receptor and dampening neuronal activity. Also, like barbiturates, they may be grouped into long-acting, intermediate-acting, and short-acting categories, based on onset and duration of activities.

The first benzodiazepine, chlordiazepoxide (LIBRUM®, Roche), was discovered accidentally by Austrian scientist Leo Sternbach, who was working for the pharmaceutical company Hoffmann-La Roche.[9] Subsequently, he discontinued his work on the compound *Ro-5-0690*, but then "rediscovered" it in 1957 when an assistant was cleaning up the laboratory. Although initially discouraged by his employer, Sternbach conducted further research that revealed the compound was a very effective tranquilizer. LIBRUM and the other benzodiazepines such as diazepam (VALIUM®, Roche) and oxazepam (SERAX®, Wyeth) were widely marketed as anxiolytics in the 1960s and 1970s. They were initially sold as substitutes for the barbiturates because they have fewer side effects, an improved safety index, and less potential for abuse. However, and with experience, practitioners and patients learned that these drugs do have a relatively high abuse potential; all are now controlled substances under the Controlled Substances Act (CSA).

More recently marketed short-acting benzodiazepines include lorazepam (ATIVAN®, Wyeth) and midazolam (VERSED®, Roche). As intravenous agents, these products are used extensively as anticonvulsants and preanesthetic medications. These agents are used in palliative care situations as antianxiety and sedative medicines, and have a very quick onset of action following oral administration.

THE DEBATE ABOUT PHYSICIAN-ASSISTED SUICIDE AND EUTHANASIA

The "right and wrong" of suicide and "mercy-killing" have been debated for centuries.[10] From Hebrew and Christian Scripture, there are three examples of suicide that are quite familiar to many: Judas, Samson, and Saul. After betraying Jesus, the guilt-ridden Judas hanged himself.[11] To some, Judeo-Christian tradition seems to pity Judas rather than condemn the manner of his death, perhaps because he was either not in his right mind, because he evidenced some remorse, or maybe sought repentance. The recorded deaths of Samson and Saul are somewhat different from Judas' suicide. Having succumbed to Delilah's entreaties and lately a blinded object of Philistine ridicule, Samson—once a proud and boastful man—ended his life by collapsing a temple on himself and those taunting him, thus killing more of his enemy at that moment than in all previous battles.[12] Scripture does not overtly criticize Samson for this act of revenge and a later passage in the New Testament, attributed to Paul in the letter to the Hebrews, lists Samson as one of the heroes of faith.[13] King Saul's death is even more dissimilar. Encircled by his foes in desperate hand-to-hand combat—and afraid that if taken prisoner, his enemies would eventually execute him after "[making] a mock" or "[making] sport" of him—Saul asked his armorbearer to kill him so that he would avoid capture.[14] There is some question as to whether Saul took his own life by falling on his sword or whether the armorbearer finished the job after Saul's botched suicide attempt.[15] Regardless, David—named king in Saul's stead—ordered the servant executed upon hearing the account because the aide admitted to having a hand in his master's death.[16]

Curiously, the Hebrew and Christian Scripture—with the descriptions of the deaths of Judas, Samson, and Saul—appears relatively neutral regarding their suicides. Moreover, some have used the analogy of Saul's suicide as an argument to support the suicide or assisted-suicide decision of a terminally ill person. Proponents see Saul as a beleaguered patient—beset with a ravaging disease (like cancer), whose body is being abused or "mocked" by a fatal illness that is "making sport" of the afflicted person's quality of life—with the realization that the disease or some other medical condition will soon take the patient's life. Supporters see suicide in this circumstance as a patient's conscious choice and a welcome option—as did Saul in his last fight with the Philistines—to foil the disease's attempt to rob the dying patient of any dignity or self-respect at life's end.

Moreover, the Judeo-Christian tradition makes allowance for some self-deaths—most dramatically that of Jesus. John 15:13 (KJV) says, "Greater love hath no man than this, that a man lay down his life for his friends." Paul writes in Romans 5:7 (KJV), "For scarcely for a righteous man will one die: yet peradventure for a good man some would even dare to die." Regardless, one is left to ponder the ambivalence and whether it is motive (self-defense or defense of others), intent (being hopeful for one's own death through self-action), act (taking one's own life or allowing death without a struggle), or the consequences (one's actual death as the result of some action) that is the key to understanding the difference between morally acceptable and unacceptable self-aware death.

The ancient Greeks and Romans also appear unsure about suicide and mercy killing. In Sparta, it was commanded by law that deformed infants be put to death; the "more enlightened" Athenians did not require infanticide of their deformed young, but there was no condemnation for parents who elected to abandon them in an open field to be exposed to the elements and certain death.[17] However, the support for infanticide was not taken as evidence for a general lack of respect for life. The great Greek philosophers Pythagoras, Plato, and Aristotle did not approve of suicide and saw it as a coward's way of avoiding life's hardships.[18] On the other hand, they did not condemn suicide in all circumstances. All three recognized the right of someone who was afflicted with an incurable disease and/or in great pain to choose an "earlier death."[19] Also, they made no distinction between suicide and euthanasia; if the dying person needed help, it was permissible for others to assist.

The Hippocratic Oath appeared about the time of Socrates' suicide and contains the sentence: "I will not give a drug that is deadly to anyone if asked, nor will I suggest the way to such a counsel."[20] Some biomedical ethics scholars have used that passage as support for the proposition that physicians should not assist patients—even dying patients who are in great pain—to an "earlier death."[21] However, Steven Miles, in his work *The Hippocratic Oath and the Ethics of Medicine,* has suggested that this may be a dogmatic misinterpretation, given the practice patterns of the time. He concluded his analysis of the relevant sentence from the Oath with this summary:

> Attempting to cure, palliating suffering, and advancing the science: these three goals defined the engagement of Greek physicians with dying persons. If medically assisted euthanasia had been a part of the care of the dying by physicians, herbalists, or midwives it seems likely that they would have noted it just as abortions would have been discussed. There is no evidence that this passage [from the Oath] spoke to an ancient debate about medical euthanasia.[22]

Moreover, Greek physicians did recognize the futility of offering ineffective and nonbeneficial treatments. *The Art*—collected medical sayings attributed to Hippocrates and his contemporaries—contains this statement: "Whenever a man suffers from an illness, which is too strong for the means at the disposal of medicine, he surely must not expect that it can be overcome by medicine."[23] The authors were trying to remind healers that to even attempt a futile treatment was to show ignorance that was "allied to madness." Others have written that Hippocrates said the *master* physician is the one who recognizes when the disease has *mastered* the case.[24]

The views of Roman philosophers seem to closely parallel those of the Greeks. The Stoics—represented by Epictetus—thought suicide was an option when one no longer cares for life: "If the room is smoky, if only moderately, I will stay; if there is too much smoke, I will go. Remember this, keep a firm hold on it, the door is always open."[25] When commenting about old age and the possibility of senility and infirmity, Seneca wrote:

> I will not relinquish old age if it leaves my better part intact. But if it begins to shake my mind, if it destroys my faculties one by one, if it leaves me not life but breath, I will depart from the putrid or the tottering edifice. If I know that I must suffer without

hope of relief I will depart not through fear of the pain but because it prevents all for which I would live.[26]

For the Greeks and the Romans, decisions regarding suicide and assisted suicide appear to focus on the impacted individual's perception of quality of life.

The late James Rachels, in his book *The End of Life: Euthanasia and Morality,* reported that "[t]he coming of Christianity caused vast changes in these attitudes."[27]

More directly, Rachels wrote:

> Infanticide was prohibited, for it was thought that all who are born of woman, no matter how monstrous or miserable, are made in God's image. Suicide was forbidden because one's life was viewed as a trust from God, and only He had the right to take it. The same was said about euthanasia. Under the influence of the Church, what for the Greek and Roman philosophers had been a compassionate solution to the problem of lingering, degrading death became a mortal sin. Suffering, no matter how horrible or seemingly pointless, came to be viewed as a burden imposed by God himself, for purposes known only to him [*sic*], which men and women must bear until the "natural" end.[28]

Similarly, the Christian view is closely aligned with Jewish and Islamic traditions on the subject.[29]

Good physicians, more recently and generally, have been guided by the patient's best interests in making decisions based on the goals of medicine.[30] The physician-patient relationship and its shared decision making regarding available medical interventions is taken to be the ethical, legal, and moral foundation for modern medical ethics.[31] Perhaps the real disagreement among various patient and physician camps is about the interpretation of the phrase, the "patient's best interests." Some physicians think they are "doing good," by helping to ease their dying patients' suffering, when assisting with an "earlier death."[32] Others question whether physicians should *ever* be perceived as actively participating in a patient's death.[33] Even with the occasional report of euthanasia—such as the death of King George V of Great Britain after a lethal injection of cocaine and morphine, timed to assure a headline in the next morning's London papers[34]—there was little public notice of the underlying professional conflict about euthanasia.

However, the 1960s and 1970s in America created a climate for changing attitudes about illness, physicians, and the limits of intervention.[35] Medicine advanced with a greater dependency on newer technologies and specialization; physicians became more determined to cure diseases than ever before. (Recall that President Nixon, in an administrative initiative, declared a "war on cancer" and was responsible for enacting the National Cancer Act with the goal of eliminating the killer disease.) In their battles to defeat illnesses, physicians were so aggressive that patients became afraid that the effects of the cures might be worse than the diseases. Patients saw their quality of life diminish with some treatments because they offered little or no benefit for recovery. Patients also saw themselves as having less and less ability to participate in the decision-making process. The rise in medical malpractice claims and the humanism movement in medicine developed at about that same time. Regarding end-of-life care, patients began completing living wills so that their loved ones (or surviving family members) would have a written expression of treatment preferences if the patients lost their own decision-making capacity.[36]

With the publication of "It's Over Debbie" in the *JAMA* on January 8, 1988, the private medical debate became far more open.[37] The article—an anonymous, first person account published as "A Piece of My Mind"—describes how a gynecology resident administered an arguably fatal dose of morphine to a twenty-year-old patient named Debbie who was dying of ovarian cancer (after having failed chemotherapy). It perhaps is the first report of euthanasia in a reputable American medical journal. The patient was clearly in her last days, hours, or minutes of life, obviously suffering, and in much distress from air hunger; she was a "supportive care only" patient. She said to the resident, "Let's get this over with." The resident interpreted the remark as a request for mercy killing (or at least a plea for comfort) and arguably complied ("I injected the morphine intravenously and watched to see if my calculations on its effect would be correct . . . With clocklike certainty, within four minutes the breathing rate slowed even more, then become irregular, then ceased.").

Publication of the Debbie case was immediately and roundly criticized by most physicians. In a later issue of the *Journal,* nationally recognized physician-medical ethicists Willard Gaylin, Leon Kass, Edmund Pellegrino, and Mark Siegler collectively condemned the publication of the article without editorial comment or rebuke, and called for identification and prosecution of the gynecology resident for murder.[38] A contrary opinion appeared immediately following that article in the same issue—authored by University of Illinois, Chicago, medical ethics consultant Kenneth Vaux—which asked if this was really a homicide or just the "double-effect" of a large dose of morphine given for palliation.[39] Regardless, the issue seemed squarely framed for more public discourse.

The Debbie case may worry many physicians—even those who favor limited euthanasia—because of the obvious lack of patient safeguards: the diagnosis and prognosis seemed clear and independently determined, and there appeared to be some family involvement and agreement in the decision-making process. However, the facts are sketchy: there appears to have been no traditional physician-patient relationship (the resident had never met the patient before); it is not clear that the patient had decision-making capacity (perhaps because of depression or discomfort); the patient's wishes were not clear (there was no informed consent); the physician's intent was not well understood; there was no opportunity for reflection about the intervention decision (the episode was over in minutes); the physician administered the lethal dose personally; and there was no opportunity for outside or regulatory oversight (with a reporting mechanism for later review).

About two years after the Debbie report in *JAMA*, Dr. Jack Kevorkian helped Janet Adkins take her life.[40] Dr. Kevorkian was a retired Michigan pathologist; Janet Adkins was a fifty-four-year-old Portland, Oregon, musician and teacher, who had been recently diagnosed with Alzheimer's disease.[41] Janet Adkins wanted to end her life because its quality—in her mind—had changed radically and she wanted to spare herself and her family a long, agonizing goodbye.

As with the Debbie case, Kevorkian's actions were almost universally condemned. The Adkins' diagnosis and prognosis seemed clear and they were independently determined, but only a few months before Kevorkian assisted with her death. It is hard to say that Adkins had an adequate understanding of the disease, its stages, and progression. (It takes months to years for some Alzheimer's disease patients to progress from one stage to the next.) There appeared to be some family involvement and tacit agreement in the decision-making process (Adkins' husband had traveled to Michigan with her and participated in the conversation with Kevorkian during dinner the day before the suicide). However, there was certainly no traditional physician-patient relationship (Adkins and Kevorkian met purely for the purpose of assisted suicide), and it is not clear that the patient had decision-making capacity (perhaps because of depression or the disease). But, if she did have that capacity, then the patient's wishes were probably as clear as possible (arguably there was informed consent). The physician's intent was undeniably unmistakable. However, because the total encounter with Kevorkian (i.e., the time between the dinner discussion the night before and the suicide) occurred within the span of a few hours, there was little opportunity for reflection about the intervention decision. Unlike Debbie, the *patient* rather than the *physician* administered the lethal dose. There was no opportunity for outside or regulatory oversight (with a reporting mechanism for later review); it seems as if was all done in relative secrecy.

Less than one year after Adkins' death, physician Timothy E. Quill wrote an article, "Death and Dignity: A Case of Individualized Decision Making," which was published in the *New England Journal of Medicine* on March 7, 1991.[42] For the second time, a reputable American medical journal published an account of a patient's death under circumstances that heretofore would have been considered unethical. Quill told how he had prescribed barbiturates so that Diane, a patient who was suffering from acute myelomoncytic leukemia, had refused chemotherapy, and was in hospice care, could use the drug to take her life when she could no longer "maintain control of herself and her own dignity." Some physicians defended Quill by saying that he only did what other physicians have done in the past to help terminally ill patients: prescribe a month's supply of sleeping pills.[43] However, by his own admission, Quill knowingly prescribed the barbiturates for his patient to commit suicide at a time of her own choosing. He then broadcasted the facts publicly in a national medical journal. After reviewing the case, a Rochester, New York, grand jury decided not to indict Quill for criminally assisting in a suicide, and a three-member panel of the New York Board of Professional Medical Conduct elected not to discipline him for unprofessional conduct.[44]

With Diane's case, there was a different response from professionals and the public than that over the Debbie and Adkins cases. Quill
was openly criticized in some quarters, and quietly praised for his
compassion and courage by others. In comparison to the other two reports of Debbie and Janet Adkins, Diane's diagnosis and prognosis
was definitively and independently determined by two oncologists
other than Quill. Diane knew about the illness (having survived vaginal
cancer), the treatment options, the possibility of long-term cure (only
25 percent), and, thus, had refused chemotherapy. It is unclear if Diane's husband and child knew of her intentions to take her life (they did
try to convince her to undergo chemotherapy, but seemed to understand her reasons for refusing curative treatment). Remarkably different from Debbie and Adkins, in Diane's case the physician and patient
knew each other well and had a strong, traditional physician-patient
relationship. Even with her history of alcoholism and depression,
Diane had decision-making capacity (in fact, she saw a psychologist
to discuss treatment options and her refusal to undergo treatment).
The patient's wishes were as clear as possible (she discussed the lethal
prescription with Quill twice; there was a period of time between the
first and second conversations; and there was informed consent), and
it was the physician's intent to prescribe a sufficient dose for a suicide. During their discussions, held over a period of several months,
there was more than ample opportunity for reflection about the decision. Like Adkins, the patient, rather than the physician, administered
the lethal dose. Also, like the other two cases, there was no opportunity
for prospective regulatory oversight (there was, however, retrospective review before a grand jury and medical board). As with the other
two cases, events transpired in secret. With the Diane case, the most
pernicious objections to the Debbie and Adkins' cases had been al-
layed. However, also with the Diane case, the behind-the-scenes physician-assisted suicide was, for all practical purposes, later sanctioned
by the state's criminal justice system and medical board. Not long
after the Diane case, Quill's patient-encounter protocol—with statutory addition of regulatory oversight and immunity provisions—was
codified in the Oregon Death With Dignity Act.

THE OREGON DEATH WITH DIGNITY ACT

In 1994, the citizens of Oregon voted to enact the Oregon Death With Dignity Act (DWDA). The Act was passed by a close 52 percent to 48 percent margin after a bitter, polarizing debate in the media, with the opposing camps nearly equally funded.[45] For the first time in the United States, physicians and pharmacists were able to legally assist terminally ill patients who wanted to take their own lives. (The voters in Washington and California defeated similar measures in 1991 and 1992, respectively.)

The DWDA is procedurally exacting for physicians who write lethal prescriptions and then seek immunity from civil or criminal sanctions and from any professional disciplinary action.[46] However, without the immunity provided by the DWDA, physicians and pharmacists would be open to prosecution or administrative sanction because Oregon still has a law that prohibits aiding another in committing suicide, under most circumstances.[47]

The DWDA's pertinent provisions may be summarized as follows:

- The terminally ill Oregon resident may make an oral request of his or her attending physician for a lethal dose of a medicine.[48] Terminal illness is defined as "an incurable and irreversible disease that has been medically confirmed and will, within reasonable medical judgment, produce death within six months."[49]
- After a 15-day waiting period, the patient must repeat the request, in written form, witnessed by at least two persons.[50]
- The attending physician and a consulting physician must determine that the patient has decision-making capacity, is suffering from a terminal illness, and is freely expressing a voluntary wish to accelerate the dying process.[51] If either physician believes that the patient has "a psychiatric or psychological disorder or depression causing impaired judgment," the patient must be referred for counseling.[52] The physicians must ascertain that the patient is making an informed choice and that the patient has been advised of the diagnosis, prognosis, possible effects associated with medicines prescribed, probable result of taking the drugs, and other available treatment options (including comfort care, hospice care, and pain management).[53]

- Only after all the preceding legal requirements have been met may the attending physician then write a prescription for a lethal dose of a drug.[54] The prescriptions are for "medications intended to facilitate the desired effect and minimize the patient's discomfort."[55] It may be that the prescription order is for sleeping pills (such as a short-acting barbiturates) and perhaps for an anti-anxiety agent and muscle relaxant (such as a benzodiazepines).[56] The physician may dispense the medicine(s) directly or deliver the prescription(s) to the patient or a pharmacist.[57]
- The attending physician must document the encounter[58] and provide a copy of the dispensing record to the state Department of Human Services.[59]
- The patient must self-administer the lethal dose "to end his or her life in a humane and dignified manner."[60]

Between 1998 (when the DWDA was first enacted) and 2004 (the latest complete reporting period), 208 Oregonians died after ingesting a self-administered lethal dose of drugs, which were prescribed under the law.[61] Not all patients who had received the lethal dose prescription(s) followed through with taking the medicine(s).[62]

The Path to the Supreme Court

In October 1997 the U.S. Supreme Court addressed the constitutionality of physician-assisted suicide in the paired opinions, *Washington v. Glucksberg* and *Vacco v. Quill*.[63] Physicians and patients brought the cases to challenge state statutes (in Washington and New York, respectively) that criminalized assisted suicide. The cases reached the Supreme Court after the Second and Ninth Circuits issued apparent conflicting decisions. The Court took the cases to clarify the constitutional law issue and reconcile the lower courts' divergent interpretations. In its opinions, the Court held that nothing in the U.S. Constitution would prohibit a state from criminalizing assisted suicide. The Court was careful, however, to make clear that, although a state could criminalize such an act, the Court itself was not banning the practice. Chief Justice Rehnquist wrote: "Throughout the nation, Americans are engaged in an earnest and profound debate about the morality, legality, and practicality of physician-assisted suicide. Our holding permits this debate to continue, as it should in a democratic society."[64]

In the wake of the *Glucksberg* and *Vacco* opinions, the Oregon voters reaffirmed their commitment to the DWDA. By a 60-40 percent margin, they defeated a ballot measure to repeal the Act. However, opponents of physician-assisted suicide—particularly at the federal level—continued in their attempts to thwart or nullify the Oregon law. Rep. Henry J. Hyde (R-Illinois), Sen. Orrin G. Hatch (R-Utah), and other federal legislators (including Senator John Ashcroft [R-Missouri]) asked Drug Enforcement Administration (DEA) Administrator Thomas Constantine about the validity of the Oregon law, in light of a possible discrepancy with federal controlled substances statutes and regulations. In response, Administrator Constantine opined that if an Oregon physician used controlled substances as suggested by the ODWDA, it would not be for a "legitimate medical purpose" as required under federal law. In June 1998, U.S. Attorney General Janet Reno, pursuant to her executive authority over the DEA, overruled Administrator Constantine and declared that the DEA lacked jurisdiction to sanction physicians acting responsibly under the Oregon statute.[65]

Members of Congress who disagreed with Attorney General Reno urged her to uphold Administrator Constantine's interpretation of "legitimate medical purpose." She responded that after a "thorough and careful review" she had concluded that the Controlled Substances Act (CSA) was intended to "prevent both the trafficking in controlled substances for unauthorized purposes and drug abuse." She said further that she could find no evidence "in the CSA [that] Congress intended to displace the states as the primary regulators of the medical profession, or to override a state's determination as to what constitutes legitimate medical purpose in the absence of a federal law prohibiting that practice."[66]

After Attorney General Reno issued her response, Rep. Hyde introduced proposed federal legislation to resolve the problem. The bill was styled the Lethal Drug Abuse Prevention Act of 1998. The proposed law would have made it a crime for a physician to prescribe controlled substances "for the purpose of causing death."[67] Speaking specifically about the DWDA, Hyde said, "Oregon decided to change the time-honored professional purpose of medicine and give doctors the option to serve no longer as healing forces, but as social engineers, messengers of death."[68] The bill passed the House, but did not pass the Senate.

Shortly after the defeat of the Lethal Drug Abuse Prevention Act, Rep. Hyde and Sen. Don Nickles (R-Okla) introduced the Pain Relief Promotion Act of 1999 (PRPA). The title notwithstanding, the PRPA appeared to be aimed at "prevent[ing] physicians in Oregon from continuing to implement the Death With Dignity Act."[69] The PRPA prohibited the use of controlled substances with the intent to "caus[e] death or assis[t] another person in causing death." The bill granted the Attorney General the right to make decisions about controlled substances more broadly, in the public interest, and instructed the incumbent to "give no force and effect to state law authorizing or permitting assisted suicide or euthanasia." Once again, the proposed legislation passed the House but did not pass the Senate.

Following the election of President George W. Bush in 2000, John Ashcroft replaced Janet Reno as Attorney General and "with a change of administrations came a change of perspectives."[70] Attorney General Ashcroft sought the opinion of the Justice Department's Office of Legal Counsel (OLC) as to the legality of the DWDA's protections for physicians who aid a patient in suicide. The OLC responded that "assisting in suicide was not a 'legitimate medical purpose' that would justify a physician's dispensing controlled substances under the Controlled Substances Act."

Based on the OLC opinion, Attorney General Ashcroft issued an Interpretive Rule, titled Dispensing of Controlled Substances to Assist Suicide,[71] in which he concluded that physicians who prescribe controlled substances that are meant to assist a patient to hasten his or her death are in violation of the CSA regulations and thereby subject to possible prosecution and sanction (such as loss of DEA controlled substances registration). Faced with an Interpretive Rule that, for all practical purposes, negated the DWDA, the State of Oregon, a physician, a pharmacist, terminally ill Oregon residents, and family members of patients filed a declaratory judgment asking the federal district court to invalidate the Attorney General's opinion.

A split three-judge panel of the Ninth Circuit struck down the Interpretive Rule on the basis that Attorney General Ashcroft did not have authority to issue it.[72] In a report that was published in the *New*

York Times[73] on the following day, three quotations from the Ninth Circuit were highlighted:

- "The attorney general's unilateral attempt to regulate general medical practices historically entrusted to state lawmakers inter-feres with the democratic debate about physician-assisted suicide and far exceeds the scope of his authority under federal law."
- "We express no opinion on whether the practice [of physician-assisted suicide] is inconsistent with the public interest or con-stitutes illegitimate medical care. This case is simply about who gets to decide."
- "The principle that state governments bear the primary respon-sibility for evaluating physician-assisted suicide follows from our concept of federalism, which requires that state lawmakers, not the federal government, are the primary regulators of profes-sional medical conduct."

The Attorney General appealed the Ninth Circuit decision to the Supreme Court. The Supreme Court accepted the case on writ of cer-tiorari on February 22, 2005,[74] and heard oral arguments on October 5, 2005.[75] (The name of the case had changed from *Ashcroft v. Oregon* to *Gonzales v. Oregon* because Alberto R. Gonzales had replaced John Ashcroft as Attorney General in the interim.)

Gonzales v. Oregon

When the case reached the Supreme Court, the key issue was a straightforward, rather dry, legal one: Did the Attorney General have authority under the Controlled Substances Act to issue an Interpretive Rule stating that assisting suicide is not a "legitimate medical pur-pose" for which federally regulated drugs may legally be prescribed?

The Supreme Court found that the Attorney General did not have such authority and struck down the Interpretive Rule by a vote of six to three. Justice Anthony M. Kennedy wrote for the majority, joined by Justices John Paul Stevens, Sandra Day O'Connor, David H. Souter, Ruth Bader Ginsburg, and Stephen G. Breyer. Justice Antonin Scalia filed a dissenting opinion in which Chief Justice John G. Roberts, Jr., and Justice Clarence Thomas joined. Justice Thomas also filed a separate dissenting opinion.

The Majority Opinion

Writing for the majority, Justice Kennedy reasoned that the Interpretive Rule was not entitled to judicial deference and Congress had not envisioned such a broad grant of authority when it enacted the CSA:

> There are two primary situations in which the judicial branch will defer to an administrative official's interpretation of a statute or regulation. The first, based on the reasoning set forth in *Auer v. Robbins,* occurs where a government official issues an explanation of a regulation or rule originally promulgated by his or her own Agency.[76] For example, where the Secretary of Labor issued an interpretation of the Fair Labor Standards Act, the original Act at issue "was a creature of the Secretary's own regulations, [and] his interpretation of it is . . . controlling unless plainly erroneous or inconsistent with the regulation."[77]

Following the line of reasoning in *Auer,* Attorney General Gonzales argued that the Interpretive Rule was merely an elaboration of the Department of Justice's own regulations contained in 21 CFR § 1306.04(a) that require that a controlled substance be issued for a "legitimate medical purpose." The Court rejected this argument and distinguished the *Gonzales* case from *Auer* because the regulation cited by Attorney General Gonzales "[did] little more than restate the terms of the [federal] statute itself. The language the Interpretive Rule addresses [came] from Congress, not the Attorney General."[78] As the Court found that the regulation simply parroted the terms of the statute, they concluded that the Attorney General did not have the type of special experience or insight necessary to warrant *Auer* deference.

The second and more frequently used rationale for according deference to an Interpretive Rule arises where the rule is promulgated by an administrative official pursuant to authority delegated to the official by Congress.[79] The Court declined to find such a delegation in the CSA, writing that:

> The Attorney General has rulemaking power to fulfill his duties under the CSA. The specific respects in which he is authorized to make rules, however, instruct us that he is not authorized to

make a rule declaring illegitimate a medical standard for care and treatment of patients that is specifically authorized under state law.[80]

In interpreting the relevant provisions of the CSA, the Court noted that the law did not give the Attorney General broad latitude to regulate medical practice. Rather, it granted "limited powers, to be exercised in specific ways"[81] to make and enforce rules relating to "registration" or "control."

The Court found that neither the registration nor the control provisions provided a sufficiently broad endowment of authority to support the Interpretive Rule. The "registration" provision of the CSA grants the Attorney General the authority to deny registration to any physician for whom registration would be "inconsistent with the public interest," while the "control" provision grants the Attorney General authority to reclassify, add, or remove drugs from the controlled substances schedules. The Interpretive Rule, the Court reasoned, could not arise from the registration authority because the Rule itself, "concerns much more than registration. . . . It is instead an interpretation of the substantive federal law requirements."[82] The Court stated that the CSA tasks the Attorney General with ensuring compliance with federal law, but does not grant him the power to "decide what the law says."[83] The Court similarly rejected a broad grant of power arising from the "control" provision because "control" is technically defined in the CSA and refers only to the power to reclassify or add drugs to a schedule.

Finding that the Interpretive Rule was not entitled to any deference, the Court turned to examining whether any provisions in the CSA supported a broad grant of authority to the Attorney General. The Court found insufficient evidence to support such a grant. Justice Kennedy emphasized that the CSA delegates decision making to the Attorney General and the Secretary of Health and Human Services, with the latter having final say as to medical and scientific conclusions regarding several issues, including the scheduling of substances. Although the Attorney General argued that the Interpretive Rule was based on legal rather than medical reasoning, the Court responded that the "Interpretive Rule, and the Office of Legal Counsel [OLC] memo it incorporates, place extensive reliance on medical judgments and the views of the medical community in concluding that assisted suicide is not a 'legitimate medical purpose.'"[84] If Congress had intended to grant the Attorney General such broad authority, the Court reasoned, then that Congress would have done so explicitly.[85] The Court further noted that the CSA manifested "no intent to regulate the practice of medicine generally,"[86] in part due to the limitations of federalism that vest such powers in the states.

The Dissenting Opinions

The dissenting opinion authored by Justice Scalia and joined by Chief Justice Roberts and Justice Thomas supported the Attorney General's interpretation of "legitimate medical purpose" and reasoned that the Interpretive Rule should be entitled to judicial deference. Unlike the majority opinion, the dissent found no relevance in the fact that the language of the regulation mirrored or incorporated the same language of the federal statute. Because the Interpretive Rule was issued to expand upon a regulation (21 CFR § 1306.04), and because that regulation was originally promulgated by the Department of Justice, the dissenting justices found all of the necessary elements required for the courts to defer to the judgment of the Attorney General.

The dissent further noted that, even if the Interpretive Rule were not entitled to any deference, the Rule still provided for the most natural interpretation of the phrase "legitimate medical purpose." Citing sources from Hippocrates to the American Medical Association, Justice Scalia argued that assisting suicide was not within the bounds of legitimate medical practice. In a scathing critique of the majority's reasoning, Justice Scalia wrote: "the Court confuses the *normative* inquiry of what the boundaries of medicine *should be* . . . with the *objective* inquiry of what the accepted definition of 'medicine' *is*." [emphasis in original][87]

Reasoning that the Controlled Substances Act (CSA) is broader than interpreted by the majority, Justice Scalia contended that the statute confers authority directly upon the Attorney General to register physicians and make rules relating to the control, manufacture, and dispensing of controlled substances. Pursuant to this authority, the Attorney General would have rule-making authority, as well as the authority as a law enforcement official to determine the standards that govern physician registration.[88]

Justice Thomas went even further and wrote a separate dissenting opinion to address what he called a "newfound understanding of the CSA as a statute of limited reach." Citing the Court's recent opinion in *Gonzales v. Raich*,[89] Justice Thomas critiqued the majority for "beat[ing] a hasty retreat"[90] from the conclusion that "the CSA is a comprehensive regulatory regime specifically designed to regulate which controlled substances can be utilized for medicinal purposes and in what manner."[91] Supporting the view of the other dissenting Justices, Justice Thomas argued that the court had construed the CSA broadly in the *Raich* case and should do so in the *Oregon* case as well.

CONTINUING DILEMMAS
WITH ASSISTED SUICIDE AND EUTHANASIA

One of the immediate concerns that many have about official recognition (legalization) of physician-assisted suicide is the fear of practice extension—from accepting and condoning the physician-assisted deaths of terminally ill patients to more widespread involuntary euthanasia (the "slippery slope" or "camel's nose under the tent" argument).[92] Opponents often point to the Dutch experience as an example how state-sanctioned toleration has been abused.[93] The Netherlands (Holland) made its first step toward decriminalization of physician-assisted suicide with the murder conviction and subsequent suspended sentence of Dr. Geertuida Postma in 1971.[94] (Recall that administering a lethal drug to hasten the death of a patient is a criminal act in Holland, punishable by imprisonment of up to twelve years.[95]) Postma notified the authorities after killing her mother with injections of morphine (to induce unconsciousness) and curare (to paralyze her voluntary and involuntary muscles). At trial, Postma described her mother as "a human wreck"—partially paralyzed after a cerebral hemorrhage, deaf, and with a gross speech deficit—merely "hanging on to life in a chair." The caring and compassionate daughter-physician told the court: "I couldn't stand it anymore." She admitted to killing her mother as an act of mercy. (In The Netherlands, there appears to be no distinction between mercy-killing and voluntary euthanasia.)

Within two years, the Dutch Medical Association had crafted a detailed protocol (in 1973) with Dutch prosecutors to prevent future criminal trials of physicians who act similarly to Postma if they followed the agreed-upon guidelines. The guidelines—which were further formalized in 1984—were drafted for persons who were competent and suffering or in unbearable pain without any prospect of improvement (though not necessarily terminally ill), whose conditions had been confirmed independently by another physician (a "second opinion"), and whose physicians documented that the patients were voluntarily making the unequivocal decision without coercion or reservation and making repeated requests over time.

Until 1990, with the publication of the Remmelink Commission Report, the full extent of euthanasia practices in The Netherlands was not widely known.[96] The commission, appointed by the Dutch government and chaired by Professor Jan Remmelink (the attorney general of the country's Supreme Court), oversaw "a careful, nationwide study of the practice." The report revealed that about 1.8 percent of the deaths in The Netherlands in 1990 (roughly 2,300 out of 130,000) were the result of euthanasia. Another 400 deaths were from physician-assisted suicide. Almost all (87 percent) of these patients were terminally ill, with death expected within a week. Of these 2,700 incidents, only 486 physician-assisted deaths (euthanasia or assisted suicide) had been properly reported on death certificates. The report concluded, however, that in "nearly all of these 2,700 cases, the guidelines seemed to be met, despite the fact that the cases were usually not reported."[97] However, the study also found an additional 1,000 cases (0.8 percent) of mercy killing in which the patient was not competent—a clear violation of the guidelines. (Note that of these, about half of the patients had expressed an interest in euthanasia while they were still competent.) One might say, then, that there was evidence for both continuing the practice and halting the "Dutch experiment" in the Remmelink report. For proponents, the "system" appeared to be working despite the nonreporting by medical practitioners; for opponents, there was absolute proof that physicians were slipping down the slope and extending the practice to "unqualified" patients. Regardless, in another study published in a 1996 *New England Journal of Medicine* article, Dutch physician-researchers showed that euthanasia practices were the same as five years earlier when reported by the Commission.[98]

In 2005, although a new report from The Netherlands shows that Dutch pediatricians have been euthanizing severely ill neonates who have "a hopeless prognosis [and] who experience what parents and medical experts deem to be unbearable suffering."[99] According to the article, "[t]wenty-two cases of euthanasia in newborns have been reported to district attorney's office during the past seven years." All of the cases involved very severe forms of spina bifida. In each case, both parents consented to the euthanasia of their child; none of the physicians involved were prosecuted. A proposed "Groningen protocol" for euthanasia of newborns has been suggested for use of parents, physicians, and prosecutors in much the same way as the formalized euthanasia guidelines for competent adults after the Postma conviction in 1971.

There have been many ethics discussions about impaired newborns over the past thirty-five years and whether physicians should intervene in some cases. Among the more notable examples sparking these periodic debates are: the Johns Hopkins Down's Syndrome newborns with life-threatening gastrointestinal defects[100] (1971); the Lorber Criteria for Spina Bifida interventions[101] (1971); the Duff and Campbell *New England Journal of Medicine* article[102] (1973); the conjoined Mueller twins[103] (1981); and the Bloomington, Indiana, Baby Doe case (1983). The last gave rise to the infamous federal Baby Doe Rules, which were eventually struck down by the courts.[104] As a general rule parents and their physicians are left to make treatment decisions for impaired newborns that are in the patient's best interests. A decade after the Baby Doe Rules debacle, pediatrician and medical ethicist Norman Fost said that "securing consensus" from all involved in such instances had led to "no reported cases of a physician being found liable, civilly or criminally, for withholding or withdrawing any kind of treatment, including food and water, from any patient of any age for any reason."[105]

Of course, the United States is different from The Netherlands in many respects: America is more populous and remarkably diverse; patients have greater access to expensive technologies; there is no governmentally operated health care system; and individuals use the legal system more frequently to protect their rights. It may not be appropriate to use the Dutch experience as a benchmark for American culture shifts. However, the humanistic claim that patients who are suffering from incurable illnesses and are in great pain are worthy of consideration by compassionate physicians is universal.

Gregory Pence made this observation regarding "slippery slopes" in his book *Classic Cases in Medical Ethics**:

> Although claims about such slopes are frequently made, the nature of this claim is often vague and ill-defined. Generally, a slippery slope argument asserts that if a preliminary neutral or good step is accepted, a series of other changes will inevitably occur, leading to a final, bad result. As a metaphor, it often sees society as a teetering ball perched atop a steep slope, but leaning downward, braced by chocks on the ground, preventing it from descending. The chocks are our basic moral principles.[106]

One might say that the Dutch euthanasia practices and the steady progression from Debbie to Adkins to Diane to Oregon's Death With Dignity Act in America are examples of slippery slope argument actualizations. However, others might make the counterargument that—at least in the United States—the Debbie-to-DWDA progression illustrates how policy makers (legislators and courts) and society have made deliberate efforts at each step to weigh the benefits and burdens of the options and have created an enlightened framework for respecting patient autonomy.

The seeming failure of living wills and other advance directives to protect patients in vulnerable situations from overzealous physicians and family members has not helped the situation.[107] Patient pressure on physicians to stretch the boundaries of assisted suicide will certainly continue.[108] As with Adkins and Diane, patients want control over their bodies and quality of life decisions. It was just such an instance that finally put Kevorkian behind bars in 1999: to wit, the case of Thomas Youk.[109]

Youk, a fifty-two-year-old Detroit-suburb accountant who worked on vintage cars as a hobby, suffered with Lou Gehrig's disease for years. He had tried experimental drugs and therapies, but he had lost almost all use of his body. His brother described him as "a prisoner in

---

*Pence GE (2004). *Classic Cases in Medical Ethics: Accounts of the Cases That Have Shaped Medical Ethics, with Philosophical, Legal, and Historical Backgrounds.* New York, NY: McGraw-Hill, pp. 241, 242. Reprinted with permission of The McGraw-Hill Companies.

his own body." His wife said he "had come to the end of his life as he chose it." In 1998, he sought out Kevorkian—who, at that time, had assisted more than 130 people with their suicides—to help him. In the Youk case though, there was a clear difference from the others. Youk did not have the muscle strength to self-administer any medicines orally or to trip a switch for intravenous delivery. Kevorkian administered the lethal injection because Youk could not. The events were aired on the national television program *60 Minutes* in late 1998; Kevorkian was prosecuted and convicted of second-degree murder in 1999.

With Youk, Kevorkian literally *pushed* the envelope when he *pushed* the syringe that contained the lethal dose. He may have been hoping that the jury would not convict him—that they would have taken the videotaped evidence of Youk's own pleas for assistance and gratitude to Kevorkian as definitive.[110] (Between the Adkins case and the Youk case, Kevorkian had been prosecuted and acquitted three times for murder or assisting in a suicide.[111]). However, the law does not permit persons to consent to their own murders. Kevorkian may have thought that the jury would be influenced by the explanations of Youk's wife and bother about his mental state and determination. Or, Kevorkian may have been hoping that the jury, or perhaps an appeals court, would be swayed by the legal arguments that, since Youk was now paralyzed from the effects of amyotrophic lateral sclerosis (ALS), he was no longer able to avail himself of the "right" to take his own life (as explicitly embodied in the Oregon DWDA). Kevorkian may have seen his action as one of justice, assisting Youk to exercise his "right" because he could not self-administer medicines. On appeal, lawyers might argue that it was unfair of Youk to be deprived of his "right" just because of his debilitating illness—a Fourteenth Amendment equal protection claim.

However, past events should have convinced Kevorkian otherwise. The judge at the sentencing hearing reminded Kevorkian that Michigan voters had rejected, by a wide margin, in November 1998 a law that would have legalized assisted suicide. The U.S. Supreme Court had considered the constitutionality of assisted suicide statutes as applied to physicians and their dying patients in Washington (*Washington v. Glucksberg* from the Ninth Circuit, considering primarily due process rights) and New York (*Vacco v. Quill* from the Second Circuit, discussing principally equal protection arguments) in 1997 and determined that it was left to the states to settle the question for themselves. With the Youk case, Kevorkian lost the gamble. One might say that with Kevorkian's conviction, society erected a barrier to prevent the further downward slide on the slippery slope toward euthanasia.

Collective societal pressure may be exerted as well regarding the increasing costs of health care, particularly at life's end. The statistical trends regarding Medicare expenditures for patients in their last year of life reportedly have not changed since program inception.[112] It is widely accepted that 27 to 30 percent of the Medicare budget is used to pay for the roughly 5 percent of enrollees who die each year. Researchers have documented that expenditures in the last month of life account for 30 to 40 percent of the total medical care expenses for the patient's last year of life. To some, this may just be common sense: sicker patients require more resources. However, it has also led some to the conclusion that if physician-assisted suicide was more available for the terminally ill, then the community might benefit from the potential savings. In a detailed analysis, noted scholars Ezekiel Emanuel and Margaret Battin have shown that this is not the case, with the most reasonable savings estimate placed at 0.07 percent of total health care expenditures.[113] However, with increasing costs the economic pressures may intensify.

Moreover, there are cultural differences in end-of-life expenditures. In 2001, a group of Medicare researchers investigated patterns in the use of care by Medicare beneficiaries in the three years before death. They found that African Americans used 25 percent less care in the three years before death than white persons, but 18 percent *more* in the last year of life. The principal reason for the higher utilization in the last year of life was more inpatient care.[114] It has recently been observed that African American, Hispanic, Asian, and North American Native Medicare beneficiaries who are in skilled nursing facilities are far less likely than Caucasians to have do-not-resuscitate (DNR) or do-not-hospitalize (DNH) directives.[115]

Many Americans are ambivalent about physician-assisted suicide, but still assert their "right" to control events at life's end as much as possible.[116] And, for that matter, Americans are just as ambivalent about assisted suicide in general. More often than not, when a person is charged with assisting another person to commit suicide, either the jury does not convict or the defendant receives a relatively light punishment, if any at all.[117] For now, however, there appears to be a clear ethical and legal distinction between suicide, assisted suicide, and murder that patients and health care providers would be advised to remember and observe.[118]

While some hail the *Gonzales v. Oregon* ruling as a victory for the right-to-die movement, others lament the opinion as one more step down the proverbial slippery slope toward euthanasia. Yet, when rhetoric and politics are put aside, the true scope of the ruling is much narrower, addressing only the "federal-state balance and the congressional role in maintaining it."[119]

In the wake of the recent rulings, the daily practice of physicians outside of Oregon will not change. Indeed, even among Oregon physicians, it remains to be seen whether there will be an increase in the number of physicians and pharmacists who avail themselves of the law's protection to assist patients who wish to die. And while the ruling may pave the way for more states to follow Oregon's lead, the prior defeat of similar initiatives in California and Washington suggests that other states may not be quick to adopt their own versions of the DWDA.[120]

Regardless of the next steps in Oregon and elsewhere, it is clear that the nation is engaged in a profound debate about the legality and morality of assisted suicide, as well as the scope of professional medical practice. Although the Supreme Court did not address the substantive questions about assisted suicide, it did provide a space for the debate surrounding legalization to continue. As U.S. Supreme Court Justice Louis D. Brandeis wrote in 1932, "[i]t is one of the happy incidents of the federal system that a single courageous state may, if its citizens choose, serve as a laboratory; and try novel social and economic experiments without risk to the rest of the country."[121] With thanks or regrets to the Court's ruling in *Gonzales v. Oregon,* Oregon's "experiment" will continue.

Chapter 7

Drug Use in "Dwindling" Patients and in Medically Futile Situations

To what extent should frail and dwindling patients be treated medically as their function continues to decline? Is it fair to allow late, end-stage patients with illnesses like Lou Gehrig's disease and Alzheimer's disease to determine for themselves the level of care necessary to support their quality of life as their muscles and capacities wane? But what if the patients lack decision-making capacity? Who will represent them and voice their treatment preferences to the health care team? What standard will legally authorized representa - tives use in making surrogate decisions? Can patients and families demand treatments that practitioners believe to be medically inappropriate as the end of their lives draw near?

In a 2003 *JAMA* article, noted end-of-life researchers June Lunney, Joanne Lynn, Daniel Foley, Steven Lipson, and Jack Guralnik offered data to support their understanding of the four typical "trajectories of dying" as seen in a cohort of patients.[1] They first reminded readers that Barney Glaser and Anselm Strauss, in their 1968 book *Time for Dying,* described three trajectories: surprise, abrupt deaths; short-term (or terminal illness) and long-term (or lingering and frailty) deaths; and "entry-reentry deaths" in which patients have multiple hospital stays over time while they progressively decline.[2] Then building on the Glaser and Strauss work, Lunney et al. theorized four end-of-life trajectories, after analyzing information gathered from the Established Populations for Epidemiologic Studies for the Elderly (EPESE). The EPESE researchers followed community-based cohorts in four populations around the country—two in urban Connecticut and Massachusetts, and two in rural Iowa and North Carolina. The cohort included 14,456 persons aged sixty-five years or more. During the study period, 4,871 (33.7 percent) died. The research team conducted baseline interviews between 1981 and 1986 and collected additional information in six to ten annual in-person or telephone follow-up conversations during the course of the study. Patient proxies provided information during the follow-up interviews for those who were either too cognitively or physically impaired to participate or had died. Interviewers asked participants if they needed help or were unable to perform seven "activities of daily living" (ADLs): walking across a small room, bathing, grooming, dressing, eating, transferring from bed to chair, and using the toilet. The interviewers also gathered information about certain functional abilities (e.g., walking a half mile, stooping, kneeling, climbing a flight of stairs, and doing heavy housework) and health status (e.g., new diagnosis of a chronic illness, hospitalization or nursing home stay, occurrence of a hip fracture, or stroke). Lunney and her group analyzed the data using a multiple logistic regression model to eliminate as much bias from confounding co-morbidities as possible. The researchers graphed the results to show trends of how dependent patients were on others for assistance or ADL function over time and identified four typical trajectory death groups: (1) sudden death; (2) terminal illness death (such as a cancer); (3) organ failure death (such as occurs in congestive heart failure and chronic obstructive pulmonary disease); and (4) frailty or "dwindling" death (such as occurs in patients with amyotrophic lateral sclerosis [Lou Gehrig's disease], Parkinson's disease, Alzheimer's disease and other dementias, and persistent vegetative state). The four theoretical trajectories of dying as described by Lunney et al. are illustrated in Figure 7.1.

For some patients, it is the fear of a frailty or "dwindling" death that is most haunting or upsetting. It was the anxiety about their illnesses taking control and leaving them with a diminished quality of life that led Janet Adkins to seek out Dr. Jack Kevorkian[3] and "Diane" to have conversations with Dr. Timothy Quill about physician-assisted suicide.[4] From the results of national opinion polls that followed the Nancy Beth Cruzan and Terri Schiavo cases, it was the concern that they too might be left in a persistent vegetative state that spurred respondents to complete living wills and advance directives forms.[5] With the advent of additional life-saving pharmaceuticals—or what others might describe as death-prolonging drugs—and other technolo-

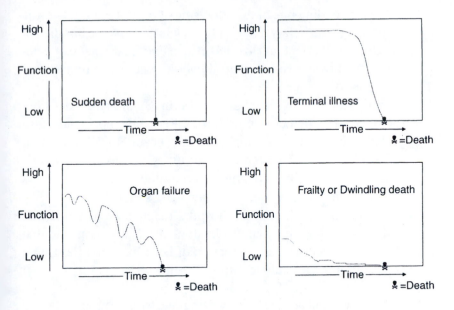

FIGURE 7.1. The four theoretical trajectories of dying are depicted graphically for patients with declining functional changes over time for sudden death, terminal illness death, organ failure death, and frailty or dwindling death. *Source:* From Lunney JR, Lynn J, Foley DJ, Lipson S, Guralnik JM. Patterns of functional decline at the end of life. *JAMA* 2003;289:2387-2392. Reprinted with permission of the American Medical Association.

gies, more of these frailty cases are becoming widely known. There are many times when the "dwindling" cases present ethical dilemmas to health care team members.

"DWINDLING" PATIENTS AND QUALITY OF LIFE

On June 8, 2005, *The Boston Globe* published a newspaper article titled "Woman Dies at MGH After Battle Over Care." The article began with these paragraphs*:

---

*Kowalczyk L. Woman dies at MGH after battle over care; daughter fought for life support. *Boston Globe.* 2005; Jun 8. Republished with permission of *The Boston Globe;* permission conveyed throught Copyright Clearance Center, Inc.

Quietly ending one of the state's most prominent right-to-die cases, a woman paralyzed with Lou Gehrig's disease has died at Massachusetts General Hospital after a two-year legal battle between the hospital and her family about whether to remove her life support.

Barbara Howe, 80, died at 11:24 p.m. Saturday, 26 days before a court settlement would have allowed the hospital to turn off her ventilator, Gary Zalkin, the lawyer for Howe's daughter, Carol Carvitt, said yesterday. Carvitt, who was her mother's healthcare proxy, had fought the recommendations of doctors at Mass. General to end her mother's life support.

In March, Carvitt and the hospital reached an agreement to withdraw Howe's life support by June 30. But Zalkin said that Howe died Saturday "as a function of her illness" while still on her ventilator. He said the family is relieved.[6]

Barbara Howe had been slowly wasting due to amyotrophic lateral sclerosis (ALS or Lou Gehrig's disease) for years, after being diagnosed in 1991. She was admitted to Massachusetts General Hospital on November 15, 1999 and by the time of her death, she had been a patient in Massachusetts General Hospital for five years. Her husband, a Boston police officer, died in 2001. For the last several years of her life, her world was the 21st floor of the hospital's Phillips House, where she was maintained on a breathing machine and fed artificially through a tube. On admission to the hospital, she had stated a desire for the most aggressive care available; this was documented in the hospital record. Undoubtedly, her treatment plan involved many drugs. During her hospitalization, she gradually lost her ability to speak, gesture, and even blink her eyes, finally leaving her unable to communicate her wishes in any manner.

One of her daughters, Carol Carvitt, visited four days a week; another daughter, Maureen Howe, came every night and spent about five hours helping to care for her mother (performing such tasks such as taking her blood pressure and suctioning mucus from her lungs). Carvitt maintained that her mother wanted to be kept alive medically as long as she could enjoy her family—and the family believed that their mother still did, up to the very end.

As Lou Gehrig's disease progresses, patients retain their abilities to think and feel, but they eventually lose all muscle function, if they survive to that point, as Howe did. They cannot breathe, move, or chew and swallow food. It is entirely probable that Howe's thinking mind was trapped or locked in the crumbling shell of a body. Because she was unable to share her thoughts, her health care team came to believe that keeping her alive was hurting her more than helping her. (Philosophically, the medical team struggled with the balance between beneficence and nonmaleficence.) The *Globe* piece concluded with additional details about the court actions and the family-versus-health care team disagreements over Howe's severely diminished (dwindling) quality of life and the medical care she would want to receive:

> In court documents and testimony, nurses referred to Howe as a "war horse" and said she "wanted everything done to maintain her, including CPR, antibiotics, and ICU." But after Howe's bones broke during routine turning and doctors had to remove her right eye because of corneal damage, her caregivers grew increasingly opposed to keeping her on a ventilator. Many believed she was in terrible pain, but had no way of communicating it. Carvitt, however, said she felt obligated to carry out her mother's wishes and did not believe that she was suffering. [Because of the circumstances, neither the medical team nor Carvitt were able to "prove" their opinion.]
>
> Unable to reach an agreement, Mass. General doctors took the rare step of going to court to try to overturn Carvitt's wishes as her mother's healthcare proxy, first in 2003. Probate and Family Court Judge John M. Smoot ruled [at the time] that there was not enough evidence to warrant taking away Carvitt's power to determine her mother's treatment.
>
> But earlier this year, Howe's doctors said her condition was deteriorating and asked the hospital's end-of-life committee to again [permit] removal of her life support. Carvitt went back to court to block the move.
>
> In March [2005], after meetings with lawyers from Mass. General and the judge, Carvitt said she believed that Smoot was going to rule against her and decided to enter into the agreement with the hospital.

In a statement at the time, the two sides tried to mend fences after two years of sometimes angry disagreement over Howe's care. The hospital "acknowledges that the family has acted out of love and concern for their mother, and the family acknowledges that the hospital acted with similar concern for their patient and that Barbara would not have received better care anywhere else."[7]

Other recent newspapers carry similar heart-wrenching stories about frail or dwindling ALS patients. The July 1, 2004 *USA Today* carried a story about sixty-year-old ALS patient John Farie, the husband of *USA Today* reporter Marilyn Adams.[8] Farie had just died after a year-long battle by the time the report appeared. The first sentence in the article ended with: "[his] neurologist said it was the worst disease he knew."[9] The initial symptoms began around Christmas 2002; Farie "had a tired foot after walking through the mall."* His wife's first person account details the progression of Farie's disease course:

> John began to fall without warning. He bloodied his head on the patio at home, crashed in the elevator at work. He lived in fear that he wouldn't be able to get up or call for help. As his left leg grew weaker and spread to the right [*sic*], he was forced to rely on a foot brace, then a cane, then a walker, then a wheelchair.
>
> The only thing he never had was pain. I prayed for pain, prayed he really had a brain tumor or a different disorder that science could attack. We traveled to the Mayo Clinic seeking a different diagnosis, but the doctor there agreed with our own.
>
> The neurologists seemed as frustrated as we were. There's no diagnostic test to detect ALS. John's doctor had to rule out everything else, then wait to see if the paralysis spread. The only drug that the Food and Drug Administration has approved for

---

*ALS typically progresses in an "ascending" fashion, often beginning in the more distal parts of the body (such as a lower extremity) and progresses bilaterally and centrally toward the chest and head. As the disease progresses, it injures and then kills motor neurons. The disease progression is uncertain. Adams M. ALS, like a terrorist, kills without partiality. *USA Today.* 2004; Jul 1:4D. From USA TODAY, a division of Gannett Co., Inc. Reprinted with permission.

ALS costs $920 a month at [the family's] local pharmacy if a patient lacks insurance. It doesn't stop the disease; it's said to slow the progression somewhat. Our insurance would have covered it.

But John couldn't fathom why anyone would want to extend the hell he was going through. He wouldn't take the drug.[10]

John Farie died one year after the first symptoms appeared during a walk in the mall. At the time of his death, he was in hospice care at home, in a hospital bed, and required to have supplemental oxygen.

Other ALS patients were featured on the front page of the *New York Times* on November 7, 2004.[11] One patient, Dr. Jules Lodish, a hematologist-oncologist, had been fighting ALS for ten years. At the time the article appeared, his family cared for him at home; his treatment plan was meticulous and exhaustive. However, the *New York Times* described his current status as "looking forward to every day"*:

> Dr. Lodish's body sits limp in a wheelchair and his tongue lolls; a machine breathes for him through a tracheostomy tube in this throat. He lost the ability to talk more than three years ago, he says, then jokes, "but not the ability to be annoying."
>
> . . .
>
> "One irony is with many people, I communicate [via a laptop computer controlled with a twitch of his cheek] now more than when I was well," Dr. Lodish said.
>
> . . .
>
> By holding on, he said, he had been able to see many of life's milestones, including the marriages of two of his children.[12]

In discussing Lodish and other ALS patients, the article said: "[P]atients and their families are forced on a daily basis to take stock of the meaning of quality of their lives and make repeated decisions about how much [care] is too much."[13] In that same vein, hematologist-oncologist Mellar P. Davis, of the Cleveland Clinic, said, "Quality of life becomes a moving target—what was one day an unacceptable quality of life becomes an acceptable quality of life."[14] Northwestern

Memorial Hospital (Chicago, Illinois) neurologist Scott Heller reported that today there are about 30,000 Americans with ALS.[15]

Besides the ALS example, one may also reflect on another devastating disease that is affecting Americans and causing them to dwindle during the latter stages of the illness: Alzheimer's disease. With ALS, patients' brain function is, for the most part, unaffected; with Alzheimer's disease, however, patients gradually lose their mental capacities while the rest of their bodily functions essentially continue intact. It may be difficult for persons to say which is worse—Lou Gehrig's disease or Alzheimer's—because to many, both are dreadful and horrifying. In 1994, the *USA Today* reported that there were 1.6 million people in the United States with Alzheimer's disease—the most common cause of dementia in old age.[16] The estimated cost (at that time) of caring for these patients was $82 billion, with only heart disease and cancer patient care costing more. However, in 2003, there were an estimated 4.5 million patients suffering from Alzheimer's disease.[17] In a 2004 study commissioned by the Alzheimer's Association, the Lewin Group stated: "Medicare costs for beneficiaries with Alzheimer's are expected to increase 75 percent, from $91 billion in 2005 to $160 billion in 2010; Medicaid expenditures on residential dementia care will increase 14 percent, from $21 billion in 2005 to $24 billion in 2010."[18]

A May 18, 2004 *New York Times* article illustrates the dilemmas facing many Alzheimer's patient families*:

> Macie Mull was 82 and had suffered from Alzheimer's disease for more than a decade when she developed pneumonia. Her nursing home rushed her to the hospital where she spent the night, receiving intravenous antibiotics. The next day she was back at the nursing home, more confused than ever.
>
> [Soon afterward] she was choking on her puréed food; eating was becoming impossible. And so, one Sunday afternoon, the administrators of the nursing home in Hickory, N.C., asked Mrs. Mull's daughter what to do: Did she want a feeding tube inserted? At that point, Ms. Mull muttered only a few random words and could no longer recognize her daughter. The feeding tube would almost certainly prolong her life, but was it worth it?

---

*Copyright © 2004 by The New York Times Co. Reprinted with permission.

The question of how aggressive to be in treating late-stage Alzheimer's patients is one of the most wrenching and contentious issues in medicine. For every patient, like Mrs. Mull, there are typically about five or six family members faced with decisions about whether to authorize medical treatments whose bodies live on though their minds are gone.[19]

At the end of the article, the reporter describes what eventually happened with Mull:

Mrs. Mull had her feeding tube for about four years, until she started to regurgitate food with episodes of choking and coughing.

Mrs. Patricia Hollar [her daughter and surrogate] spoke with her sister and brothers. "I don't want to put her through any more discomfort," she recalled. "It's time to let her go."

Her sister, she said, agreed, but one of her brothers had doubts. "He was hoping that she would just drift off," Mrs. Hollar said.

Finally, [Patricia] had the tube removed. Two weeks later, her mother died [at age 86].

"It was not an easy decision," she said. "But I don't look back, and I don't ever regret it."[20]

Certainly, not all the dilemmas with Alzheimer's patients are end-of-life issues or concern withdrawing life-sustaining medical interventions. Another dilemma might be labeled as identifying the "least restrictive" appropriate care for the patient, even more so when drugs are used to calm and sedate patients who are aggressive and combative. Some concerns may involve whether patients still have some decision-making capacity to make decisions for themselves. A primary means of classifying the three stages of Alzheimer's disease is based on whether the patient still has capacity (Early Stage), whether capacity is waxing-and-waning (Middle Stage), and when the patient clearly does not have capacity (Late Stage).[21]

A very interesting story that illustrates this point was published in the *New York Times* on January 3, 2005.[22] The article was about former North Dakota U.S. District Judge Bruce M. Van Sickle. One of Judge Van Sickle's sons was asking the North Dakota Supreme Court to release his father from a Bismarck nursing home "so he could be given the same individual care that [the judge] once ordered for other disabled people."[23] The incident was ironic because Judge Van Sickle, twenty years earlier in a sweeping decision, ruled that North Dakota's institutions were systematically violating the rights of the mentally disabled. The brief filed in support of releasing Judge Van Sickle said*:

> The limitation of visitors, *use of chemical restraints in the form of psychotropic drugs,* and a temporary admission to a psychiatric ward of the local hospital demonstrated he was restricted by more than a security net. Each is a restraint on the liberty Judge Van Sickle fought so hard to protect for others [emphasis added].[24]

Also, many Alzheimer's patients have concurrent medical problems—high blood pressure, diabetes, and kidney disease—and are given drugs for these chronic conditions. Many likewise receive drugs to help elevate their mood or improve their brain function in an effort to slow down the progression of the disease. Some medical and ethics experts state that additional treatment in cases of Late Stage Alzheimer's patients is "inappropriate, even cruel, [especially when the] costs are excessively high."[25]

After considering the Howe, Farie, Lodish, Mull, and Van Sickle cases, one may more fully understand the concept of frailty or dwindling patients as described by Lunney et al. and how drugs and other medical interventions impact quality of life. For physicians, pharmacists, and other caregivers, the medical uncertainty of the disease process itself, and often unpredictable progression in spite of therapy adds doubt and ambiguity to making recommendations that hopefully benefit rather than further harm the patient.

MEDICAL FUTILITY

Closely associated with debates about continued treatment for frail and dwindling patients is the concept of medical futility, particularly as a patient's level of function trails toward death, as in the Lunney

---

et al. frailty trajectory graph. Occasionally, the discussions between caregivers and family members begin with the rhetorical question "When is enough enough?"[26]

Much has been written about medical futility, especially in recent years. It is certainly important to consider medical futility, conceptually, because near the very end of the dwindling curve, one may come to the realization that additional treatment is futile and, therefore, quite legitimately question the appropriateness of further medical intervention. Several early medical futility articles focused simply on the various definitions of the term *medical futility*, as were commonly used.[27] Later definitions dealt with the importance of *who* defined the phrase[28] or considered the ethical implications of medical futility.[29] More authors tried to demonstrate the importance of the definition and its implications by emphasizing what they would term the false allusion of medical futility in clinical practice.[30] Still others queried the soundness of a specific approach in practice by discussing special instances or situations, such as: cardiopulmonary resuscitation (CPR) decisions[31] and other life-sustaining treatment interventions;[32] settings such as the adult[33] and neonatal intensive care units,[34] the emergency department,[35] or even the scene of an accident;[36] individual cases of notoriety like Helga Wanglie,[37] Baby K.,[38] and Sun Hudson;[39] the impact of possible savings by avoiding futile treatments on health care economics[40] or societal justice;[41] and hospital policies[42] or medical society policy statements.[43]

As with any philosophical debate, it is critically essential that discussants be clear about key definitions. A dictionary-based definition of "futility" early in the conversation may offer some advantage to developing common ground:

> **fu•tile** *adj.* **1.** Having no useful result. **2.** Trifling and frivolous, idle: *the futile years after her artistic peak.* [Latin *futilis.*]— **fu´tile•ly** *adv.* —**fu´tile•ness** *n.*
>
> **fu•til•i•ty** *n., pl.* —**ites** 1. The quality of having no useful result; uselessness. **2.** Lack of importance or purpose: frivolousness. **3.** A futile act.[44]

Regarding the etymology of the word *futile*, emergency physician Michael Ardagh wrote in a *Journal of Medical Ethics*[45] article:*

> The word "futile" is derived from the Latin word *"futilis,"* meaning that which easily melts or pours, but its common usage stems from the Greek legend in which the daughters of Danaus, the King of Argos, murdered their husbands and for their crime, were condemned to [carry] water for eternity in leaking buckets.[46,47] To arrive at the destination with an empty bucket when the intention of the journey was to bring water, gives a definition of futile as something which is "useless" or "ineffectual."[48] Futility then, is the nominal form which describes a uselessness or an absence of any effect. Specifically it describes the absence of any desired effect and if we assume that the desired effect of medical interventions is to benefit the patient, (by direct benefit, by avoidance of harm, or by respecting the patient's autonomous choices), then futility describes an absence of benefit.

McMaster University philosopher Sophie Kasimow explained the mythological root of the word when she wrote:

> The word "futility" comes from the Latin word for leaky *(futilis)*, and can be found in ancient texts such as the Greek myth of the daughters of Danaus who were condemned for eternity in Hades to draw water in leaky buckets. A futile action, as exemplified in this story, is one that will never *achieve the goals* of the action, no matter for how long or how often it is repeated.[49] To deem a medical treatment futile requires considerable clarification [emphasis added].[50]

As underscored by both Ardagh and Kasimow, when one modifies *futility* with the adjective *medical,* an entirely different set of issues arise in their opinion—issues related to the benefits or *goals of medicine.* Albert Jonsen, Mark Siegler, and William Winslade, in their

---

*Ardagh M. Futility has no utility in resuscitation medicine. *J Medl Ethics.* 2000;26:396-399. Reproduced with permission from the BMJ Publishing Group.

pocket handbook *Clinical Ethics,* listed what they considered to be
the goals of medicine:

> The practice of medicine consists of a relationship between a
> patient and a physician. The goals and benefits of medicine are
> optimal in relationships where physicians and other health pro-
> fessionals demonstrate a professionalism that includes honesty
> and integrity, respect for patients, a commitment to patients' wel-
> fare, a compassionate regard for patients, and a dedication to
> maintaining competency in knowledge and technical skills. The
> physician's central responsibility is to use that medical compe-
> tence to respond to the patient's need for help. The physician
> makes a diagnosis and recommends a course of action.
>
> That course of action will have some or all of the following
> goals:
>
> 1. Promotion of health and prevention of disease
> 2. Relief of symptoms, pain, and suffering
> 3. Cure of disease
> 4. Prevention of untimely death
> 5. Improvement of functional status or maintenance of com-
>   promised status
> 6. Education and counseling of patients regarding their con-
>   dition and prognosis
> 7. Avoidance of harm to the patient in the course of care
>
> The achievement of these goals is the benefit of medicine.[51]

In describing the goals and benefit of medicine with specific reference to medical futility, Jonsen, Siegler, and Winslade also stated that:

> In the clinical situation, futility more often designates an effort
> to provide a benefit to a patient, which reason and experience
> suggest is highly likely to fail and whose rare exceptions cannot
> be systematically produced. Here the judgment of futility is
> probabilistic, and its accuracy depends on empirical data drawn
> from clinical trials and from clinical experience. This is the so-
> called quantitative futility, which we prefer to call "probabilistic
> futility." . . . [Also,] futility has a qualitative meaning: the judg-
> ment that the goal that might be attained is not worthwhile. All

uses of the term "futility" represent value judgments based on the preferences of clinicians and patients.[52]

For some, reflecting on the Danaides' sieves and their inability to accomplish *the* goal of filling a cistern from a distant water source, and then comparing physicians' attempts to accomplish *their* stated medical goals for patients using the ineffectual technological means at hand (their "leaky buckets"), may more clearly and directly spotlight the "medical futility" quandary.

Correlatively, physician-medical ethicist Steven Miles has suggested four possible "types" of medical futility.[53] He has remarked that when a physician uses the phrase *medical futility* it may mean a proposed medical intervention or treatment is (1) not offered, recommended, or even contemplated because it is "physiologically impossible" (e.g., effective cardiopulmonary resuscitation when the patient's aortic aneurysm has ruptured is not possible, antibiotics will not kill viruses in patients with a viral upper respiratory tract infection[54]); (2) "in the physician's opinion, nonbeneficial" (e.g., dialysis for a patient who is in a permanent coma may prevent uremia but will not improve neurological status[55]); (3) "very unlikely to produce a desired physiological or personal benefit" (e.g., continuing extracorporeal membrane oxygenation or heart-lung bypass after a two-week therapeutic trial when there has been no improvement in the patient's condition[56]); or (4) "plausible, but nonvalidated" (e.g., bone marrow transplant for a patient who has extensive metastases of her breast cancer[57]). Miles said, too, that the four categories of medical futility he described are not mutually exclusive; that is, a medical treatment may be medically futile because it is both unlikely to work and nonvalidated (e.g., transplanting a baboon heart in a baby born with a fatal heart anomaly[58]).

More recently, philosopher Mark Wicclair—in his attempt to define medical futility[59]—collapsed Miles' four categories into three. He labeled his first as "physiologic futility." His second category is one in which the proposed treatment "will not achieve the goals of the patient"; and the third, is one in which "there is no reasonable chance [the proposed treatment] will achieve any goals that are consistent with the rules of professional integrity." (One might legitimately wonder if Wicclair's "rules of professional integrity" are to be interpreted as the "minimally required legal standard of care" alone or something more, perhaps the legal minimum with an aspirational ethical standard conjoined.) The second and third categories truly beg additional questions: futile in whose opinion, the patient's or the doctor's? How are disagreements about medical futility to be mediated or resolved? With the first category—physiologic futility—the answer seems more objective (a substantive medical issue); with the latter two, more subjective (and procedural). Wicclair, using his three categories, stresses that (1) it does not seem reasonable for anyone to argue that physicians should attempt an intervention when there is incontrovertible evidence that it is useless (recalling the "leaky" bucket analogy), and (2) with both subjective categories centering on *goals,* whether it is the "patient's goals" or "goals consistent with the rules [standards] of professional integrity," there must be some mechanism to resolve disputes.

Carrying these points further, in an article about ethics and communication in do-not-resuscitate (DNR) orders, ethicist Tom Tomlinson and physician-ethicist Howard Brody wrote:*

> When the decision [to write a DNR order] is based on there being no medical benefit [i.e., physiologic futility or unable to achieve goals consistent with the rules of professional integrity] in resuscitation,** then the value that the patient or the patient's family might place on the patient's life after an arrest is irrelevant: resuscitation would not provide any meaningful prolongation of the patient's life and so could not provide anything that the patient or his family could reasonably value. Consequently, when resuscitation offers no medical benefit, the physician can make a reasoned determination that a DNR order should be written without any knowledge of the patient's values in the matter. The decision that CPR [i.e., resuscitation] is unjustified because it is futile is a judgment that falls entirely within the physician's technical expertise.[60]

---

*Tomlinson T, Brody H. Ethics and communication in do-not-resuscitate orders. *N Engl J Med.* 1988;318:43-46. Copyright © 1988 Massachusetts Medical Society. All rights reserved. Reprinted with permission.

**Many resuscitation efforts involve drugs—oxygen, epinephrine, vasopressin, amiodarone, lidocaine, to name just a few. Hazinski MF, Cummins RO, Field JM, eds. *Handbook of Emergency Cardiovascular Care for Healthcare Providers.* Dallas, Tex: American Heart Association, 2004, pp. 6-8.

Following the more philosophical reasoning of Miles, Wicclair, Tomlinson, and Brody as gleaned from their writings, one may correspondingly come to the same conclusion as did Jonsen, Siegler, and Winslade: (1) determinations about medical futility should be made with reference to a physician's ability to achieve a goal of medicine for the benefit of a particular patient, given a specific clinical context; and (2) a physician should use reasonable medical judgment about the limits of one's technical expertise in being able to accomplish an expressed medical goal.

Of course, the patient must be involved in establishing the goal(s) of treatment. Because of the nature of the physician-patient relationship, the health care team must come to some accommodation with the patient about goals of treatment and benefits of medicine because of their respect for the patient's autonomy and personal values.[61] However, there is no *real* decision for a patient if the proffered alternatives are unreasonable and the goal(s) cannot be achieved given the clinical circumstances. There is no *real* choice if there are no bona fide options. Any discussion about possibilities makes a mockery of respect for the patient and the patient's autonomy without reasonable and legitimate treatment alternatives. Likewise, if the health care team comes to the understanding—using reasonable medical judgment—that an intervention just will not work, they have a responsibility to so advise the patient. Leslie Blackhall wrote about this duty in a 1987 *New England Journal of Medicine* article regarding the clinical appropriateness of CPR, a very specific treatment intervention:

> The issue of patient autonomy is irrelevant, however, when CPR has no potential benefit. Here, the physician's duty to provide reasonable medical care precludes CPR, either as a routine process in the absence of a decision by a patient or as a response to a patient's misguided request for such treatment in the absence of adequate information. In such cases it is not the physician's responsibility to offer CPR. Both physicians and patients must come to terms with the inability of medicine to postpone death indefinitely.[62]

If an attending physician believes that a medical intervention should not be attempted because it cannot reverse or ameliorate a physiologic process or because it will not accomplish a stated goal of medicine, then the physician should share that information with the patient and resist any pleas or entreaties to the contrary.[63] There is no health care team *obligation* to provide medically inappropriate care. To give in to unreasonable patient demands for medical care that is inappropriate raises serious distributive justice problems for the attending physician and team, as well as the entire health care delivery system.[64]

Some hospitals have found it helpful—for both practical and educational purposes—to formalize a process through a hospital policy to resolve medical futility cases and assure appropriate medical care.[65] There are several reasons why hospitals and physicians might support the adoption of such a policy: it proactively expresses the hospital's concern for the issue and makes their stand open and the process transparent; it legitimates an approved and fair decision-making approach; and it aligns hospital and physician staff values into one legally defensible position, firmly grounded on community standard of care, as set by consultants and experts. An example of a very direct and relatively simple policy may suffice to illustrate a typical approach:

Policy Statement

[Hospital Name] is committed to providing appropriate, affordable, and compassionate care in an environment that supports patients and their families.

Based on the advice and recommendations of the patient's physician, medical care decisions are made by the patient. If the patient lacks decision-making [*sic*] capacity, such decisions generally are made in accordance with the patient's advance directive and by the patient's surrogate.

If the patient or the patient's surrogate has difficulty in accepting the limitations of appropriate medical care, full discussion of all concerns is encouraged and supported. Participation of the Ethics Committee and medical consultants is desirable. If appropriate, legal counsel may make application for a court-appointed guardian to make medical care decisions for the patient. If agreement cannot be reached, discussion should include exploration of available options, including transfer to another physician or hospital if necessary.

All services at [Hospital Name] shall be respectful of life. No action directly intended to terminate life is permitted. Supportive care shall always be provided.

Definitions

"Decision making capacity" means the ability to fully appreciate and understand one's medical condition and the probable consequences of medical care and the withholding/withdrawal of medical care. [Decision making capacity is determined] by [the] patient's attending physician.

"Medical care" means any procedure or treatment designed to diagnose, assess, or treat a disease, illness, or injury such as surgery, drugs, transfusions, cardiopulmonary resuscitation (CPR), mechanical ventilation, dialysis, artificial or forced feeding of nourishment, hydration, or other basic nutrients, regardless of the methods used, or any other medical act designed for diagnosis, assessment, or treatment or to sustain, restore, or supplant vital body function. If CPR is medically futile (see below), it is not included in this definition.

"Appropriate medical care" means medical care that confers greater proportional benefits than burdens to the patient within reasonable medical judgment; medical care is considered inappropriate or futile if it cannot be expected to restore function to the patient or to achieve the expressed goals of the informed patient. [Appropriate medical care is determined] by [the] patient's attending physician.

"Supportive care" means measures designed to primarily maintain the patient's comfort, including hygienic care, suctioning, oral feeding and hydration that is not artificial, and sedatives, and pain-killing drugs.[66]

Because the term "futility" itself is so charged and open to misinterpretation, Jonsen, Siegler, and Winslade have suggested that the term not even be used in some conversations because of the possibility of confusion:

[E]ven when the facts of the case support a judgment of physiologic or probabilistic futility, [Jonsen-Siegler-Winslade] suggest that it may be advisable to avoid the actual word "futility" in discussions with patients and families. Many persons may interpret this word as an announcement that the physician is "giving up" on the patient. We suggest that the futility situation be discussed in terms of the principle of proportionality, that is, the imbalance of expected benefit over burdens imposed by continued interventions.[67]

From a legal point of view, an argument about whether an intervention is futile may be ill-focused. Physicians and other health care professionals are legally required to meet a standard of care in practice. In defining the phrase, nationally recognized health lawyer-bioethicist George Annas wrote:

> "Standard of care" is a legal term denoting the level of conduct a physician or health care provider must meet in treating a patient so as not to be guilty of negligence, usually called malpractice. That standard is generally defined simply as what a reasonably prudent practitioner (or specialist) would do in the same or similar circumstances. This is a profession-centered standard and encompasses a wide range of practices.[68]

The standard of care is established by peers, not by physicians who act independently of others as did the Lone Ranger. It is not what a majority of physicians would do, and it is certainly not what a single physician would do, in providing care for a patient. The fact that there might be *one* physician somewhere who would be willing to provide care when others would not should not be interpreted as imposing an obligation on a treating physician to provide that same treatment or intervention. (In fact, to do so might be interpreted as substandard practice.) "Standard of care" is a collective ideal based on what prudent practitioners in a given area would provide similarly situated patients. Standard of care embodies reasonable medical judgment and does not require physicians to attempt the physiologically impossible or to institute or continue a treatment that will not reasonably achieve a stated goal of medicine. Some third-party or government payers and regulators might question the legitimacy of a medical treatment that a number of physicians would believe to be medically inappropriate in a specific clinical situation. Should a malpractice or quality assurance claim result because of a disagreement about the appropriateness of care, one would think it may be very difficult for a physician to defend inappropriate care or substandard practice. Moreover, how can patients make a legal claim or demand for inappropriate care when, in America, they do not have a legal right to appropriate care except as provided by law?*

Again, because of the nature of the physician-patient relationship, both patient and physician are usually at liberty to terminate their relationship when they disagree profoundly about the achievable goals of medicine and available reasonable treatment options. If the physician does not agree with a patient that an intervention is appropriate within reasonable medical judgment, then the patient is free to find another physician who might be willing to provide that service, if available. If the patient makes inappropriate demands, then the physician should perhaps suggest terminating the relationship and assist the patient in some reasonable way to find alternative care options without technically abandoning the patient.** (If the disagreement between doctor and patient is so strained that there is no authentic trust between the two, then one might characterize this collapsed partnership as "no relationship at all." In this case, terminating the relationship and transferring care to another may simply formalize the reality, like a divorce decree officially recognizes that a marriage has ended.)

SURROGATE MEDICAL DECISION MAKING

Quite often frail and dwindling patients do not have decision--making capacity. Typically, patients who lack decision-making capacity are not able to reflect on their treatment options (such as with Mull and Van Sickle cases) or communicate their preferences (as with the

---

*One might make the claim that the federal Emergency Medical Treatment and Active Labor Act (EMTALA) creates a "right to health care" in a limited way (or perhaps more pointedly, a "right" to an emergency department "screening examination" within the capability of the facility; "necessary stabilizing treatment" if available; and "appropriate transfer") and that some federal entitlement programs and contractual arrangements also create some "right" or claim to health care services. Furrow BR, Greaney TL, Johnson SH, Jost TS, Schwartz RL. *Health Law: Cases, Materials, and Problems.* 5th ed. St. Paul, Minn: Thomson-West, 2001, pp. 538-565.

**"*Abandonment* occurs when a physician unilaterally severs the doctor-patient relationship at a time when continued care is needed. If injury results to the patient because of the abandonment, a patient may sue the doctor for damages." Annas GJ. *The Rights of Patients: The Authoritative ACLU Guide to the Rights of Patients.* 3rd ed. New York, NY: New York University Press, 2004, p. 162.

Howe case). As a general rule in these situations (as with minors), physicians, nurses, therapists, and pharmacists must obtain valid informed consent from the patient's legally authorized representative (surrogate) before touching or treating incapacitated patients, unless there is an emergency.

The "idea of informed consent" is both a theoretical and practical concept. The theory—according to such authors as psychiatrist-law Professor Jay Katz and multidisciplinary bioethics scholars Jessica Berg, Paul Appelbaum, Charles Lidz, and Lisa Parker—may be stated briefly:

> This idea is the core notion that decisions about medical care that a person will receive, if any, are to be made in a collaborative manner between the patient and the physician. The concept also implies that the physician must be prepared to engage in—indeed to initiate—a discussion with the patient about the available therapeutic options and to provide relevant information on them.[69]

In order to obtain informed consent, the practitioner should be assured that the patient fully comprehends and understands the nature of the proposed encounter; the diagnosis (diagnoses); the prognosis (prognoses); and the available, reasonable evaluation and treatment options and the benefits and risks of each (including the possibility of forgoing any treatment at all). Many would say that informed consent is actually a *process* rather than either a single event, a signed document acknowledging permission to proceed with a treatment, or a refusal that stops the intervention.*

One cannot ignore the legal requirement of informed consent without there being possible, perilous consequences. Informed consent, at its crux, serves as a physician's defense against a charge of assault or battery. Further, according to Berg, Appelbaum, Lidz, and Parker:

---

*There are a number of additional excellent references that more fully explain the doctrine of informed consent: Katz J. *The Silent World of Doctor and Patient.* New York, NY: Free Press, 1984; Faden RR, Beauchamp TL. *A History and Theory of Informed Consent.* New York, NY: Oxford University Press, 1986; and Schneider CE. *The Practice of Autonomy: Patients, Doctors, and Medical Decisions.* New York, NY: Oxford University Press, 1998.

Law has also played an important role in nourishing the idea of informed consent. In fact, it is probably from the law that the term informed consent originated. Legally protected interests—primarily bodily integrity and individual autonomy—have contributed to the idea of informed consent. The right of bodily integrity is largely a common-law one, embodied in the protections conferred by both the civil and criminal law of assault and battery. There are also important constitutional underpinnings to this right. Individual autonomy, or the right to choose or decide, has similar common-law and constitutional antecedents.... The idea of informed consent is made operational by means of the *legal doctrine of informed consent.* The doctrine, which prevails in all American jurisdictions, requires that informed consent be obtained before a physician is legally entitled to administer treatment to a patient. This requirement is actually composed of two separate but related legal duties imposed on physicians: the duty first to disclose information to patients, and the duty subsequently to obtain their consent before administering treatment.[70]

Individual autonomy and common-law and constitutional rights were the primary themes that came before the U.S. Supreme Court in the Nancy Beth Cruzan case, decided in 1990.[71] One should recall that *Cruzan* dealt most fundamentally and immediately with whether the state of Missouri violated the federal Constitution when it held that clear and convincing evidence was required in determining an incapacitated patient's wishes regarding the continued use of life-sustaining medical treatment. Some say that it was the first "right to die" case to be heard by the Supreme Court.

The facts of the *Cruzan* case are instructive for a number of reasons, but are particularly helpful when considering proxy decision making because, in this case, the patient lacked capacity and a surrogate was involved in communicating her preferences to the medical team. Following an automobile accident, Nancy Beth Cruzan remained in a permanent coma (or persistent vegetative state, PVS) for more than three years, sustained only by medically mediated nutrition and hydration, before her parents requested that the medical team remove the feeding tube and let her die. The doctors at the state hospital where Cruzan was a patient refused their request. Her parents filed a lawsuit, asserting Cruzan's common-law and constitutional right to refuse unwanted medical treatment (in essence, asserting the mirror right of informed consent: informed refusal). The probate court judge at trial authorized removal; the state objected and appealed.* The Missouri Supreme Court ruled against the parents because they were not able to show—by clear and convincing evidence—what Cruzan's preferences were regarding artificial nutrition and hydration. The parents appealed the Missouri Supreme Court decision to the U.S. Supreme Court.

On June 25, 1990, the Court decided the case in Missouri's favor (i.e., against the parents of Nancy Beth Cruzan), but—by way of dictum**—held that competent adults have a "liberty interest" to accept or refuse medical treatment. Regarding proxy decision making, Chief Justice William H. Rehnquist questioned the contention that incapacitated patients automatically possess the same rights as patients who have the capacity to refuse treatment:

> [Cruzan's parents] go on to assert that an incompetent person should possess the same right in this respect as is possessed by a competent person . . .
>
> The difficulty with the petitioners' claim is that in a sense it begs the question: an incompetent person is not able to make an informed and voluntary choice to exercise a hypothetical right to refuse treatment or any other right. Such a "right" must be exercised for her, if at all, by some sort of surrogate. Here, Missouri has in effect recognized that under certain circumstances a surrogate may act for the patient in electing to have hydration and nutrition withdrawn in such a way as to cause death, but it has established a procedural safeguard to assure that the action of the surrogate conforms as best it may to the wishes expressed by the patient while competent.[72]

---

*At the time of the trial, John Ashcroft served as Missouri's attorney general and was responsible for the legal department that represented the hospital. He then served as governor of Missouri from 1985 to 1993.

**Obiter dictum* may be referred to as dictum or dicta. It is a statement made by the judge or a court, often in a written opinion, which is incidental to the decision or resolution of a case. It is an aside or ancillary statement that may or may not be related to the question before the court and it is usually not binding as precedent for future cases.

However, going further in the analysis, Justice Sandra Day O'Connor, in her concurring opinion, wanted to emphasize the importance of a surrogate decision maker in such cases:

> In my view, such a duty [that would require the state to recognize the decisions of a patient's appointed surrogate] may well be constitutionally required to protect the patient's liberty interest in refusing medical treatment. Few individuals provide explicit or written instructions regarding their intent to refuse medical treatment should they become incompetent. States which decline to consider any evidence other than such instructions may frequently fail to honor a patient's intent. Such failures might be avoided if the State considered an equally probative source of evidence: the patient's appointment of a proxy to make health care decisions on her behalf.[73]

After the Supreme Court's decision was announced, Cruzan's parents filed another petition with the probate court—in fact, they came back to the same judge who ruled seven years earlier that the feeding tube should be removed—to now show, by clear and convincing evidence, that their daughter would not want to be artificially maintained in a permanent coma.[74] After another evidentiary hearing (in which additional witnesses testified about Cruzan's wishes), the court ruled that the patient would refuse medical treatment under the circumstances and, for the second time, ordered the physicians to comply. The state did not appeal this decision. The feeding tube was removed on December 13, 1990; Nancy Beth Cruzan died on December 26, 1990.[75] The *Cruzan* case demonstrates how important surrogate decision making is to the health care delivery of many patients, including those who are frail and dwindling.

In the wake of the *Cruzan* case, Congress passed the Patient Self-Determination Act[76] and approximately three-fourths of the states have enacted proxy health care decisions statutes[77] to assure that incapacitated patients' rights to informed consent (and the refusal of unwanted medical treatments) are recognized and honored. A very progressive example of a state law of this type is the Tennessee Health Care Decisions Act.[78] Notable major provisions of this law* include:

---

*Selected sections of the Tennessee Health Care Decisions Act (2004) are reprinted at the end of this chapter.

- Definitions to be used in interpreting the act (including "capacity");
- Authority for the patient to appoint an agent for proxy health care decision making via a durable power of attorney for health care;
- Superiority of an agent's decision-making authority over that of a court-appointed guardian or surrogate;
- Oral or written designation of a surrogate if the patient does not execute a durable power for health care and does not have a court-appointed guardian;
- Requirement that "the patient's surrogate shall be identified by the supervising health care provider and documented in the current clinical record of the institution or institutions at which the patient is then receiving health care";
- Primary criterion for the designation of a surrogate decision maker as "an adult who is familiar with the patient's personal values, who is reasonably available, and who is willing to serve";
- Non-binding, descending priority listing of preferred relatives or interested individuals for consideration in the designation of a surrogate;
- Criteria to be considered in identifying the most appropriate individual to serve as surrogate;
- Fail-safe possibility of asking for recommendations from the institution's ethics mechanism or involving a second physician if no individual is otherwise identified, available, or willing to serve as surrogate;
- Creation of a rebuttable presumption in favor of the one designated as surrogate in the event of a challenge;
- Surrogate's obligation to make decisions in accord with the patient's instructions (legally, the substituted judgment standard), or in the alternative, in the patient's best interests (best interests standard);
- Inability to withdraw artificial nutrition or hydration unless certain safeguards are met;
- Recognition of surrogate decision-maker's authority without court approval; and
- Civil and criminal immunity for those who identify and designate the surrogate and for those who make decisions under the law.

CONTINUING DILEMMAS INVOLVING DRUG USE IN "DWINDLING" PATIENTS AND MEDICALLY FUTILE SITUATIONS

Some experts believe that only about 15 percent of the population has completed their living wills or any other type of advance directives.[79] (One might wonder what percentage of patients who are frail or dwindling has advance directives and if the percentage is the same as or different than the general population.) After the Terri Schiavo fiasco, there was a surge of interest in memorializing personal preferences regarding end-of-life care.[80] Moreover, several organizations have proposed simpler forms than the commonly available lawyer-drawn documents with which to record care wishes and/or appoint surrogates. Notable among these is the less legalistic and more user-friendly, but still rather lengthy, *Five Wishes.* * Similar documentation efforts, like the Oregon POLST Paradigm, are more for health care providers rather than patients, but are still exceedingly helpful.** However, there remains much work in educating the public about the importance of executing medical directives prior to there being a need for them.[81] For patients, recording end-of-life preferences for use at a time when they lack decision-making capacity is a most important issue; but somehow assuring patients that advance directives will be followed when they become operative in the future is yet another.[82] These are critical concerns as physicians and health care team members struggle with providing tender, compassionate, and hopeful care in accord with dying patients' express wishes.[83]

The challenge is certain to intensify as novel therapies appear on the horizon. One recent report noted that there are several promising drugs (prostate cancer pharmaceutical R-flurbiprofen, intravenous

---

*"*Five Wishes* lets your family and doctors know: (1) Which person you want to make health care decisions for you when you can't make them. (2) The kind of medical treatment you want or don't want. (3) How comfortable you want to be. (4) How you want people to treat you. (5) What you want your loved ones to know." *Five Wishes.* Tallahassee, Fla: Aging With Dignity, 2005. Available at http://www.agingwithdignity.org/5wishes.html (accessed Mar 19, 2006).

**POLST is an anagram for "Physician Orders for Life-Sustaining Treatment." Information about the POLST Paradigm is sponsored by the Center for Ethics in Healthcare at the Oregon Health Sciences University. Available at http://www.ohsu.edu/ethics/polst/ (accessed Mar 19, 2006).

immunoglobin, and nasally administered insulin) in the pipeline that remarkably slow the progression of Alzheimer's disease.[84] Pressures are also intensifying as technologies improve; imaging studies that more clearly demonstrate brain changes with cognitive impairment over time will bolster gene therapy and stem cell experiments.[85]

The additional associated financial costs that accrue in caring for frail and dwindling patients are sure to increase as well. In February 2006, a judge in Great Britain ruled against a fifty-four-year-old cancer patient and refused to order her clinic and primary care trust to provide the high-priced drug Herceptin® (trastuzumab, Genentech).[86] "The ruling has potentially serious consequences across the taxpayer-financed National Health Service."[87] A report in the *New York Times* stated that the treatment "is an expensive drug, costing $36,000 to $47,000 a year for each patient."[88] After the ruling, the patient's lawyer remarked that "the decision by this primary care trust to pit one cancer patient against another and decide on their personal circumstances is just quite simply unfair." However, one must wonder if this may not be an example of the way cases will be resolved in the future as the financial burden of caring for frail and dwindling patients rises. However, on appeal, judges declared that the "local health service had acted illegally" and ordered a full course of treatment for the patient.[89]

The federal government will also be involved in more issues than just funding Medicare and Medicaid budgets for frail and dwindling patients. State agencies have been cited for failing to meet their legal responsibilities in monitoring care for the elderly and disabled.[90] It may be that adult protective services are over-stretched and operating with thin and exhausted staffs, but citizens are bound to question failures when civil service fail-safe mechanisms falter. Likewise, patients who have court-appointed guardians are at similar risk for fraud and abuse when there is no effective oversight to protect the vulnerable.[91]

Frail and dwindling pediatric patients remain a special worry. End-of-life care may be improving for adults, but much needs to be done to advance the quality of palliative and hospice services for children.[92] Just one statistic may frame the need: It is reported that in the United States there are 10,000 to 35,000 adult PVS patients (i.e., patients who are in a persistent vegetative state), as well as 6,000 to 10,000 children.[93] The story about eleven-year-old child abuse victim Haleigh Poutre (Boston, Massachusetts) may highlight some of the dilemmas involved.[94] When the article appeared in the *New York Times* on December 6, 2005, she had been in a hospital on life support for more than three months. One of her injuries was a sheared brain stem, which left her in PVS. It was reported that her aunt—who had adopted Haleigh in 2001—and the aunt's husband may have been responsible for her multiple injuries. The Massachusetts Department of Social Services, acting as the child's legal custodian, petitioned the juvenile court for permission to remove Haleigh's life support; the court granted the petition and the patient died after support was withdrawn. Cases such as this are very sad and often leave the bedside team groping for answers. One recent study concluded that "[t]here is a need for more hospital-based education and more interdisciplinary and cross-subspecialty discussion of inherently complex and stressful pediatric end-of-life cases. Education should focus on establishing appropriate goals of care, as well as on pain management [and] medically supplied nutrition and hydration."[95]

When there is medical uncertainty surrounding the diagnoses, prognoses, and treatment options for frail and dwindling patients, the public is often confused about patients who are minimally functional, in a persistent vegetative state (PVS), or declared dead by neurological criteria (i.e., "brain-dead"). Recent stories such as the sudden awakening of a brain-injured Buffalo (New York) firemen, who had been minimally functional for ten years following an injury when a burning roof collapsed on him, served to fuel the confusion.[96] In this case, public bewilderment became even more confounded due to the reports that his physicians had no explanation for his arousal from or the subsequent lapse back into his previous semi-conscious state. Even after his death from pneumonia—about ten months after his arousal and relapse—his neurologist was unable to account for the episode.[97] Uncertainty and confusion such as this can lead to more misapprehensions about diagnoses and prognoses.

Misunderstanding may be even worse when the patient's family will not believe the attending physician and health care team when they tell them that the patient is dead. Occasionally, there are newspaper stories that highlight the perplexities involved, like the one in 1996 about New York Roman Catholic Archbishop John Cardinal O'Connor helping to arrange the transfer of a brain-dead baby maintained on a ventilator from a Long Island hospital to St. Vincent's in Manhattan to accommodate the Jamaican-born parents.[98] Unfortunately, health care providers and hospitals sometimes fail to make much progress with some routine processes—like notifying families that their loved ones have died—that seem quite settled. One would think that doctors and hospitals would be able to remove dead patients from life support after the declaration of death without much ado, but in some cases it remains an effort even in the most sophisticated facilities because of strained relations and unusual circumstances. For example, in 2005, the family of a thirteen-year-old boy filed a lawsuit in New York to keep the physicians at Montefiore Medical Center from disconnecting the ventilator from the deceased patient more than a week after he died from a severe brain infection.[99] The *New York Times* article reported that "[t]he arguments over [the patient Teron Francis'] treatment were marked by what both sides called miscommunications. Lawyers for the Francis family said their clients felt mistreated by hospital officials, particularly when two doctors told family members that Teron would be taken off life support without their consent, an assertion the hospital denies."[100] One might ask if the "miscommunications" disagreement was over whether the family had a choice in continuing treatment. It is absolutely clear that the team had no legal or moral obligation to continue treating a corpse (recall the physiologic futility arguments); moreover, the hospital in fact may have had a legal and moral obligation to cease treatments after the patient died. Third-party payers would clearly not have a financial obligation to pay for unnecessary medical care. Undoubtedly, when the team harkens to the family's wishes to maintain support, it does so in an attempt to be sensitive and compassionate; however, the family may misinterpret compassionate delays and demand inappropriate care because of the mixed message the health care team may be sending.

Health care providers, hospitals, and state legislatures still have a long way to go in helping resolve ethical dilemmas regarding the treatment of frail and dwindling patients, but are taking steps forward. Ten years before the Barbara Howe case, Massachusetts General Hospital faced a similar crisis with the Catherine Gilgunn matter.[101] As disclosed at the 1995 jury trial, Gilgunn was in a persistent vegetative state and her wishes about continued care were not completely known. Her daughter, Joan Gilgunn, was her surrogate. The seventy-one-year-old patient's medical problems were numerous when she entered the hospital on June 7, 1989 for the treatment of a hip fracture. She was in very poor health, and suffered from heart disease, diabetes, and Parkinson's disease; she had had a mastectomy for breast cancer and suffered a stroke about a year before her admission to the hospital in June. Following the orthopedic surgery to repair her hip fracture, she began having seizures, which progressed to status epilepticus. When the seizures were finally controlled, she was left with irreversible brain damage and in a coma. On August 7, despite the objections of her surrogate, but with the agreement of the hospital's optimum care committee, Gilgunn's attending physician wrote a do-not-resuscitate (DNR) order because he felt that a resuscitation attempt would be futile and inappropriate. Catherine Gilgunn died on August 10, 1989. At the conclusion of the two-week 1995 trial, the jury found the hospital and doctors were not negligent and refused to award damages for mental anguish to Gilgunn's daughter.[102]

In a more concerted effort to help patients, hospitals, and providers, the Texas legislature amended their Advance Directives Act[103] to provide for a "due-process mechanism that empowers physicians . . . to limit life-sustaining treatments that are deemed futile by the medical team."[104] The law was successfully invoked, in 2005, by providers at Texas Children's Hospital regarding their care of Sun Hudson.[105] The infant was born at twenty-five weeks' gestation. During his birth, he suffered respiratory distress and was subsequently placed on a ventilator. In the first week of life, he had a grade III intraventricular hemorrhage and then developed severe progressive post-hemorrhagic hydrocephalus. Over the next few months, he contracted necrotizing enterocolitis (for which he underwent laparotomy with bowel resection), pneumonia, an abdominal abscess, and several other infections (including fungemia from *Candida albicans*, which required weeks of antifungal therapy). During the treatment course, the team learned that he also had a fatal genetic disorder, thanatophoric dysplasia (a rare form of dwarfism that would leave him with a tiny chest too small to support life without mechanical ventilation).[106] The hospital discussed Sun's situation with his mother. She wanted treatment continued, but the hospital—pursuant to the Texas futility law—determined that additional interventions would be futile and called other hospitals to ask if they would accept the child in transfer in order to resolve the disagreement they had with Sun's mother. After contacting thirty-nine other institutions and not securing alternative care, the hospital informed the mother that the team was going to discontinue support. The hospital's ethics committee reviewed the case and agreed that life support should be discontinued. When the mother filed a lawsuit to block the hospital, the court ruled in the hospital's favor. Sun's medical team discontinued life support and the five-month-old died on March 15, 2005.

Noteworthy in the Gilgunn and Hudson cases is the role of the institutional ethics committees in drawing the decision-making process to a conclusion. In both cases, the committee supported the health care team in trying to do what was in the patient's best interests—over the objections of the patients' surrogates—given that future medical interventions would be futile. Ethics committees include doctors, nurses, bioethicists, and others "trained in resolving disputes" as best they can when the patient or surrogate and health care team reach an impasse.[107] Nancy Neveloff Dubler, director of the Montefiore Medical Center (Bronx, New York) bioethics consultation service, has remarked that the caregivers should "avoid the disputes that can arise from poor communication between members of the medical team and family members, and to defuse tense situations with straight talk and empathy."[108]

Without a doubt, the problems of how best to deal with frail and dwindling patients, medical futility, and surrogate decision making are as old as caregiving, medicine, and pharmacy. One may look to Hippocrates for words of advice about these complex modern day issues: It is the "master physician" who learns the signs and "refus[es] to treat those [patients] over-mastered by their illness."[109] Fortunately (or perhaps unfortunately), due to ever-advancing science and technology, with developing drug therapies, and innovative health care possibilities, frail and dwindling patients will have increasing numbers of treatment options that will impact their quality of life. And for patients, surrogates, and health care team members, there will be new dilemmas to resolve as the efforts to balance beneficence, nonmaleficence, autonomy, and justice mature while we move forward with providing for those who are in desperate straits at their end of life.[110]

APPENDIX:
TENNESSEE HEALTH CARE DECISIONS ACT (2004)

Codified at Tenn. Code Ann. §§ 68-11-1701 *et seq.* (2005)

Section 68-11-1702

(a) As used in this [act], unless the context clearly requires otherwise:
   (1) "Advance directive" means an individual instruction or a written statement relating to the subsequent provision of health care for the individual, including, but not limited to, a living will or a durable power of attorney for health care.
   (2) "Agent" means an individual designated in an advance directive for health care to make a health care decision for the individual granting the power.
   (3) "Capacity" means an individual's ability to understand the significant benefits, risks, and alternatives to proposed health care and to make and communicate a health care decision.
   (4) "Designated physician" means a physician designated by an individual or the individual's agent, guardian, or surrogate, to have primary responsibility for the individual's health care or, in the absence of a designation or if the designated physician is not reasonably available, a physician who undertakes such responsibility.
   (5) "Guardian" means a judicially appointed guardian or conservator having authority to make a health care decision for an individual.
   (6) "Health care" means any care, treatment, service or procedure to maintain, diagnose, treat, or otherwise affect an individual's physical or mental condition, and includes medical care as defined in § 32-11-103(5).
   (7) "Health care decision" means consent, refusal of consent or withdrawal of consent to health care.
   (8) "Health care institution" means a health care institution as defined in § 68-11-1602.
   (9) "Health care provider" means a person who is licensed, certified or otherwise authorized or permitted by the laws of this state to administer health care in the ordinary course of business of practice of a profession.
   (10) "Individual instruction" means an individual's direction concerning a health care decision for the individual.
   (11) "Person" means an individual, corporation, estate, trust, partnership, association, joint venture, government, governmental subdivision, agency, or instrumentality, or any other legal or commercial entity.

(12) "Personally informing" means a communication by any effective means from the patient directly to a health care provider.

(13) "Physician" means an individual authorized to practice medicine or osteopathy under Tennessee Code Annotated, Title 63, Chapters 6 or 9.

(14) "Power of attorney for health care" means the designation of an agent to make health care decisions for the individual granting the power.

(15) "Reasonably available" means readily able to be contacted without undue effort and willing and able to act in a timely manner considering the urgency of the patient's health care needs. Such availability shall include, but not be limited to, availability by telephone.

(16) "State" means a state of the United States, the District of Columbia, the Commonwealth of Puerto Rico, or a territory or insular possession subject to the jurisdiction of the United States.

(17) "Supervising health care provider" means the designated physician or, if there is no designated physician or the designated physician is not reasonably available, the health care provider who has undertaken primary responsibility for an individual's health care.

(18) "Surrogate" means an individual, other than a patient's agent or guardian, authorized under this part to make a health care decision for the patient.

(19) "Treating health care provider" means a health care provider who at the time is directly or indirectly involved in providing health care to the patient.

(b) The terms "principal," "individual," and "patient" may be used interchangeably in this part unless the context requires otherwise.

Section 68-11-1706

(a) An adult or emancipated minor may designate any individual to act as surrogate by personally informing the supervising health care provider. The designation may be oral or written.

(b) A surrogate may make a health care decision for a patient who is an adult or emancipated minor if and only if: (1) the patient has been determined by the designated physician to lack capacity, and (2) no agent or guardian has been appointed or the agent or guardian is not reasonably available.

(c) (1) In the case of a patient who lacks capacity, has not appointed an agent, has not designated a surrogate, and does not have a guardian, or whose agent, surrogate, or guardian is not reasonably available, the patient's surrogate shall be identified by the supervising health care provider and documented in the current clinical record of the institution or institutions at which the patient is then receiving health care.

(2) The patient's surrogate shall be an adult who has exhibited special care and concern for the patient, who is familiar with the patient's personal values, who is reasonably available, and who is willing to serve. No person who is the subject of a protective order or other court order that directs that person to avoid contact with the patient shall be eligible to serve as the patient's surrogate.

(3) Consideration may be given in order of descending preference for service as a surrogate to:

(A) the patient's spouse, unless legally separated;

(B) the patient's adult child;

(C) the patient's parent;

(D) the patient's adult sibling;

(E) any other adult relative of the patient; or

(F) any other adult who satisfies the requirements of subdivision (c)(2) of this section.

(4) The following criteria shall be considered in the determination of the person best qualified to serve as the surrogate:

(A) Whether the proposed surrogate reasonably appears to be better able to make decisions either in accordance with the known wishes of the patient or in accordance with the patient's best interests;

(B) The proposed surrogate's regular contact with the patient prior to and during the incapacitating illness;

(C) The proposed surrogate's demonstrated care and concern;

(D) The proposed surrogate's availability to visit the patient during his or her illness; and

(E) The proposed surrogate's availability to engage in face-to-face contact with health care providers for the purpose of fully participating in the decision-making process.

(5) If none of the individuals eligible to act as a surrogate under this subsection (c) is reasonably available, the designated physician may make health care decisions for the patient after the designated physician either:

(A) Consults with and obtains the recommendations of an institution's ethics mechanism; or

(B) Obtains concurrence from a second physician who is not directly involved in the patient's health care, does not serve in a capacity of decision-making, influence, or responsibility over the designated physician, and is not under the responsibility.

(6) In the event of a challenge, there shall be a rebuttable presumption that the selection of the surrogate was valid. Any person who challenges the selection shall have the burden of proving the invalidity of that selection.

(d) A surrogate shall make a health care decision in accordance with the patient's individual instructions, if any, and other wishes to the extent known to the surrogate. Otherwise, the surrogate shall make the decision in accordance with the surrogate's determination of the patient's best interest. In determining the patient's best interest, the surrogate shall consider the patient's personal values to the extent known to the surrogate.

(e) A surrogate who has not been designated by the patient may make all health care decisions for the patient that the patient could make on the patient's own behalf, except that artificial nutrition and hydration may be withheld or withdrawn for a patient upon a decision of the surrogate only when the designated physician and a second independent physician certify in the patient's current clinical records that the provision or continuation of artificial nutrition or hydration is merely prolonging the act of dying and the patient is highly unlikely to regain capacity to make medical decisions.

(f) A health care decision made by a surrogate for a patient is effective without judicial approval.

. . .

(h) A health care provider may require an individual claiming the right to act as surrogate for a patient to provide a written declaration under penalty of perjury stating facts and circumstances reasonably sufficient to establish the claimed authority.

Section 68-11-1707

(a) Absent a court order to the contrary, a guardian shall comply with the patient's individual instructions and may not revoke the patient's advance directive.

(b) Absent a court order to the contrary, a health care decision of an agent takes precedence over that of a guardian.

(c) A health care decision made by a guardian for the patient is effective without judicial approval.

Section 68-11-1708

(a) A designated physician who makes or is informed of a determination that a patient lacks or has recovered capacity, or that another condition exists which affects an individual instruction or the authority of an agent, guardian, or surrogate, shall promptly record the determination in the patient's current clinical record and communicate the determination to the patient, if possible, and to any person then authorized to make health care decisions for the patient.

(b) Except as provided in subsections (c), (d), and (e) of this section, a health care provider or institution providing care to a patient shall:

(1) comply with an individual instruction of the patient and with a reasonable interpretation of that instruction made by a person then authorized to make health care decisions for the patient; and

(2) comply with a health care decision for the patient made by a person then authorized to make health care decisions for the patient to the same extent as if the decision had been made by the patient while having capacity.

(c) A health care provider may decline to comply with an individual instruction or health care decision for reasons of conscience.

(d) A health care institution may decline to comply with an individual instruction or health care decision if the instruction or decision:

(1) is contrary to a policy of the institution which is based on reasons of conscience, and

(2) the policy was timely communicated to the patient or to a person then authorized to make health care decisions for the patient.

(e) A health care provider or institution may decline to comply with an individual instruction or health care decision that requires medically inappropriate health care or health care contrary to generally accepted health care standards applicable to the health care provider or institution.

(f) A health care provider or institution that declines to comply with an individual instruction or health care decision pursuant to subsections (c), (d), or (e) of this section shall:

(1) promptly so inform the patient, if possible, and any person then authorized to make health care decisions for the patient;

(2) provide continuing care to the patient until a transfer can be effected or until the determination has been made that transfer cannot be effected;

(3) unless the patient or person then authorized to make health care decisions for the patient refuses assistance, immediately make all reasonable efforts to assist in the transfer of the patient to another

health care provider or institution that is willing to comply with
the instruction or decision; and

(4) if a transfer cannot be effected, the health care provider or institution shall not be compelled to comply.

Section 68-11-1709

   Unless otherwise specified in an advance directive, a person then authorized to make health care decisions for a patient has the same rights as the
patient to request, receive, examine, copy, and consent to the disclosure of
medical or any other health care information.

Section 68-11-1710

(a) A health care provider or institution acting in good faith and in accor-
    dance with generally accepted health care standards applicable to the
    health care provider or institution is not subject to civil or criminal lia-
    bility or to discipline for unprofessional conduct for:
    (1) complying with a health care decision of a person apparently hav-
        ing authority to make a health care decision for a patient, includ-
        ing a decision to withhold or withdraw health care;
    (2) declining to comply with a health care decision of a person based
        on a belief that the person then lacked authority; or
    (3) complying with an advance directive and assuming that the direc-
        tive was valid when made and has not been revoked or terminated.
(b) An individual acting as agent or surrogate under this part is not sub-
    ject to civil or criminal liability or to discipline for unprofessional
    conduct for health care decisions made in good faith.
(c) A person identifying a surrogate under this part is not subject to civil
    or criminal liability or to discipline for unprofessional conduct for
    such identification made in good faith.

PART III:
DRUG EXPERIMENTATION

Chapter 8

Gene Therapy and Experimentation

Human drug experimentation is just that, experimentation. *One may wonder, and rightly so, if potential drugs can ever be evaluated without there being risk to research subjects and patients. Even more, how can the hazards of experimentation be minimized when a proposed therapeutic intervention is so new and novel—as is gene therapy—that the risks to humans are virtually unknown? And then, what happens (and who should bear the blame) if the experiment goes awry?*

Eighteen-year-old Jesse Gelsinger died September 17, 1999.* At the time of his death, he was a research subject in a gene therapy experiment at the University of Pennsylvania.[1] It was reported that his was the first death "attributed by doctors to a burgeoning field of research that seeks to cure people by giving them new genes."[2]

Gelsinger had been diagnosed at age two with ornithine transcarbamylase (OTC) deficiency syndrome. OTC is one of six essential liver cell enzymes in the cyclic pathway, called the urea cycle, that is needed by humans to convert waste nitrogen products (toxic ammonia) into a water-soluble and nontoxic derivative (urea) that can be excreted into the urine.[3] If there is defective function in any of these six enzymes, patients accumulate the poisonous ammonia instead of making urea. An "inborn error of metabolism" (or "metabolic disease

---

*Stolberg SG. The biotech death of Jesse Gelsinger. *New York Times Magazine* 1999; Nov. 28: 136-150. Copyright © 1999 by The New York Times Co. Excerpts reprinted with permission.

state") has been identified for each of the six enzymes when there is a deficiency.

Ornithine transcarbamylase deficiency is the most common urea cycle disorder; it is the only one that is inherited on the X chromosomes, which geneticists refer to as X-linked. (The other five urea cycle enzyme deficiencies are transmitted to descendants through an autosomal recessive inheritance pattern.) OTC deficiency occurs in about one of every 40,000 births.[4] Because the gene for OTC deficiency is X-linked, male offspring primarily suffer with the disease although female carriers can have the disease too. Severely affected newborns appear normal at birth and develop symptoms soon after taking in dietary protein. Typically, these infants will then begin to refuse milk or formula, vomit, breathe faster, and become increasingly sleepy and eventually comatose within just a few days if undiagnosed and untreated. About half of those with OTC deficiency die in the first month of life; half of those who survive will die by age five.

Some heterozygous females and some males have a less severe form of the disease. In the case of females, who have two X chromosomes, the disease results because one of the X chromosomes usually has a normal OTC gene which lessens the symptoms due to the abnormal OTC gene on the other X chromosome. Males, on the other hand, have only one X chromosome and milder cases are due to genetic changes different from those causing the more severe disease. In fact, Gelsinger had what geneticists refer to as a mosaic OTC deficiency.[5] His gene material (DNA) was analyzed in 1988 and it was learned that some of his cells had normal OTC DNA while other cells had genetic change called a deletion. This genetic change could only have occurred very early in fetal development. Gelsinger had a "mixture" of normal and abnormal OTC genes, this likely accounted for his milder clinical presentation. These milder cases are characterized by episodic symptoms caused by the hyperammonemia (or elevated blood levels of ammonia): vomiting and neurological abnormalities such as ataxia (unsteady gait), confusion, agitation, irritability, combativeness, seizures, and somnolence. (This is how Gelsinger showed disease symptoms initially.) If not identified and treated, these symptoms progress to lethargy, coma, and death. Almost any catabolic condition (or a problem that causes body protein to break down)—even a relatively benign viral illness like a common cold—can trigger hyperammonemia in OTC deficiency patients.

Conventional treatment for OTC deficiency focuses on preventing excess ammonia accumulation.[6] To reduce the possible nitrogen load, OTC deficiency patients must follow special diets that have very little protein and are not very palatable. These low-protein diets consist of a mixture of regular foods, such as fruits, and specially made synthetic foodstuffs that include essential and nonessential amino acids combined with carbohydrate and fat. Patients also take drugs—such as sodium benzoate, sodium phenylacetate or phenylbutyrate, citrulline, and arginine (collectively called "ammonia scavengers")—several times a day to keep ammonia levels within the normal range by ridding the body of waste nitrogen through mechanisms other than urea excretion. Patients report that these chemicals have offensive odors and very unpleasant tastes. Some OTC deficiency patients have received a liver transplant and this intervention has proven to be a curative treatment as the transplanted liver is capable of forming urea through its normally functioning urea cycle. Often there are, however, problems with rejection of the transplant which introduces additional medical problems for patients. For the future, therapy to correct the genetic defect at the cellular level—that is, gene therapy—holds great promise for urea cycle enzyme deficiency patients like Gelsinger.

Historically, researchers and physicians can easily manipulate DNA for transfer into cells where the recombinant gene can then be transcribed and function. One of the great leaps toward genetic engineering took place in 1973: "Herbert Boyer, a researcher at the University of California, San Francisco, and Stanley Cohen, at Stanford University, succeeded in ferrying a recombinant DNA molecule containing DNA sequences from a toad, and a bacterium into a living bacterial cell."[7] Other breakthroughs soon followed in rapid succession:

- In 1981, for the first time, a human disease was identified prenatally by analyzing DNA;
- In 1982, human insulin was produced using recombinant DNA techniques;
- In 1989, genetically engineered cells were injected into a human being;[8] and

- In 1990, Dr. W. French Anderson performed the first gene therapy experiment, "curing" a four-year-old girl with an immune system disorder.[9]

Presently, genes are being transferred by scientists for many uses. This is particularly evident in the pharmaceutical industry where movement of human genes into organisms such as bacteria and yeast enable large-scale production of important biopharmaceuticals. In plants, gene manipulation allows introduction of genes for resistance to pests and herbicides. So transfer of genetic material between different organisms is highly successful.

For purposes of human gene therapy, the creation of genetic material shuttle systems—specialized viral and plasmid vectors—to transfer the important recombinant DNA splices into cells is necessary.[10] (One of the researchers involved in the Gelsinger case at the University of Pennsylvania—Dr. James Wilson—was recognized by the scientific world at the time for his legendary research efforts to perfect a gene therapy adenovirus delivery vehicle.) For those with genetic and genetically influenced disease, gene therapy offers hope for a "cure" and an improved, symptom-free quality of life. By correcting the genetic defect present in their bodies, this would eliminate the disease so that they would not have to continue the onerous ongoing treatments like Gelsinger had endured and tolerated since age two. On April 30, 2000, the *New York Times* reported "from France that several infants with severe immune disorders have apparently been cured by gene therapy [and this] is a dramatic breakthrough in a field that is in desperate need of one" after numerous false starts.[11] These children would otherwise have had to live a life similar to that experienced by David Phillip Vetter, Houston's "Bubble Boy, who died at age 12 in 1984."[12]

In April 2003, scientists announced that the human genome was completely mapped.[13] Genetic tests are currently available for about 1,100 genetic diseases, which are done by more than 550 laboratories across the United States.[14] With all the significant forces coming together and aligning, it was simply a matter of time before physicians began investigating the possibility of treating OTC deficiency with gene therapy.

THE FEDERAL DRUG RESEARCH
AND PATIENT SAFETY FRAMEWORK

Medicine, pharmacy, and drug delivery, in general, are highly regulated activities in America; one can demonstrate "highly regulated" by simply listing the numerous federal and state written laws—both statutory and administrative—that cover almost every aspect of product research or other means of testing, manufacture, storing, marketing, shipping, administering, sale, and dispensing medicines and their precursor chemicals. (The practice of medicine is certainly tightly controlled, but not with the same degree of statutory and administrative oversight as is pharmacy practice. Carl DeMarco wrote in his *Pharmacy and the Law* that "[s]ociety regulates the practice of pharmacy more than it does any health care profession."[15]) The recurring theme—or justification—for governmental intervention in drug delivery is patient safety. If one were to review a history of federal drug regulation, a periodic succession of tragedies or near-catastrophic public health scares would be easily identified. These calamitous events gave rise to punctuated legal and regulatory frenzies. Notable along the timeline—for purposes of considering drug regulation historically—are the key dates 1906, 1938, 1951, and 1962.

In 1906, Congress enacted the federal Pure Food and Drugs Act.[16] Some feel that publication in that year of the novel *The Jungle* by Upton Sinclair—which described the unsanitary and unsafe conditions in Chicago's stockyards and meat-packing factories—led to a federal investigation into the nation's food-processing industry and passage of the first broad federal law to regulate food wholesomeness and distribution, as well as drugs.[17] This statute prohibited the manufacture or sale of food or drugs that were "adulterated" or "misbranded." However, the law did not cover premarketing investigation or testing of drugs and could only be applied after the product entered the distribution chain. In 1937, the sulfanilamide episode brought public attention to the need for more rigorous drug product regulation.[18] In an effort to find a better oral antibiotic formulation for younger patients, the S.E. Massengill Company experimented with developing a liquid sulfa, which they eventually sold as Elixir of Sulfanilamide. The company's chemists found that diethylene glycol* was the best

---

*Diethylene glycol is a highly water soluble compound and like ethylene glycol is used as a coolant in commercial automobile antifreeze products.

liquid vehicle for stabilization and long-term storage (i.e., shelf life). Unfortunately, the company did not test the product specifically for safety *inter vivos* before it was sold. Only after patients began using the medicine to treat infections did company officials learn about its potential toxicity. It is reported that, nationwide, at least 107 individuals died after consuming the product. Under the 1906 Pure Food and Drugs law, regulators did not have the authority to ban or confiscate unsafe products. Only after the federal government established that the liquid sulfa was technically misbranded—it was not really an "elixir" as labeled because elixirs have alcohol as a base, not glycol—did they show that they had a legal right to condemn* and remove the product from the market. As a consequence, the Congress enacted the expanded federal Food, Drug, and Cosmetic Act (FDCA) of 1938. This statute required that before new drugs could be marketed, it must be shown that they are "safe" for the use intended and approved by the Food and Drug Administration (FDA).

In the 1940s, because some of the FDCA's provisions were unclear about how the law changed previous drug sales practices, there was intense confusion about which pharmaceuticals pharmacists could sell or refill without a prescription order.[19] The FDA felt that certain drugs, like antibiotics, could only be sold or refilled upon a physician's prescription; pharmacists did not agree and sold most medicines to whoever they pleased, just as druggists had for centuries. Physicians and the FDA felt that the unrestricted sale of dangerous drugs by pharmacists to consumers was harmful to the public. The FDA asserted that certain drugs sold to patients without a prescription were technically "misbranded" if not labeled properly with adequate directions for use.[20] (The FDA was making a purely legal argument—as they did in the sulfanilamide elixir case—using a strict reading of the statutory language in an attempt to assert authority to control perceived unsafe prac-

---

*The FDCA is, at its core, a criminal statute that prohibits the introduction into interstate commerce products that are adulterated or misbranded. The act's enforcement provisions are archaic, awkward, and time-consuming. For the Food and Drug Administration (FDA) to remove a product from the market, agents are required to obtain a process from the courts in order to seize goods ("condemnation" proceedings). Typically, the questionable product's manufacturer is very cooperative and has already issued a recall, asking suppliers and retailer to send the product back to the company for credit. Wetherbee H, White BD. *Pharmacy Law: Cases and Materials.* St. Paul, Minn: West Publishing Co., 1980, pp. 168-181.

tice.) In 1951, two pharmacists who served in the Congress—Rep. Carl Durham (D-NC) and Sen. Hubert Humphrey (D-MN)—proposed amending the FDCA to clarify that prescription drugs* could be dispensed or refilled only pursuant to an order or prescription from a practitioner authorized by state law to administer such drugs. The Congress enacted the bill into law as the Durham-Humphrey Amendment to the FDCA (1951).[21]

In 1962, another near-tragedy was barely averted when FDA physician/new drug application reviewer Frances Kelsey delayed approval for a new sedative-antiemetic to be marketed by Richardson-Merrell, a Cincinnati pharmaceutical manufacturer. The application was not expected to be controversial, but Kelsey personally wanted more safety data in light of reports from Britain and other European countries about some curious neurological side effects observed in patients taking the drug. The delay probably avoided birth defects (notably limb deformities like phocomelia or "seal limbs") in thousands of children in the United States since the drug—thalidomide—is teratogenic. Shortly afterward, Congress enacted the Kefauver-Harris Drug Amendments of 1962 to hopefully prevent a similar risk in the future.[22] These amendments strengthened the FDCA by requiring: (1) premarket testing for drug product effectiveness as well as safety; (2) procedures to investigate "new drugs"; (3) informed consent for those patients involved in drug studies; (4) a balanced representation of benefits and risks in a new drug application; (5) reporting of adverse drug events (ADEs); (6) implementation of standardized "good manufacturing practices" for the industry with periodic factory inspections; and (7) use of established (generic) names in product labeling and advertising.

Over the years the FDA, pharmaceutical manufacturers, and investigators have developed a very elaborate system to establish that new drugs are both safe and effective before they are marketed in the United States. Occasionally, and often vehemently, critics question the system's efficiency, value, and success;[23] however, time has shown that the present system does have many critical and essential safeguards.

---

*Prescription drugs are also referred to as "legend drugs" because their containers bear the printed legend: "Caution: Federal law prohibits dispensing without prescription." Non-prescription drugs are also called over-the-counter (OTC) drugs because patients may purchase them without a prescription or "over the counter" at a pharmacy cashier checkout station.

The schema's foundation rests on altruism, private enterprise and investment, research integrity, and cooperation in protecting patients as potential new drugs are evaluated.

Parallel with the regulatory framework for new drug approval runs the federal control of human subject research, albeit more broadly. The history of government regulation of human research in the United States might also be characterized as a spotty patchwork of legislative and administrative efforts to remedy problems identified through tragedy and scandal. Most noteworthy among the many unfortunate events include: the crimes against humanity trials of the Nazi doctors, which led to the Nuremberg Code (1948),[24] the publication of Henry Beecher's seminal article "Ethics and Clinical Research" in the *New England Journal of Medicine* (1966),[25] and the sensationalized news in the 1960s and 1970s of the Willowbrook hepatitis investigations, the Jewish Chronic Disease Hospital cancer work, the infamous Tuskegee syphilis study, and like stories.[26] Because of these widespread and notorious reports of abusive research practices "the American public [became convinced] that human subjects were being exploited and harmed on a regular basis by both biomedical and social science researchers."[27] Sens. Walter Mondale (D-Minn) and Edward Kennedy (D-Mass) convened congressional hearings in 1968[28] and 1973,[29] respectively, to explore remedies.[30] As a direct result of the latter investigation, Congress enacted the National Research Act of 1974. This statute had two immediate and far-reaching effects: (1) the provision for the establishment of institutional review boards (IRBs) within local organizations to approve and oversee federally funded research projects that involve human subjects; and (2) the creation of the National Commission for the Protection of Human Subjects of Biomedical and Behavioral Research.

Although a comprehensive discussion of IRBs and their role and function is beyond the scope of any introductory medical and pharmacy ethics text, IRBs may be defined as "'administrative bod[ies]' composed of scientists and nonscientists 'established to protect the rights and welfare of human research subjects recruited to participate in research activities conducted under the auspices of the institution with which it is affiliated.'"[31] Local IRBs share accountability with their sponsoring institutions and associated investigators for compliance with applicable federal regulations.[32] Within the federal government, the Office for Human Research Protections (OHRP) in the office of Public Health and Science, which is housed in the office of the Secretary of the Department of Health and Human Services (DHHS), and the FDA monitor local IRB activities. Even though the OHRP and FDA systems of compliance and assurance differ, both have authority to restrict or suspend human subject research activities for noncompliance with regulations. "Suspension of DHHS approval of an institution's OHRP assurance means that, with the stroke of a pen, DHHS funding [often in the millions of dollars] for ongoing or previously approved research is [immediately] halted."[33] In May 2000, the Clinton administration, reacting to widely publicized lapses, "announced . . . that it would seek additional authority from Congress to levy fines of up to $250,000 on scientists who violate federal rules for human research and $1 million on the universities that employ them."[34]

In establishing the National Commission for the Protection of Human Subjects of Biomedical and Behavioral Research (the Commission), Congress charged the commissioners with (1) identifying and explaining the principles that govern ethically appropriate and defensible human research, and (2) developing guidelines to assure that human research is conducted in a way that is consistent with upholding the principles. The Commission was appointed by the Secretary of the Department of Health, Education, and Welfare and met often.[35] The Commission published several reports, the last of which was the *Belmont Report* (named after the conference center site where the Commission met near Baltimore in 1978). The *Belmont Report* discussed three basic ethical principles that undergird all human subject research activities: respect for persons, beneficence, and justice.[36] The first principle—*respect for persons*—encompasses many critical aspects of human research, including the autonomous right to self-determination in making medical decisions, voluntary informed consent, protection of vulnerable populations, and the right to privacy and confidentiality. *Beneficence* connotes the critical process of investigators, and subjects and patients balancing the benefits and risks of the proposed project. *Justice* implies that the clinical research infrastructure has the responsibility of treating subjects and patients fairly, including individuals systematically selected as appropriate candidates and excluding from the project those who may bear undue burdens or hardship.[37]

In addition, new drug investigations or clinical trials in great part are regulated directly by the FDA.[38] The process to approve a new drug is slow and arduous. Potential new drugs are extensively studied in animals (preclinical trials) before being given to human research subjects. Human clinical studies are classified as phased trials. Phase I ("first-in-human") studies are basically clinical pharmacology evaluations of potential therapies and little else. Robert Levine, in his *Ethics and Regulation of Clinical Research* describes the four phases of human subject clinical research:

> *Phase I Clinical Pharmacology* is intended to include the initial introduction of a drug into [humans]. It may be in the usual "normal" volunteer subjects to determine the levels of toxicity and, when appropriate, pharmacologic effect and be followed by early dose-ranging studies in patients for safety and, in some cases, for early evidence of effectiveness.
>
> Alternatively, with some new drugs, for ethical or scientific considerations, the initial introduction into [humans] is more properly done in selected patients. When normal volunteers are the initial recipients of a drug, the very early trials in patients which follow are also considered part of Phase I.
>
> Drug dynamic and metabolic studies, in whichever stage of investigation they are performed, are considered to be Phase I clinical pharmacological studies. While some, such as absorption studies, are performed in early stages, others, such as efforts to identify metabolites, may not be performed until later in the investigations.
>
> *Phase II* ["proof of concept"] *Clinical Investigation* consists of controlled clinical trials designed to demonstrate effectiveness and relative safety. Normally, these are performed on closely monitored patients of limited number.
>
> *Phase III* ["safety and efficacy"] *Clinical Trials* are the expanded and controlled and uncontrolled trials. These are performed after effectiveness has been basically established, at least to a certain degree, and are intended to gather additional evidence of effectiveness for specific indications and more precise definition of drug-related adverse effects.
>
> *Phase IV Postmarketing Clinical Trials* are of several types:

1. Additional studies to elucidate the incidence of adverse reactions, to explore a specific pharmacologic effect, or to obtain more information of a circumscribed nature.
2. Large-scale, long-term studies to determine the effect of a drug on morbidity and mortality.
3. Additional clinical trials similar to those in Phase III, to supplement premarketing data where it has been deemed in the public interest to release a drug prior to acquisition of all data which would ordinarily be obtained before marketing.
4. Clinical trials in a patient population not adequately studied in the premarketing phase, e.g., children.
5. Clinical trials for an indication for which it is presumed that the drug, once available, will be used.[39]

In summary, Phase I studies are usually conducted in normal volunteers, while Phases II through IV are carried out in patients with disease. Phase I studies are primarily done to evaluate toxicity and safety; Phase II: safety, effectiveness, and appropriate dose; Phase III: safety, effectiveness, and adverse effects. Phase I studies are typically completed in the 10s of normal volunteers or patients; Phase II: in the 100s of patients; Phase III: in the 1,000s of patients; and Phase IV: the 10s or 100s of thousands of patients.

GELSINGER V. UNIVERSITY OF PENNSYLVANIA

From a clinical researcher's point of view, Jesse Gelsinger may have been an ideal Phase I gene therapy trial research subject. He was not a normal volunteer, but he had a relatively mild form of the disease, which was controlled reasonably well by eating a special low-protein diet and taking from thirty to fifty pills a day. Gelsinger's parents followed a very strict regimen with him as a child and he developed normally. As a teenager, and more responsible for his own care, he did not stick to his diet as closely and he resisted taking his medicines, using them only when he felt unwell.[40] Occasionally, he suffered life-threatening ammonia buildups that required hospitalization. He saw his metabolic doctor twice a year at a state-funded clinic in his hometown of Tucson, Arizona.

In late 1998 or early 1999, Gelsinger and his family learned about a gene therapy trial being conducted in Philadelphia for patients with

OTC deficiency. Gelsinger's specialist received a mailing describing the trial from University of Pennsylvania pediatrician and metabolic specialist Dr. Mark Batshaw.[41] However, Gelsinger was not eligible to participate in the Pennsylvania research project at that time because he was under eighteen years old (thus, a minor) and not technically of age to give consent personally. Batshaw was a recognized expert in OTC deficiency disease having developed diet and medication regimens which had helped hundreds of patients. He was a coinvestigator on the research trial with the Institute of Gene Therapy physician Dr. James Wilson who was developing techniques to transfer corrective genes to patients via adenovirus vectors. Batshaw, Wilson, and coinvestigator surgeon Dr. Steven Raper—the physician who actually administered intravenously the new genes bound to the virus vectors to study subjects through a groin catheter threaded to a point near the liver—formed the core project team. The Gelsingers considered meeting with the Philadelphia team during a trip to New York in the summer of 1999.

As events developed, the next few months were very painful for Gelsinger and his family. He was hospitalized almost continuously for several weeks beginning December 22, 1998, when his ammonia level reached six times that of normal.[42] He spent Christmas 1998 in an intensive care unit. On December 29, 1998, he became comatose because of the severe elevation of ammonia and required intubation with breathing machine support. He spent the next two days in a drug-induced coma so that the medical team could better control his breathing on a ventilator. In the hospital, his weight fell from 120 to 97 pounds. By switching Gelsinger's medications from sodium benzoate and arginine to sodium phenylbutyrate and citrulline, his ammonia levels improved and he awoke from the coma. Unfortunately, these new medicines were much more expensive than his previous regimen and cost nearly $3,300 a month. By February 1999, he was almost well enough to go back to school and his part-time job, but he then contracted influenza, which further delayed his recovery. On February 27, 1999, Gelsinger and his father had a quarrel—about his illness and restricted lifestyle—and the teenager threw a soda bottle into a car windshield. Within minutes of the that argument, when the two were in a moving vehicle, Gelsinger jumped out of the van and became pinned under the right rear wheel, suffering a broken arm. After emergency treatment, he required a month of physical therapy. Still, Gelsinger was much more compliant after his hospitalization, with his medicines and diet and his ammonia levels remaining in the normal range, an indication of excellent medical control.

When Gelsinger met with his local metabolic disease specialist again in April 1999, the University of Pennsylvania study participation idea came up again. Gelsinger was very interested and his metabolic physician provided him with the solicitation for participation from Batshaw. (Coincidentally, he initially was diagnosed at The Children's Hospital of Philadelphia which is physically connected to the Hospital at the University of Pennsylvania, so the family was very familiar and comfortable with these medical facilities.) He and his father made arrangements to meet with the Pennsylvania research team on June 22, during a scheduled family trip to the New York area. At that meeting, investigators thoroughly explained the study and the associated risks. The laboratory took blood samples and confirmed that Gelsinger had only 6 percent OTC enzyme function. Following his visit, the project group asked Gelsinger to enroll. He agreed. His father was involved in all conversations and discussions, and characterized Gelsinger's motive and intent: "When I presented . . . what the OTC specialist had to say, he knew the right thing to do. He signed on to help everybody and, hopefully, himself in the long run."[43] A *New York Times* story later described Gelsinger's reasons more fully:

> He knew when he signed up for the experiment at the University of Pennsylvania that he would not benefit; the study was to test the safety of a treatment for babies with a fatal form of his disorder. Still, it offered hope, the promise that someday Jesse might be rid of the cumbersome medications and diet so restrictive that half a hot dog was a treat. "What's the worst that can happen to me?" he told a friend shortly before he left for the Penn hospital, in Philadelphia. "I die, and it's for the babies."[44]

The research team asked Gelsinger to come to Philadelphia in September 1999 to participate in the study.

On Monday, September 13, 1999, Dr. Raper personally administered the adenovirus with the attached new OTC gene to Jesse Gelsinger. Within twenty-four hours, Jesse's temperature rose to 104.5 degrees; after the fever subsided, he became jaundiced and a bit

confused, and his ammonia levels were rising. This immediate response was not totally unexpected: "Gene therapy experts have known
for some time that adenovirus provokes an immune response that
frequently includes high fevers."[45] However, before another twenty-
four hours passed, Gelsinger was in a coma, his liver was failing
(with an ammonia level ten times that of normal and associated
blood-clotting problems), and he was intubated and breathing on
a ventilator. Approximately twelve hours later, his ventilation on the
respirator began to worsen and the team placed him on a heart-lung
by-pass machine (a treatment known as extracorporeal membrane
oxygenation, or ECMO) to rest his shocked lungs. Soon thereafter,
Gelsinger's kidney function began to falter ("he was bloated beyond recognition").[46] The following morning—about four days after
Gelsinger had received the gene therapy infusion—the doctors told
his family that "Jesse had suffered irreparable brain damage and that
his vital organs were all shutting down. They wanted to [take him] off
life support."[47] After a brief service in the room and with the father's
consent, the physicians withdrew life support. Moments later Jesse
Gelsinger was pronounced dead. The news broke nationally within a
few days.[48]

Seven weeks later, on a clear Sunday morning in November,
Gelsinger's father and two dozen mourners—including the Arizona
metabolic disease physician who had told him about the Philadelphia
OTC gene therapy trial and coinvestigator Raper—scattered Jesse
Gelsinger's ashes on Mount Wrightson, a high mountain overlooking
Tucson.[49]

Initially, Gelsinger's family deeply appreciated what the research
team had done in caring for Jesse;[50] sadly, as more detailed information became available, that gratitude soon turned into frustration, an-
ger, and then resolve, which ultimately manifested itself as a personal
injury lawsuit filed on September 18, 2000, in the Philadelphia Court
of Common Pleas trial division.[51] The legal complaint* named as
defendants: the Trustees of the University of Pennsylvania and The
Children's Hospital of Philadelphia (which shared institutional responsibility and IRB oversight for the research project); Drs. Wilson,
Batshaw, and Raper; William Kelley, MD (the dean of the University's medical school and the administrator who recruited and

---

*A copy of the complaint may be found online at http://www.sskrplaw.com/
links/healthcare2.html (accessed May 7, 2007).

hired Dr. Wilson); Arthur Caplan, PhD (the University bioethicist who offered consultative ethics advice to the research team); Genovo, Inc. (a biotech firm—founded by lead scientist Wilson—that had a financial stake in the successful outcome of the experiment); and the Children's National Medical Center in Washington, DC (Dr. Batshaw's employer at the time of the action; he had gone there to serve as Chief Academic Officer and Chairman of Pediatrics at The George Washington University School of Medicine and Health Sciences after leaving the University of Pennsylvania). The plaintiffs—the court-appointed administrator of Jesse Gelsinger's estate, John Gelsinger (his uncle), and Paul Gelsinger (Jesse's father)—asked for unspecified compensatory and punitive damages for the research team's allegedly negligent, reckless, and fraudulent acts in recruiting and treating Gelsinger.

In the news that appeared during the year immediately following the death, outrageous reports surrounding the University of Pennsylvania OTC gene therapy trial and Gelsinger's participation surfaced continually. A listing of the more significant revelations included:

- At the time of his enrollment into the study, Jesse Gelsinger was not an appropriate research subject, according to project selection criteria as approved by the oversight IRB (his blood ammonia level was too high).[52]
- Gelsinger received a significantly higher dose of the viral vector than all but one other subject (a female) in the experimental group of nineteen individuals; it was the highest dose given under the protocol (and from a different batch than that given the other patient who had received a similarly high dose).[53]
- When considering the project proposal, two members* of the National Institutes of Health Recombinant DNA Advisory Committee (or RAC, the multidisciplinary federal panel that oversees gene therapy research) thought the project was too risky for

---

*Interestingly, one of the two who voted to reject the proposal was Dr. Robert Erickson, a medical geneticist who was a member of the faculty of The University of Arizona College of Medicine and had an office two doors away from Jesse Gelsinger's Tucson metabolic specialist, Dr. Randy Heidenreich. Stolberg SG. The biotech death of Jesse Gelsinger. The *New York Times Magazine*. 1999; Nov 28: 136-150. Neither Gelsinger nor his father ever spoke to Erickson about the study. Nelson D. Family's debate mirrored scientists' on gene therapy risk. *The Washington Post*. 1999;Sep 30:A7.

asymptomatic volunteers and recommended the research not be approved; as a compromise, the Batshaw-Wilson team agreed to modify the protocol so that the viral vector would be infused into a peripheral vein rather than almost directly into the liver via a femoral catheterization. (However, this modification was changed back later by the FDA, after a determination that the original delivery method was safer; the RAC, however, was not informed of the protocol detail reversal.)[54]

- The adenovirus was infused intravenously just below Gelsinger's liver rather than in a peripheral vein per the FDA recommendation but contrary to the recommendation by the RAC.[55] (This may or may not be material because the investigators—most certainly—would have been interested in proceeding in a manner that all considered the safest possible. It remains unclear as to why the FDA did not advise—nor suggest that the investigators notify—the RAC of the change.)
- Researchers failed to disclose that their previous testing with the adenovirus vector in mice and monkeys showed potentially lethal side effects, similar to those Gelsinger and one previous research subject in the study group experienced.[56]
- The adenovirus infusion material used in the animal tests was old (injected into the monkeys after its expiration date) and had not been stored properly, leading to a possible overdosing error when compared to fresher viral material infused into the human subjects.[57]
- The research team had not complied with FDA regulations requiring immediate notification of adverse events that arose during the study (the team failed to report that two patients—long before Gelsinger's death—had experienced severe side effects).[58]
- Bioethicist Caplan had urged the research team to consider conducting the Phase I trials in either female carriers or men like Gelsinger rather than in seriously ill infants as originally planned by Wilson. (Caplan argued that the parents of dying babies were incapable of giving voluntary informed consent: "They are coerced by the disease of their child.")[59]
- "Volunteers were recruited in ways that federal officials had explicitly precluded as being potentially too coercive, with direct appeals [by Batshaw][60] on a patient advocacy Web site that heralded 'promising' early results from the clinical trials and

said the experiment used 'very low doses' when in fact they were relatively high."[61]

- Genovo (and Wilson as a stockholder and the University of Pennsylvania as a business associate) stood to benefit financially in a substantial way from gene therapy successes because the company had exclusive rights to develop any of Wilson's discoveries into commercial products. ("'The relationship [was] so entangled,' said Peter Erichsen, the [University of Pennsylvania] general counsel, 'that the university set up two committees to oversee it.'")[62]

When it became known that the university team had not adhered meticulously to federal regulations in clinical research, the medical school's senior vice dean Richard Tannen said, "It is not acceptable to follow the rules and regulations to a level less than 100 percent perfection, and we regret that we haven't done that and are going to take a variety of follow-up steps to assure that happens."[63] In an unsigned letter released near the same time as Tannen's comment, the University also said, "As deeply regrettable as Jesse Gelsinger's death was, it was simply not foreseeable based on informed medical judgment and the best scientific information available at the time."[64]

On November 4, 2000, less than two months after the Gelsingers filed their civil action, *The Washington Post* announced that the University of Pennsylvania and the family had reached an out-of-court settlement for an undisclosed amount.[65] The plaintiffs also released from the lawsuit defendants (then former medical school dean) William Kelley (who himself held several patents on gene therapy technique and was a strong advocate for the University moving into the gene therapy field) and bioethicist Caplan. According to the article*:

Gelsinger's death drew widespread attention to shortcomings in the federal system for protecting research volunteers. It prompted several congressional hearings and various ongoing efforts by the FDA, the National Institutes of Health, and the Department of Health and Human Services to improve human subject protections.[66]

---

*© 2000 *The Washington Post*. Reprinted with permission.

The newspaper piece ended with these sentences:

> The university also said it hoped the agreement would "enable the Gelsingers to bring a small measure of closure to their loss."
> [Paul] Gelsinger said closure was unlikely. "There's never really any satisfaction to be had," he said. But he said he was gratified that in the aftermath of Jesse's death, some wheels of change had begun to turn.
> "I am amazed at the impact my boy has had," he said.[67]

CONTINUING DILEMMAS WITH GENE THERAPY AND EXPERIMENTATION

In commenting to a news reporter about the Gelsinger death in November 1999, LeRoy Walters, a philosopher-bioethicist at Georgetown University and former chairman of the RAC, said:

> I think it's a perilous time for gene therapy . . . Until now, we have been able to say, "Well, it hasn't helped many people, but at least it hasn't hurt people." That has changed.[68]

Closer scrutiny and investigation of scientific and regulatory lapses in human gene therapy with decisive corrective actions soon followed Gelsinger's death. In December 1999, after three days of public hearings, the FDA took the very unusual step to begin proceedings to disqualify Dr. Wilson—accused by the government as having "repeatedly or deliberately [violated] regulations governing the proper conduct of clinical studies"—as a clinical investigator, thus attempting to effectively end his involvement in any human subject research trials.[69] In January 2000, the FDA suspended seven active or pending gene therapy experiments at the University of Pennsylvania.[70] In March 2000, the FDA halted four gene therapy experiments led by physician Jeffery Isner at Tufts University School of Medicine and St. Elizabeth's Medical Center in Boston because the teams had not followed exact protocol by immediately reporting a number of study "adverse events."[71] In May of that same year, the University of Pennsylvania announced that it would no longer conduct gene therapy experiments in humans.[72] Given these responses, it may be valid to ask whether the government has prospective solutions—rather than bandaids or retrospective rules—that can be considered and applied without tragic backdrops (just like the sulfanilamide and thalidomide disasters sixty-five and forty years before, respectively). Perspective, however, is always important; as U.S. Supreme Court Justice Oliver Wendell Holmes, Jr., wrote:

> Great cases like hard cases make bad law. For great cases are called great, not by reason of their importance in shaping the law of the future, but because of some accident of immediate overwhelming interest which appeals to the feelings and distorts the judgment. The immediate interests exercise a kind of hydraulic pressure which makes what was previously clear seem doubtful, and before which even well settled principles of law [and conduct] will bend.[73]

The Gelsinger case occurred in 1999, just three-and-a-half years *after* the death of Hoiyan Wan, a nineteen-year-old nursing student and healthy volunteer who underwent a bronchoscopy at the University of Rochester; her death was attributed to a fatal dose of lidocaine administered during the procedure.[74] In addition, the Gelsinger case was almost two years *before* a death at Johns Hopkins involving a fatal inhalation of hexamethonium by Ellen Roche, a healthy volunteer and twenty-four-year-old lab technician participating in an asthma study.[75] All three projects—with the unexpected deaths of Wan, Gelsinger, and Roche—were approved by local IRBs and were funded with federal research dollars. Inquiring minds are left to ponder whether it is even possible to minimize human research subject risk to zero (or near zero), and whether the present system of monitoring human subject investigations is so broken that it is completely beyond repair. Moreover, physicians, pharmacists, and manufacturers seem, at times, to have a difficult time eliminating risks even for drugs that have been approved after extensive testing in Phase I, II, and III trials, as is shown with the deaths of two radiology patients and the severe reactions in twenty other patients who received the medical imaging contrast agent NeurtoSpec® (Technetium 99m Tc fanolesomab, Palatin Technologies) in 2005.[76] In spite of the seemingly authoritarian inactivity until, or unless, a tragedy occurs, it should be noted that many thoughtful, reflective, and often quite expensive innovations have been undertaken with an eye toward being as proactive as possible in protecting human research subjects.[77]

One of the more worrisome aspects of the Gelsinger case—one extremely difficult to deal with and occasionally simply ignored—centers on Dr. Wilson's conflicts of interest with Genovo. One year after Gelsinger's death, a *New England Journal of Medicine* Sounding Board, written by then Secretary of Health and Human Services Donna Shalala, observed:

> Unfortunately, the public's confidence in [medical researchers' work, competence, and ethics] has been seriously shaken by the death of 18-year-old Jesse Gelsinger in a gene-transfer trial at the University of Pennsylvania in which human subjects were not adequately protected and which presented the appearance of substantial conflicts of interest.[78]

The Institute for Human Gene Therapy-University of Pennsylvania-Genovo joint venture arrangement may not be that unusual. Venture capitalists and old-line pharmaceutical companies (such as Merck and Eli Lilly) appreciate the fact that universities and university faculty are phenomenal research and innovation resources, and thus invest heavily in these potentials.[79] There are great success stories with new drugs that fuel the profit-motive dreams of many (e.g., the hepatitis B vaccine).[80] In one article*, it was revealed that:

> [f]orty percent of gene therapy protocols approved in the past three years have had corporate sponsors. Wilson and others argue that sponsorship provides an important source of funding for research and an eventual pipeline to get cures to the public. Yet the business-academia pipeline has been the subject of much criticism in recent years, because it may sometimes force scientists to choose between good science and good business.[81]

Given what surfaced in the Gelsinger case, something is obviously muddled and, to the informed public, reeks with a foul stench.[82] In an attempt to remedy this state of affairs, universities and academic medical centers, like the government, are tightening restrictions.[83] Scholars themselves see that it is "[s]candals [that are] driving these escalating restrictions."[84] However, the paper trail may never uncover real motives, financial or otherwise*:

> "What effect, if any, such relationships have on the outcome of clinical studies is difficult to evaluate," said Dr. Mildred Cho, a bioethicist at Stanford University who studied conflict-of-interest policies at the 100 largest research institutions in the country. "There is almost never a smoking gun," she said. "You can't say Jesse Gelsinger died because Jim Wilson had stock in Genovo."[85]

Researchers too—as illustrated in the Gelsinger case—unwittingly rationalize and characterize their reasons for involvement differently**:

> [Dr. James] Wilson said that he went to great pains to ensure that his business interests would not influence his judgment during the OTC adenovirus trial. Although he was a senior scientist, for example, he gave Raper control over medical and patient care decisions. "To suggest that I acted or was influenced by money is really offensive to me," he said. "I don't think about how my doing this work is going to make me rich. It's about leadership and notoriety and accomplishment. Publishing in first-rate journals. That's what turns us on. You've got to be on the cutting edge and take risks if you're going to stay on top." Nevertheless, Wilson's own financial disclosure statement says Wilson and Genovo "have a financial interest in a successful outcome from the research involved in this study." Wilson acknowledged that the ties with Genovo are tight enough to require him to include that statement on research papers and the consent forms that patients sign when entering his clinical trials, including the OTC experiment.[86]

---

*Copyright © 2000 by The New York Times Co. Reprinted with permission.
**1999 *The Washington Post.* Reprinted with permission.

Thus, for celebrated scientist- and physician-investigators, fame, position, status, and prestige may be more seductive motivators than fortune. Of course, the question of research legitimacy in such situations may arise in numerous other ways as well—for example, medical journals worry about the validity of the peer-review process and financial influences in much the same vein, and have tried to create safeguards to protect reputation and the publication selection process from corruption.[87]

Dr. Art Caplan's suggestions to the research team in the study's informed consent approval process highlights that there are palpable autonomy, beneficence, and justice issues—for example, in actually obtaining voluntary informed consent for Phase I studies and in allowing at-risk children to participate as subjects—have not been addressed adequately with respect to gene therapy research.[88] In recalling one of Caplan's rationales for suggesting that patients like Jesse Gelsinger be enrolled in the trial instead of dying babies, some might say that Gelsinger, in his circumstances, was "coerced" by the desire to improve his quality of life, just like the parents of seriously ill newborns with OTC deficiency are coerced to agree to almost anything to save their children.[89] However, also, Caplan's advice was not limited to the problem of parental consent (written communication, May 14, 2006). It was based, too, on the ethics of doing nontherapeutic research on a baby when there were alternative subjects available. Caplan did not think that the federal research rules would permit the research under such circumstances. (Subsequently, his belief was validated by both the University of Pennsylvania and Children's Hospital of Philadelphia IRBs.) Also, according to Caplan, it would not have been practical to try to do the experiments on newborns—the diagnosis would have required a team to be ready to fly to the babies wherever they were and quickly set up in an "emergency" situation to deliver the vector. Of course, these are not new issues, but the novelty of gene therapy adds fresh twists.[90] It may be that creative solutions will still be found to help patients and researchers, but it may also be that all are left with simply fine-tuning what is acknowledged as an inexact solution to an insoluble problem.[91]

Entwined with the informed consent concern is the notion of "therapeutic misconception":

The therapeutic misconception is a widely recognized problem in informed consent that occurs when subjects consent to participate in clinical research and who fail to appreciate the distinction between research and treatment will inevitably not understand some of the consequences of their decision.[92]

It appears that Gelsinger most likely knew that his disease would not be "cured" by participating in the gene therapy trial. Paul Gelsinger said his son's "pure intent" was to benefit the "babies" born with more severe forms of OTC deficiency who are at great risk of early death.[93] However, it may be hard to believe that Gelsinger did not harbor slight hope of personal benefit that his condition might be ameliorated to some degree after the gene therapy infusion, even to the point of being able to eat a whole hot dog rather than just half of one. It may be that the mere *hope* of an improved quality of life is difficult to factor out entirely from the consent equation. At present, perhaps the best way for researchers to address therapeutic misconception is to: raise the issue directly in the informed consent process; tease the nuances of decision making as thoroughly as possible; and discuss the consequences until completely satisfied that the subject's purpose and expectations are unequivocally clear. The informed consent form and process used when Dr. Barney Clark agreed to receive the experimental Jarvik-7 artificial heart* at the hands of University of Utah surgeon William DeVries in 1982 may serve as a model.[94]

To escape stifling regulation and possibly the reach of American courts, some drug companies and researchers have moved their clinical trials offshore or overseas.[95] The resulting ethical dilemmas are legion and extend far past the notion of reducing bureaucratic oversight, lessening liability risks, considerably lowering research costs, and exploiting vulnerable individuals. A *New York Times* article added**:

The issue [about where to conduct pharmaceutical research] is especially difficult when it comes to drugs . . . that do not save lives but can vastly improve the quality of life. Nobody knows for sure how many patients in other countries have had to forgo drugs

*See FDA Center for Devices and Radiological Health home page on the Internet. Available at http://www.fda.gov/cdrh/ (accessed May 12, 2006).
**Copyright © 2004 by The New York Times Co. Reprinted with permission.

that improved their lives when clinical trials ended, and companies do not give out patients' names, to protect their privacy. . . . . Ethicists say that they, too, are troubled, but that their field has reached no consensus on what companies should do.

"Do we have an obligation to everyone in the trial or to everyone in the community, the province, the nation, the region of the world?" asked Dr. Ruth Faden, the director of the Phoebe R. Berman Bioethics Institute at Johns Hopkins University. "We haven't really figured this out."

Yet, Dr. Faden said, "Many physician investigators feel uncomfortable with the idea of using patients in studies and then not being able to continue to help them when the trial ends."[96]

Some may think that the Gelsinger case and discussing the adequacy of informed consent for human gene therapy trials is the opening salvo in a much broader debate (or war) about genetic testing generally and the medical decision making that follows more particularly. The prospect of aborting "defective" fetuses stirs emotions and polarizes deliberations.[97] A recent wrongful life case in California over whether—under state law—the obstetrician should have informed a pregnant woman of the results of prenatal tests that showed that her fetus was at high risk to be born with spina bifida has recently been settled and only draws attention to the difficulties for clinicians and patients.[98] Hundreds of reliable tests are available to those interested in obtaining specific patient genetic information; the results are "just a swab away."[99] However, for patients, the decisions about what to do once the information is obtained are often agonizing.[100] Many feel that not having the information—and, thus, not having to deal with the consequences when there are other intervention options—is much better.[101] Simple, painless genetic tests and individualized drug therapy—even for ethnic groups within the population—are now a reality.[102]

Pharmacogenomics—the ability to tailor drugs to specific human genomes—is dawning. According to Dr. Susan Hellmann, the chief medical officer at Genentech, a biotech company pioneer: "It's as if our old weapon was an ax, and now we have a scalpel."[103] Unfortunately and regrettably, more deaths of human research subjects while enrolled in clinical trials—like Jesse Gelsinger's—are probable. According to another bioethicist:

"Scientists call gene therapy 'elegant,'" said Thomas Murray, president of the Hastings Center, a bioethics institute in Garrison, N.Y. "But obviously it is not elegant at this point. It is damn messy, and in fact we now see it can be dangerous. Patients and research subjects need to be told about the risks, and protocols need to be approved or denied in full knowledge of those risks."[104]

Ruth Macklin, a bioethicist at Albert Einstein College of Medicine in New York and also a member of the RAC, puts it more bluntly: "Gene therapy is not yet therapy." The take-away is that the hope and promise of pharmacogenomics, through continued drug experimentation, is still years, perhaps *decades,* away from actualization, and there is still much investigational work to be done.

Afterword

John Lachs

In the complex contemporary world, the problems faced by such professionals as physicians, pharmacists, and nurses converge with vexing issues of public policy and the agonized choices of ordinary people. Whatever our social position and political persuasion, we are constantly bombarded with decisions about medical treatment and the sensible use of drugs. As the case of COX-2 inhibitors shows, it is difficult enough to know the long-term effects of medications, yet we are also called on to be familiar with the laws governing drug use and the moral considerations that motivate individual choice and the creation of regulations. The demand for knowledge, the desire to do what is right, and the drive for living well create a great deal of uncertainty in modern life.

The knowledge we need is multidisciplinary and cannot be partisan. It must be provided by someone who has faced the problems and integrated the proposed solutions of a variety of professions, a person who is both well informed and morally sensitive. Finding such a guide is all the more difficult because each profession is a world unto itself, offering its own perspectives and demanding allegiance in word and thought. The vast growth and consequent fragmentation of knowledge make it an unusual achievement to master two disciplines; excellence in three professions is nearly unknown.

What is so remarkable about Bruce White, the author of this volume, is that in addition to being a physician and a pharmacist, he is also a lawyer. His professional qualifications in these three fields are supplemented by work in ethics. The multidisciplinary approach is evident throughout the book: the author addresses students and practitioners of each profession from a standpoint developed by reference to all. The perspective of the physician is supplemented by that of the pharmacist and modified by the views of the lawyer, creating an account of problems that does justice to their complexity. Moreover, White's sensitivity to issues relating to the quality of life lifts problems out of the realm of abstraction and situates them in the real world of human suffering. Yet there is no preaching here: White is keenly aware that individuals must make their own choices and face the consequences that follow.

Many writers on health care get entangled in the unruly details of the problems and forget that they deal not with intellectual conundrums but with practical matters requiring choice and action. A great virtue of White's text is that it never loses sight of the real-life context of problems. He provides vast amounts of information about the issues he tackles, lays bare the reasons for the choices people make, and prepares his readers for intelligent decisions. His approach makes it clear that the stakes are high, that even inaction involves a value-commitment and that what we do is largely irreversible. Yet we must act and act expeditiously, too often without having all the necessary evidence in hand.

Precisely because the problems are difficult and we make decisions under less than ideal conditions, it is better to arm ourselves with critical skills and sound principles rather than broad ideological commitments. White is masterful at avoiding the easy generalization and partisan conclusion, dispassionately exhibiting every side of the moral problems he considers. The overwhelming impression conveyed is that of good sense supported by careful reasoning. The best reason for reading this book is its calm thoughtfulness. It educates in a context of caring, convinced that if enough information is provided, it is safe to trust human intelligence to make the right decisions.

Appendix 1

Law and Decisions

OBJECTIVES

After completing this appendix, the reader should be able to:

- Define *law.*
- List and explain the four primary sources of law.
- Recognize the differences between and interrelationships of the federal and state governments.
- Explain the following federal constitutional principles: interstate commerce and police power.
- Explain the relevance of statutes to medical practice.
- Illustrate the relevance by discussing the statutory definitions of death.
- Understand the difference between statutes and regulations.
- Explain the relevance of regulations to medical practice.
- Illustrate the relevance by discussing the Baby Doe regulations.
- Explain the concept *common law.*
- Explain the relevance of appellate judicial opinions to medical practice.
- Illustrate the relevance by discussing the right to refuse life-sustaining treatments.

WHAT DOES LAW MEAN?

The first definition of law that appears in the third edition of *The American Heritage Dictionary of the English Language* is very short: "[a] rule of conduct established by custom, agreement, or authority."[1] *Webster's Seventh New Collegiate Dictionary* defines *law* as "a binding custom or practice of a community: a rule of conduct or action prescribed or formally recognized as binding or enforced by a controlling authority."[2] The important elements of the *Webster's* definition are: (1) *"a rule of conduct"* [or community custom or practice]; (2) *adopted by the community,* or an authoritative body representing the community; (3) prescribing or formally *identifying some specific activity;* (4) *which is binding* on the whole community or a limited, defined group within the community; and (5) *enforceable by a controlling authority.*

However, a single definition may not be as helpful as understanding a few of the purposes, functions, or roles of law in society. (It is just as important to know what the law *does* and how it *operates* as it is to know its elementary definitions.) Some of the broad functions of law are:

- *Law prescribes conduct, both positively and negatively.* Some rules command and some forbid specified activities within the community (broadly called public law). Some establish the legitimate boundaries of required personal conduct; some permit unregulated individual interchanges (sometimes termed private law). The criminal statutes create penalties for conduct that violate societal and accepted interests (the field of criminal law, a subset of public law). Damages for personal injuries can be awarded in civil actions upon a finding of liability for tortuous conduct (the sphere of *tort law,* a subset of private law).

- *Law authorizes the creation and protection of individual rights and privileges.* Some rules allow parties to contract for real property, goods, and services and govern the performance of bargains (an area of law governed by *property law* and *contract law*). Some rules allow for liberty of travel, assembly, and speech; the unfettered ability to transport personal effects; or emancipation from unwarranted governmental intrusions (usually discussed within the context of individual rights as derived from *substantive constitutional law*). Some rules protect individuals from others' interference or harmful actions (again, tort law). Some rules permit workers to labor at their public trades (normally a feature of contract law and *substantive administrative law*). In all these situations, a controlling authority may impose reasonable conditions to assure public safety and security.

- *Law assists in the resolution of conflicts between competing interests.* Because disagreements and differences of opinion must be resolved in order to maintain relationships between individuals and groups, there must be some way of peacefully and deliberately settling disputes. Written rules coupled with a mechanism to interpret the rules and to resolve situations in which there are no written rules has proven to be a progressive and widely accepted method. (In the United States, this mechanism—which some feel to be far from perfect—is represented by an independent and respected judiciary.) Law then sets the stage for orderly dispute resolution through published rules that govern proceedings (hence, *civil* and *criminal procedure* and *procedural constitutional* and *administrative law*). Law allows for orderly social change. Stability in the law is essential; without knowing the limits of permissibility, some would almost always be at risk of crossing the barrier. However, without flexibility and the capability to modify the limits as conditions merit, social and economic stagnation would occur. For example, technological advances continually prompt the creation of new rules.

- *Law provides a means to achieve the community's goals.* It allows, in most instances, a self-imposed and regulated system through identified institutions and conventions for sovereign control so that citizens can work toward meeting their own objectives. As a corollary, government then acts to characterize and prioritize aims to best meet perceived community and individual needs.

WHAT ARE THE FOUR PRIMARY SOURCES OF LAW IN THE UNITED STATES?

Enforceable rules of conduct (i.e., laws) are primarily created in the United States by four recognized authorities: (1) *the people,* the nation's citizens, usually acting through their representatives, and also by public referenda; (2) *legislative bodies,* the federal Congress and primarily the 50 state legislatures or general assemblies; (3) *federal and state administrative agencies;* and (4) *federal and state judges,* when they render opinions after making decisions in trial and appeals courts.

The first three categories create law that is written and published prospectively. Constitutions, statutes, and regulations, for the most part, specifically describe expected community behaviors or norms (i.e., responsibilities to be met, or activities to be avoided, or conduct to be observed). The fourth produces law retrospectively. Only after someone does something that is offensive or causes harm to another, who then asks the proper authorities (usually the courts) for redress or compensation, does law (or a particular rule of conduct) follow. For this reason, case or judge-made law may appear indiscriminate and punitive (more like punishment). However, case law really allows for the creation of new communitywide rules while also helping individuals solve their own unique problems with the least governmental involvement.

The first three categories are derivative and hierarchical. Law is derivative in that constitutions permit statutes, which in turn allow regulations. Citizens ordain constitutions and forms of government. Constitutions provide for legislatures. Legislatures enact statutes. Special statutes (enabling acts) authorize and empower administrative agencies. Administrative agencies function executively, adopt rules and regulations, and hold hearings. And, law is hierarchical in that regulations must be consistent with, and be drafted in conformity to, their enabling statutes. In turn, statutes must be consistent with, and conform to, the constitutions that authorized the legislative actions. A regulation that goes beyond the scope of what was intended by the legislature that permitted the rule is not valid. A statute that is inconsistent with the constitution is unconstitutional. Of course, it may take a court case to determine invalidity or unconstitutionality. In an effort to make this point absolutely clear for all time, Article VI of the Constitution states:

> This Constitution, and the Law of the United States which shall be made in Pursuance thereof; and all Treaties made, or which shall be made, under the Authority of the United States, shall be *the supreme Law of the Land;* and the Judges in every State shall be bound thereby, any Thing in the Constitution, or Laws of any State to the Contrary notwithstanding [emphasis added].[3]

It is, in the final analysis, the interpretation of this authority that allows the U.S. Supreme Court to declare a law—such as one enacted by the federal or a state legislature, one promulgated by an executive or an administrative agency, or one handed down through any federal or state lower court ruling—*unconstitutional* because it violates, or is repugnant to, one of the principles as written in the federal Constitution.

All four sources of law are relatively flexible; that is, constitutions can be amended by the people, statutes can be revised by the respective legislatures, regulations can be changed by the appropriate administrative agencies, and court decisions can be overturned on appeal by a higher court or by actions of the people (by amending constitutions) or their representatives (through statutes). Yet all four provide some stability and security once the rules of conduct are established and become known.

The Constitution states clearly that state judges—not just federal judges—are "bound" by controlling federal law. State court judges, therefore, have the authority to rule on questions of federal law, but only in a manner consistent with federal judiciary interpretation of the same issue. State judges are thus empowered to make decisions based on federal law rights and principles in addition to state law. Federal judges may not have as much latitude in contrary cases; when applying state law in federal cases, they are bound by the decisions of the state's court of last resort.

Similarly, in a country with concurrent federal and state governments, sometimes both bodies of government act to adopt enforceable rules that govern particular activities. Both may have valid jurisdiction or authority to do so. For example, both the federal government and the fifty state governments have jurisdiction over the distribution of controlled substances. The Constitution gives Congress the power to regulate interstate commerce (or the transportation of market goods across state lines) and states possess the "police power" (the authority to protect the health, safety, and welfare of citizens, which is one of the powers the Constitution reserved for the individual states). As a general rule, both governments may enact laws necessary to execute their powers without impinging on the authority of the other. However, if there is a conflict between federal and state law, the federal law usually takes precedence or supersedes state law because of the federal *preemption doctrine* (i.e., by implication, since the federal legislature is attempting to regulate a field, the state government is preempted from attempting the same enterprise).

Further, with regard to the conflict between federal and state law, there sometimes appears to be a conflict where one truly does not exist. For example, an accused drug dealer might be subject to ten-year imprisonment if convicted in federal court and a five-year imprisonment if convicted in state court. No conflict exists in this situation. The defendant can be prosecuted by both governments and if convicted by both, would serve both sentences. As another example, under federal law, physicians must keep records associated with the use or prescription of controlled substances for two years. A state law may require that the records be kept five years. There is a conflict here; however, compliance with the more strict state law assures compliance with the less strict federal law.

HOW DO THE PEOPLE
(THE NATION'S CITIZENS) CREATE LAW?

The preamble of the federal Constitution reads:

> *We the People* of the United States, in Order to form a more perfect Union, establish Justice, insure domestic Tranquility, provide for the common defense, promote the general Welfare, and secure the Blessings of Liberty to ourselves and our Posterity, do ordain and establish this Constitution for the United States of America [emphasis added].[4]

In a very real sense, it was the people—the citizens of the United States— who created the fundamental law of the land and they ordained the federal Constitution in 1787. The federal and subsequent state constitutions created the general framework required for the proper exercise of governmental authority at the central and state levels.

The Founding Fathers agreed that a *written* Constitution—which clearly delineates the powers of government and formulates a system of checks and balances within the three branches of a federal government—was preferable to the "*unwritten* constitution" of Great Britain. In the Mother Country, it is accepted that an unwritten constitution (really, little more than traditions or non-statutory binding conventions and prerogatives; i.e., accepted governmental practice) controls the reigning King's (or Queen's) actions. This concept is relatively modern because in ancient England, the King owned all property and possessed all governmental authority without limit; he had absolute power to make, to execute (or enforce), and to interpret (or adjudge) the law. (These legal functions—legislative, executive, and judicial—are the essential capacities or branches of government). However, as Lord Acton said, ". . . absolute power corrupts absolutely."[5] For all practical purposes, it was abuse of power that led to three radical, but integral changes in English government over the years:

1. Magna Carta (1215) forced King John to recognize that the barons and freemen had rights independent of him;
2. the English Civil Wars (1642-1651) settled against the monarchy the Stuart kings' contention that they were subject only to God's, and not the House of Commons', law (a repudiation of the "divine right of kings"); and
3. the Glorious Revolution (1688-1689) resulted in the Commons replacing James II with William (of Orange) and Mary (James' daughter) and a Bill of Rights.

Certainly by the early 1700s, the English kings had recognized that they alone could not maintain a functioning government without considerable assistance. By that time, successive monarchs had more or less split governmental service into three areas and delegated responsibility to others: legislative responsibilities were performed by the hereditary House of Lords (including the Lords Spiritual and Temporal) and the elected House of Commons; executive responsibilities were exercised through appointed ministers; and judicial responsibilities were effected through an appointed judiciary. The king still maintained strong control by designating and dismissing governmental officials.

The Founding Fathers, as English citizens, were very comfortable with the King's representatives exercising legislative, executive, and judicial powers in the Colonies. However, they felt that allowing one person (such as the King) to hold complete governmental autonomy might lead to abuse of power. (An enumeration of George III's abuses within the Thirteen Colonies can be found in America's Declaration of Independence.[6]) Therefore, the Framers separated the powers of government into three distinct authorities through a written Constitution: a federal Congress (with an elected Senate and House of Representatives) to exercise legislative powers; an elected President to exercise executive powers; and an independent judiciary (appointed by the President with the advice and consent of the Senate) to exercise judicial powers. This view of segregated governmental control is termed the "separation of powers" doctrine. To further prevent abuse of power, the Constitution establishes a system of checks and balances within the three branches of government so that no one branch can dominate the others. For example, Congress has authority to establish budgets, the president usually appoints (and removes) departmental officers who oversee spending, while the U.S. Supreme Court decides whether constitutional authority was exceeded in the process. If the citizenry are disturbed by the Court's interpretation of the Constitution, then that document can be amended to reflect their will. The Constitution is not easily changed—certainly for good reasons—but the fact that it *can* be changed indicates that ultimate governmental control rests with the people.

The Constitution not only establishes a central national government, but it also limits the central government's authority by denying it powers other than those expressly granted, thereby reaffirming that state governments, local governments, and the people retain the rest. The Constitution thus promotes effective regional governments (to deal with relatively local issues like crime and public safety) and significant personal liberty. More directly, the national government has exclusive authority by specific grant—over the individual states—to regulate interstate commerce, coin money, establish postal services, maintain national defenses, and regulate naturalization and immigration. Both national and state governments may collect taxes, borrow money, create and maintain court systems, and hold elections. By implication, the states have full control over intrastate commerce, protection of the state's public health and welfare (the so-called police power), school systems, local political subdivisions, and state voter qualifications (save for the later amendments to the Constitution that deal with this issue). The Constitution also specifically denies some powers to the central and state governments, independently and collectively. The national government may not tax exports, suspend the writ of habeas corpus, unilaterally modify state boundaries, or abridge the Bill of Rights. State governments may not tax imports, exports, federal properties, and reservations, or make treaties. Neither the federal or state governments may enact ex post facto laws nor bills of attainder, deny due process of law to its citizens, or grant titles.

Parenthetically, an understanding of the federal government's power to regulate interstate commerce and the states' inherent police power is very important for physicians and pharmacists. It is through these two powers (one exercised at the federal level and one at the state level) that government usually controls the practice of medicine and pharmacy. For example, it is the authority to regulate interstate commerce that allowed Congress to enact the Food, Drug and Cosmetic Act in 1938 (that allows for prescription drugs) and the Controlled Substances Act in 1970 (that schedules narcotics and dangerous drugs and limits their manufacture, distribution, and use). It is through the states' authority to protect the safety, health, and welfare of its citizens (the "police power") that state legislatures enact medical and pharmacy practice acts (which permit the licensure of physicians and pharmacists and limit the practice of medicine and pharmacy to those licensed under the law).

HOW DO LEGISLATIVE BODIES CREATE LAW?

Legislatures create law when they enact bills (articles of legislation proposed by legislators) and forward them to the executive for approval. When the President or governor signs a bill, or when the legislature properly overrides an executive's veto, a bill becomes a statute. (Individual statutes are also termed legislative acts, such as the federal Emergency Medical Treatment and Active Labor Act, and the federal Americans With Disabilities Act, or the medical practice or pharmacy act of a particular state.) These statutes, when categorized topically and officially published (i.e., codified), are collectively called a code. Statutes of the United States Congress are codified in the *United States Code* (abbreviated U.S.C.). Sometimes parts of statutes are commonly referred to by their article number (such as Title XVIII [the Medicare provisions] and Title XIX [the Medicaid provisions] of the Social Security Act).

Ordinance is a term usually reserved for local legislative acts (such as law enacted by a city council), but is used occasionally at the national level (e.g., through the Ordinance of 1787 the Congress opened up for settlement the Territory Northwest of the River Ohio).

Illustrating Statutory Law in Practice:
Definitions of Death

In 1979, President Jimmy Carter appointed the President's Commission for the Study of Ethical Problems in Medicine and Biomedical and Behavioral Research. The Commission was authorized by Congress in

1978 to study the ethical and legal implications of a number of pressing issues in medicine and research that might be the subject of federal or state legislation or regulation. One of the questions posed for the Commission's consideration was "whether the law ought to recognize new means for establishing that human death has occurred."[7]

It may seem surprisingly strange that suddenly in 1978, there appeared to be a pressing need to reevaluate the way physicians were able to legally declare that persons had died. After all, doctors had been "pronouncing" persons "dead" long before there were even statutes that recognized the practice. And before that, physicians were not required for a legal determination of death, laypersons understood that when someone's breathing ceased and heart stopped that that individual was dead (or would be shortly thereafter). The legal determination followed the physiological event for legal purposes (so that an undertaker could bury the body, a beneficiary could collect life insurance proceeds, or a district attorney could prosecute an assailant for murder). Over the years, all states had enacted statutes that required a medical determination of death based on irreversible cessation of cardiopulmonary function. However, in the 1960s and 1970s, two important national phenomenon were radically changing medicine and society in the United States: (1) physicians were able to artificially maintain beating hearts (with electrical shocks and drugs) and breathing lungs (with ventilators) in patients who had suffered total and irreversible loss of all brain function; and (2) physicians were beginning to surgically transplant a dead person's vital organs (for example, kidneys, corneas, and hearts) into dying patients.

In its final report, the Commission made the following recommendations regarding a statutory definition of death:

Recent developments in medical treatment necessitate a restatement of the standards traditionally recognized for determining that death has occurred.

1. Such a restatement ought preferably be a matter of statutory law.
2. Such a statute ought to remain a matter for state law, with federal action at this time being limited to areas under exclusive federal jurisdiction.
3. The statutory law ought to be uniform for all the several states.
4. The "definition" contained in the statute ought to address general physiological standards rather than medical criteria and tests, which will change with advances in biomedical knowledge and refinements in technique.

5. Death is a unitary phenomenon that can be accurately demon-strated either on the traditional grounds of irreversible cessation of heart and lung functions or on the basis of irreversible loss of all functions of the entire brain.

6. Any statutory "definition" should be kept separate and distinct from provisions governing the donation of cadaver organs and from any legal rules on decisions to terminate life-sustaining treatment.

To embody these conclusions in statutory form, the Commission worked with the major professional bodies in medicine, law, and legislative reform to develop a proposed statute. The American Bar Association, the American Medical Association, and the National Conference of Commissioners on Uniform State Laws joined the Commission in endorsing the Uniform Determination of Death Act, to replace their previous separate proposals:

An individual who has sustained either (1) irreversible cessation of circulatory and respiratory functions, or (2) irreversible cessation of all functions of the entire brain, including the brain stem, is dead. A determination of death must be made in accordance with accepted medical standards.[8]

Suggestion for Additional Reading. President's Commission for the Study of Ethical Problems in Medicine Biomedical and Behavioral Research. *Defining Death.* Washington, D.C.: U.S. Government Printing Office, 1980.

HOW DO FEDERAL AND STATE ADMINISTRATIVE AGENCIES CREATE LAW?

Administrative agencies exist at the federal and state level; they were established by their respective legislatures by law. This is usually done via the enactment of an "enabling act" (i.e., a statute to enable or empower the given agency to act for the legislature). With this enabling legislation, the Congress or a state legislature usually creates a board or commission of individuals to act as a composite body, or agency, in order to accomplish specific objectives. In essence, the legislature delegates some of its law-making authority to another body so that it can act as the legislature's proxy in a clearly defined and limited manner. (Recall that if the legislature delegates power inappropriately, or tries to delegate power that it really does not possess under the constitution, the enabling act may be declared unconstitutional by a court with proper jurisdiction.)

Some areas of activity in society—like the practice of medicine, dentistry, pharmacy, or nursing—are highly specialized and technical. (Individuals spend countless hours learning, in the classroom and by working with others, the skills necessary to practice these professions proficiently.) It is the responsibility of the state legislatures (because they possess the police power to protect the health, safety, and welfare of its citizens) to insure that only competent persons practice these professions within their borders. However, to effectively exercise this authority, it would take a great deal of time for the legislators to learn the nuances of these disciplines and properly license and then monitor those who practice these healing arts. So, the general assemblies have created state boards of medical and dental examiners and state boards of pharmacy and nursing to perform these duties in their stead. Each board is composed of respected and able professionals who understand the elements of good and bad practice, and who can more appropriately assess the qualifications of applicants and discipline licensees for improprieties.

Because of their responsibilities, administrative agencies have a great deal of broad powers and discretionary authority. To use the state board of medical examiners as an example, the board:

- Promulgates regulations (a rule-making authority) necessary to its licensure and disciplinary functions (e.g., it determines which tests are most appropriate for initial licensure by examination and sets the minimum qualifying score, and it specifies conduct which might subject licensees to sanction);
- Administers and enforces the rules (an executive authority) (e.g., makes inspections of practice premises to insure compliance with board mandates, and assists in the prosecution of individuals who are practicing without a license); and
- Holds hearings, reviews circumstances, determines whether licensees have violated board rules, and imposes sanctions for violations (an adjudicatory authority).

One can easily identify the three essential elements of governmental responsibility—legislative, executive, and judicial—in the workings of administrative agencies. One might just as easily wonder about the possibilities of abuse of power in such an arrangement (just as did occur when the English monarchy ruled the Thirteen Colonies). To balance these potentialities, there exists a system of checks on administrative agencies as there does among the three constitutional branches of government. Most directly, because the agency is a creature of the legislature, it can be dissolved by the same assembly that created it (this happens periodically and automatically through the effect of many state's "Sunset Laws," commanding the abolishment of identified agencies by operation of law unless the entities are specifically reauthorized to continue). The state legislature can write the enabling acts in a very detailed manner, disallowing some agency discretion (thereby legislating particularly on some issues that might have been the subject of board regulation). The legislature can increase or decrease the number of board members and uniquely detail the process for appointment and removal. If the legislature so desires, it may allow the state's governor to appoint and remove board members. Since most state administrative agencies are housed within the executive branch of government, the governor may enlarge or shrink agency budgets and expand or limit cooperation with other executive departments (such as providing legal counsel and prosecutors from the attorney general's office for the agency's operations). And, almost all administrative agency actions (including the promulgation of regulations and adjudicatory proceedings) are subject to judicial review by courts of competent jurisdiction. Courts may set aside agency regulations, and reverse or modify determinations and rulings. As noted earlier, judges even have the authority to determine whether the legislature acted appropriately in creating and enabling the administrative agency in the first place.

There are a number of federal administrative agencies (i.e., authorities created by the Congress) that affect the practice of medicine and pharmacy in the United States. Some are:

- the Drug Enforcement Administration (DEA), an agency within the Department of Justice, is responsible for enforcing the Controlled Substances Act;
- the Food and Drug Administration (FDA), a unit of the Department of Health and Human Services (DHHS), insures compliance with the requirements of the Food, Drug and Cosmetic Act;
- the Centers for Medicare and Medicaid Services (CMS), also in DHHS, oversees federally funded health care operations (primarily— as the name implies—the Medicare and Medicaid programs) by developing appropriate reimbursement policies and procedures; and
- the Federal Trade Commission (FTC), a freestanding agency independent of the executive branch, administers the Federal Trade Commission Act, which essentially deals with unfair business practices and antitrust law.

Regulation is a term used synonymously with *rule* when discussing a law adopted or promulgated by an administrative agency (just as statute is used to describe the law enacted by a legislature). At the federal level, administrative regulations are published in the *Federal Register,* a daily journal that records federal agencies' actions (such as meetings and hearings, and proposed and final rules). Federal regulations are codified in the *Code of Federal Regulations* (abbreviated C.F.R), an annual set of paperbacks containing collected agency rules with revisions, and cataloged under the same fifty titles as the *United States Code.*

Illustrating Administrative Law in Practice:
The Baby Doe Rules

Baby Doe died April 15, 1982, aged six days. At birth, his parents learned he had Down's syndrome and a tracheoesophageal fistula. In agreement with the medical and surgical team, they decided not to consent to the necessary corrective surgery. Baby Doe was provided comfort care, including phenobarbital and morphine, but not artificially fed. After the parents refused surgery, the hospital filed a suit in a local court to override that decision. The court declined to order surgery over the parents' informed and expressed objections. The Indiana Supreme Court denied an extraordinary writ on appeal. Hospital attorneys were in the process of seeking a stay from the U.S. Supreme Court when the issue became moot due to the patient's death.

Several advocacy groups were outraged regarding the circumstances of the child's death when the story became more widely known. Within weeks, the Department of Health and Human Services issued emergency regulations ("Baby Doe I") to prevent a similar episode from occurring again in the United States. Acting under the authority of § 504 of the Rehabilitation Act of 1973 (which forbids any entity that receives federal funds from discriminating against handicapped persons), the Secretary, by regulation, instituted a nationwide enforcement mechanism—including (1) a toll-free telephone hotline— for reporting alleged discriminatory conduct against handicapped newborns; (2) "Baby Doe squads" to act immediately upon notification to investigate allegations of discrimination; and (3) required poster displays in all maternity, nursery, and pediatric units that alert staff, parents, and visitors of the regulation and its purposes.

The American Academy of Pediatrics challenged the regulations in federal court. The regulations were struck down because of a procedural defect: the Secretary issued the rules without providing due notice and offering a period for public comment (a violation of the federal Administrative Procedures Act).[9]

The Secretary later issued new regulations properly following the Administrative Procedures Act guidelines ("Baby Doe III"). Under these new regulations the Department maintained its investigatory and enforcement roles, but mandated that state child protective services develop processes to review such cases and local health care institutions were encouraged to establish "Infant Care Review Committees."

In time these regulations were also struck down. The American Medical Association and the American Hospital Association filed suit asserting that § 504 of the Rehabilitation Act of 1973 did not authorize the Secretary's actions in promulgating the regulations in the first place. After making its way through the lower courts, in 1986 the case was ultimately decided against the Department by the U.S. Supreme Court.[10] The Court said that the hospital did not discriminate against Baby Doe by refusing treatment because it was the parents who refused to authorize the recommended surgery. The Court also agreed with the Associations that the Secretary had exceeded statutory authority in adopting the Baby Doe regulations.

Suggestion for Additional Reading. Pence GE. *Classic Cases in Medical Ethics: Accounts of the Cases That Have Shaped Medical Ethics, with Philosophical, Legal, and Historical Backgrounds.* New York: McGraw Hill, 2004, pp. 219-226.

HOW DO FEDERAL
AND STATE JUDGES CREATE LAW?

In medieval England, the King personally settled disputes between his subjects, often openly in the company of courtiers (his court). When unable to sit in judgment himself, the monarch appointed a deputy to try (or judge) the case. The judge sometimes traveled the countryside on a prearranged visitation schedule (or circuit) so that parties would not have to attend the King at court (instead the circuit court would meet near them, saving time and expense, and permitting poorer subjects the same right to be heard as those who could afford to travel greater distances). Moreover, after the judges rendered decisions, they explained their reasons—based on findings of fact and beliefs about the area's customary practices—to those in court so that subjects could come to understand the rules (really what proved to be binding conventions) necessary to live peaceably with one another. As the judges journeyed from one locale to another, they confronted similar cases and usually made decisions involving like circumstances in the same way as they had earlier in other sites (the previous decisions serving as precedents for later ones). Over time, the people came to understand the rules that were common to them all (the "common law"). Therefore, common law evolved from judicial decisions as opposed to royal proclamations. It became a set of rules (based on custom) that grew—in a case-by-case fashion—from the experiences of the people and the collective wisdom of their ruler's authorized representatives.

Later, lawyers and clerks (reporters) began to compile recollections or reports of these oral decisions in case books (law reports) for future reference by other subjects, their attorneys, and judges and for educational purposes (to train judges and lawyers). Even later, the judges themselves wrote down their grounds for making decisions; these opinions were published in official reports. If more than one judge was asked to help in resolving a case, there might be multiple opinions. If the judges were split on deciding a case in a particular way, then one judge wrote a majority opinion (for those judges who voted in the majority) while another wrote the minority or dissenting view (for those judges voting in the minority). Occasionally, there would be a number of majority and minority opinions or plurality decisions. Sometimes, judges would agree on the result of a case, but not on the legal reasoning that lead to the result; thus, some would write concurring opinions to record the differences in interpretation.

When concerns about bias and unfairness surfaced, the King instituted a mechanism to review individual judges' decisions. If subjects were not satisfied with the ruling in a circuit court, they could appeal directly to the King for redress. The King might affirm (uphold) or reverse or modify or remand (send back for another determination) the lower court judgment. As the population grew, and the King no longer had time to be involved with appeals personally, he appointed a group of experienced judges to hear the appeals (an appeals court). The King, however, retained ultimate judicial authority by appointing the judges and maintaining final appellate jurisdiction. By the Victorian era, the House of Lords had become the appeals court of last resort for the realm.

Over the centuries, much of the common law—as administered by the King's Bench judges—became relatively fixed and inflexible. Judges had agreed that future decisions should be based on previous opinions or precedents (requiring judges to decide similar cases in similar ways). They felt this would ensure stability in the law. They felt this legal doctrine (called *stare decisis,* Latin for "let the decision stand") best allowed subjects to understand legal limits and accepted standards. In such a system though, judges were not always willing to change prior interpretations of the law to meet different circumstances (i.e., to overturn prior precedents). Some appeals cases resulted because this stern judicial interpretation of the law caused unfair hardships (e.g., a judge might order the sale of a sentimental heirloom, distributing equal shares to beneficiaries because the family could not agree on an acceptable disposition). By the early 1600s, the King's chancellor (often a church officer, sometimes called the "King's conscience") began hearing these "fairness" appeals. Shortly afterward, the chancellor's court (or chancery court) was formally empowered to hear cases in which there was no adequate remedy at law (e.g., partition of land, specific performance of contracts, adoption, divorce, probate, and estate settlements—cases in which one needed redress for circumstances that money damages could not be calculated easily or would be inadequate). It was this need for nonmonetary judgments that led to the development of "courts of equity" to ensure justice to litigants.

At the time the Thirteen Colonies declared their independence from Great Britain, most states had sophisticated, separate—and quite functional—circuit (law) and chancery (equity) trial courts, with higher courts to hear appeals. Different law and equity subject matter jurisdiction for each court flowed along the historical lines that had evolved in England over the centuries. Circuit courts exercised authority over the traditional law cases: punishing offenders for crimes against the state (criminal trials) and awarding money damages between litigants (civil trials). Chancery courts awarded judgments in cases for which there was no exact remedy of law. Over the past two hundred years, however, the stark distinction between *law* and *equity* has blurred to the point that most states have one trial level court with general jurisdiction (in some states it is called the circuit court, in others it is the district court or court of common pleas). All states have an appeals court of last resort, though called by various names (e.g., the supreme court, the supreme judicial court, or the court of appeals).

Parallel with state courts are federal courts. In the federal courts system, there is one trial level court that has civil, criminal, and equity jurisdiction—the U.S. district court. Each state has at least one. Aggrieved parties may appeal to the U. S. Circuit Court of Appeals for the particular circuit (area of the country) in which the district court is located. Appeals from the circuit courts are made to the U.S. Supreme Court. Appeals to the Supreme Court are discretionary; the nine justices decide which appeals to hear. They usually hear cases of important national interest or cases that are problematic because of inter-circuit conflicts (which result from varying interpretations of the same federal law by circuit judges in different circuits).

Not every case is a "federal case"; that is, not every possible disagreement can be litigated in a federal court. Federal court jurisdiction extends to cases and controversies that involve (1) a specified monetary amount, and (2) a federal question or has opposing parties that have diversity of citizenship. By federal question jurisdiction, the case must involve interpretation of a federal law (e.g., a Constitutional provision, a federal statute or regulation, or a treaty section). By diversity of citizenship, the opposing parties must be residents of different states (out-of-state litigants might prefer a federal court forum over a state court to lessen risk of local bias). By a vast margin, state courts hear the majority of cases tried in the United States. Appeals from state courts of last resort may be made to the U.S. Supreme Court if a federal question is involved.

Illustrating Case Law in Practice:
The Right to Refuse Medical Treatment

The *Cruzan* case[11] offers a remarkable example of how the courts create law. Before the landmark (i.e., precedent-setting) case was decided, it was not unequivocally clear that Americans had a federal constitutional right to refuse medical treatment. (Remember that individual liberties and rights emanate from some legal authority: constitution, statute, regulation, or common law.) Since the federal Constitution is "the supreme law of the land," personal rights derived directly from the Constitution are of special importance. Many of the most treasured personal liberties of U.S. citizens are specifically enumerated in the Constitution (e.g., the freedom to assemble, to worship, and to speak). Other rights, though not expressly stated in the original 1787 document (or as amended), have been recognized over the years—by the courts, most particularly by the U.S. Supreme Court—as being the freedoms understood by the Framers as essential for "life, liberty, and the pursuit of happiness" (e.g., the right to privacy[12]). These constitutional rights are sometimes labeled "fundamental rights" or "liberty interests." Fundamental constitutional rights cannot be abridged by governments without demonstrating some even greater countervailing state interest that has to be defended. So, if it were determined—in the last analysis by the U.S. Supreme Court—that the Constitution guarantees citizens the right to refuse medical treatment, then governments would not only be prohibited from creating barriers to its effective free exercise, but should fiercely protect it.

At the time of the *Cruzan* case (1990), it was universally understood that physicians could not touch patients without permission, except in cases of emergency (and even then, the law presumes the permission of the patient). To do so would be a battery, an act that might subject those involved to civil damages and criminal prosecution. In fact, during the time period known as the Medical Malpractice Crisis I (1972-1974), when the number of malpractice cases against physicians rose sevenfold, many liability cases turned on whether the doctor had obtained informed consent from the patient prior to surgery or initiating the proffered treatment. (The doctrine of informed consent had evolved in the common law and was recognized by all the states either by statute or case law.)

It seems a reasonable corollary that patients—who have the right to *accept* medical treatment by giving informed consent—have a corresponding and comparable right to *refuse* treatment, even life-sustaining treatment. (This is widely-accepted in the case of competent, adult Jehovah's Witnesses who—in the free exercise of their fundamental constitutional right to religious freedom—may refuse life-saving blood transfusions.) However, because (1) there was a slight factual difference between the two—requiring informed *consent* before proceeding with treatment versus insuring informed *refusal* before withholding or withdrawing treatment—and (2) there were no statutes and very few court cases that addressed the issues precisely, it was not crystal clear that patients could refuse life-sustaining treatment without some risk—civil, criminal, or administrative—attaching to those providing (ergo subsequently withholding) health care. After all, many thought physicians were obligated to act to preserve life (i.e., physiologic life) if at all possible (and at all costs), and felt they might be liable if they did not. Besides physicians and hospitals, others were uncomfortable with the lack of legal lucidity: special interest groups (including right-to-life organizations, handicapped persons associations, terminally ill patients' representatives, and euthanasia advocates), health care malpractice defense attorneys, and prosecutors. Compounding the uncertainty associated with the varying legal worries was the confusion that resulted from diverse state courts and lower federal courts opinions in the few "right to die" or treatment refusal cases[13] with similar, but not quite exact, fact patterns (notably the early ones: *Quinlan*,[14] *Saikewicz*,[15] *Dinnerstein*,[16] *Eichner*,[17] *Storar*,[18] *Conroy*,[19] *Brophy*,[20] and *Bouvia*[21]).

Parenthetically, the differing fact pattern (or contextual variations) issue is very important to judges and attorneys who search for precedents in the law; the closer the particular facts of the case at bar to the facts of a previously reported case, the greater its precedent value. Consequently, the fact that the patient is incompetent versus competent when the treatment decision has to be made matters a good deal if there is no prior decision on that point of law. It would be correspondingly important to compare facts of cases to learn if the patient were a child versus an adult, or had ever had legal capacity to make treatment decisions versus had capacity at one time but now has lost that capacity, or had an independent legal guardian versus a guardian ad litem (a guardian appointed just for the lawsuit) or was a ward of the state.

The *Cruzan* case did provide the unchallengeable answer to the federal constitutional right question (via one grudging sentence given as if not really wanting to address the point directly) in the Court's majority opinion, written by Chief Justice William H. Rehnquist, to wit: "The principle that a competent person has a constitutionally protected liberty interest in refusing unwanted medical treatment may be inferred from our prior decisions."[22] Moreover, the one sentence that answered the question was dicta. (Dictum or the plural dicta—Latin for "saying" or "sayings"—is used by lawyers to describe statements appearing in reported opinions that are instructive for purposes of interpreting the law, but were not actually used by the court in making the decision about that case. Dicta are useful in making legal analyses, but not as helpful as finding a precedent in which the point of law under discussion is the point of law the judge or judges used making the decision.) And, unfortunately, the federal interpretation of the right to refuse medical treatment was not beneficial to the *Cruzan* plaintiffs who sought relief from the courts.

The facts of *Cruzan* are straightforward. Around midnight, on January 10-11, 1983, the car that Nancy Beth Cruzan was driving skidded on an icy road in rural Missouri. There was an unwitnessed accident. The state trooper who came upon the scene some minutes later found Cruzan face down in a shallow, water-filled ditch, about thirty-five feet from her overturned automobile. She had no pulse or respirations at that time. Emergency medical technicians arrived shortly afterward and began resuscitative efforts. It is believed that she was anoxic for approximately twelve to fourteen minutes. She was removed to the nearest acute care hospital for treatment. By the time she arrived at that facility, she had heart and respiratory function. She never regained consciousness after the accident.

Approximately three weeks later, while Cruzan was still in a coma, a feeding tube was placed for artificial delivery of fluids and food (with the consent of her then-husband). She remained in the acute care facility for some time, but was later moved to a rehabilitation hospital. After eight months in the rehabilitation unit, she was taken to a state long-term care facility. She was artificially provided nutrition and (food and water) thereafter. Throughout this entire timeframe, she remained in a coma. Undoubtedly, she met the criteria of being in a persistent vegetative state (PVS). No one questioned the medical conclusion that she would never awaken or that if fluids and food were withheld she would die shortly thereafter.

In 1988—five years after the accident, with Nancy Beth Cruzan still comatose (in PVS)—her parents and co-guardians, Lester and Joyce

Cruzan, asked the facility staff (primarily, the physicians and administrators) to withhold the artificial feedings and let their daughter die. The staff, however, would not do so without express permission from a court. The Cruzans filed their complaint (really, their request for relief) in the Jasper County Probate Court. After an evidentiary hearing (in which the parents and a friend testified that Cruzan would not want to be maintained as she was in PVS), Judge Charles E. Teel, Jr. ruled that Nancy Beth Cruzan had a fundamental right, under the Missouri and United States Constitutions, to refuse medical treatment or direct the withdrawal of "death-prolonging procedures." He issued an opinion to that effect and absolved the facility staff of any liability that might arise as a result of her death from withholding life-sustaining treatment. The state attorney general (as counsel for the state hospital) appealed this decision to the Missouri Supreme Court.

The Missouri Supreme Court, in a contentious 4 to 3 decision, reversed Judge Teel's ruling.[23] This court agreed that Cruzan did have the right to refuse medical treatment—a right they found in Missouri common law and in the U.S. Supreme Court's *Roe v. Wade* opinion (which established the federal constitutional right to abortion). However, the judges also said that the right to refuse medical treatment was an inherently personal right, one that could only be exercised by the individual personally, or by another acting with the express authority of the individual, or by one who could show by "clear and convincing" evidence the individual's wishes regarding treatment. The court held that there were four counterbalancing "state interests" (adopted from the *Quinlan* case years before) that weighed in their judgment against permitting the parents "absolute" freedom in making the decision for their incompetent daughter: the state's obligation to preserve life, the need to prevent homicide and suicide, the protection of innocent third parties from potential abuse, and the maintenance of the ethical integrity of the medical profession. They found that the Missouri legislature intended to protect life as much as possible when it enacted the Missouri Uniform Rights of the Terminally Ill Act in 1986 after substantially revising the recommended uniform statute (so as to specifically exclude medical procedures to provide nutrition and hydration from the definition suggested for "death-prolonging procedure"). The judges further held that the evidence offered at trial was not "clear and convincing" as to Nancy Beth Cruzan's wishes regarding refusal of life-sustaining medical treatment. ("Clear and convincing" is an evidentiary standard required for proof in some instances just as evidence "beyond a reasonable doubt" is essential for a criminal conviction, "a preponderance of the evidence" is necessary in most civil trials, and "suspicion" is all that is needed to report child or elder abuse.)

The three dissenting justices (who authored two opinions) were very quick to point out problems with the majority view and appeared quite frustrated with their colleagues.

On appeal, the U.S. Supreme Court affirmed the Missouri Supreme Court in a narrow five to four decision. At the very end of their written opinion the majority justices said:

> In sum, we conclude that a State [like Missouri] may apply a clear and convincing evidence standard in proceedings where a guardian seeks to discontinue nutrition and hydration of a person diagnosed to be in a persistent vegetative state. . . . The Supreme Court of Missouri held in this case the testimony adduced at trial did not amount to clear and convincing proof of the patient's desire to have hydration and nutrition withdrawn. . . . The testimony adduced at trial consisted primarily of Nancy Cruzan's statements made to a housemate about a year before her accident that she would not want to live should she face life as a "vegetable," and other observations to the same effect. The observations did not deal in terms with withdrawal of medical treatment or hydrations or nutrition. We cannot say that the Supreme Court of Missouri committed constitutional error in reaching the conclusion that it did.
>
> Petitioners [Cruzan's parents] alternatively contend that Missouri must accept the "substituted judgment" of close family members even in the absence of substantial proof that their views reflect the views of the patient. . . . [W]e do not think the Due Process Clause [of the Fourteenth Amendment to the Constitution] requires the State to repose judgment on these matters with anyone but the patient herself. Close family members may have a strong feeling—a feeling not at all ignoble or unworthy, but not entirely disinterested, either—that they do not wish the continuation of the life of a loved one which they regard as hopeless, meaningless, and even degrading. But there is no automatic assurance that the view of close family members will necessarily be the same as the patient's would have been had she been confronted with the prospect of her situation while competent. All the reasons previously discussed for allowing Missouri to require clear and convincing evidence of the patient's wishes lead us to conclude that the State may choose to defer only to those wishes, rather than confide the decision to close family members.[24]

As one can read, the Court really only considered whether the Missouri Supreme Court's holding violated the federal Constitution (a very narrow procedural question). The Court did not deal chiefly with the federal constitutional right of competent adult citizens to refuse medical treatment; had the Chief Justice not stated, almost as an aside, that one existed by inference from previous decisions, it still might be unclear. However, now it has been delineated by an authority recognized by the people to make such a determination. Of course, other questions remain. Whether a future court in another jurisdiction will rule similarly—for other patients who lack capacity, for children (or others who have never been competent), for patients with terminal illness or infirmities not the result of accident—is open for debate. Also, notably the Court said the right to refuse treatment was its own "liberty interest," not one derived from the "right to privacy."

Suggestion for Additional Reading. Pence GE. *Classic Cases in Medical Ethics: Accounts of the Cases That Have Shaped Medical Ethics, with Philosophical, Legal, and Historical Backgrounds.* New York: McGraw Hill, 2004, pp. 40-43; and White BD, Singer PA, Iserson KV, Siegler M. What does *Cruzan* mean to the practicing physician? *Arch Intern Med* 1991;151:5:925-928.

Appendix 2

Continuing Dilemmas Involving Drugs, Ethics, and Quality of Life: An Outline for Further Discussion

Legal cases that pose ethical dilemmas may be quite informative and enlightening in discussing moral problems, but there are many other instructional possibilities as well. In their book *A Philosophical Basis of Medical Practice,* Edmund Pellegrino and David Thomasma wrote that "any act which applies knowledge to persons involves values and consequently falls into the moral realm."[1] It is a very broad characterization, one encompassing many endeavors and professional fields. Because of the nature of the "calling" of medicine and pharmacy and the intimacy of the provider-patient relationship Pellegrino and Thomasma describe, the message is applicable to all those practicing the healing arts. Their statement established their foundational argument for the overarching theme that doctors need to think about and understand ethics as applied to medicine and medical encounters in order to be good physicians.

Robert Buerki and Louis Vottero quoted this very sentence as the ultimate justification for pharmacists likewise to study ethics, and they continued:

> While some pharmacists may feel uncomfortable using the term "moral" to describe their everyday behavior toward their patients, most would agree that they often make professional decisions based upon what is "good" for the patient, rather than upon what may be scientifically or legally "correct."[2]

(With this pithy introduction to philosophical concepts, Buerki and Vottero went on in the pages immediately following to discuss beneficence, non-maleficence, justice, autonomy, veracity, confidentiality, ideals, and virtues.[3] One might note too that their philosophical discussion as such only began about halfway through their text, relatively long after they considered various decision-making frameworks and hypothetical scenarios.)

Regardless, one might take issue with the Buerki and Vottero rationalization and extension into professional morals for at least four reasons. *First,* those making decisions that resolve ethical or moral dilemmas may never be completely "comfortable" with the results. *Comfort* denotes "ease" or "relief," not necessarily peace of mind.[4] Decision makers may be uneasy about the resolution of an ethics question for many weeks, months, years, perhaps for the remainder of their lives. For some decision makers the resolution may be quite troubling, even haunting. Thus, it might be better for those making decisions to think in terms of "being at peace" with the resolution, rather than being "comfortable." Being at peace with their motive, or intent, or an act, or the consequences, or all or some of these elements, implies that decision makers made a better rather than a worse decision— perhaps even the best decision instead of the worst-given the circumstances, the context (as Jonsen-Siegler-Winslade would phrase it[5]) of the case. "Being at peace" also expresses the notion that the decision makers at least tried or made a laudable effort to do the best they could in resolving the dilemma, and can live with the resulting outcome better than another.

Second, "what is 'good' for the patient" may be beyond the decisional reach of any particular pharmacist, physician, drug manufacturer, regulator, or anyone else in the drug distribution chain. True, making a decision in the patient's best interests seems essential in resolving a moral dilemma. However, often the facts are not completely known and what the patient thinks is "good" may be entirely different from what the professionals believe. *Third,* there may not be a "scientifically . . . 'correct'" resolution, or even the best statistical approximation. The scientific evidence in many cases remains uncertain. Respected scientific investigators may be completely opposite one another in reaching conclusions. There may never be scientific agreement on a particular issue. And *fourth,* the "legally 'correct'" decision may not be the morally acceptable one. The law may not be a better guide for decision makers. Or, the legal—like the scientific—answer too may be uncertain. One might reason from the Buerki-Vottero statements that they thoroughly understood that the scientific or legal solution might be at odds with the patient's "good."

In the end though, the Buerki-Vottero resolution quatrad (being at peace-believing that one acted beneficently-assuring scientific rigor—meeting legal requirements) allows decision makers some supporting construct in troublesome cases. It may even prove a quick check to certify a decision. Moreover, the Buerki-Vottero reflection demonstrates again how pervasive drug availability and use ethical dilemmas are in American society today and how difficult it is to settle some of the questions, at least in the short term.

However, the paradigm still begs the question: So what additional moral dilemmas do pharmacists, physicians, and those providing drugs to patients confront in practice? One only has to consider a few newspaper, journal, or Internet articles to establish the range and offer additional topics for discussion about drugs, ethics, and quality of life.

TOPICS RELATED TO DRUG USE

Quality of Life Generally

- Pollack A. Quality of life found equal with 2 breast cancer drugs; but kind of side effects varies, study says. *New York Times.* 2006;Jun 6:A19.
- Carey B. Mute 19 years, he helps reveal brain's mysteries. *New York Times.* 2006;Jul 4:A1, A12.

Drugs that Prevent Illness

Immunizations Generally

- Manning A. Polio vaccine hits landmark; disease nearly gone thanks to efforts launched in 1954. *USA Today.* 2004;Apr 20:6D.
- Zhou F, Harpaz R, Jumaan AO, Winston CA, Shefer A. Impact of varicella vaccination on health care utilization. *JAMA.* 2005;294: 797-802.
- McNeil DG Jr. Rotavirus drugs deemed safe and effective; 2 vaccines treat top cause of diarrhea in infants worldwide. *New York Times.* 2006;Jan 6:A12.
- Harris G. Vaccine against diarrhea-causing virus is approved. *New York Times.* 2006;Feb 4:A10.
- Stone A. Senate provision would inoculate vaccine makers; lawsuit protection has staunch allies, vehement critics. *USA Today.* 2005;Dec 15:8A.

Immunizations and Autism

- Manning A. Autism's surge mystifies; broader definition of disorder fails to explain dramatic rise in number of children afflicted. *USA Today.* 2004;May 18:8D.
- Harris G, O'Connor A. On autism's cause, it's parents v. research. *New York Times.* 2005;Jun 25:A1, A10.

- Manning A. Mistrust rises with autism rate; role of vaccines still disputed [Cover Story]. *USA Today.* 2005;Jul 5:1D, 2D.
- Autism link unproven [Editorial]. *USA Today.* 2005;Jul 6:14A.
- Diekema DS and the Committee on Bioethics [Clinical Report]. Responding to parental refusals of immunization in children. *Pediatrics.* 2005;115:1428-1431.

Epidemics, Vaccines, and Preventative Drugs

- Santora M. How New York City coped with the flu vaccine scare: It scrounged. *New York Times.* 2005;Jan 10:A17.
- Schmit J. USA got improperly made flu vaccine; FDA reports recurring problems at British plant since 1999 [Cover Story]. *USA Today.* 2005;Feb 10:1A, 10A.
- Schmit J. Tamiflu maker treads minefield; profit, global reputation depend on drug's ability to counter avian flu. *USA Today.* 2005;Dec 7:A1.

Drugs that Impact Pregnancy

Drugs that Enhance the Possibility of Pregnancy

- Szabo L. America's first "test-tube baby" [Cover Story]. *USA Today.* 2004;May 13:8D.
- Leigh S. Fertility patients deserve to know the odds—and the risks. *USA Today.* 2004;Jul 7:11A.

Drugs that Prevent Pregnancies

- Clot risk for birth-control patch is found to be double that of pill. *New York Times.* 2006;Feb 18:A9.

Drugs that Terminate Pregnancies

- Johnson K. Harm to fetuses becomes issue in Utah and elsewhere. *New York Times.* 2004;Mar 27:A9.
- Biskupic J. Abortion-notification case could test changing court. *USA Today.* 2005;Nov 30:4A.
- Greenhouse L. Justices to review federal ban on disputed abortion method. *New York Times.* 2006;Feb 22:A1, A14.
- Greenberger SS. Romney vetoes law on pill, takes aim at Roe vs. Wade. Boston.com. 2005; Jul 26. Available at http://www.boston.com/news/local/articles/2005/07/26/romney_vetoes_law_on_pill_takes_aim_at_roe_v_wade/ (accessed July 3, 2006).

Drugs that Cure or Minimize Acute Illnesses

- Blumenthal R. Hodgkin's returns to girl whose parents fought state. *New York Times.* 2005;Jun 11:A8.
- Driggs AE. The mature minor doctrine: do adolescents have the right to die. *JAMA.* 2001;291:687-717.
- Wilson B. The rise and fall of laetrile. Quackwatch.org. 2004; Feb. 17. Available at http://www.quackwatch.org/01QuackeryRelatedTopics/Cancer/laetrile.html (accessed July 3, 2006).
- F.D.A. approves new antibiotic from Wyeth. *New York Times.* 2005; Jun 17:C4.

Drugs that Minimize Symptoms in Chronic Conditions

- Berenson A. A ray of hope for diabetes. *New York Times.* 2006;Mar 2:C1, C4.
- Stolberg SG. House rejects coverage of impotence pills. *New York Times.* 2005;Jun 25:A8.
- Berenson A. A daily pill to combat impotence? Makers of Cialis foresee a market. *New York Times.* 2006;Jun 16:C1, C4.
- Pollack A. Viagra gains some advocates as treatment for lung disease. *New York Times.* 2004;Apr 10:B1, B4.
- Grady D. Doctors put hope in thin wires for a life in epilepsy's clutches. *New York Times.* 2004;May 24:A1, A19.
- Saul S. F.D.A. panel approves heart remedy for Blacks. *New York Times.* 2005;Jun 17:C4.

Drugs that Control Symptoms of Mental Illness

- Mahler J. The antidepressant dilemma. *New York Times Magazine.* 2004;Nov 21. Available at http://www.nytimes.com/2004/11/21/magazine/21TEENS.html?ex=1258693200&en=c6fb4c379526cff0&ei=5090&partner=rssuserland (accessed July 3, 2006).
- Meier B. Boy's murder case entangled in fight over antidepressants. *New York Times.* 2004;Aug 23:A1, A14.
- Elias M. Company hid link between Prozac, suicide. *USA Today.* 2005;Jan 6:2A.
- Carey B. Little difference found in schizophrenia drugs. *New York Times.* 2005;Sep 20:A1.
- Elias M. More kids get multiple psychiatric drugs. *USA Today.* 2005; Aug 2:6D.

Drugs that Control Exaggerated Behaviors

- Elias M. Number of adults on ADHD drugs doubles. *USA Today.* 2005;Sep 15:8D.
- Rubin R. Warnings advised on ADHD drugs [Cover Story]. *USA Today.* 2006;Feb 10-12:1A.
- Rubin R. "Smart Pills" make headway [Cover Story]. *USA Today.* 2004;Jul 8:D1.
- Elliott VS. Genetic profile may clarify ADHD drug response. *American Medical News.* 2005;Sep 26:26.
- Elliott VS. Marked increase shown in adult ADHD drug treatment. *American Medical News.* 2005;Oct 10:28-29.

Drugs that Relieve Relatively Minor Symptoms (Over-the-Counter or OTC Drugs)

- Kaplan T. The Tylenol crisis: How effective public relations saved Johnson & Johnson. The Pennsylvania State University, 1998. Available at http://www.personal.psu.edu/users/w/x/wxk116/tylenol/crisis.html (accessed July 3, 2006).
- Tahmincioglu E. Over the counter, yes, but out of the insurance plan. *New York Times.* 2004;Jul 4:B5.
- Chan, AT. Long-term use of aspirin and nonsteroidal anti-inflammatory drugs and risk of colorectal cancer. *JAMA.* 2005:294:914-923.
- Saul S. F.D.A. panel votes against sale of statins over counter. *New York Times.* 2005;Jan 15:B1, B2.
- Hampton T. More scrutiny for dietary supplements? *JAMA.* 2005; 293:27-28.

Drugs Used for Nonmedical Purposes

Recreational Drugs

- Butterfield F. Fighting an illegal drug through its legal source. *New York Times.* 2005;Jan 30:18B.
- Leinwand D. Drug makers take action to foil meth cooks. *USA Today.* 2005;Jun 29:3A.
- Davey M. Grisly effect of one drug: "meth mouth." *New York Times.* 2005;Jun 11:A1, A10.
- Kilgannon C. Methadone as ingredient for a cross-addiction. *New York Times.* 2005;Oct 6:A31.

- Rubin R. Addiction has many fathers, science finds [Cover Story]. *USA Today.* 2005;Oct 10:D1, D2.
- Zernike K. F.D.A.'s report illuminates wide divide on marijuana. *New York Times.* 2006;Apr 22:A9.
- Healy M. Drug ecstasy may help cancer patients. *USA Today.* 2004; Dec 28:7D.

Performance-Enhancing Drugs

- Dreifus C. Olympian talent, and a little artificial help. *New York Times.* 2004;Aug 3:D5.
- Mehlman MJ. What's wrong with using drugs in sports? nothing. *USA Today.* 2004;Aug 1:2:13A.
- Kepner T. Baseball sets tougher policy on steroid use. *New York Times.* 2005;Jan 14:1A, C19.
- Moore DL. As steroid use doubles, a school fights back [Cover Story]. *USA Today.* 2005;May 5:1A, 2A.

Generics

- Feder BJ. When F.D.A. says yes, but insurers say no. *New York Times.* 2005;Jul 6:C1, C5.
- Harris G. Lucrative drug, danger signals and the F.D.A. *New York Times.* 2005;Jun 10:C1, C6.
- Harris G. New drugs hit the market, but promised trials go undone. *New York Times.* 2006;Mar 4:A8.

Drugs as "Market Goods"

Drugs and the Marketplace

- Willing R. Patients' case gets cool response. *USA Today.* 2004;Mar 24:B1.
- Hubbard W. End to ban on reimported drugs is good medicine. *USA Today.* 2004;Aug 23:10A.
- Pear R. U.S. appeals court backs state effort at drug cost control. *New York Times.* 2004;Apr 6:A19.
- Pear R, Dao J. States trying new tactics to reduce spending on drugs. *New York Times.* 2004;Nov 21:27.
- Pear R. Administration gives mixed views on drug imports. *New York Times.* 2004;Dec 22:A1, A20.

- Hallam K. PacifiCare has eye on Medicare drug benefit. *The Orange County Register.* 2005;Jun 11:B3.
- Tadesse LB, Goldblatt J. Many farmers can't afford health insurance coverage. *USA Today.* 2004;Mar 23:6B.
- Cauchon D. Workers swelling rolls of Medicaid; many choose it over private health plans. *USA Today.* 2005;Aug 2:1A.

Worldwide Drug Availability in an Open Market

- Scott J. Drug trials on children violated rules, federal officials say. *New York Times.* 2005;Jun 17:A21.
- Sternberg S. HIV hits a new plateau. *USA Today.* 2005;Jun 14:9D.
- Santora M. US is close to eliminating AIDS in infants, officials say. *New York Times.* 2005;Jan 30:A1, A22.
- Dee J. I was an AIDS baby. *New York Times Magazine.* 2005;Jun 26:2:35-41.
- Reynolds G. Will any organ do? *New York Times Magazine.* 2005;Jul 10:37.

TOPICS RELATED TO PROFESSIONAL VIRTUES

- Draper R. The toxic pharmacist. *New York Times Magazine.* 2003; Jun 8. Available at http://query.nytimes.com/gst/fullpage.html?sec= health&res=9502E2DA1230F93BA35755C0A9659C8B63 (accessed July 4, 2006).
- Thirty year sentence for druggist. *New York Times.* 2002;Dec. 6. Available at http://query.nytimes.com/gst/fullpage.html?res=980CE 3D8133BF935A35751C1A9649C8B63 (accessed July 4, 2006).
- Lawyers say drug makers know of dilute products. *New York Times.* 2002;Aug 7. Available at http://query.nytimes.com/gst/fullpage.html? res=980CE3D8133BF935A35751C1A9649C8B63 (accessed July 4, 2006).
- Grady D. Doctors see way to cut risks of suffering in lethal injection. *New York Times.* 2006;Jun 23:A1, A25.
- Walsh MW. Wide U.S. inquiry into purchasing for health care; subpoenas to suppliers; case appears to focus on possible overcharging in sales to hospitals. *New York Times.* 2004;Aug 21:A1, B14.
- Saul S. Senate leader calls for limits on drug ads. *New York Times.* 2005;Jul2:B13.
- Berenson A. Pfizer fires a vice president who criticized the company's sales practices. *New York Times.* 2005;Dec 5:C3.

- Appleby J. States want to know more about drugmakers' gifts to doctors; nine consider bills requiring disclosure. *USA Today.* 2006; Feb 17:4B.
- Robezneiks A. Would you fib for your patient? *American Medical News.* 2005;Jun 13:13-14.
- Croasdale M. Psychologists in La., N.M. are certified to prescribe. *American Medical News.* 2005;May 16:7-8.
- Smith EB, Rubin R, McCoy K. Medical journal says Vioxx data withheld. *USA Today.* 2005;Dec 9:1B.

Notes

PREFACE

1. Zernike K. A drug scourge creates its own form of orphan; methamphetamine is sending children to strained agencies. *New York Times*. 2005;Jul 11:A1, A11.

2. Szabo L. "Targeted" cancer treatment effective in older patients. *USA Today*. 2005;Dec 14:9D.

3. Pear R. President tells insurers to aid new drug plan; confusion over benefits; cost caps for the poor and 30 days of medicine ordered. *New York Times*. 2006;Jan 16:A1, A12.

4. Pollack AW, Berenson A. U.S. regulators approve insulin in inhaled form; alternative to injection; some doctors concerned about lung impact—Pfizer to sell soon. *New York Times*. 2006;Jan 28:A1, A11.

INTRODUCTION

1. Pellegrino ED. Character, virtue, and self-interest in the ethics of the professions. The Jack W. Provonsha Lecture. Given at Loma Linda, Calif, on Feb 15, 1989.

2. Pellegrino ED, Thomasma DC. *A Philosophical Basis of Medical Practice*. New York, NY: Oxford University Press, 1981, p. 193.

3. Pellegrino ED. Character, virtue, and self-interest in the ethics of the professions. The Jack W. Provonsha Lecture. Given at Loma Linda, Calif, on Feb 15, 1989.

4. Pellegrino ED, Thomasma DC. *For the Patient's Good*. New York, NY: Oxford University Press, 1988, p. 50.

5. Pellegrino ED. Character, virtue, and self-interest in the ethics of the professions. The Jack W. Provonsha Lecture. Given at Loma Linda, Calif, on Feb 15, 1989.

6. Pellegrino ED. Professionalism, profession and virtues of the good physician. *Mount Sinai J. Med*. 2002;69:378-384.

7. Pellegrino ED. Professionalism, profession and virtues of the good physician. *Mount Sinai J. Med*. 2002;69:378-384.

8. Pellegrino ED. Professionalism, profession and virtues of the good physician. *Mount Sinai J. Med*. 2002;69:378-384.

9. Pellegrino ED, Thomasma DC. *For the Patient's Good*. New York, NY: Oxford University Press, 1988, p. 66.

10. Pellegrino ED, Thomasma DC. *For the Patient's Good*. New York, NY: Oxford University Press, 1988, p. 32.

11. Pellegrino ED, Thomasma DC. *The Virtues in Medical Practice*. New York, NY: Oxford University Press, 1993, p. 173.

12. Pellegrino ED, Thomasma DC. *The Virtues in Medical Practice*. New York, NY: Oxford University Press, 1993, p. 76.

13. Pellegrino ED, Thomasma DC. *The Virtues in Medical Practice*. New York, NY: Oxford University Press, 1993, pp. 78-80.

14. Pellegrino ED. Professionalism, profession and virtues of the good physician. *Mount Sinai J. Med.* 2002;69:378-384.

15. Pellegrino ED, Thomasma DC. *The Virtues in Medical Practice*. New York, NY: Oxford University Press, 1993, p. 92.

16. Pellegrino ED, Thomasma DC. *The Virtues in Medical Practice*. New York, NY: Oxford University Press, 1993, p. 94.

17. Pellegrino ED, Thomasma DC. *The Virtues in Medical Practice*. New York, NY: Oxford University Press, 1993, p. 109.

18. Pellegrino ED, Thomasma DC. *The Virtues in Medical Practice*. New York, NY: Oxford University Press, 1993, p. 122.

19. Pellegrino ED, Thomasma DC. *The Virtues in Medical Practice*. New York, NY: Oxford University Press, 1993, p. 157.

20. Pellegrino ED, Thomasma DC. *The Virtues in Medical Practice*. New York, NY: Oxford University Press, 1993, p. 127.

21. Pellegrino ED, Thomasma DC. *The Virtues in Medical Practice*. New York, NY: Oxford University Press, 1993.

SPECIAL ADDITIONAL INTRODUCTION

1. Buerki RA, Vottero, LD. *Ethical Responsibility in Pharmacy Practice*. 2nd ed. Madison, Wis: American Institute of the History of Pharmacy, 2002, p. 233.

2. Fink III JL. Updating pharmacy's code of ethics. *US Pharm.* 1992;17:53-54.

3. Fink III JL. Updating the code of ethics. *Am Pharm.* 1994;NS34:80.

4. Buerki RA, Vottero LD. *Ethical Responsibility in Pharmacy Practice*. 2nd ed. Madison, Wis: American Institute of the History of Pharmacy, 2002, p. 42.

5. Buerki RA, Vottero LD. *Ethical Responsibility in Pharmacy Practice*. 2nd ed. Madison, Wis: American Institute of the History of Pharmacy, 2002, pp. 42-44.

6. Buerki RA, Vottero LD. *Ethical Responsibility in Pharmacy Practice*. 2nd ed. Madison, Wis: American Institute of the History of Pharmacy, 2002, p. 57.

7. *Code of Ethics for Pharmacists*. Washington, DC: American Pharmacists Association, 1994.

CHAPTER 1

1. 61 Fed. Reg. 44619-45318 (Aug 25, 1996).

2. *Food and Drug Administration (FDA), et al. v. Brown & Williamson Tobacco Corp. (Brown & Williamson), et al.*, 529 U.S. 120, 120 S.Ct. 1291 (2000).

3. 60 Fed. Reg. 41314-41787 (Aug 11, 1995).

4. *FDA v. Brown & Williamson,* 120 S.Ct. 1291 (2000) at 1297.

5. 61 Fed. Reg. 44619 (Aug 25, 1996) at 44397 and 44402.

6. 21 U.S.C. § 321(g)(1)(C).

7. *FDA v. Brown & Williamson,* 120 S.Ct. 1291 (2000) at 1296.

8. *FDA v. Brown & Williamson,* 120 S.Ct. 1291 (2000) at 1298, citing the regulation at 61 Fed. Reg. 44398 (Aug 25, 1996).

9. *FDA v. Brown & Williamson,* 120 S.Ct. 1291 (2000) at 1298, citing the regulation at 61 Fed. Reg. 44398 (Aug 25, 1996).

10. *FDA v. Brown & Williamson,* 120 S.Ct. 1291 (2000) at 1298, citing the regulation at 61 Fed. Reg. 44398-44399 (Aug 25, 1996).

11. *FDA v. Brown & Williamson,* 120 S.Ct. 1291 (2000) at 1298, citing the regulation at 61 Fed. Reg. 44398 (Aug 25, 1996).

12. *FDA v. Brown & Williamson,* 120 S.Ct. 1291 (2000) at 1320 (Breyer, J., dissenting), citing the regulation at 60 Fed. Reg. 41579 (Aug 11, 1995).

13. *FDA v. Brown & Williamson,* 120 S.Ct. 1291 (2000) at 1320 (Breyer, J., dissenting), citing the regulation at 61 Fed. Reg. 44814 (Aug 25, 1996).

14. *FDA v. Brown & Williamson,* 120 S.Ct. 1291 (2000) at 1298, citing the regulation at 61 Fed. Reg. 44398-44399 (Aug 25, 1996).

15. *FDA v. Brown & Williamson,* 120 S.Ct. 1291 (2000) at 1320 (Breyer, J., dissenting), citing the regulation at 61 Fed. Reg. 44704 (Aug 25, 1996).

16. *FDA v. Brown & Williamson,* 120 S.Ct. 1291 (2000) at 1298, citing the regulation at 61 Fed. Reg. 44399 (Aug 25, 1996).

17. *Coyne Beahm, Inc. v. FDA,* 966 F. Supp. 1374 (1997).

18. 2nd Bf. in Support of Plfs' Motion for Summary Judgment in No. 2:95CV 00591 (MDNC), in 3 Rec. in No. 97-1604 (CA4), Tab No. 40; and 3rd Bf. in Support of Plfs' Motion for Summary Judgment in No. 2:95CV00591 (MDNC), in 3 Rec. in No. 97-1604 (CA4), Tab No. 42.

19. 153 F.3d 155 (1998).

20. 526 U.S. 1086 (1999).

21. *FDA v. Brown & Williamson,* 120 S.Ct. 1291 (2000) at 1313-1314.

22. *FDA v. Brown & Williamson,* 120 S.Ct. 1291 (2000) at 1308.

23. *FDA v. Brown & Williamson,* 120 S.Ct. 1291 (2000) at 1306-1307.

24. *FDA v. Brown & Williamson,* 120 S.Ct. 1291 (2000) at 1308-1313.

25. *FDA v. Brown & Williamson,* 120 S.Ct. 1291 (2000) at 1301-1306.

26. *FDA v. Brown & Williamson,* 120 S.Ct. 1291 (2000) at 1301.

27. *FDA v. Brown & Williamson,* 120 S.Ct. 1291 (2000) at 1315.

28. *FDA v. Brown & Williamson,* 120 S.Ct. 1291 (2000) at 1317, 1319-1321 (Breyer, J., dissenting).

29. *FDA v. Brown & Williamson,* 120 S.Ct. 1291 (2000) at 1317, 1322-1327 (Breyer, J., dissenting).

30. *FDA v. Brown & Williamson,* 120 S.Ct. 1291 (2000) at 1331 (Breyer, J., dissenting).

31. Soukhanov AH, ex ed. *The American Heritage Dictionary of the English Language.* 3rd ed. Boston, Mass: Houghton Mifflin Company, 1992, p. 565.

32. Ansel HC, Allen LV Jr, Popovich NG. *Pharmaceutical Dosage Forms and Drug Delivery Systems.* 7th ed. Philadelphia, Pa: Lippincott Williams & Wilkins, 1999, p. 1.

33. Clark WG, Brater DC, Johnson AR. *Goth's Medical Pharmacology.* 13th ed. St. Louis, Mont Mo.: Mosby Year Book, 1992, p. 1.

34. Weil A, Rosen W. *From Chocolate to Morphine,* rev updated. Boston, Mass: Houghton Mifflin Company, 1993, p. 9.

35. Williams DA, Lemke TL. *Foye's Principles of Medicinal Chemistry.* 5th ed. Philadelphia, Pa: Lippincott Williams & Wilkins, 2002, p. 1.

36. Brecher EM, ed. *Licit and Illicit Drugs.* Mount Vernon, NY: Consumers Union, 1972, p. 209.

37. Brecher EM, ed. *Licit and Illicit Drugs.* Mount Vernon, NY: Consumers Union, 1972, p. 210.

38. Brecher EM, ed. *Licit and Illicit Drugs.* Mount Vernon, NY: Consumers Union, 1972, p. 220.

39. Vergano D. Study: Tobacco firms tried to weaken anti-smoking aids. *USA Today.* 2002;Aug 14:D7.

40. Soukhanov AH, ex ed. *The American Heritage Dictionary of the English Language.* 3rd ed. Boston, Mass: Houghton Mifflin Company, 1992, p. 630.

41. Ingram DB, Parks JA. *The Complete Idiot's Guide to Understanding Ethics.* Indianapolis, Ind: Alpha Books, 2002, p. 6.

42. Morris T. *Philosophy for Dummies.* Foster City, Calif: IDG Books Worldwide, Inc., 1999, p. 84.

43. Ingram DB, Parks JA. *The Complete Idiot's Guide to Understanding Ethics.* Indianapolis: Alpha Books, 2002, p. 19.

44. Ingram DB, Parks JA. *The Complete Idiot's Guide to Understanding Ethics.* Indianapolis, Ind: Alpha Books, 2002, p. 21.

45. Aristotle, *The Nicomachean Ethics* (Welldon JEC trans.). Amherst, NY: Prometheus Books, 1987.

46. Pence GE. *Classic Cases in Medical Ethics: Accounts of the Cases That Have Shaped Medical Ethics, with Philosophical, Legal, and Historical Backgrounds.* New York, NY: McGraw Hill, 2004, pp. 10-11.

47. Morris T. *Philosophy for Dummies.* Foster City, Calif: IDG Books Worldwide, Inc., 1999, p. 327.

48. Buerki RA, Vottero LD. *Ethical Responsibility in Pharmacy Practice.* Madison, Wis: American Institute of the History of Pharmacy, 1994.

49. Pence GE. *Classic Cases in Medical Ethics: Accounts of the Cases That Have Shaped Medical Ethics, with Philosophical, Legal, and Historical Backgrounds.* New York, NY: McGraw Hill, 2004, pp. 11-13.

50. Ingram DB, Parks JA. *The Complete Idiot's Guide to Understanding Ethics.* Indianapolis, Ind: Alpha Books, 2002, p. 9.

51. Pence GE. *Classic Cases in Medical Ethics: Accounts of the Cases That Have Shaped Medical Ethics, with Philosophical, Legal, and Historical Backgrounds.* New York, NY: McGraw Hill, 2004, pp. 13-14.

52. Butler J. *Five Sermons* (Darwall SL ed.). Indianapolis, Ind: Hackett Publishing Company, Inc., 1983.

53. Pence GE. *Classic Cases in Medical Ethics: Accounts of the Cases That Have Shaped Medical Ethics, with Philosophical, Legal, and Historical Backgrounds*. New York, NY: McGraw Hill, 2004, pp. 14-16.

54. Pence GE. *Classic Cases in Medical Ethics: Accounts of the Cases That Have Shaped Medical Ethics, with Philosophical, Legal, and Historical Backgrounds*. New York, NY: McGraw Hill, 2004, pp. 16-18.

55. Kant I. *Groundwork of the Metaphysic of Morals* (Paton HJ trans.). New York, NY: Harper & Row Publishers Inc. (Harper Torchbooks Imprint), 1964.

56. Pence GE. *Classic Cases in Medical Ethics: Accounts of the Cases That Have Shaped Medical Ethics, with Philosophical, Legal, and Historical Backgrounds*. New York, NY: McGraw Hill, 2004, pp. 18-21.

57. Lyons D. *The Forms and Limits of Utilitarianism*. Oxford, London: Clarendon Press, 1965.

58. Nietzsche F. *Beyond Good and Evil: Prelude to a Philosophy of the Future* (Kaufmann W, trans.). New York, NY: Random House (Vintage Books imprint), 1966.

59. Pence GE. *Classic Cases in Medical Ethics: Accounts of the Cases That Have Shaped Medical Ethics, with Philosophical, Legal, and Historical Backgrounds*. New York, NY: McGraw Hill, 2004, pp. 15-16.

60. Pence GE. *Classic Cases in Medical Ethics: Accounts of the Cases That Have Shaped Medical Ethics, with Philosophical, Legal, and Historical Backgrounds*. New York, NY: McGraw Hill, 2004, pp. 23-24.

61. Sherwin S. Feminist and medical ethics: Two different approaches to contextual ethics. In: Jecker NS, Jonsen AR, Pearlman RA, eds. *Bioethics: An Introduction to History, Methods, and Practice*. Sudbury, Mass: Jones and Bartlett Publishers, 1997, pp. 184-189.

62. Nelson HL. *Stories and Their Limits: Narrative Approaches to Bioethics (Reflective Bioethics)*. London, England: Routledge, 1997.

63. Pence GE. *Classic Cases in Medical Ethics: Accounts of the Cases That Have Shaped Medical Ethics, with Philosophical, Legal, and Historical Backgrounds*. New York, NY: McGraw Hill, 2004, pp. 24-25.

64. Jonsen AR, Toulmin S. *The Abuse of Casuistry: A History of Moral Reasoning.* Berkeley: University of California Press, 1988.

65. Jonsen AR, Siegler M, Winslade WJ. *Clinical Ethics: A Practical Approach to Ethical Decisions in Clinical Medicine.* 5th ed. New York, NY: McGraw-Hill, 2002.

66. Pence GE. *Classic Cases in Medical Ethics: Accounts of the Cases That Have Shaped Medical Ethics, with Philosophical, Legal, and Historical Backgrounds*. New York, NY: McGraw Hill, 2004, pp. 21-23.

67. Soukhanov AH, ex ed. *The American Heritage Dictionary of the English Language.* 3rd ed. Boston, Mass: Houghton Mifflin Company, 1992, p. 1479.

68. Jonsen AR, Siegler M, Winslade WJ. *Clinical Ethics: A Practical Approach to Ethical Decisions in Clinical Medicine.* 5th ed. New York, NY: McGraw-Hill, 2002, pp. 1-2.

69. Jonsen AR, Siegler M, Winslade WJ. *Clinical Ethics: A Practical Approach to Ethical Decisions in Clinical Medicine.* 5th ed. New York, NY: McGraw-Hill, 2002, pp. 105-146.

70. Jonsen AR, Siegler M, Winslade WJ. *Clinical Ethics: A Practical Approach to Ethical Decisions in Clinical Medicine.* 5th ed. New York, NY: McGraw-Hill, 2002, p. 7.

71. Jonsen AR, Siegler M, Winslade WJ. *Clinical Ethics: A Practical Approach to Ethical Decisions in Clinical Medicine.* 5th ed. New York, NY: McGraw-Hill, 2002, pp. 106-107.

72. Rapley M. *Quality of Life Research: A Critical Introduction.* London, England: SAGE Publications, 2003, pp. 139-166.

73. Bowling A. *Measuring Disease: A Review of Disease-Specific Quality of Life Measurement Scales.* 2nd ed. Buckingham, England: Open University Press, 2001.

74. Szabo L. Quality of life falls for prostate cancer survivors. *USA Today.* 2004;May 11:7D.

75. Quality of life [Patient Page]. *JAMA.* 2002;288:3070.

76. Tobacco state takes aim at smoking. *USA Today.* 2005;Jul 5:3A.

77. Shamasunder B, Bero L. Financial ties and conflicts of interest between pharmaceutical companies and tobacco companies. *JAMA.* 2002;288:738-744.

78. Hulse C. Senate approves tobacco buyout and new curbs. *New York Times.* 2004;Jul 16:A1, A20.

79. Zoroya G. Smoking bans spread to prisons. *USA Today.* 2004;Jul 22:3A.

80. Gillum J. Strong words, images target smoking. *USA Today.* 2004;Jul 13:10D.

81. Janofsky M. Tobacco trial ends, but the arguing does not. *New York Times.* 2005;Jun 10:A14.

82. Smoking fight goes on [Editorial]. *USA Today.* 2005:Nov 4:11A.

83. Szabo L. Flavored cigarettes, colorful wrappers ignite ire. *USA Today.* 2005;Jan 5:11D.

84. Szabo L. Smoking makes the campus scene. *USA Today.* 2004;Dec 29:7D.

85. Cooper M. Post Office stays out of fray on online cigarette sales. *New York Times.* 2005;May 29:24.

86. Szabo L. California says its long anti-tobacco campaign has paid off: cancers have dropped sharply. *USA Today.* 2005;Jan 26:7D.

CHAPTER 2

1. Kolata G. Merck and VIOXX: The overview; a widely used arthritis drug is withdrawn. *New York Times.* 2004;Oct 1:1A.

2. Gilmartin RV. Open letter to patients entitled "Merck voluntarily withdraws VIOXX." Sep 30, 2004. Available at: www.merck.com/newsroom.vioxx_withdrawal/ (accessed Dec 10, 2005).

3. Feder BJ. Federal panel consolidates Vioxx suits. *New York Times.* 2005;Feb 17:C1.

4. Berenson A. Chief executive quits at Merck; insider steps up. *New York Times.* 2005;May 6:C1.

5. Berenson A, Gardiner, H. Pfizer says 1999 trials revealed risks with Celebrex. *New York Times.* 2005;Feb 1:C3.

6. Berenson A, Harris G, Meier B, Pollack A. Despite warnings, drug giant took long path to Vioxx recall. *New York Times.* 2004;Nov 11:1, 20-21.

7. Berenson A, Harris G, Meier B, Pollack A. Despite warnings, drug giant took long path to Vioxx recall. *New York Times.* 2004;Nov 11:1, 20-21.

8. Wolfe MM, Lichtenstein DR, Singh G. Gastrointestinal toxicity of nonsteroidal antiinflammatory drugs. *N Engl J Med.* 1999;340:1888-1899. [Erratum, *N Engl J Med.* 1999;341:548.]

9. Waxman HA. The lessons of Vioxx—Drug safety and sales. *N Engl J Med.* 2005;352:2576-2778.

10. Berenson A, Harris G, Meier B, Pollack A. Despite warnings, drug giant took long path to Vioxx recall. *New York Times.* 2004;Nov 11:1, 20-21.

11. Berenson A, Harris G, Meier B, Pollack A. Despite warnings, drug giant took long path to Vioxx recall. *New York Times.* 2004;Nov 11:1, 20-21.

12. Mukherjee DM, Nissen SE, Topol EJ. Risk of cardiovascular events associated with selective COX-2 inhibitors. *JAMA.* 2001;286:954-959.

13. Berenson A, Harris G, Meier B, Pollack A. Despite warnings, drug giant took long path to Vioxx recall. *New York Times.* 2004;Nov 11:1, 20-21.

14. *United States Pharmacopoeia Drug Information (USP DI): Drug Information for the Healthcare Professional, Vol. I,* Rofecoxib—Systematic. Greenwood Village, Colo: Thomson Micromedix, 2004, pp. 2635-2638.

15. Rubin R. Painkillers hang in the balance: Heart risk causes FDA to scrutinize COX-2 inhibitors. *USA Today.* 2005;Feb 10:8D.

16. Angell M. *The Truth About the Drug Companies: How They Deceive Us and What to Do About It.* New York, NY: Random House, 2004, pp. 21-36.

17. Use of approved drugs for unlabeled indications. *FDA Drug Bull.* 1982;12:4-5.

18. Salis S. FDA warning letter regarding Vioxx (rofecoxib) tablets. Dec 16, 1999. Available at http://www.fda.gov/cder/warn/dec99/dd121699.pdf (accessed Dec 10, 2005).

19. Meier B, Saul S. Marketing of Vioxx: How Merck played the game of catch-up. *New York Times.* 2005;Feb 11:A1.

20. Berenson A, Harris G, Meier B, Pollack A. Despite warnings, drug giant took long path to Vioxx recall. *New York Times.* 2004;Nov 11:1, 20-21.

21. Topol EJ. Rofecoxib, Merck and the FDA [Letter]. *N Engl J Med.* 2005;352:1163.

22. Berenson A, Harris G, Meier B, Pollack A. Despite warnings, drug giant took long path to Vioxx recall. *New York Times.* 2004;Nov 11:1, 20-21.

23. Abrams TW. FDA warning letter regarding Vioxx (rofecoxib) tablets. Sep 17, 2001. Available at http://www.fda.gov/cder/warn/2001/9456.pdf (accessed Dec 10, 2005).

24. Ray WA, Stein CM, Daugherty JR, Hall K et al. COX-2 selective non-steroidal anti-inflammatory drugs and risk of serious coronary heart disease. *Lancet.* 2002;360:1071-1073.

25. Berenson A, Harris G, Meier B, Pollack A. Despite warnings, drug giant took long path to Vioxx recall. *New York Times*. 2004;Nov 11:1, 20-21.

26. Kweder S. Statement of the Deputy Director, Office of New Drugs, Center for Drug Evaluation and Research, Food and Drug Administration, before the United States Senate Committee on Finance. Nov 18, 2004. Available at http://www.fda.gov/ola/2004/vioxx1118.html (accessed Dec 10, 2005).

27. Graham DJ. Memorandum to Paul Seligman, MD, MPH, Acting Director, Office of Drug Safety, Food and Drug Administration, with attached manuscript entitled "Risk of Myocardial Infarction and Sudden Cardiac Death in Patients Treated with COX-2 Selective and Non-Selective NSAIDs." 2004;Sep 30.

28. Harris G. F.D.A. failing in drug safety, official asserts. *New York Times*. 2004;Nov 19:A1, C3. Copyright 2004 by The New York Times Co. Reprinted with permission.

29. Mission Statement [Merck & Company Inc.] Available at http://www.merck.com/about/mission.html (accessed Dec 10, 2005).

30. Soukhanov AH, ex ed. *The American Heritage Dictionary of the English Language*. 3rd ed. Boston, Mass: Houghton Mifflin Company, 1992, p. 173.

31. Soukhanov AH, ex ed. *The American Heritage Dictionary of the English Language*. 3rd ed. Boston, Mass: Houghton Mifflin Company, 1992, p. 1088.

32. Smith MC, Knapp DA. *Pharmacy, Drugs and Medical Care*. 5th ed. Baltimore, Md: Williams & Wilkins, 1992, pp. 56-57.

33. Ingram DB, Parks JA. *The Complete Idiot's Guide to Understanding Ethics*. Indianapolis, Ind: Alpha Books, 2002, pp. 217-218.

34. Annas GJ. *The Right of Patients: The Authoritative ACLU Guide to the Rights of Patients*. 3rd ed. New York: New York University Press, 2004, pp. 19-24.

35. Buerki RA, Vottero LD. *Ethical Responsibility in Pharmacy Practice*. Madison, Wis: American Institute of the History of Pharmacy, 1994, pp. 102-115.

36. Russell LB, Gold MR, Siegel JE, Daniels N et al. The role of cost-effectiveness analysis in health and medicine. *JAMA*. 1996;276:1172-1177.

37. Weinstein MC, Stasson WB. Foundations of cost-effectiveness analysis for health and medical practice. *N Engl J Med*. 1977;296:716-721.

38. Lieu TA, Ray GT, Black SB, Butler JC et al. Projected cost-effectiveness of pneumococcal conjugate vaccination of healthy infants and young children. *JAMA*. 2000;283:1460-1468.

39. U.S. Centers for Disease Control and Prevention (CDC). Responses to cigarette prices by race/ethnicity, income, and age groups—United States 1976-1993. *Morbidity and Mortality Weekly Report (MMWR)*. 1998;47:605-609. Available at http://www.cdc.gov/mmwr/preview/mmwrhtml/00054047.htm (accessed Dec 10, 2005).

40. Hellmich N. Health spending soars for obesity. *USA Today*. 2005;Jun 27:1A.

41. Pellegrino ED, Thomasma D. *The Virtues in Medical Practice*. New York, NY: Oxford University Press, 1993, p. 35.

42. Pellegrino ED. Medical professionalism: Can it, should it survive? *J Amer Board Fam Prac*. 2000;13:148.

43. Weiss JW. *Business Ethics: A Stakeholder and Issues Management Approach*. 3rd ed. Mason, Ohio: South-Western, a division of Thomson Learning, 2003.

44. Rubin R. Scientist says FDA system "broken": Doubts agency ability to stop another Vioxx. *USA Today.* Nov 19-21:1A.

45. Appleby J, Schmit J, Rubin R, Manning A. FDA asks Pfizer to suspend Bextra sales. *USA Today.* 2005;Apr 8:1B-2B.

46. Herper M. Face of the Year. Dec 13, 2004. Available at http://www.forbes.com/home/sciencesandmedicine/2004/12/13/cx_mh_1213faceoftheyear.html (accessed Dec 10, 2005).

47. Rubin R. He's still the whistle-blower; dissatisfied with the FDA, Graham seeks real solutions. *USA Today.* 2005;Nov 17:D7.

48. Szabo L. Tough choice: Pain or risk? *USA Today.* 2004;Dec 23:11D.

49. Pollack A. Removal of Vioxx shifts drug landscape. *New York Times.* 2004, Dec 1:C2.

50. Deadlines set in Vioxx cases. *New York Times.* 2005;Feb 19:C3.

51. Weiss JW. *Business Ethics: A Stakeholder and Issues Management Approach.* 3rd ed. Mason, Ohio: South-Western, a division of Thomson Learning, 2003, p. 95.

52. Gilmartin RV. An open letter from Merck (advertisement). *New York Times.* 2004;Nov 14:26.

53. Gilmartin RV. An open letter from Merck (advertisement). *New York Times.* 2004;Nov 14:26.

54. Harris G. Drug trial finds big health risks in 2nd painkiller; Pfizer shares plummet; company has no plans to withdraw Celebrex from the market. *New York Times.* 2004;Dec 18:A1, B3.

55. Appleby J, Schmit J, Rubin R, Manning A. FDA asks Pfizer to suspend Bextra sales; withdrawal means Celebrex only available COX-2 inhibitor. *USA Today.* 2005;Apr 8:1B-2B.

56. Rubin R. More evidence links Celebrex to heart problems; group: Pfizer hid unfavorable study. *USA Today.* 2005;Feb 1:6D.

57. Feder BJ. Criticism of drug may leave Pfizer awash in lawsuits. *New York Times.* 2004;Dec 18:B1, B3.

58. Rubin R. Painkillers hang in the balance: heart risk causes FDA to scrutinize COX-2 inhibitors. *USA Today.* 2005;Feb 10:8D.

59. Harris G. F.D.A. is advised to let pain pills stay on the market. *New York Times.* 2005;Feb 19:A1.

60. Schmit J. A winded FDA races to keep up with drug ads that go to far. *USA Today.* 2005;May 31:1A, 4A.

61. Appleby J, Manning A. For those in pain, relief trumps risks. *USA Today.* 2005;Jan 5:1A, 2A.

62. Harris G. Drug safety system is broken, a top F.D.A. official says. *New York Times.* 2004;Nov 19:A1, C3.

63. Schmit J. Some drug prices go up after rivals leave market; drugmakers say increases aren't linked to withdrawals. *USA Today.* 2005;Jun 6:1B.

64. Astra Zeneca L.P. advertisement. *USA Today.* 2005:Jan 10:3D.

65. Nexium. Available at http://www.purplepill.com/ (accessed Dec 10, 2005).

66. McCoy K, Schmit J. Jury sides with Merck in 2nd Vioxx trial; outcome likely means legal war. *USA Today.* 2005;Nov 5:B1.

67. Prakash S. Merck rests its defense in Federal Vioxx Trial. Dec 7, 2005. Available at http://www.npr.org/templates/story/story.php?storyId=5043658 (accessed Dec 12, 2005).

68. Available at http://news.yahoo.com/s/ap/20051206/ap_on_bi_ge/vioxx_federal_trial_5 (accessed Dec 12, 2005).

69. Available at http://www.npr.org/templates/story/story.php?storyId=5039151 (accessed Dec 12, 2005).

70. Available at http://www.npr.org/templates/story/story.php?storyId=5039151 (accessed Dec 12, 2005).

71. Curfman D, Morrissey S, Drazen JM. Expression of concern: Bombardier et al., "Comparison of upper gastrointestinal toxicity of rofecoxib and naproxen in patients with rheumatoid arthritis," *N Engl J Med,* 2000;343:1520-1528. *N Engl J Med.* 2005;353:2813-2814.

72. Smith EB, Rugin R, McCoy K. Medical journal says Vioxx data withheld. *USA Today.* 2005;Dec 9:B1.

73. Merck loses Vioxx verdict; will consumers also lose? *USA Today.* 2005;Aug 23:A11.

74. McCoy K. Merck plans to cut jobs, close plants doesn't help stock. *USA Today.* 2005;Nov 29:B1.

75. Rubin R. Drug industry takes its pulse. *USA Today.* 2005;May 17:9D.

76. Rubin R. Drugmakers to voluntarily post information. *USA Today.* 2005;Jan 7:7B.

77. Meier B. Contracts keep drug research out of reach. *New York Times.* 2004;Nov 29:A1, A16.

78. Drugmakers slow on follow-up tests; lawmaker says fast-track process is breaking down. *USA Today.* 2005;Jun 2:9D.

79. U.S. Food and Drug Administration, FDA News. FDA seeks input on communication of drug safety information. Available at http://www.fda.gov/bbs/topics/NEWS/2005/NEW01269.html (accessed Dec 10, 2005).

80. Available at http://www.fda.gov/bbs/topics/NEWS/2005/NEW01269.html (accessed Dec 10, 2005).

81. Available at http://bmj.bmjjournals.com/cgi/content/full/331/7528/1310?ehom (accessed Dec 10, 2005).

82. McConnaughy J. Jury sides with Merck in Vioxx trial. *USA Today.* 2005;Feb 20:5B.

CHAPTER 3

1. Codified at Calif Health & Safety Code § 11362.5 *et seq.* (West 2004).

2. Calif Public Acts of 2003, ch. 875.

3. Willing R. Medical-pot fight goes to justices; patients say they need it; feds say it does no good. *USA Today.* 2004;Nov 26:3A.

4. Biskupic J, Koch W, Ritter J. Patients who use marijuana fear worst if forced to stop; their dilemma: Break law or be in pain. *USA Today.* 2005;Jun 7:1A-2A.

5. Ritter R. Supreme court will take on medical-marijuana lawsuit. *USA Today.* Jun 29, 2004, 11A.

6. Supreme Court is set to consider medical marijuana. *New York Times.* 2004; Nov 28:22.

7. *Gonzales v. Raich,* 545 U.S., 125 S.Ct. 2195 (2005) at 2200.

8. Willing R. Medical-pot fight goes to justices; patients say they need it; feds say it does no good. *USA Today.* 2004;Nov 26:3A.

9. *Gonzales v. Raich,* 545 U.S., 125 S.Ct. 2195 (2005) at 2195.

10. Soukhanov AH, exec ed. *The Dictionary of the English Language.* 3rd ed. Boston, Mass: Houghton Mifflin Company, 1992, p. 1401.

11. Brecher EM, ed. *Licit and Illicit Drugs: The Consumers Union on Narcotics, Stimulants, Depressants, Inhalants, Hallucinogens, and Marijuana—Including Caffeine, Nicotine, and Alcohol.* Mount Vernon, NY: Consumers Union, 1972, pp. 395-472.

12. Weil A, Rosen W. *From Chocolate to Morphine,* rev and updated. Boston, Mass: Houghton Mifflin Company, 1993, pp. 114-125.

13. Brecher EM, ed. *Licit and Illicit Drugs: The Consumers Union on Narcotics, Stimulants, Depressants, Inhalants, Hallucinogens, and Marijuana—Including Caffeine, Nicotine, and Alcohol.* Mount Vernon, NY: Consumers Union, 1972, pp. 395-472.

14. Brecher EM, ed. *Licit and Illicit Drugs: The Consumers Union on Narcotics, Stimulants, Depressants, Inhalants, Hallucinogens, and Marijuana—Including Caffeine, Nicotine, and Alcohol.* Mount Vernon, NY: Consumers Union, 1972, pp. 395-472.

15. Weil A, Rosen W. *From Chocolate to Morphine,* rev and updated. Boston, Mass: Houghton Mifflin Company, 1993, pp. 114-125.

16. Brecher EM, ed. *Licit and Illicit Drugs: The Consumers Union on Narcotics, Stimulants, Depressants, Inhalants, Hallucinogens, and Marijuana—Including Caffeine, Nicotine, and Alcohol.* Mount Vernon, NY: Consumers Union, 1972, pp. 395-472.

17. *Gonzales v. Raich,* 545 U.S., 125 S.Ct. 2195 (2005) at 2198.

18. *Marijuana: Our Newest Narcotic Menace.* Sacramento, Calif: California Division of Narcotic Enforcement, 1940.

19. Erlen J, Spillane JF eds. *Federal Drug Control: The Evolution of Policy and Practice.* New York Pharmaceutical Products Press (an imprint of The Haworth Press, Inc.), 2004, pp. 66-76.

20. Harrison Narcotic Act of 1914, Pub. L. No. 63-223, 38 Stat. 785 (1914).

21. Erlen J, Spillane JF eds. *Federal Drug Control: The Evolution of Policy and Practice.* New York Pharmaceutical Products Press (an imprint of The Haworth Press, Inc.), 2004, pp. 66-76.

22. *Gonzales v. Raich,* 545 U.S., 125 S.Ct. 2195 (2005) at 2201.

23. *Leary v. United States,* 395 U.S. 6 (1969).

24. 84 Stat. 1236 (1970).

25. *Gonzales v. Raich,* 545 U.S., 125 S.Ct. 2195 (2005) at 2203.

26. Drug Enforcement Administration Mission Statement. Available at http://www.dea.gov/agency/mission.htm (accessed Oct 11, 2005).

27. Tenn. Pub. Acts 1998. ch. 1079, amending Tenn. Code Ann. § 39-17-417(g)(2). (2004).

28. Abood R. *Pharmacy Practice and the Law.* 4th ed. Sudbury, Mass: Jones and Bartlett Publishers, 2005, pp. 185-200.

29. Gieringer DH. The origins of cannabis prohibition in California. *J Contemp Drug Problems.* 1999;26:237-288.

30. Steinbrook R. Medical marijuana, physician-assisted suicide, and the Controlled Substances Act. *N Engl J Med.* 2004;351:1380-1383.

31. Beauchamp TL, Childress JF. *Principles of Biomedical Ethics.* 5th ed. New York. NY: Oxford University Press, 2001. pp. 57-68.

32. Leo RJ. Competency and the capacity to make treatment decisions: A primer for primary care physicians. *Primary Care Companion J Clin Psychiatry.* 1999;1:131-144.

33. The National Commission for the Protection of Human Subject of Biomedical and Behavioral Research. The Belmont Report: Ethical Principles and Guidelines for the Protection of Human Subjects of Biomedical and Behavioral Research (1979). In: Emanuel EJ, Crouch RA, Arras JD, Moreno JD, Grady C, eds. *Ethical and Regulatory Aspects of Clinical Research: Readings and Commentary.* Baltimore, Md: Johns Hopkins University Press, 2003, pp. 33-38.

34. Black HC. *Black's Law Dictionary.* 5th ed. St. Paul, Minn: West Publishing Co., 1979, p. 257.

35. Appelbaum PS, Grisso T. Assessing patients' capacities to consent to treatment. *N Engl J Med.* 1988;319:1635-1638.

36. Leo RJ. Competency and the capacity to make treatment decisions: A primer for primary care physicians. *Primary Care Companion J Clin Psychiatry.* 1999;1:131-144.

37. Leo RJ. Competency and the capacity to make treatment decisions: A primer for primary care physicians. *Primary Care Companion J Clin Psychiatry.* 1999;1:131-144.

38. United States Constitution, preamble.

39. White BD, Siegler M, Singer PA, Iserson KV. What does *Cruzan* mean to the practicing physician? *Arch Intern Med.* 1991;151:925-928.

40. *U.S. v. Oakland Cannabis Buyers' Cooperative,* 532 U.S. 483 (2001), reversing 190 F.3d 1109 (1999).

41. Willing R. Medical-pot fight goes to justices; patients say they need it; feds say it does no good. *USA Today.* 2004; Nov 26:3A.

42. Older Americans' attitudes on medical marijuana. *AARP the Magazine,* Mar & Apr, 2005. Available at http://www.aarpmagazine.org/health/Articles/a2005-01-18-mag-marijuana.html (accessed Oct 11, 2005).

43. 1996 California ballot initiative statute text codified as Calif Health & Safety Code §§ 11362.5 *et seq.* (West Publishing Co. edition, 2004).

44. *The Federalist Papers.* Available at http://www.law.ou.edu/history/federalist.html (accessed Oct 17, 2005).

45. *Raich v. Ashcroft,* 248 F. Supp. 2d 918 (N.D. Cal. 2003).

46. *Gonzales v. Raich,* 545 U.S., 125 S.Ct. 2195 (2005) at 2200.

47. United States Constitution. Art. I, Section 8.

48. *United States v. Lopez,* 459 F.2d 949 (9th Cir. 1972).
49. United States Constitution, Art. I, Section 8.
50. *Gonzales v. Raich,* 545 U.S., 125 S.Ct. 2195 (2005) at 2200.
51. *Raich v. Ashcroft,* 248 F. Supp. 2d 918 (N.D. Cal. 2003).
52. *Raich v. Ashcroft,* 352 F.3d 1222 (9th Cir. 2003).
53. *Raich v. Ashcroft,* 352 F.3d 1222 (9th Cir. 2003) at 1227.
54. *Gonzales v. Raich,* 545 U.S., 125 S.Ct. 2195 (2005) at 2201.
55. *U.S. v. Lopez,* 514 U.S. 549, 115 S.Ct. 1624 (1995) and *U.S. v. Morrison,* 529 U.S. 598, 120 S.Ct. 1740 (2000).
56. *Gonzales v. Raich,* 545 U.S., 125 S.Ct. 2195 (2005) at 2209.
57. *Gonzales v. Raich,* 545 U.S., 125 S.Ct. 2195 (2005) at 2210.
58. Greenhouse L. Justices will hear argument on medical marijuana. *New York Times.* 2004;Jun 29: A17.
59. Supreme court is set to consider medical marijuana. *New York Times.* 2004; Nov 28:22.
60. Greenhouse L. Justices say U.S. may prohibit the use of medical marijuana; federal law prevails in 11 states with legislation. *New York Times.* 2005; Jun 7:1A, A15.
61. *Gonzales v. Raich,* 545 U.S., 125 S.Ct. 2195 (2005) at 2208.
62. *Gonzales v. Raich,* 545 U.S., 125 S.Ct. 2195 (2005) at 2211.
63. *Gonzales v. Raich,* 545 U.S., 125 S.Ct. 2195 (2005) at 2214.
64. *Gonzales v. Raich,* 545 U.S., 125 S.Ct. 2195 (2005) at 2221 (O'Connor, J., dissenting).
65. *Gonzales v. Raich,* 545 U.S., 125 S.Ct. 2195 (2005) at 2229-2230 (O'Connor, J., dissenting).
66. *Gonzales v. Raich,* 545 U.S., 125 S.Ct. 2195 (2005) at 2215 (Scalia, J., concurring).
67. United States Constitution, Fifth Amendment.
68. United States Constitution, Ninth Amendment.
69. United States Constitution, Tenth Amendment.
70. *United States v. Oakland Cannabis Buyers' Cooperative,* 532 U.S. 483, 121 Sup. Ct. 1711 (2001) at 1717, fn.1 (Stevens, J., concurring).
71. *Gonzales v. Raich,* 545 U.S., 125 S.Ct. 2195 (2005) at 2215.
72. Biskupic J, Koch W, Ritter J. Patients who use marijuana fear worst if forced to stop; their dilemma: Break law or be in pain. *USA Today.* 2005;Jun 7:1A-2A.
73. Biskupic J, Koch W, Ritter J. Patients who use marijuana fear worst if forced to stop; their dilemma: Break law or be in pain. *USA Today.* 2005;Jun 7:1A-2A.
74. Biskupic J, Koch W, Ritter J. Patients who use marijuana fear worst if forced to stop; their dilemma: Break law or be in pain. *USA Today.* 2005;Jun 7:1A-2A.
75. Biskupic J, Koch W, Ritter J. Patients who use marijuana fear worst if forced to stop; their dilemma: Break law or be in pain. *USA Today.* 2005;Jun 7:1A-2A.
76. Biskupic J, Koch W, Ritter J. Patients who use marijuana fear worst if forced to stop; their dilemma: Break law or be in pain. *USA Today.* 2005;Jun 7:1A-2A.
77. Biskupic J, Koch W, Ritter J. Patients who use marijuana fear worst if forced to stop; their dilemma: Break law or be in pain. *USA Today.* 2005;Jun 7:1A-2A.

78. Murphy DE. Arrests follow searches in medical marijuana raids. *New York Times*. 2005;Jun 23:A12.

79. Crackdown on medical marijuana yields 20 indictments. *USA Today*. 2005; Jun 23:A3.

80. Murphy DE. Drug's users say ruling won't end their efforts. *New York Times*. 2005;Jun 7:A15.

81. When marijuana is misused [Editorial]. *New York Times*. 2005;Jun 24:A22.

82. Koch W. States still push for medical pot. *USA Today*. 2005;Jun 16:3A.

83. Gostin LO. Medical marijuana, American federalism, and the Supreme Court. *JAMA*. 2005;294:842-844.

84. Koch W. Court's pot ruling won't apply to patients in federal programs. *USA Today*. 2005;Jun 8:3A.

85. Pols have no taste for pot. *USA Today*. 2005;Jul 1:3A.

86. Koch W. Spray alternative to pot on the market in Canada. *USA Today*. 2005;Jun 24:4A.

87. Szabo L. Pot studies difficult to organize, analyze. *USA Today*. 2005;Jun 7:2A.

CHAPTER 4

1. Ruethling G. Illinois pharmacist sues over contraceptive rule. *New York Times*. 2005:Jun 10:A16.

2. *Moor-Fitz, Inc. v. Blagojevich,* Complaint, No. 05-MR47, Circuit Court for the 14th Judicial Circuit, Whiteside County, Illinois, Illinois, Jun 8, 2005.

3. News Release, Office of Governor Rod R. Blagojevich of Illinois, Apr 1, 2005.

4. Illinois Gov. orders pharmacists to dispense morning-after pills. *Catholic World News*, Apr 13, 2005. Available at http://www.cwnews.com/news/viewstory.cfm?recnum=36493 (accessed Oct 11, 2005).

5. Stern A. US pharmacist sues, refusing to sell contraceptive. *Reuters Foundation AlertNet*, Jun 10, 2005. Available at http://alertnet.org/thenews/newsdesk/N10662043.htm (accessed Oct 11, 2005).

6. News Release, Office of Governor Rod R. Blagojevich of Illinois, Apr 1, 2005.

7. American Pharmacists Association (APhA) News Release, "Illinois Governor Modifies Emergency Order on Contraceptive Prescriptions," dated Apr 11, 2005. Available at http://www.aphanet.org/AM/Template.cfm?Template=/CM/Content Display.cfm (accessed Oct 11, 2005).

8. News Release, Office of Governor Rod R. Blagojevich of Illinois, Apr 1, 2005.

9. Ruethling G. Illinois pharmacist sues over contraceptive rule. *New York Times*. 2005;Jun 10:A16.

10. *Moor-Fitz, Inc. v. Blagojevich,* Complaint, No. 05-MR47, Circuit Court for the 14th Judicial Circuit, Whiteside County, Illinois, Illinois., Jun 8, 2005, p. 3.

11. Vander Bleek LD. Letter to pharmacists employed by Morr-Fitz, Inc. and L. Doyle, Inc., dated Jun 7, 2005.

12. Stern A. US pharmacist sues, refusing to sell contraceptive. *Reuters Foundation AlertNet,* Jun 10, 2005. Available at http://alertnet.org/thenews/newsdesk/N10662043.htm (accessed Oct 11, 2005).

13. Litt IF. Placing emergency contraception in the hands of women. *JAMA.* 2005;293:98-99.

14. Bucci KK, Downing D, Reed KL, Steward FH, ed board. *Emergency Contraception: The Pharmacist's Role* (an American Pharmaceutical Association [APhA] special report). Washington, DC: American Pharmaceutical Association, 2000, p. ii.

15. Bucci KK, Downing D, Reed KL, Steward FH (adv board). *Emergency Contraception: The Pharmacist's Role* (an American Pharmaceutical Association [APhA] special report). Washington, DC: American Pharmaceutical Association, 2000, p. 1.

16. Yuzpe AA, Thurlow HJ, Ramzy I, Leyshon JI. Post coital contraception—A pilot study. *J Reprod Med.* 1974;13:53-58.

17. Prescription drug products; certain combined oral contraceptives for use as postcoital emergency contraception. *Fed Reg.* 1997;62:8610-8612.

18. Office of Population Research at Princeton. *Provider Search in the United States and Part of Canada.* Available at http://ec.princeton.edu/providers/ (accessed Nov 14, 2005).

19. Bucci KK, Downing D, Reed KL, Steward FH (adv board). *Emergency Contraception: The Pharmacist's Role* (an American Pharmaceutical Association [APhA] special report). Washington, DC: American Pharmaceutical Association, 2000, p. 1.

20. Cates W, Ellertson C. Abortion. In: Hatcher RA, Trussell J, Stewart F, eds. *Contraceptive Technology.* 16th ed. New York, NY: Ardent Media, 1998, pp. 679-700.

21. Grimes DA. Emergency contraception—Expanding opportunities. *N Engl J Med.* 1997;337:1078-1079.

22. Audet MC, Moreau M, Koltun WD, Waldbaum AS, Shangold G, Fisher AC, Creasy GW. Evaluation of contraceptive efficacy and cycle control of a transdermal contraceptive patch vs. an oral contraceptive: A randomized controlled trial. *JAMA.* 2001;285:2347-2354.

23. Roberts CJ, Lowe CR. Where have all the conceptions gone? *Lancet.* 1975; 305:498-499.

24. PLAN B brochure, Duramed Pharmaceuticals, Inc., 2005. Available at http://www.go2planb.com/Plan_B.pdf (accessed Oct 11, 2005).

25. Ingram DB, Parks JA. *The Complete Idiot's Guide to Understanding Ethics.* Indianapolis, Ind: Alpha Books, 2002, pp. 255-256.

26. Ingram DB, Parks JA. *The Complete Idiot's Guide to Understanding Ethics.* Indianapolis, Ind: Alpha Books, 2002, p. 255.

27. Jones C. Druggists refuse to give out pill. *USA Today.* 2004;Nov 9:A3.

28. Soukhanov AH, exec ed. *The American Heritage Dictionary of the English Language.* 3rd ed. Boston, Mass: Houghton Mifflin Company, 1992, p. 1553.

29. News Release, Office of Governor Rod R. Blagojevich of Illinois, Apr 1, 2005.

30. Vivian JC. Refusal to fill. *U.S. Pharmacist.* 2000;Aug:73.

31. Abood R. *Pharmacy Practice and the Law.* 4th ed. Boston, Mass: Jones and Bartlett Publishers, 2005, pp. 188-190.

32. *Powers v. Thobani,* No. 4D04-2601, Fla. Dist. Ct. Appeal, Fourth Dist., decided Jun 1, 2005 (holding the dismissal of a cause of action against the defendant pharmacies for failing to properly monitor and warn about the decedent's prescription drug use improper).

33. Buerki RA, Vottero LD. *Ethical Responsibility in Pharmacy Practice.* Madison, Wis: American Institute of the History of Pharmacy, 1994, pp. 127-143.

34. 1997-98 Ill. Pub. Acts, 90th Gen. Assembly, ch. 246 (eff. Jan 1, 1998); codified at 745 Ill. Comp. Stat. 70/1 *et seq.*

35. Stein R. Pharmacists' right at front of new debate; because of beliefs, some refuse to fill birth control prescriptions. *Washington Post.* 2005;Mar 28:A1.

36. Soukhanov AH, exec ed. *The American Heritage Dictionary of the English Language.* 3rd ed. Boston, Mass: Houghton Mifflin Company, 1992, p. 400.

37. Annas GJ, Glantz LH, Katz BF. *The Rights of Doctors, Nurses, and Allied Health Professionals: A Health Law Primer.* New York, NY: Avon Books, 1981, pp. 208-209.

38. Soukhanov AH, exec ed. *The American Heritage Dictionary of the English Language.* 3rd ed. Boston, Mass: Houghton Mifflin Company, 1992, p. 979.

39. Ingram DB, Parks JA. *The Complete Idiot's Guide to Understanding Ethics.* Indianapolis, Ind: Alpha Books, 2002, p. 208.

40. Soukhanov AH, exec ed. *The American Heritage Dictionary of the English Language.* 3rd ed. Boston, Mass: Houghton Mifflin Company, 1992, p. 979.

41. Statement by National Association of Chain Drug Stores (NACDS) President and CEO Craig L. Fuller on Medicaid Prescription Drugs before the House Energy and Commerce Health Subcommittee, Jun 22, 2005. Available at http://www.nacds.org/wmspage.cfm?parm1=3821 (accessed Oct 11, 2005).

42. Ingram DB, Parks JA. *The Complete Idiot's Guide to Understanding Ethics.* Indianapolis, Ind: Alpha Books, 2002, p. 136.

43. Ingram DB, Parks JA. *The Complete Idiot's Guide to Understanding Ethics.* Indianapolis, Ind: Alpha Books, 2002, p. 138.

44. Ingram DB, Parks JA. *The Complete Idiot's Guide to Understanding Ethics.* Indianapolis, Ind: Alpha Books, 2002, p. 174.

45. Ingram DB, Parks JA. *The Complete Idiot's Guide to Understanding Ethics.* Indianapolis, Ind: Alpha Books, 2002, p. 14.

46. Jonsen AR, Siegler M, Winslade WJ. *Clinical Ethics: A Practical Approach to Ethical Decisions in Clinical Medicine.* 5th ed. New York, NY: McGraw-Hill, 2002, pp. 16-17.

47. Buerki RA, Vottero LD. *Ethical Responsibility in Pharmacy Practice.* Madison, Wis: American Institute of the History of Pharmacy, 1994, pp. 44-50.

48. Jonsen AR, Siegler M, Winslade WJ. *Clinical Ethics: A Practical Approach to Ethical Decisions in Clinical Medicine.* 5th ed. New York, NY: McGraw-Hill, 2002, p. 12.

49. Higginbotham A. Doctor Feelgood. [London *Guardian* and] *Observer.* 2002; Aug 11:6-9.

50. Buerki RA, Vottero LD. *Ethical Responsibility in Pharmacy Practice.* Madison, Wis: American Institute of the History of Pharmacy, 1994, pp. 152-153 (quoting the 1922 American Pharmaceutical Association Code of Ethics).

51. Patton M (Executive Director, Illinois Pharmacists Association), Gans JA (Executive Vice President, American Pharmacists Association), Manasse HR Jr (Executive Vice President and Chief Operating Officer, American Society of Health-System Pharmacists). Letter to Illinois Governor Rod R. Blagojevich, dated Apr 5, 2005. Available at http://www.ashp.org/news/Show/Article.cfm?id=11476 (accessed Oct 11, 2005).

52. American Pharmacists Association (APhA) News Release, "Illinois Governor Modifies Emergency Order on Contraceptive Prescriptions," dated Apr 11, 2005. Available at http://www.aphanet.org/AM/Template.cfm?Template=/CM/Content Display.cfm (accessed Oct 11, 2005).

53. Griffith W. Bad medicine: "morning after" pill creates moral dilemma in Ill. *CBN News,* undated. Available on the Internet at http://www.cbn.news/cbnnews/news/050512a.asp (accessed Oct 11, 2005).

54. *Moor-Fitz, Inc. v. Blagojevich,* Complaint, No. 05-MR47, Circuit Court for the 14th Judicial Circuit, Whiteside County, Illinois, Illinois., Jun 8, 2005, p. 14, identifying counsel for plaintiff as Mailee R. Smith, Americans United for Life, Chicago, Illinois.

55. Ruethling G. Illinois pharmacist sues over contraceptive rule. *New York Times.* 2005;Jun 10:A16.

56. Ruethling G. Illinois pharmacist sues over contraceptive rule. *New York Times.* 2005;Jun 10:A16.

57. Furrow BR, Greaney TL, Johnson SH, Jost TS, Schwartz RL. *Health Law: Cases, Materials, and Problems.* 5th ed. St. Paul, Minn: Thomson-West, 2004, p. 1154.

58. *Griswold v. Connecticut,* 381 U.S. 479, 85 S.Ct. 1678 (1965).

59. United States Conference of Catholic Bishops. *Ethical and Religious Directives for Catholic Health Care Services.* 4th ed. rev. Washington, DC: United States Catholic Conference, Inc., 2001.

60. United States Conference of Catholic Bishops. *Ethical and Religious Directives for Catholic Health Care Services.* 4th ed. rev. Washington, DC: United States Catholic Conference, Inc., 2001, p. 17.

61. United States Conference of Catholic Bishops. *Ethical and Religious Directives for Catholic Health Care Services.* 4th ed. rev. Washington, DC: United States Catholic Conference, Inc., 2001, p. 20.

62. United States Conference of Catholic Bishops. *Ethical and Religious Directives for Catholic Health Care Services.* 4th ed. rev. Washington, DC: United States Catholic Conference, Inc., 2001, p. 16.

63. *Moor-Fitz, Inc. v. Blagojevich,* Complaint, No. 05-MR47, Circuit Court for the 14th Judicial Circuit, Whiteside County, Illinois, Ill., Jun 8, 2005, p. 3.

64. United States Conference of Catholic Bishops. *Ethical and Religious Directives for Catholic Health Care Services.* 4th ed. rev. Washington, DC: United States Catholic Conference, Inc., 2001, pp. 19-20 (Directive 47).

65. Sulmasy DP, Pellegrino ED. The rule of double effect: Clearing up the double talk. *Arch Intern Med.* 1999;159:545-550.

66. Jonsen AR, Siegler M, Winslade WJ. *Clinical Ethics: A Practical Approach to Ethical Decisions in Clinical Medicine.* 5th ed. New York, NY: McGraw-Hill, 2002, pp. 122-123.

67. United States Conference of Catholic Bishops. *Ethical and Religious Directives for Catholic Health Care Services.* 4th ed. rev. Washington, DC: United States Catholic Conference, Inc., 2001, p. 15.

68. Abortion performed on Miami disabled rape victim; similar case still in Orlando court. CNN.com, dated May, 30, 2003. Available at http://www.cnn.com/2003/LAW/05/30/florida.abortion (accessed Oct 11, 2005).

69. United States Constitution, First Amendment, "Free Exercise Clause."

70. 775 Ill. Comp. Stat. 35/1 *et seq.*

71. *Catholic Charities of Sacramento, Inc., v. California,* 32 Cal.4th 527, 85 P.3rd 67 (2004).

72. Strom S. Catholic group is told to pay for birth control. *New York Times.* 2004;Mar 2:A14.

73. Vander Bleek LD. Letter to pharmacists employed by Morr-Fitz, Inc. and L. Doyle, Inc., dated Jun 7, 2005.

74. Asim J. Conscience behind the counter. washingtonpost.com, dated Apr 4, 2005. Available at http://www.washingtonpost.com/wp-dyn/articles/A24809-2005Apr4.html (accessed Oct 11, 2005).

75. Asim J. Conscience behind the counter. washingtonpost.com, dated Apr 4, 2005. Available at http://www.washingtonpost.com/wp-dyn/articles/A24809-2005Apr4.html (accessed Oct 11, 2005).

76. Davey M. Illinois pharmacies ordered to provide birth control. *New York Times.* 2005;Apr 2:A10.

77. When pharmacists refuse, market is best medicine. *USA Today.* 2005;Apr 5:A14.

78. Mesich J. Emergency contraception: U.S. out of step. Available at http://www.now.org/issues/reproductive/ec_worldwide.html (accessed Nov 4, 2005).

79. Harris G. Drugs, politics, and the F.D.A.; abortion issue hovers over the morning-after pill. *New York Times.* 2005;Aug 28:1, 13.

80. Drazen JM, Greene MF, Wood AJJ. The FDA, politics, and Plan B. *N Engl J Med.* 2004;350:1561-1562.

81. Stanford JB, Hager WD. Crockett SA. The FDA, politics, and Plan B. *N Engl J Med.* 2004;350:2413-2414.

82. Harris G. F.D.A. puts off decision on sale of birth control; morning-after pill fight; Democrats angered by new delay on labeling for teenage women. *New York Times.* 2005;Aug 27:A1, A11.

83. Cash S. New AAP policy advises on emergency contraception use. *AAP News.* 2005;Sep:1, 15.

84. Bucci KK, Downing D, Reed KL, Steward FH (adv board). *Emergency Contraception: The Pharmacist's Role* (an American Pharmaceutical Association [APhA] special report). Washington, DC: American Pharmaceutical Association, 2000, pp. 11-12.

85. Belluck P. Massachusetts veto poses hurdle to morning-after pill; action by Romney, a possible '08 hopeful. *New York Times.* 2005;Jul 26:A12.

86. Baker A, Hernandez R. Both parties attack Pataki's stand on the morning-after pill. *New York Times.* 2005;Aug 2:A20.

87. Illinois Administrative Procedures Act, 5 Ill. Comp. Stat. 100/5-5 *et seq.*

88. Pharmacists sue over birth control policy. *USA Today.* 2006;Jan 28:3A.

CHAPTER 5

1. Chapman CR, Gavrin J. Suffering and the dying patient. In: Battin MP, Lipman AG, eds. *Drug Use in Assisted Suicide and Euthanasia.* New York, NY: Pharmaceutical Products Press, 1996, p. 68.

2. Chapman CR, Gavrin J. Suffering and the dying patient. In: Battin MP, Lipman AG, eds. *Drug Use in Assisted Suicide and Euthanasia.* New York, NY: Pharmaceutical Products Press, 1996, pp. 67-90.

3. Ariès P (Ranum PM, tr). *Western Attitudes Toward Death: From the Middle Ages to the Present* (Johns Hopkins Symposia in Comparative History). Baltimore, Md: Johns Hopkins University Press, 1974.

4. Weil A, Rosen W. *From Chocolate to Morphine.* Boston, Mass: Houghton Mifflin Company, 1993.

5. Lallanilla M. *A brief history of pain.* Available at http://abcnews.go.com/Health/PainManagement/story?id=731553&page=1 (accessed Sep 4, 2005).

6. Brecher EM, ed. *Licit and Illicit Drugs.* Mount Vernon, NY: Consumers Union Reports. 1972.

7. Brody JE. A doctor's duty, when death is inevitable. *New York Times.* 2004;Aug 10:D7.

8. Jonsen AR, Siegler M, Winslade WJ. *Clinical Ethics: A Practical Approach to Ethical Decisions in Clinical Medicine.* 5th ed. New York, NY: McGraw-Hill, Inc., 2002.

9. Kuebler KK, Berry PH. End-of-life care. In: Kuebler KK, Berry PH, Heidrich DE, eds. *End-of-Life Care: Clinical Practice Guidelines.* Philadelphia, Pa: Saunders, 2002, pp. 23-37.

10. Tolstoy L. *The Death of Ivan Ilyich.* New York, NY: Bantam Books, 1991.

11. Hyman CS. Pain management and disciplinary action: How medical boards can remove barriers to effective treatment. *J. Law, Med Ethics.* 1996;24:338-342.

12. Hill CS Jr. When will adequate pain treatment be the norm? *JAMA.* 1995; 274:1881-1882.

13. Jadad AR, Bowman GP. Bowman. The WHO analgesic ladder for cancer pain management: Stepping up the quality of its evaluation. *JAMA.* 1995;274:1870-1873.

278 DRUGS, ETHICS, AND QUALITY OF LIFE

14. American Pain Society Quality of Care Committee. Quality improvement guidelines for the treatment of acute pain and cancer pain. *JAMA*. 1995;274: 1874-1880.

15. Hill CS Jr. When will adequate pain treatment be the norm? *JAMA*. 1995; 274:1881-1882.

16. Jury awards $1.5 million in elder abuse case against physician. Available at http://www.braytonlaw.com/news/verdicts/2001bergman.htm (accessed May 18, 2004).

17. Troy T. New type of suit: Pain treatment; California verdict against doctor is based on law against abuse of the elderly. *Natl Law J.* 2001;23:45.

18. Okie S. California jury finds doctor negligent in managing pain. *Washington Post.* 2001;Jun 15:A3.

19. Codified at Calif. Welfare & Institutions Code §§ 15600 *et seq* (West 2004).

20. Jury awards $1.5 million in elder abuse case against physician. Available at http://www.braytonlaw.com/news/verdicts/2001bergman.htm (accessed May 18, 2004).

21. Troy T. New type of suit: Pain treatment; California verdict against doctor is based on law against abuse of the elderly. *Natl Law J.* 2001;23:45.

22. Troy T. New type of suit: Pain treatment; California verdict against doctor is based on law against abuse of the elderly. *Natl Law J.* 2001;23:45.

23. Crane M. Treating pain: Damned if you don't? *Med Econ.* 2001;Nov:53-54.

24. Jonsen AR, Siegler M, Winslade WJ. *Clinical Ethics: A Practical Approach to Ethical Decisions in Clinical Medicine.* 5th ed. New York, McGraw-Hill, Inc., 2002.

25. White BD, Siegler M, Singer PA, Iserson KV. What does Cruzan mean to the practicing physician? *Arch Intern Med.* 1991;151:925-928.

26. von Gunten CF. Secondary and tertiary palliative care in US hospitals. *JAMA*. 2002;287:875-881.

27. Lynn J. Serving patients who may die soon and their families: The role of hospice and other services. *JAMA*. 2001;285:925-932.

28. Freidrich MJ. Hospice care in the United States: A conversation with Florence S. Wald. *JAMA*. 1999;281:1983-1685.

29. Hospice services. Available at http://www.cms.hhs.gov/medicaid/services/hospice.asp (accessed Sep 17, 2005).

30. Texas Health & Safety Code, ch. 166. (2005).

31. An explanation of palliative care. Available at http://www.nhpco.org/i4a/pages/index.cfm (accessed Sep 13, 2005).

32. World Health Organization. WHO definition of palliative care. Available at http://www.who.int/cancer/palliative/definition/en.html (accessed Sep 18, 2005).

33. United States Conference of Catholic Bishops. *Ethical and Religious Directives for Catholic Health Care Services.* 4th ed. rev. Washington, DC: United States Catholic Conference, 1995, pp. 14-15.

34. Alpers A. Criminal act or palliative care? *J Law, Med, Ethics.* 1998;26: 308-331.

35. Kaufman M. Worried pain doctors decry prosecutions. *Washington Post.* 2003;Dec 29:A1.

36. Hurwitz WE. Open letter to supporters. Available at http://www.drhurwitz.com/2005_letters.htm (accessed Feb 2, 2005).

37. Satel S. Doctors behind bars: Treating pain in now risky business. *New York Times*. 2004;Oct 19:D6, D10.

38. Kaufman M. Worried pain doctors decry prosecutions. *Washington Post*. 2003;Dec 29:A1.

39. United States Attorney for the District of Arizona. Press release: Tucson doctor Jeri B. Hassman pleads guilty. Tucson, Ariz: Office of the United States Attorney for the District of Arizona, Jan 29, 2004.

40. Brushwood DB. The pharmacist's duty to dispense legally prescribed and therapeutically appropriate opioid analgesics. *Pharmacy Times*. Available at https://secure.pharmacytimes.com/lessons/200506-03.asp (accessed Sep 18, 2005).

41. Drug maker named in lawsuits over OxyContin. *New York Times*. 2005; Aug:B1.

42. Abood RR. *Pharmacy Practice and the Law*. 4th ed. Boston, Mass: Jones and Bartlett Publishers, 2005, pp. 145-147.

43. Abood RR. *Pharmacy Practice and the Law*. 4th ed. Boston, Mass: Jones and Bartlett Publishers, 2005, pp. 150-155.

44. Abood RR. *Pharmacy Practice and the Law*. 4th ed. Boston, Mass: Jones and Bartlett Publishers, 2005, pp. 146-147.

45. Abood RR. *Pharmacy Practice and the Law*. 4th ed. Boston, Mass: Jones and Bartlett Publishers, 2005, pp. 159-160.

46. Adams D. Physicians told not to fear discipline for pain treatment. *American Medical News*. 2003;Jun 16:16-17.

47. Adams D. Preventing undertreatment of pain: Model policy on controlled substances. *American Medical News*. 2004;May 17:17.

48. Abood RR. *Pharmacy Practice and the Law*. 4th ed. Boston, Mass: Jones and Bartlett Publishers, 2005, pp. 187-192.

49. Rubin R. Pain experts, DEA seek consensus on abuse: Document aims to ease "aura of fear." *USA Today*. 2004;Aug 12:7D.

50. In a conversation with David B. Brushwood, BS Pharm, J.D. (May 2007) who restated what he had written earlier for an online continuing pharmacy education feature in 2002. Brushwood DB. The pharmacist's duty to dispense legally prescribed and therapeutically appropriate opioid analgesics. *Pharmacy Times*. Available at https://secure.pharmacytimes.com/lessons/200506-03.asp (accessed Sep 18, 2005). Reprinted with permission.

51. Abood RR. *Pharmacy Practice and the Law*. 4th ed. Boston, Mass: Jones and Bartlett Publishers, 2005, pp. 190-191.

52. 21 C.F.R. § 1306.07 (2005).

53. Abood RR. *Pharmacy Practice and the Law*. 4th ed. Boston, Mass: Jones and Bartlett Publishers, 2005, pp. 166-168.

54. 21 C.F.R. § 1300.01(b)(26) (2005).

55. 21 C.F.R. § 1300.01(b)(10) (2005).

56. Public Law 106-310 (2000)

57. Title IV of Public Law 99-660, The Health Care Quality Improvement of 1986, as amended, codified at 42 U.S.C. § 11101 *et seq*.

58. National Practitioner Data Bank and Healthcare Integrity and Protection Data Bank. Available on the Internet at http://www.npdb-hipdb.com (accessed Sep 19, 2005).

59. Adams D. Iowa doctor fights making charges public. *American Medical News.* 2005;Sep 12:13.

60. Brody JE. Let's get serious abut relieving chronic pain. *New York Times.* 2006;Jan 10:D6.

61. Okie S. California jury finds doctor negligent in managing pain. *Washington Post.* 2001; Jun 15:A3.

62. Once again—Accountability for poor pain care. *Connections* (a Compassion in Dying newsletter). 2003;11:5-7.

63. Barnett EH. Case marks big shift in pain policy; in apparent first for nation, an Oregon medical board acts against a doctor primarily for undertreatment. [Portland] *Oregonian.* 1999;Sep 2:A1.

64. Oregon Board of Medical Examiners. Board actions, 2003. Available on the Internet at http://www.bme.state.or.us/NewActions.html (accessed Sep 19, 2005).

65. *Hook's-Superx, Inc. v. McLaughlin,* 642 N.E.2d 514 (Ind. 1994).

66. *Ryan v. Dan's Food Stores, Inc.,* 972 P.2d 395, 401 (Utah 1998).

67. In shielding addicted doctors, programs put patients at risk [editorial]. *USA Today.* 2004;Jul 13:14A.

68. Stolberg SG. Doctor who treated Cheney has had an addiction problem. *New York Times.* 2004;Jul 5:A9.

69. Prescription for pain care. *American Medical News.* 2004;Dec13:11-12.

70. Survey: Chronic pain often goes untreated. *USA Today.* 2005;May 25:6D.

71. Brody JE. A doctor's duty, when death is inevitable. *New York Times.* 2004; Aug 10:D7.

CHAPTER 6

1. The Hippocratic Oath. Wikipedia, the free encyclopedia. Available at http://en.wikipedia.org/wiki/Hippocratic_oath (accessed Apr 15, 2006).

2. Brecher EM, ed. *Licit and Illicit Drugs: The Consumers Union Report on Narcotics, Stimulants, Depressants, Inhalents, Hallucinogens, and Marijuana— including Caffeine, Nicotine, and Alcohol.* Mount Vernon, NY: Consumers Union, 1972, pp. 247-259.

3. Weil AT, Rosen W. *From Chocolate to Morphine*, rev updated ed. New York, NY: Houghton Mifflin Company, 1998, pp. 69-77.

4. *United States Pharmacopeia Dispensing Information (USP DI)* 21st ed— *Volume 1: Drug Information for the Healthcare Professional.* Englewood, Colo: MICROMEDEX Thomson Healthcare, 2001, pp. 538-542.

5. Pence GE. *Classic Cases in Medical Ethics: Accounts of the Cases That Have Shaped Medical Ethics, with Philosophical, Legal, and Historical Backgrounds.* New York, NY: McGraw Hill, 2004, p. 97.

6. Sullivan AD, Hedberg K, Fleming DW. Legalized physician-assisted suicide in Oregon—The second year. *N Engl J Med.* 2000;342:598-604.

7. Humphry D. Lethal drugs for assisted suicide: How the public sees it. In: Battin MP, Lipman AG, eds. *Drug Use in Assisted Suicide and Euthanasia*. New York, NY: Pharmaceutical Products Press, 1996, p. 181.

8. *United States Pharmacopeia Dispensing Information (USP DI)*. 21st ed—Volume I: *Drug Information for the Healthcare Professional*. Englewood, Colo: MICROMEDEX Thomson Healthcare, 2001, pp. 566-588.

9. Sternbach LH. The discovery of Librium. *Agents Actions* 1972;2:193-196.

10. Rachels J. *The End of Life: Euthanasia and Morality*. Oxford, England: Oxford University Press, 1986, pp. 7-19.

11. Matthew 27:3-7 (KJV).

12. Judges 16:25-31 (KJV).

13. Hebrews 11:32 (KJV).

14. 1 Samuel 31: 1-6 (ASV, BBE, JPS).

15. 2 Samuel 1:1-6 (KJV).

16. 2 Samuel 1:1-16 (KJV).

17. Rachels J. *The End of Life: Euthanasia and Morality*. Oxford, London: Oxford University Press, 1986, pp. 7-8.

18. Rachels J. *The End of Life: Euthanasia and Morality*. Oxford, London: Oxford University Press, 1986, p. 8.

19. Rachels J. *The End of Life: Euthanasia and Morality*. Oxford, London: Oxford University Press, 1986, p. 8.

20. Rachels J. *The End of Life: Euthanasia and Morality*. Oxford, London: Oxford University Press, 1986, p. 8.

21. Miles SH. *The Hippocratic Oath and the Ethics of Medicine*. New York, NY: Oxford University Press, 2004, pp. 66-68.

22. Decisions near the end of life. *JAMA*. 1992;267:2229-2233.

23. Miles SH. *The Hippocratic Oath and the Ethics of Medicine*. New York, NY: Oxford University Press, 2004, p. 71.

24. Hippocratic corpus: The Art. In: Reiser SJ, Dyck AJ, Curran WJ, eds. *Ethics in Medicine: Historical Perspectives and Contemporary Concerns*. Cambridge, Mass: MIT Press, 1977, pp. 6-7.

25. Sulmasy DP. Clinical bioethics. In: Stein JH, ed. *Internal Medicine*. 5th ed. St. Louis, Mont Mo.for Missouri: Mosby, Inc., 1998, p. 11.

26. Pence GE. *Classic Cases in Medical Ethics: Accounts of the Cases That Have Shaped Medical Ethics, with Philosophical, Legal, and Historical Backgrounds*. New York, NY: McGraw-Hill, 2004, p. 59.

27. Rachels J. *The End of Life: Euthanasia and Morality*. Oxford, London: Oxford University Press, 1986, p. 9.

28. Rachels J. *The End of Life: Euthanasia and Morality*. Oxford, London: Oxford University Press, 1986, p. 9.

29. Rachels J. *The End of Life: Euthanasia and Morality*. Oxford, London: Oxford University Press, 1986, p. 10.

30. Rachels J. *The End of Life: Euthanasia and Morality*. Oxford, London: Oxford University Press, 1986, p. 17.

31. Pellegrino ED, Thomasma DC. *For the Patient's Own Good: The Restoration of Beneficence in Health Care*. New York, NY: Oxford University Press, 1988.

32. Jonsen AR, Siegler M, Winslade WJ. *Clinical Ethics: A Practical Approach to Ethical Decisions in Clinical Medicine.* 5th ed. New York, NY: Mc-Graw Hill, 2002.

33. Quill TE. Dying and decision making—Evolution of end-of-life options. *N Engl J Med.* 2004;350:2029-2032.

34. Gaylin W, Kass LR, Pellegrino ED, Siegler M. Doctors must not kill. *JAMA.* 1988;259:2139-21-40.

35. Hayden I. *Symbol and Privilege: The Ritual Context of British Royalty.* Tucson: University of Arizona Press, 1987, p. 125.

36. Jonsen AR. *The Birth of Bioethics.* New York, NY: Oxford University Press, 1998, pp. 3-33.

37. Fagerlin A, Schneider CE. Enough: The failure of the living will. *Hastings Center Report.* 2004;Mar-Apr:30-42.

38. It's over Debbie [A Piece of My Mind]. *JAMA.* 1988;259:272.

39. Gaylin W, Kass LR, Pellegrino ED, Siegler M. Doctors must not kill. *JAMA.* 1988;259:2139-21-40.

40. Vaux KL. Debbie's dying: Mercy-killing or the good death. *JAMA.* 1988;259:2140-2141.

41. Oregon woman who chose death is remembered at upbeat service. *New York Times.* 1990;Jun 11:A14.

42. Castaneda C, Davis R. Kevorkian: Death must be an option. *USA Today.* 1993;Feb 22:1A-2A.

43. Quill TE. Death and dignity: A case of individualized decision making [Sound Board]. *N Engl J Med.* 1991;324:691-694.

44. Castaneda C, Davis R. Kevorkian: Death must be an option. *USA Today.* 1993;Feb 22:1A-2A.

45. Foderaro LW. New York will not discipline doctor for his role in suicide. *New York Times.* 1991;Aug 17:A16.

46. Dowling C. Doctors in Oregon may assist suicide. *USA Today.* 1994: Nov 11,1A.

47. Or. Rev. Stat. § 127.815(1)(j) (2005); § 127.855; § 127.865.

48. Or. Rev. Stat. § 163.125(1)(b) (2005); § 127.880.

49. Or. Rev. Stat. § 127.810 (2005).

50. Or. Rev. Stat. § 127.800 (12).

51. Or. Rev. Stat. § 127.840 (2005).

52. Or. Rev. Stat. § 127.805 (2005); § 127.815; § 127.820.

53. Or. Rev. Stat. § 127.825 (2005).

54. Or. Rev. Stat. § 127.815 (2005).

55. Or. Rev. Stat. § 127.815 (2005).

56. *Gonzales v. Oregon,* Docket No. 04-623 (Jul 21, 2005), brief for Respondents Rasmussen and Hochhalter at 19.

57. Chin AE, Hedberg K, Higginson GK, Fleming DW. Legalized physician-assisted suicide in Oregon—The first year's experience. *New Engl J Med.* 1999; 340: 577-583.

58. *Gonzales v. Oregon,* Docket No. 04-623 (Jul 21, 2005), brief for Respondents Rasmussen and Hochhalter at 19.

59. Or. Rev. Stat. § 127.855(1)-(7) (2005).

60. Or. Rev. Stat. § 127.865(3) (2005).

61. Or. Rev. Stat. § 127.815(1)(k) (2005).

62. Oregon Department of Human Services. Seventh Annual Report on Oregon's Death with Dignity Act. Available at http://egov.oregon.gov/DHS/ph/pas/docs/year7.pdf (accessed Jul 18, 2005).

63. Hedberg K, Hopkins D, Kohn M. Five years of legal physician-assisted suicide in Oregon. New *Engl J Med.* 2003;348:961-964.

64. *Washington v. Glucksberg,* 521 U.S. 702 (1997); *Vacco* v. *Quill,* 521 U.S. 793 (1997).

65. Greenhouse L. Justices accept case weighing assisted suicide. *New York Times.* Feb 23, 2003:A1, A14 quoting from *Washington v. Glucksberg,* 521 U.S. 702 (1997) at 735.

66. Press Release: Statement of Sen. Jud. Comm. Orrin G. Hatch (R-Utah) (Jul 31, 1998). Available at http://judiciary.senate.gov/oldsite/ogh73198.htm (accessed Dec 1, 2005).

67. *Oregon v. Ashcroft,* 368 F.3d 1118, 1123 (9th Cir. 2004).

68. H.R. 4006, 105th Cong. (1998) ("Lethal Drug Abuse Prevention Act of 1998").

69. Statement of Rep Henry J. Hyde (R-Ill.). H.R. Subcomm. on the Constitution of the Jud. Comm., 105th Cong. (Jul 14, 1998). Available at http://commdocs.house.gov/committees/judiciary/hju59931.000/hju59931_0.HTM (accessed Dec 5, 2005).

70. Orentlicher D, Caplan A. The Pain Relief Promotion Act of 1999: A serious threat to palliative care. *JAMA.* 2000;283:255-258.

71. *Oregon v. Ashcroft,* 368 F.3d 1118,1123 (9th Cir. 2004).

72. 66 Fed. Reg. 56607 (Nov 6, 2001).

73. *Oregon v. Ashcroft,* 368 F.3d 1118 (9th Cir. 2004).

74. Liptak A. Ruling upholds law authorizing assisted suicide; judge rebukes Ashcroft; attorney general's edict exceeds authority in Oregon, panel says. *New York Times.* 2004;May 27:A1, A24. Copyright 2004 by The New York Times Co. Reprinted with permission.

75. Greenhouse L. Justices accept case weighing assisted suicide. *New York Times.* 2005;Feb 23:A1, A14.

76. Greenhouse L. Justices explore U.S. authority over states on assisted suicide. *New York Times.* 2005;Oct 6:A1, A30.

77. *Auer v. Robbins,* 519 U.S. 452 (1997)

78. *Auer v. Robbins,* 519 U.S. 452 (1997) at 461.

79. *Gonzales v. Oregon,* No. 04-623, 2006 WL 89200 at *13 (U.S. Jan 17, 2006).

80. *Chevron U.S.A., Inc. v. Natural Resources Defense Council,* 467 U.S. 837 (1984).

81. *Gonzales v. Oregon,* No. 04-623, 2006 WL 89200 at *10 (U.S. Jan 17, 2006).

82. *Gonzales v. Oregon,* No. 04-623, 2006 WL 89200 at *10 (U.S. Jan 17, 2006).

83. *Gonzales v. Oregon,* No. 04-623, 2006 WL 89200 at *12 (U.S. Jan 17, 2006).

84. *Gonzales v. Oregon,* No. 04-623, 2006 WL 89200 at *13 (U.S. Jan 17, 2006).

85. *Gonzales v. Oregon,* No. 04-623, 2006 WL 89200 at *15 (U.S. Jan 17, 2006).

86. *Gonzales v. Oregon,* No. 04-623, 2006 WL 89200 at *16 (U.S. Jan 17, 2006).

87. *Gonzales v. Oregon,* No. 04-623, 2006 WL 89200 at *17 (U.S. Jan 17, 2006).

88. *Gonzales v. Oregon,* No. 04-623, 2006 WL 89200 at *27 (U.S. Jan 17, 2006) (emphasis in original).

89. *Gonzales v. Oregon,* No. 04-623, 2006 WL 89200 at *32 (U.S. Jan 17, 2006).

90. *Gonzales v. Raich,* 125 S. Ct. 2195 (2005).

91. *Gonzales v. Oregon,* No. 04-623, 2006 WL 89200 at *34 (U.S. Jan 17, 2006).

92. *Gonzales v. Oregon,* No. 04-623, 2006 WL 89200 at *21 (U.S. Jan 17, 2006).

93. Gomez CF. *Regulating Death: Euthanasia and the Case of the Netherlands.* New York, NY: Free Press, 1991.

94. Keown J. Dutch slide down euthanasia's slippery slope. *Wall Street Journal.* 1991;Nov 5:A18.

95. Pence GE. *Classic Cases in Medical Ethics: Accounts of the Cases That Have Shaped Medical Ethics, with Philosophical, Legal, and Historical Backgrounds.* New York, NY: McGraw-Hill, 2004, p. 93.

96. Angell M. Euthanasia in the Netherlands—Good or bad? [Editorial]. *N Engl J Med.* 1996;335:1676-1678.

97. Angell M. Euthanasia in the Netherlands—Good or bad? [Editorial]. *N Engl J Med.* 1996;335:1676-1678.

98. Angell M. Euthanasia in the Netherlands—Good or bad? [Editorial]. *N Engl J Med.* 1996;335:1676-1678.

99. Va der Maas PJ, van der Wal G, Haverkate I et al. Euthanasia, physician-assisted suicide, and other medical practices involving the end of life in the Netherlands, 1990-1995. *N Engl J Med.* 1996;335:1699-1705.

100. Verhagen E, Sauer PJJ. The Groningen protocol—Euthanasia in severely ill newborns [Perspective]. *N Engl J Med.* 2005;352:959-962.

101. Joseph P. Kennedy Jr. Foundation, prod. *Who Should Survive?* Harford, MD: Film Service, 1971.

102. Lorber J. Results of treatment of myelomingocele: An analysis of 524 unselected cases, with special reference to possible selection for treatment. *Dev. Med. Child Neurol.* 1971;13:279-303.

103. Duff RS, Campbell AGM. Moral and ethical dilemmas in the special-care nursery. *N Engl J Med.* 1973;289:890-894.

104. Steinbock B. Whatever happened to the Danville Siamese Twins? *Hastings Center Reports.* 1987;17 (Aug-Sep):3-4.

105. Pence GE. *Classic Cases in Medical Ethics: Accounts of the Cases That Have Shaped Medical Ethics, with Philosophical, Legal, and Historical Backgrounds.* New York, NY: McGraw-Hill, 2004, pp. 117-222, 225-243.

106. Pence GE. *Classic Cases in Medical Ethics: Accounts of the Cases That Have Shaped Medical Ethics, with Philosophical, Legal, and Historical Backgrounds.* New York, NY: McGraw-Hill, 2004, pp. 241, 242.

107. Pence GE. *Classic Cases in Medical Ethics: Accounts of the Cases That Have Shaped Medical Ethics, with Philosophical, Legal, and Historical Backgrounds.* New York, NY: McGraw-Hill, 2004, p. 112.

108. Fagerlin A, Schneider CE. Enough: The failure of the living will. *Hastings Center Report.* 2004;Mar-Apr:30-42.

109. Emanuel LL. Facing requests for physician-suicide: Toward a practical and principled clinical skill set. *JAMA.* 1988;280:643-647.

110. Johnson D. Kevorkian sentenced to 10 to 15 years in prison. *New York Times.* 1999;Apr 14:A23.

111. Ganzini L, Johnston WS, McFarland BH, Tolle SW, and Lee MA. Attitudes of patients with amyotrophic lateral sclerosis and their care givers toward assisted suicide [Special Article]. *N Engl J Med.* 1998;339:967-973.

112. Pence GE. *Classic Cases in Medical Ethics: Accounts of the Cases That Have Shaped Medical Ethics, with Philosophical, Legal, and Historical Backgrounds.* New York, NY: McGraw-Hill, 2004, p. 99.

113. Lubitz JD, Riley GF. Trends in Medicare payments in the last year of life. *N Engl J Med.* 1993;328:1092-1096.

114. Emanuel EJ, Battin MP. What are the potential cost savings from legalizing physician-assisted suicide. *N Engl J Med.* 1998;339:167-172.

115. Hogan C, Lynn J, Gabel, Lunney J, O'Mara A., Wilkinson A. *Medicare beneficiaries' costs and use of care in the last year of life* (Medicare Payment Advisory Commission, Report No. 00-1). Washington, DC: Medicare Payment Advisory Commission, 2001.

116. Levy CR, Fish R, Kramer A. Do-not-resuscitate and do-not-hospitalize directives of persons admitted to skilled nursing facilities under the Medicare benefit. *J Amer Geriatr Soc.* 2005;53:2060-2068

117. Kristof ND. Jack's death, his choice. *New York Times.* 2005:Jul 10:12. Yardley W. Probation for Connecticut man, 74, who aided suicide. *New York Times.* 2005;Apr 8:A24.

118. Asch DA. The role of critical care nurses in euthanasia and assisted suicide [Special Article]. *N Engl J Med.* 1996;334:1374-1379.

119. *Gonzales v. Oregon,* No. 04-623, 2006 WL 89200 at *21 (U.S. Jan 17, 2006).

120. See information online at the Death with Dignity National Center web site for activities across the country. Available at http://www.deathwithdignity.org/ (accessed Feb 11, 2006).

121. *New State Ice Co. v. Liebmann,* 285 U.S. 262, 311 (1932).

CHAPTER 7

1. Lunney JR, Lynn J, Foley DJ, Lipson S, Guralnik JM. Patterns of functional decline at the end of life. *JAMA*. 2003;289:2387-2392.

2. Glaser B, Strauss AL. *Time for Dying*. Chicago: Aldine Publishing Co., 1968.

3. Oregon woman who chose death is remembered at upbeat service. *New York Times*. 1990;Jun 11:A14.

4. Quill TE. Death and dignity: A case of individualized decision making. *N Engl J Med*. 1991;324:691-694.

5. Campo-Flores A. The Legacy of Terri Schiavo; one woman's journey from marital bliss to medical darkness—And the forces that made her story a political and ethical watershed. *Newsweek*. 2005;Apr 4:22-24.

6. Kowalczyk L. Woman dies at MGH after battle over care; daughter fought for life support. *Boston Globe*. 2005;Jun 8. Available at http://www.boston.com/yourlife/health/other/articles/2005/06/08/woman_dies_at_mgh_after_battle_over_care/ (accessed Mar 12, 2005).

7. Kowalczyk L. Woman dies at MGH after battle over care; daughter fought for life support. *Boston Globe*. 2005;Jun 8. Available at http://www.boston.com/yourlife/health/other/articles/2005/06/08/woman_dies_at_mgh_after_battle_over_care/ (accessed Mar 12, 2005).

8. Adams M. ALS, like a terrorist, kills without partiality. *USA Today*. 2004;Jul 1:4D.

9. Adams M. ALS, like a terrorist, kills without partiality. *USA Today*. 2004;Jul 1:4D.

10. Adams M. ALS, like a terrorist, kills without partiality. *USA Today*. 2004;Jul 1:4D.

11. Fackelmann K. Scientists work to slow "this heinous disease." *USA Today*. 2004;Jul 1:4D.

12. Schwartz J, Estrin J. Living for today, locked in a paralyzed body. *New York Times*. 2004;Nov 7:1, 20.

13. Schwartz J, Estrin J. Living for today, locked in a paralyzed body. *New York Times*. 2004;Nov 7:1, 20.

14. Schwartz J, Estrin J. Living for today, locked in a paralyzed body. *New York Times*. 2004;Nov 7:1, 20.

15. Fackelmann K. Scientists work to slow "this heinous disease." *USA Today*. 2004;Jul 1:4D.

16. Painter K. Alzheimer cost: $82 billion. USA Today. 1994;Aug 17:1A.

17. Hebert LE, Scherr PA, Bienias JL, Bennett DA, Evans DA. Alzheimer disease in the U.S. population: Prevalence estimates using the 2000 census. *Archives of Neurology*. 2003;60:1119-1122.

18. Lewin Group. *Saving Lives, Saving Money: Dividends for Americans Investing in Alzheimer Research*. Washington, DC: Alzheimer's Association, 2004.

19. Kolata G. When Alzheimer's steals the mind, how aggressively to treat the body. *New York Times*. 2004;May 18:D1, D6. Copyright 2004 by The New York Times Co. Reprinted with permission.

20. Kolata G. When Alzheimer's steals the mind, how aggressively to treat the body. *New York Times*. 2004;May 18:D1, D6.

21. Brown JB, Bedford NK, White SJ. *Gerontological Protocols for Nurse Practitioners*. Philadelphia, Pa: Lippincott Williams & Wilkins, Inc., 1999, pp. 453-460.

22. Kinzer S. Judge in mental-capacity case is now focus on one. *New York Times*. 2005;Jan 3:A12.

23. Kinzer S. Judge in mental-capacity case is now focus on one. *New York Times*. 2005;Jan 3:A12.

24. Kinzer S. Judge in mental-capacity case is now focus on one. *New York Times*. 2005;Jan 3:A12.

25. Kolata G. When Alzheimer's steals the mind, how aggressively to treat the body. *New York Times*. 2004;May 18:D1, D6.

26. White BD, Hickson GB, Theriot R, Zaner RM. A medical ethics issues survey of five pediatrics residency programs. *Am J Dis Child*. 1991;145:161-164.

27. Miles SH. Medical futility. In: Monagle JF, Thomasma DC, eds. *Health Care Ethics*. Gaithersburg, Md: Aspen Publishers, Inc., 1994, pp. 233-240.

28. Younger SJ. Who defines futility? *JAMA*. 1988;260:2094-2095.

29. Schneiderman LJ, Jecker NS, Jonsen AR. Medical futility: Its meaning and ethical implications. *Ann Intern Med*. 1990;112:949-954.

30. Lantos JD, Singer PA, Walker RM, Gramelspacher GP et al. The illusion of futility in clinical practice [Special Article]. *Amer J Med*. 1989;87:81-84.

31. Tomlinson T, Brody H. Futility and the ethics of resuscitation [Special Communication]. *JAMA*. 1990;254:1276-1280.

32. Murphy DJ, Matchar DB. Life-sustaining therapy: A model for appropriate use. *JAMA*. 1990;264:2103-2108.

33. Gilmer T, Schneiderman LJ, Teetzel H, Blustein J et al. The costs of non-beneficial treatment in the intensive care unit. *Health Aff* (Millwood). 2005;24:976-979.

34. Lantos JD, Miles SH, Silverstein MD, Stocking CB. Survival after cardio-pulmonary resuscitation in babies of very low birth weight: is CPR futile therapy. *N Engl J Med*. 1988;318:91-95.

35. Gray WA, Capone RJ, Most AS. Unsuccessful emergency medical resuscitation—Are continued efforts in the emergency department justified? *N Engl J Med*. 1991;325:1393-1398.

36. Jecker NS, Schneiderman LJ. Ceasing futile resuscitation in the field: Ethical considerations [Commentary]. *Arch Intern Med*. 1992;152:2392-2397.

37. Miles SH. Informed demand for "non-beneficial" medical treatment. *N Engl J Med*. 1991;325:512-515.

38. Annas GJ. Asking the courts to set the standard of emergency care: The case of Baby K. *N Engl J Med*. 1994;330:1542-1545.

39. Hopper L. Baby dies after hospital removes breathing tube. *Houston Chronicle*. 2005;Mar 16:A1.

40. Emanuel EJ, Emanuel LL. The economics of dying; the illusion of cost savings at the end of life [Special Article]. *N Engl J Med*. 330:540-544.

41. Jecker NS, Schneiderman LJ. Futility and rationing [Special Article]. *Amer J Med.* 1992;92:189-196.

42. Lundberg GD. American health care system management objectives: The aura of inevitability becomes incarnate. *JAMA.* 1993;269:2554-2555.

43. Rosner F, Kark PR, Bennett AJ, Buscaglia A et al. Medical futility [Committee Report]. *New York State J Med.* 1992;Nov:485-488.

44. Soukhanov AH, ex ed. *The American Heritage Dictionary of the English Language.* 3rd ed. Boston, Mass: Houghton Mifflin Company, 1992, p. 738.

45. Ardagh M. Futility has no utility in resuscitation medicine. *J Clin Ethics.* 2000:26:396-399.

46. Luce JM. Physicians do not have a responsibility to provide futile or unreasonable care if a family insists. *Critical Care Medicine* 1995;23:760-766.

47. Halliday R. Medical futility and the social context. *J Med Ethics* 1997; 23:148-153.

48. Sykes JB, ed. *The Concise Oxford Dictionary.* Oxford, London: Oxford University Press, 1986.

49. Schneiderman LJ, Jecker NS, Jonsen AR. Medical futility: Its meaning and ethical implications. *Ann Int Med.* 1990:112:949-954.

50. Kasimow S. A new approach to the issue of medical futility: Reframing the debate. *McMaster J Philos.* 2005;14:112-119.

51. Jonsen AR, Siegler M, Winslade WJ. *Clinical Ethics: A Practical Approach to Ethical Decisions in Clinical Medicine.* 5th ed. New York, NY: McGraw-Hill, 2002, p. 15.

52. Jonsen AR, Siegler M. Winslade WJ. *Clinical Ethics: A Practical Approach to Ethical Decisions in Clinical Medicine.* 5th ed. New York, NY: McGraw-Hill, 2002, p. 25.

53. Miles SH. Medical futility. In: Monagle JF, Thomasma DC, eds. *Health Care Ethics.* Gaithersburg, Md: Aspen Publishers, Inc, 1994, pp. 233-240.

54. Pendergast TJ. Futility and the common cold: How requests for antibiotics can illuminate care at the end of life. *Chest.* 1995;107:836-844.

55. Angell M. The case of Helga Wanglie. *N Engl J Med.* 1991;325:511-512.

56. Paris JJ, Schreiber MD, Statter M, Arensman R, Siegler M. Beyond autonomy—Physicians' refusal to use life-prolonging extracorporeal membrane oxygenation [Sounding Board]. *N Engl J Med.* 1993;329:354-357.

57. Larson E. The soul of an HMO. *Time.* 1996;Jan 22:44-52.

58. Pence GE. *Classic Cases in Medical Ethics: Accounts of Cases That Have Shaped Medical Ethics, with Philosophical, Legal, and Historical Backgrounds.* New York, NY: McGraw-Hill, 2004, pp. 345-347.

59. Wicclair MR. Medical futility: A conceptual and ethical analysis. In: Mappes TA, DeGrazia D, eds. *Biomedical Ethics.* 4th ed. New York, NY: McGraw-Hill, Inc., 1996, p. 346.

60. Tomlinson T, Brody H. Ethics and communication in do-not-resuscitate orders. *N Engl J Med.* 1988;318:43-46.

61. Siegler M. The physician-patient accommodation: A central event in clinical medicine. *Arch Intern Med.* 1982;142:1899-1902.

62. Blackhall LJ. Must we always use CPR? [Sounding Board]. *N Engl J Med.* 1987;317:1281-1284.

63. Paris JJ, Schreiber MD, Statter M, Arensman R, Siegler M. Beyond autonomy—Physicians' refusal to use life-prolonging extracorporeal membrane oxygenation [Sounding Board]. *N Engl J Med.* 1993;329:354-357.

64. Daniels N. Why saying no to patients in the United States is so hard; cost containment, justice, and provider autonomy [Sounding Board]. *N Engl J Med.* 1986;314:1380-1383.

65. Tan SY, Chun B, Kim E. Creating a medical futility policy; physicians at a [Catholic] Honolulu hospital describe the experience. *Health Progress.* 2003;Jul/Aug:14-20.

66. Administrative Policy W-1 "Withholding/Withdrawal of Treatment—Appropriate Medical Care." Nashville, Tenn: Saint Thomas Hospital, 1994.

67. Jonsen AR, Siegler M, Winslade WJ. *Clinical Ethics: A Practical Approach to Ethical Decisions in Clinical Medicine.* 5th ed. New York, NY: McGraw-Hill, 2002, p. 29.

68. Annas GJ. *Standard of Care: The Law of American Bioethics.* New York, NY: Oxford University Press, 1993, p. 4.

69. Berg JW, Appelbaum PS, Lidz CW, Parker LS. *Informed Consent: Legal Theory and Clinical Practice.* 2nd ed. New York, NY: Oxford University Press, 2001, p. 11.

70. Berg JW, Appelbaum PS, Lidz CW, Parker LS. *Informed Consent: Legal Theory and Clinical Practice.* 2nd ed. New York, NY: Oxford University Press, 2001, pp. 11, 12.

71. White BD, Siegler M, Singer PA, Iserson KV. What does Cruzan mean to the practicing physician? *Arch Intern Med.* 1991;151:925-928.

72. *Cruzan v. Director, Missouri Department of Health,* 110 S.Ct. 2841 (1990) at 2852.

73. *Cruzan v. Director, Missouri Department of Health,* 110 S.Ct. 2841 (1990) at 2858 (O'Connor, J., concurring).

74. Malcolm AH. Missouri renews battle over right to die. *New York Times.* 1990; Nov 12:A12.

75. Lewin T. Cruzan dies, outlived by debate over right to die. *New York Times.* 1990; Dec 26:A1.

76. White BD, Singer PA, Siegler M. Continuing problems with self-determination. *Am J Med Qual.* 1993;8:187-193.

77. Menikoff JA, Sachs GA, Siegler M. Beyond advance directives—Health care surrogate laws. *N Engl J Med.* 1992;327:1165-1169.

78. Tenn. Public Acts (2004), ch. 862.

79. Fagerlin A, Schneider CE. Enough: The failure of the living will. *Hastings Center Report.* 2004;Mar-Apr:30-42.

80. Schwartz J, Estrin J. Many seeking one final say on end of life. *New York Times.* 2005;Jun 17:A1, A12.

81. Emanuel LL, Emanuel EJ. The medical directive: A new comprehensive advance care document. *JAMA.* 1989;261:3288-3293.

82. Fagerlin A, Schneider CE. Enough: The failure of the living will. *Hastings Center Report.* 2004;Mar-Apr:30-42.

83. Hoffman J. Doctors' delicate balance of keeping hope alive. *New York Times.* 2005;Dec 24:A1, A14.

84. Fackelmann K. Three novel therapies could slow progress of Alzheimer's; drugs promising in small trials. *USA Today.* 2005;Jul 21:7D.

85. Fackelmann K. Researchers' new goal: Hold line on Alzheimer's; treatments at mild stage could amount to a "cure." *USA Today.* 2004;Jul 15:4D.

86. Lyall S. British clinic is allowed to deny medicine; decision on cost has broad impact. *New York Times.* 2006;Feb 16:A6.

87. Lyall S. British clinic is allowed to deny medicine; decision on cost has broad impact. *New York Times.* 2006;Feb 16:A6.

88. Lyall S. British clinic is allowed to deny medicine; decision on cost has broad impact. *New York Times.* 2006;Feb 16:A6.

89. Lyall S. Court backs Briton's right to a costly drug. *New York Times.* 2006;Apr 13:A8.

90. Blumenthal R, Novovitch B. Texas agency for elderly under fire over neglect; judge spurs inquiry, citing mismanagement. *New York Times.* 2004;Apr 20:A10.

91. Eaton L. In the hands of a troubled system, a son's guardianship is at issue; lawyer appointed for disabled man is accused of losing funds. *New York Times.* 2004;Mar 29:A18.

92. Himelstein BP, Hilden JM, Boldt AM, Weissman D. Pediatric palliative care [Review Article: Medical Progress]. *N Engl J Med.* 2004;350:1752-1762.

93. Multi-Society Task Force on PVS. Medical aspects of the persistent vegetative state (First of Two Parts). *N Engl J Med.* 1994;330:1499-1508.

94. Belluck P. Custody and abuse cases swirl around a troubled girl on life support. *New York Times.* 2005;Dec 6:A18.

95. Solomon MZ, Sellers DE, Heller KS, Dokken DL, Levetown M, Rushton C, Truog RD, Fleishchman AR. New and lingering controversies in pediatric end-of-life care. *Pediatrics.* 2005;116:872-883.

96. McFadden RD, Staba D. Buffalo fireman regains long-lost memories. *New York Times.* 2005;May 3:B1.

97. Staba D. Firefighter who awoke after 10-year gap dies in Buffalo. *New York Times.* 2006;Feb 22:A21.

98. Bruni F. Baby's move ends a battle over her fate. *New York Times.* 1996; Mar 1. Available at http://query.nytimes.com/gst/fullpage.html?sec=health&res=9F00E4DE1E39F932A35750C0A960958260 (accessed Mar 19, 2006).

99. Kalkut G, Dubler ND. The line between life and death. *New York Times.* 2005;May 10:A21.

100. Fahim K. Boy, 13, dies after dispute over life support is settled. *New York Times.* 2005;Apr 29:B3.

101. Kolata G. Withholding care from patients: Boston case asks, who decides? *New York Times.* 1995;Apr 3:A1, B8.

102. Mass jury: Doctors were right to withdraw life support. *Amer Med News.* 1995;May 8:10.

103. Texas Health & Safety Code, ch. 166 (2003).

104. Fine RL, Whitfield JM, Carr BL, Mayo TW. Medical futility in the neonatal intensive care unit: Hope for a resolution. *Pediatrics.* 2005;116:1219-1222.

105. Hopper L. Baby dies after hospital removes breathing tube. *Houston Chronicle.* 2005;Mar 16:A1.

106. Houston mother loses fight to keep baby on life support: Baby Sun born with fatal genetic disorder. www.NBC5.com. Available at http://www.nbc5.com/health/4286333/detail.html??z=dp&dpswid=1167317&dppid=65194 (accessed Mar 19, 2006).

107. Schwartz J. At life's end, hospital finds junction of ethics and medicine; team effort to resolve bedside conflicts. *New York Times.* 2005;Jul 5:A13.

108. Schwartz J. At life's end, hospital finds junction of ethics and medicine; team effort to resolve bedside conflicts. *New York Times.* 2005;Jul 5:A13.

109. Hippocrates. Aphorisms. In: Chadwick J, Mann WN, trans. *The Medical Works of Hippocrates.* Oxford, London: Blackwell Scientific Publications, 1950, p. 149.

110. Carey B. In the hospital, a degrading shift from person to patient. *New York Times.* 2005;Aug 16:A1, A12.

CHAPTER 8

1. Stolberg SG. The biotech death of Jesse Gelsinger. *New York Times Magazine.* 1999:Nov 28:136-150.

2. Weiss R. Teen dies undergoing experimental gene therapy. *Washington Post.* 1999;Sep 29:A1.

3. Avery ME, First LR. *Pediatric Medicine.* 2nd ed. Baltimore, Md: Williams & Wilkins, 1994, pp. 1063-1067.

4. Nelson D, Weiss R. Hasty decisions in race to a cure? Gene therapy study preceded despite safety, ethics concerns. *Washington Post.* 1999;Nov 21:A1. © 1999, *Washington Post.*

5. Maddalena A, Sosnoski DM, Berry GT, Nussbaum RL. Mosaicism for an intragenic deletion in a boy with mild ornithine transcarbamylase deficiency. *N Engl J Med.* 1988;319:999-1003.

6. Behrman RE, Kliegman RM, Jenson HB, eds. *Nelson Textbook of Pediatrics.* 16th ed. Philadelphia, Pa: W.B. Saunders Company, 2000, pp. 370-371.

7. Suzuki D, Knudtson P. *Genetics: The Ethics of Engineering Life,* rev ed. Cambridge, Mass: Harvard University Press, 1990, p. 98.

8. Suzuki D, Knudtson P. *Genetics: The Ethics of Engineering Life,* rev ed. Cambridge, Mass: Harvard University Press, 1990, p. 26.

9. Stolberg SG. Five questions for Dr. W. French Anderson; the long horizon of gene therapy. *New York Times.* 1999;Dec 12:A15.

10. Fackelmann K. Gene therapy appears to relieve Parkinson's symptoms. *USA Today.* 2005;Dec 20:9D.

11. Success in gene therapy, at last [Editorial]. *New York Times.* 2000; Apr 30:18.

12. *The Boy in the Bubble.* Washington, DC: Public Broadcasting Service (PBS) (American Experience), first aired Apr 10, 2006. *See* the PBS "The Boy in the Bubble" website. Available at http://www.pbs.org/wgbh/amex/bubble/ (accessed Jun 3, 2006).

13. Human map complete. *New York Times.* 2003;Apr 15:F1.

14. See www.genetests.org, a medical genetics information resource maintained by the University of Washington, Seattle, and funded by the National Institutes of Health.

15. DeMarco CT. *Pharmacy and the Law.* Rockville, Md: Aspen Publishers, Inc., 1984, p. 1.

16. Pray WS. *A History of Nonprescription Product Regulation.* New York, NY: Pharmaceutical Products Press, 2003, pp. 33-75.

17. Wetherbee H, White BD. *Pharmacy Law: Cases and Materials.* St. Paul: West Publishing Co., 1980, pp. 90-94.

18. Pray WS. *A History of Nonprescription Product Regulation.* New York, NY: Pharmaceutical Products Press, 2003, pp. 91-129.

19. Swann JP. The FDA and the practice of pharmacy: Prescription drug regulation before 1968. In: Erlen J, Spillane JF, eds. *Federal Drug Control: The Evolution of Policy and Practice.* New York, NY: Pharmaceutical Products Press, 2004; pp. 147-174.

20. *U.S. v. Sullivan,* 332 U.S. 689, 68 S.Ct. 331 (1948).

21. Pray WS. *A History of Nonprescription Product Regulation.* New York, NY: Pharmaceutical Products Press, 2003, pp. 131-145.

22. Pray WS. *A History of Nonprescription Product Regulation.* New York, NY: Pharmaceutical Products Press, 2003, pp. 147-172.

23. Harris G. New drugs hit market, but promised trials go undone. *New York Times.* 2006;Mar 4:A8.

24. Annas GJ, Grodin MA. *The Nazi Doctors and the Nuremberg Code: Human Rights in Human Experimentation.* New York, NY: Oxford University Press, 1992.

25. Beecher HK. Ethics and clinical research. *N Engl J Med.* 1966;274:1354-1360.

26. Amdur R. *Institutional Review Board Member Handbook.* Sudbury, Mass: Jones and Bartlett Publishers, 2003, pp. 9-21.

27. Amdur R. *Institutional Review Board Member Handbook.* Sudbury, Mass: Jones and Bartlett Publishers, 2003, pp. 19.

28. Jonsen AR. *The Birth of Bioethics.* New York, NY: Oxford University Press, 1998, pp. 90-94.

29. Jonsen AR. *The Birth of Bioethics.* New York, NY: Oxford University Press, 1998, pp. 94-98.

30. Amdur R. *Institutional Review Board Member Handbook.* Sudbury, Mass: Jones and Bartlett Publishers, 2003, p. 19.

31. Peckman S. A shared responsibility for protecting human subjects. In: Bankart EA, Amdur RJ, eds. *Institutional Review Board: Management and Function.* 2nd ed. Sudbury, Mass: Jones and Bartlett Publishers, 2006, p. 16.

32. Peckman S. A shared responsibility for protecting human subjects. In: Bankart EA, Amdur RJ, eds. *Institutional Review Board: Management and Function.* 2nd ed. Sudbury, Mass: Jones and Bartlett Publishers, 2006, pp. 16-20.

33. Amdur RJ, Bankert EA. The institutional review board: Definition and federal oversight. In: Bankart EA, Amdur RJ, eds. *Institutional Review Board: Management and Function.* 2nd ed. Sudbury, Mass: Jones and Bartlett Publishers, 2006, p. 25.

34. Stolberg SG. Fines proposed for violations of human research rules. *New York Times.* 2000;May 24:A23.

35. Jonsen AR. *The Birth of Bioethics.* New York, NY: Oxford University Press, 1998, pp. 99-106.

36. Childress JF, Meslin EM, Shapiro HT, eds. *Belmont Revisited: Ethical Principles for Research with Human Subjects.* Washington, DC: Georgetown University Press, 2005.

37. Amdur R. *Institutional Review Board Member Handbook.* Sudbury, Mass: Jones and Bartlett Publishers, 2003, pp. 23-31.

38. Abood R. *Pharmacy Practice and the Law.* 4th ed. Sudbury, Mass: Jones and Bartlett Publishers, 2005, pp. 63-72.

39. Levine RJ. *Ethics and Regulation in Clinical Research.* 2nd ed. Baltimore, Md: Urban and Schwarzenberg, 1986, pp. 3-10.

40. Gelsinger P. Jesse's intent. In: Bankart EA, Amdur RJ, eds. *Institutional Review Board: Management and Function.* 2nd ed. Sudbury, Mass: Jones and Bartlett Publishers, 2006, pp. xi-xix.

41. Batshaw ML. Memorandum to members of the American Society of Human Genetics regarding "Gene Therapy for Ornithine Transcarbamylase Deficiency," dated Mar 18, 1998.

42. Gelsinger P. Jesse's intent. In: Bankart EA, Amdur RJ, eds. *Institutional Review Board: Management and Function.* 2nd ed. Sudbury, Mass: Jones and Bartlett Publishers, 2006, pp. xi-xix.

43. Gelsinger P. Jesse's intent. In: Bankart EA, Amdur RJ, eds. *Institutional Review Board: Management and Function.* 2nd ed. Sudbury, Mass: Jones and Bartlett Publishers, 2006, p. xv.

44. Stolberg SG. The biotech death of Jesse Gelsinger. *New York Times Magazine.* 1999;Nov 28:136-150.

45. Stolberg SG. F.D.A. officials fault Penn team in gene therapy death. *New York Times.* 1999;Dec:A15.

46. Gelsinger P. Jesse's intent. In: Bankart EA, Amdur RJ, eds. *Institutional Review Board: Management and Function.* 2nd ed. Sudbury, Mass: Jones and Bartlett Publishers, 2006, p. xviii.

47. Gelsinger P. Jesse's intent. In: Bankart EA, Amdur RJ, eds. *Institutional Review Board: Management and Function.* 2nd ed. Sudbury, Mass: Jones and Bartlett Publishers, 2006, p. xviii.

48. Wade N. Patient dies during a trial of therapy using genes. *New York Times.* 1999;Sep 29:

49. Stolberg SG. The biotech death of Jesse Gelsinger. *New York Times Magazine.* 1999;Nov 28:136-150.

294 *DRUGS. ETHICS. AND QUALITY OF LIFE*

50. Stolberg SG. Tribute and apologies in gene therapy death. *New York Times.* 1999;Dec 10:A16.
51. Nelson D. Penn researchers sued in gene therapy death; teen's parents also name ethicist as defendant. *Washington Post*. 2000;Sep 19:A3.
52. Stolberg SG. F.D.A. officials fault Penn team in gene therapy death. *New York Times*. 1999;Dec:A15.
53. Stolberg SG. The biotech death of Jesse Gelsinger. *New York Times Magazine*. 1999;Nov 28:136-150.
54. Stolberg SG. The biotech death of Jesse Gelsinger. *New York Times Magazine*. 1999;Nov 28:136-150.
55. Stolberg SG. The biotech death of Jesse Gelsinger. *New York Times Magazine*. 1999;Nov 28:136-150.
56. Weiss R, Nelson D. FDA faults Penn animal tests that led to fatal human trial. *Washington Post*. 2000;Jul 12:A9.
57. Weiss R, Nelson D. FDA faults Penn animal tests that led to fatal human trial. *Washington Post*. 2000;Jul 12:A9.
58. Stolberg SG. F.D.A. officials fault Penn team in gene therapy death. *New York Times*. 1999;Dec:A15.
59. Stolberg SG. The biotech death of Jesse Gelsinger. *New York Times Magazine*. 1999;Nov 28:136-150.
60. Nelson D. Weiss R. Hasty decisions in race to a cure? Gene therapy study preceded despite safety, ethics concerns. *Washington Post.* 1999;Nov 21:A1.
61. Nelson D, Weiss R. Hasty decisions in race to a cure? Gene therapy study preceded despite safety, ethics concerns. *Washington Post.* 1999;Nov 21:A1.
62. Stolberg SG. Biomedicine is receiving new scrutiny as scientists become entrepreneurs. *New York Times.* 2000;Feb 20:Section 1, 26.
63. Nelson D. Gene researchers admit mistakes, deny liability. *Washington Post*. 2000;Feb 15:A3.
64. Nelson D. Gene researchers admit mistakes, deny liability. *Washington Post*. 2000;Feb 15:A3.
65. Weiss R. Nelson D. Penn settles gene therapy suit; university pays undisclosed sum to family of teen who died. *Washington Post*. 2000;Nov 4:A4. © 2000, *Washington Post*. Reprinted with permission.
66. Weiss R, Nelson D. Penn settles gene therapy suit; university pays undisclosed sum to family of teen who died. *Washington Post*. 2000;Nov 4:A4.
67. Weiss R, Nelson D. Penn settles gene therapy suit; university pays undisclosed sum to family of teen who died. *Washington Post*. 2000;Nov 4:A4.
68. Stolberg SG. The biotech death of Jesse Gelsinger. *New York Times Magazine*. 1999;Nov 28:136-150.
69. Weiss R. FDA seeks to penalize gene scientist. *Washington Post*. 2000;Dec 12:A14.
70. Nelson D. Penn ends gene trials on humans. *Washington Post.* 2000;May 25:A1.
71. Nelson D, Weiss R. FDA stops researcher's human gene therapy experiments. *Washington Post*. 2000;Mar 2:A8.

72. Nelson D. Penn ends gene trials on humans. *Washington Post.* 2000;May 25:A1.

73. *Northern Securities Co. v. U.S.*, 193 U.S. 197 at 300-401 (Holmes, J., dissenting).

74. Steinbrook R. Improving protection for research subjects [Health Policy Report]. *New Engl J Med.* 2002;346:1425-1430.

75. Kolata G. Johns Hopkins death brings halt to U.S.-financed human studies. *New York Times.* 2001;Jul 20:A1.

76. Harris G. F.D.A. bars imaging drug after deaths. *New York Times.* 2005;Dec 20:A22.

77. Abzug MJ, Esterl EZ. Establishment of a clinical trials office at a children's hospital. *Pediatrics.* 2001;108:1129-1134.

78. Shalala D. Protecting research subjects—What must be done [Sounding Board]. *N Engl J Med.* 2000;Sep 14:808-810.

79. Hopkins J. Biotech upstarts get injection of capital; money flows into start-up that move fast, take risks. *USA Today.* 2004;Mar 23:1B, 2B.

80. Stossel TP. Regulating academic-industrial research relationships—Solving problems or stifling progress? [Sounding Board]. *N Engl J Med.* 2005;Sep 8:1060-1065.

81. Nelson D, Weiss R. Hasty decisions in race to a cure? gene therapy study preceded despite safety, ethics concerns. *Washington Post.* 1999;Nov 21:A1.

82. Johns MME, Barnes M, Florencio PS. Restoring balance to industry-academia relationships in an era of institutional financial conflicts of interest: Promoting research while maintaining trust. *JAMA.* 2003;289:741-746.

83. Cho MK, Ryo S, Schissel A, Rennie D. Policies on faculty conflicts of interest at US universities. *JAMA.* 2000;284:2203-2208.

84. Stossel TP. Regulating academic-industrial research relationships—Solving problems or stifling progress? [Sounding Board]. *N Engl J Med.* 2005;Sep 8:1060-1065.

85. Stolberg SG. Biomedicine is receiving new scrutiny as scientists become entrepreneurs. *New York Times.* 2000;Feb 20:Section 1, 26.

86. Nelson D, Weiss R. Hasty decisions in race to a cure? gene therapy study preceded despite safety, ethics concerns. *Washington Post.* 1999;Nov 21:A1.

87. Meier B. A medical journal quandary: Hot to report on drug trials. *New York Times.* 2004;Jun 21:C1, C5.

88. Hamvas A, Madden KK, Nogee LM, Trusgnich MA, Wegner DJ, Heins HB, Cole FS. Informed consent for genetic research. *Arch Pediatr Adolesc Med.* 2004;158:551-555.

89. Cooke RE. Vulnerable children. In: Grodin MA, Glantz LH, eds. *Children as Research Subjects: Science, Ethics & Law.* New York, NY: Oxford University Press, 1994, pp. 206-212.

90. Mastroianni A, Kahn J. Swinging on the pendulum: Shifting views of justice in human research subjects research. In: Lemmons TM, Waring DR, eds. *Law and Ethics in Biomedical Research: Regulation, Conflict of Interest, and Liability.* Toronto: University of Toronto Press, 2006, pp. 47-60.

91. Annas GJ. Reforming informed consent to genetic research. *JAMA*. 2001; 286:2326-2328.

92. Lidz CW, Appelbaum PS. The therapeutic misconception: Problems and solutions. *Med Care*. 2002;40:V55-V63.

93. Gelsinger P. Jesse's intent. In: Bankart EA, Amdur RJ, eds. *Institutional Review Board: Management and Function*. 2nd ed. Sudbury, Mass: Jones and Bartlett Publishers, 2006, pp. xi-xix.

94. Pence GE. *Classic Cases in Medical Ethics: Accounts of Cases That Have Shaped Medical Ethics, with Philosophical, Legal, and Historical Backgrounds*. New York, NY: McGraw Hill, 2004, pp. 307-312.

95. Kolata G. Companies facing ethical issue as drugs are tested overseas. *New York Times*. 2004;Mar 5: A1, A15. Copyright 2004 by The New York Times Co. Reprinted with permission.

96. Kolata G. Companies facing ethical issue as drugs are tested overseas. *New York Times*. 2004;Mar 5: A1, A15.

97. Tribe LH. *Abortion: The Clash of Absolutes*. New York, NY: W. W. Norton & Company, Inc., 1992.

98. Precious child, impossible choice. *People*. 2006;May 15:123-124.

99. Freundlich N. Genetic predictions: Just a swab away. *New York Times*. 2004;Mar 21:2004.

100. Harmon A. In new tests for fetal defects, agonizing choices for parents. *New York Times*. 2004;Jun 20:1, 19.

101. Rubin R. Science chips away at ALD; adult trial of Lorenzo's oil offers hope. *USA Today*. 2005;Sep 26:5D.

102. Bamshad M. Genetic influence on health: Does race matter? *JAMA*. 2005; 294:937-946.

103. Lappin T. The year in ideas: A to Z; pharmacogenomics. *New York Times*. 2001;Dec 9:Health Section, 3.

104. Weiss R. Gene therapy's troubling crossroads. *Washington Post*. 1999;Dec 31:A3.

105. Stolberg SG. The biotech death of Jesse Gelsinger. *New York Times Magazine*. 1999;Nov 28:136-150.

APPENDIX I

1. Soukhanov AH, ex ed. *The American Heritage Dictionary of the English Language*. 3rd ed. Boston, Mass: Houghton Mifflin Company, 1992, p. 1020.

2. *Webster's Seventh New Collegiate Dictionary*. Springfield, Mass: G. & c. Merriam Company, 1965, p. 478.

3. *The Constitution of the United States*. Washington, DC: The Commission on the Bicentennial of the United States Constitution, 1986, pp. 15-16.

4. *The Constitution of the United States*. Washington, DC: The Commission on the Bicentennial of the United States Constitution, 1986, p. 1.

5. In a letter to Bishop Mandell Creighton, Apr 5, 1887. In: Beck EM ed. *Bartlett's Familiar Quotations.* 15th ed. Boston, Mass: Little, Brown and Company, 1980, p. 615.

6. Maier P. *American Scripture: Making the Declaration of Independence.* New York, NY: Alfred A. Knopf, Inc., 1997, pp. 105-123.

7. President's Commission for the Study of Ethics Problems in Medicine and Biomedical and Behavioral Research, *Summing Up.* Washington, DC: Government Printing Office, 1983, p. 14.

8. President's Commission for the Study of Ethics Problems in Medicine and Biomedical and Behavioral Research, *Summing Up.* Washington, DC: Government Printing Office, 1983, pp. 15-16.

9. *American Academy of Pediatrics v. Heckler,* 561 F.Supp. 395 (D.D.C.).

10. *Bowen v. American Hospital Association,* 476 U.S. 610, 106 S.Ct. 2101 (1986).

11. *Cruzan v. Director, Missouri Dept. of Health,* 497 U.S. 261, 110 S.Ct. 2841 (1990).

12. *Griswold v. Connecticut,* 381 U.S. 479, 85 S.Ct. 1678 (1965).

13. Weir RF, Gostin L. Decisions to abate life-sustaining treatment for non-autonomous patients: Ethical standards and legal liability for physicians after *Cruzan. JAMA.* 1990;264:1846-1853.

14. Pence GE. *Classic Cases in Medical Ethics: Accounts of the Cases That Have Shaped Medical Ethics, with Philosophical, Legal, and Historical Backgrounds.* New York, NY: McGraw Hill, 2004, pp. 29-39.

15. *Superintendent of Belcherton State School v. Saikewicz,* 370 N.E. 2d 417 (1977).

16. *In the Matter of Shirley Dinnerstein,* 380 N.E. 2d 134 (Mass. App. 1978).

17. *Eichner v. Dillon,* 426 N.Y. Supp. 2d 517 (App. Div. 1980).

18. *Matter of Storar,* 52 N.Y. 2d 363, 420 N.E. 2d 64, cert. denied 454 U.S. 858 (1981).

19. *In re Conroy,* 98 N.J. 321, 486 A. 2d 1209 (1985).

20. *Brophy v. New England Sinai Hosp., Inc.,* 398 Mass. 417, 497 N.E. 2d 626 (1986).

21. Pence GE. *Classic Cases in Medical Ethics: Accounts of the Cases That Have Shaped Medical Ethics, with Philosophical, Legal, and Historical Backgrounds.* New York, NY: McGraw Hill, 2004, pp. 64-71.

22. *Cruzan v. Director, Missouri Dept. of Health,* 497 U.S. 261, 110 S.Ct. 2841 (1990) at 2854.

23. *Cruzan v. Harmon,* 760 S.W. 2d 408 (Mo. 1989).

24. *Cruzan v. Director, Missouri Dept. of Health,* 497 U.S. 261, 110 S.Ct. 2841 (1990) at 2851.

APPENDIX 2

1. Pellegrino ED, Thomasma DC. *A Philosophical Basis of Medical Practice: Toward a Philosophy and Ethic of the Healing Professions.* New York, NY: Oxford University Press, 1981, p. 71.

2. Buerki RA, Vottero LD. *Ethical Responsibility in Pharmacy Practice.* Madison, Wis: American Institute of the History of Pharmacy, 1994, p. 71.

3. Buerki RA, Vottero LD. *Ethical Responsibility in Pharmacy Practice.* Madison, Wis: American Institute of the History of Pharmacy, 1994, pp. 72-78.

4. The word *comfort* is derived from two Latin words for "come with" (*cum*) and "strong" (*fortis*) and may be translated literally "to come alongside with strength." Soukhanov AH, ex ed. *The American Heritage Dictionary of the English Language.* 3rd ed. Boston, Mass: Houghton Mifflin Company, 1992, pp. 378-379.

5. Jonsen AR, Siegler M, Winslade WJ. *Clinical Ethics: A Practical Approach to Ethical Decisions in Clinical Medicine.* 5th ed. New York, NY: McGraw-Hill, 2002.

Index

Page numbers followed by the letter "f" indicate figures.

American Academy of Pediatrics, 107
American Association of Retired
    Persons, 71–72
American Bar Associations, 236
American Center for Law and Justice,
    102
American Hospital Association, 240
American Medical Association, 2n,
    5–6, 236, 240
American Medical News, 131, 254, 257
American Medical Women's
    Association, 91
American Pharmacists Association, 7,
    10–12, 101, 106
American Society of Health-System
    Pharmacists, 101
Americans United for Life, 102
Americans With Disabilities Act, 234
Ammonia scavengers, 201
Amyotrophic lateral sclerosis. *See* ALS
Analgesics, 40, 55–56
Anderson, W. French, 202
Annas, George, 177, 178
Anorexia, marijuana and, 61
Ansel, Howard, 21
Anslinger, Harry J., 66
Antianxiety agents, 135, 136, 145
Antibiotics, 253
Anti-clotting drugs, 38–39
Anticonvulsants, 135
Antidepressants, 253
Anti-ethics, 28
Anti-inflammatory drugs, 254
Anti-platelet drugs, 38–39
Antipyretics, 40
APhA. *See* American Pharmacists
    Association
Appelbaum, 179–180
Appleby, J., 257
APPROVe, 39
Aquinas, Thomas (Saint), 26–27
ARCOXIA, 41
Ardagh, Michael, 170
Arginine, 201, 210
Ariès, Philippe, 113
Aristotle, 4–5, 25, 26, 137
Arthritis, marijuana and, 61
Asclepius, 49–50
Ashcroft, John, 146, 147
Ashcroft v. Oregon, 148. *See also*
    Gonzales v. Oregon

ASHP. *See* American Society of
    Health-System Pharmacists
Aspirin, 38–39, 58, 133–134, 254
Assisted suicide
    continuing dilemmas regarding,
        152–158
    debate about, 136–143
    overview of, 133–136
Astra Zeneca International, 56
ATIVAN, 135
Attention-deficit/hyperactivity
    disorder, 254
Auer v. Robbins, 149
Autism, 251–252
Autonomy
    Buerki and Vottero on, 249
    decision-making and. *See* Decision-
        making
    defined, 69
    defining, 29
    experimentation and, 220
    pharmacy practice and, 8, 11
    protection/limitation of, 70–71

Babies
    assisted suicide and, 153–154
    medical futility and, 169
Baby Doe, 154, 239–240
Baby K., 169
Bacon, Sir Francis, 23
Balances, checks and, 233
Barbiturates, 133–135, 145
Barbituric acid, 133–134
Batshaw, Mark, 210, 212–214
Baylor College of Medicine, 56
BCPs. *See* Birth control pills
Beechers, Henry, 206
Belladonna, as drug, 22
Belmont Report, 69–70, 207
Beneficence
    Buerki and Vottero on, 249
    COX-2 inhibitors and, 44–46
    defined, 45
    defining, 29
    emergency contraception and, 99
    implications of, 207
    palliative care and, 127
Benefit, maximizing, 28
Bentham, Jeremy, 28

University of Rochester, 217
University of Wisconsin, 125
Urea, 133–134
Urea cycle enzyme deficiency. *See*
 OTC deficiency syndrome
U.S. Court of Appeals
 history of, 242
 marijuana and, 75
 ruling on tobacco/nicotine and, 18
U.S. District Court, ruling on
 tobacco/nicotine and, 17–18
U.S. Federal Bureau of Narcotics,
 marijuana and, 64
USA Today
 addiction and, 255
 Alzheimer's disease and, 166
 COX-2 inhibitors and, 57, 59
 drug availability and, 256
 emergency contraception and, 91,
  106–107
 end-stage patients and, 164–165
 immunizations and, 251, 252
 marijuana and, 79, 80
 marketplace and, 255, 256
 mental illness and, 253
 performance-enhancing drugs and,
  255
 pregnancy and, 252
 virtues and, 257
U.S.P. *See United States
 Pharmacopoeia*
Utilitarianism, 28

Vaccinations. *See* Immunizations
Vacco v. Quill, 145–148, 156–157
Valdecoxib, 41
VALIUM, 135
Value, defining, 25
Van Sickle, Bruce M., 167–168, 178
Vander Bleek, Luke D., 85, 87,
 101–103
Vaux, Kenneth, 141
Ventilation, Test of, 53
Veracity, Buerki and Vottero on,
 249
VERONAL, 134
VERSED, 135
Viagra, 253

VICODIN, 115
Victoria (Queen), marijuana and, 63
VIOXX. *See* COX-2 inhibitors
Virtues
 Buerki and Vottero on, 249
 professional, 4–5
 topics for further inquiry, 256–257
Vivian, Jesse, 8
Volstead Act of 1920, marijuana and,
 65
von Bayer, Aldolph, 133–134
von Guten, Charles, 119
von Mering, Joseph, 134
Vottero, Louis, 8, 26, 99, 249

Wade, Roe v., 246, 252
Waite, Rogene, 81
Walgreens Co., 97, 108
Wal-Mart Stores, Inc., 97
Walsh, M.S., 256
Walters, John, 80
Walters, LeRoy, 216
Wan, Hoiyan, 217
Wanglie, Helga, 169
War on drugs, 67
Warning labels, tobacco and, 34
Washington
 assisted suicide and, 144
 marijuana and, 71
Washington, George, 63
Washington Post, gene therapy and,
 213, 215
The Washington Post, palliative care
 and, 123, 129
Washington v. Glucksberg, 145–148,
 156
Wealth, 27
Webber, Carolyn A., 91
Weil, Andrew, 21
Weiss, Joseph, 50
Wetherbee, H., 204
Wheeler, Thomas, 56
White, Bruce, 204, 225–226
White House National Drug Control
 Policy, 81
WHO. *See* World Health Organization
Wicclair, Mark, 172–173, 174
William (of Orange), 232